The Global Middle Classes

Publication of this book and the SAR seminar from which it resulted were made possible with the generous support of the SAR President's Council and The Brown Foundation, Inc., of Houston, Texas.

School for Advanced Research
Advanced Seminar Series

James F. Brooks
General Editor

The Global Middle Classes

Contributors

Krisztina Fehérváry
Department of Anthropology, University of Michigan

Carla Freeman
Departments of Anthropology and Women's, Gender, and Sexuality Studies, Emory University

Rachel Heiman
Department of Social Sciences, The New School

Carla Jones
Department of Anthropology, University of Colorado at Boulder

Cindi Katz
Doctoral Programs in Environmental Psychology and Geography, The Graduate Center, City University of New York

Mark Liechty
Departments of Anthropology and History, University of Illinois at Chicago

Samuli Schielke
Zentrum Moderner Orient, Berlin

Sanjay Srivastava
Antropológicos Institute of Economic Growth, Delhi

Rihan Yeh
Centro de Estudios Antropológicos, El Colegio de Michoacán

Li Zhang
Department of Anthropology, University of California at Davis

The Global Middle Classes
Theorizing through Ethnography

Edited by Rachel Heiman, Carla Freeman,
and Mark Liechty

School for Advanced Research Press
Santa Fe

School for Advanced Research Press
Post Office Box 2188
Santa Fe, New Mexico 87504-2188
sarpress.sarweb.org

Managing Editor: Lisa Pacheco
Editorial Assistant: Ellen Goldberg
Designer and Production Manager: Cynthia Dyer
Manuscript Editor: Merryl Sloane
Proofreader: Kate Whelan
Indexer: Catherine Fox
Printer: Sheridan Books, Inc.

Library of Congress Cataloging-in-Publication Data
The global middle classes : theorizing through ethnography / edited by Rachel Heiman,
Carla Freeman, and Mark Liechty.
    p. cm. — (Advanced seminar series)
Includes bibliographical references and index.
ISBN 978-1-934691-53-3 (alk. paper)
1. Middle class—Cross-cultural studies. 2. Ethnology. I. Heiman, Rachel. II. Freeman, Carla.
III. Liechty, Mark, 1960-
HT684.G54 2012
305.5'5—dc23
                    2011047607

 This book was printed on paper containing 30% PCW and FSC certified.

Cover illustration: Indonesian model Aditya and her family display pious Muslim clothing at the
pre-Ramadan fashion show of designer Shafira at the Hotel Dharmawangsa on July, 6, 2011,
Jakarta, Indonesia. Photograph courtesy of Arselan Ganin (arselan_ganin@yahoo.com).

Contents

List of Figures ix

1. Introduction: Charting an Anthropology of the Middle Classes 3
   Rachel Heiman, Mark Liechty, and Carla Freeman

2. Living in the Future Tense: Aspiring for World and Class
   in Provincial Egypt 31
   Samuli Schielke

3. National Identity, Bedrooms, and Kitchens: Gated
   Communities and New Narratives of Space in India 57
   Sanjay Srivastava

4. Neoliberal Respectability: Entrepreneurial Marriage,
   Affective Labor, and a New Caribbean Middle Class 85
   Carla Freeman

5. The Postsocialist Middle Classes and the New "Family House"
   in Hungary 117
   Krisztina Fehérváry

6. Women in the Middle: Femininity, Virtue, and Excess
   in Indonesian Discourses of Middle Classness 145
   Carla Jones

7. Just Managing: American Middle-Class Parenthood in
   Insecure Times 169
   Cindi Katz

8. A Middle-Class Public at Mexico's Northern Border 189
   Rihan Yeh

9. Private Homes, Distinct Lifestyles: Performing a New Middle
   Class in China   213
   Li Zhang

10. Gate Expectations: Discursive Displacement of the "Old
    Middle Class" in an American Suburb   237
    Rachel Heiman

11. Middle-Class Déjà Vu: Conditions of Possibility, from
    Victorian England to Contemporary Kathmandu   271
    Mark Liechty

    References   301
    Index   339

Figures

2.1	Teachers and children at a government school, Alexandria	38
2.2	Dining table used as a computer desk, Alexandria	41
5.1	Panel-construction apartment buildings, Dunaújváros	121
5.2	New family house under construction, near Dunaújváros	123
5.3	Before and after of a room transformed into a "modern" apartment	128
5.4	Self-built houses with older peasant houses	134
5.5	Neighborhood of new family houses outside Dunaújváros	135
6.1	Chic, elaborate Islamic fashion	160
9.1	Upscale, gated condominium complex	223
9.2	Lower-income housing compound	226
9.3	Social life and public space in a *gongxin jieceng* community	227
10.1	Completed homes in Tarragon Hills	241
10.2	Proposed 6-foot-high gate	243
10.3	Flag lot	249
10.4	Typical stanchions	256
10.5	The gate, as built	264

The Global Middle Classes

1

Introduction

Charting an Anthropology of the Middle Classes

Rachel Heiman, Mark Liechty, and Carla Freeman

In recent years, there has been a constant stream of media attention to the condition of the middle classes. On the one hand, there has been curious fascination with (and competitive envy of) places where middle classes are expanding, particularly India and China. At the same time, there has been escalating concern about the cultural, political, and economic implications of the fragility of the middle classes in the United States and Western Europe and the shrinking middle in Latin America. On the fringes of these discussions have been hints of attention to sites in Eastern Europe where the configuration of postsocialist middle classes looms large and to areas of the Middle East where the composition of the middle classes is changing. In 2011, of course, the revolutionary potential and religious orientation of middle classes in North Africa took center stage. Public intellectuals, policy makers, and academics from a variety of disciplines and interdisciplinary locations have been debating these issues in an effort to discern rhetoric from reality and to understand the implications of these shifts for the global economy and for people's everyday lives. Anthropology—a discipline uniquely poised to complicate this discourse—has not, until this book, offered a collective contribution to this theorizing.

This volume emerged out of an advanced seminar at the School for Advanced Research and brings together ethnographers who have been doing research on the middle classes in a range of nation-states. The impetus for the seminar was our desire to explore global economic changes through the lens of the middle classes and to engage universal theories through ethnographies of everyday life. A series of key questions guided our early discussions: How does close attention to the middle classes broaden our understanding of contemporary forms of globalization? What analytical questions are raised about the category of "middle class" when its diverse referents, multifaceted uses, and different historical contexts of emergence are brought into view? In what ways might we need to reconfigure our concept of "class" once the middle classes are given their due place in class relations? And finally, how can anthropology's particular theoretical approaches and empirical methods contribute to these debates?

Since the mid-1980s, anthropologists have been at the forefront of theorizing contemporary forms of globalization through examining its local articulations and cultural formations (for example, Appadurai 1996; Ferguson 2006; Ong 1987, 2006; Rouse 1995; Stephens 1995). Not content with universal theories that fail to attend to the range of lived experiences, subject formations, and local epistemologies, anthropologists have conducted in-depth ethnographic and historical research to offer nuance to our understanding of everything from the gendering of global divisions of labor (Fernández-Kelly 1983) to the production of locality (Appadurai 1996) to the nature of transnational citizenship (Ong 1998) to the emergence of multi-scalar activist networks and coalitions (Tsing 2005). Starting in the late 1980s and the 1990s, the middle classes began to emerge as a critical site for considering the implications of globalization, particularly the rise and spread of neoliberal logics, with the end of the Cold War, economic crises in Latin America and Asia, the movement of white-collar jobs from the United States and Western Europe to India and China, and now the current global economic crisis. In the years leading up to this seminar, a burgeoning number of anthropologists were tackling these concerns head-on (such as Caldeira 2000; Freeman 2000; Guano 2003; Heiman 2004; Liechty 2003; Lomnitz 2003; Mazzarella 2005; O'Dougherty 2002; Ortner 2003; Patico 2008). The time was ripe for anthropologists to come together not only to think deeply about the relationship between global economic shifts and middle-class formations but also to interrogate our understanding of what constitutes a "middle class"—and class politics more broadly—in this pivotal historical moment.

The chapters in this volume span the globe in their portrayal of the middle classes, with pieces that focus on Barbados, China, Egypt, Hungary, India, Indonesia, Mexico, Nepal, and the United States. Our introduction is framed around a series of five questions that emerged when the ethnographic material and theoretical insights from each of the chapters came together within a shared analytical purview. With so much contextual particularity, along with striking comparative resonances, our discussion here addresses how anthropology can contribute to theorizing middle-class culture and history within global capitalist relations. Our goal is less to defend a particular answer to any of these questions than to lay out a range of intellectual lineages and analytical concerns with which anyone attempting to study middle classes will have to contend.

First, why have the middle classes become such an important focus in anthropology, and what has hindered—both from within the discipline and from without—anthropological efforts to shift the theoretical terrain on which middle classness is understood? Second, how does the incorporation of the middle classes into our theorizing of capitalist relations enable us to transform conventions of class analysis and our understanding of class politics? Third, how can we theorize the differences and similarities among middle-class formations through time and across space in a way that does not fall into a teleological understanding of the history of class? Fourth, while keeping in focus different conditions of possibility in which middle classes emerge, grow, and contract, how can we conceptualize the relationship between states and capitalism, particularly the role of the state in the formation, management, and privileging of the middle classes? Fifth, what practices, affects, and spaces are most associated with middle-class forms of labor, consumption, and citizenship, and how might we better understand ever-changing structures of capitalism and class relations if we place middle-class subjects and middle-class subjectivities at the center of our class theorizing?

ANTHROPOLOGY OF THE MIDDLE CLASSES: FROM AN AMBIVALENT TO A CRITICAL DOMAIN

The ethnographic analyses of middle classes around the world offered in this volume highlight a formerly ambivalent domain for anthropology. As a field whose origins rest upon a commitment to the holistic study of non-Western and small-scale societies, with sociologists and political scientists having traditionally focused primarily on industrialized, class-based societies, anthropology's engagement with class analysis has mainly taken the peasant, the lower classes, and the oppressed as its central protagonists. Indeed, while some anthropologists have taken the charge to "study up" (Nader 1972)—generating ethnographies of elites and the powerful (Marcus 1983; Marcus and Hall 1991; Ong 1998), as well as studies of middle classes, particularly in the United States and Europe (Frykman and

5

Löfgren 1987; Newman 1988, 1993; Ortner 2003)—the field as a whole has traditionally privileged the powerless ethnographic subject as indicative of a more purposeful, "morally engaged" scholarship (Scheper-Hughes 1995:420). Middle classes and upward mobility into the middle classes were viewed as tainted not only by implicit exploitation of their lower-class counterparts but also by cultural inauthenticity and mimicry of (often foreign, colonial) elites.

This previous anthropological avoidance of the middle-class subject reflects the dominance of certain gatekeeping concepts in anthropology and also other analytical traditions in which anthropologists are engaged, particularly geographic areas of study. Today, in an era of the global, it may seem overly traditional to return to region or "culture area" as significant analytical lenses, yet we suggest that some of the legacies of area studies offer indispensable clues to the ways in which middle classes have been left out of the analytical frame and how they have been articulated in the contemporary context of globalization. Not surprisingly, these traditions and concepts are, themselves, framed differently in the world areas in which anthropologists have worked (Appadurai 1986; Fardon 1990). For example, in Caribbean social science, the dominant paradigm for analyzing class has been Marxist political economy. This is due, in large part, to the historically close fit between the Marxist framework and the region's plantation economy, in which a small, white, planter/corporate elite and the region's black or nonwhite laboring masses constituted the fundamental struggle and the middle strata garnered only marginal interest. For this part of the world, a Marxist reading of class struggle has shaped not only the enterprise of academic inquiry but also politics more generally (Freeman, chapter 4, this volume). By contrast, in Indonesia, once home to the largest communist party outside the socialist bloc, class analysis by Indonesian and foreign scholars alike was explicitly silenced under the Suharto regime precisely because of its political threat (Jones, chapter 6, this volume). That is to say, state politics and local histories, as well as the power of academic gatekeeping concepts and theoretical trends, have contributed in particular ways in the past to the marginality of the middle classes as worthy ethnographic subjects and of class analysis that engages these groups as central actors.[1]

At the same time, the growing interest in contemporary middle classes reflects a long tradition of anthropological inquiry in which fieldworkers are driven to topics both that their subjects make imperative and that geopolitics bring to the fore. Indeed, amid escalating contemporary economic flux, neoliberal restructuring, and the extensive reach of global media, surging middle-class aspirations and anxieties throughout the world have compelled our attention to this emic preoccupation with middle-class life-styles, spaces, sentiments, careers, and civic engagements. Not only has middle classness become an increasingly powerful category for aspiration, longing, and anxiety in many parts of the world, but "the middle classes" are also an increasingly common subject/citizenry hailed by political and corporate leaders. The global political-economic transformations that are giving rise to a renewed interest in class require an explicit theorization of the middle. Meanwhile, this stratum is susceptible to a wide range of assumptions and meanings, depending upon the local specificities of what it means to be middle-class—apathy, industriousness, fiscal irresponsibility, thrift, political conservatism, progressivism, cultural inauthenticity, and national character, among them—in part because of the analytical vagueness that has framed the usage of "middle class."

With these groups increasingly in the public eye, their changing structures of work; changing patterns of consumption, reproduction, and citizenship; and associated middle-class subjectivities are imperative domains of ethnographic inquiry. The chapters in this collection demonstrate striking resonances: aspiring middle classes in Egypt, for example, bear notable similarities to middle classes in China and Hungary in their longing for middle-class lifestyles, spaces, and modes of consumption and in the ways in which middle classness is now achieved by new means. At the same time, the chapters expose critical differences arising from divergent histories, colonial traditions, and political-economic formations. The anthropological lens on the global middle classes that lies at the heart of this collective enterprise thus foregrounds cultural specificity, presents new logics of class itself, and offers the kind of powerful comparative analysis and theorizing that is most richly produced through ethnographic research. In so doing, this ethnographic perspective offers not only a glimpse of emergent groups and changing economic arrangements across the world but also a unique set of tools for analyzing middle classness itself as a culturally specific position and set of subjectivities, articulated in and through shifting terrains of gender, nation, race, caste, ethnicity, and empire. The manner in which these transformations are unfolding has urged anthropologists studying middle classes and the practices, ideologies, and meanings associated with middle classness to provide a more nuanced theorization of "middle class" and to rethink traditional tools of class analysis.

For anthropologists concerned with class, the rich tradition of Marxist political economy has offered a critical lens through which struggles between a ruling class and a subordinated class, bourgeoisie and proletariat, have constituted the central drama of capitalism. For many of us, our own political sympathies made this framework additionally compelling: it made sense of our ethnographic projects, whether of nationalisms, state socialism, postcolonial politics, global labor restructuring, or new urban landscapes. Yet, just as Marx provided little insight into the position of middle classes—envisioning their eventual dissolution into either owning or laboring groups—many anthropologists have viewed these groups with trepidation. But in the contemporary period, globalization and neoliberalism have pushed our analyses to include not just the expanding realms of multinational capital and global factory labor (and associated migrations), but a widening array of immaterial and affective labor and the mounting significance of consumption and new forms of citizen action. It is time for anthropologists to collectively delve into the murky plurality of the global middle classes.

THE MATERIALITY OF MIDDLE CLASSNESS; OR, WHY MIDDLE CLASSES MATTER FOR THEORY AND POLITICS

The contemporary expanding fields on which new middle classes enact themselves call for analytical tools that highlight the complexities and inextricable dimensions of economy and culture, labor and subjectivity, in the production of class. Although broadening materialist readings of class to examine its cultural and affective underpinnings illuminates all class positionings, we find that these complexities are made especially salient in the longings and entailments associated with middle classness. For here, as many of the chapters in this collection make plain, styles of consumption, modes of production (immaterial and material), approaches to reproduction, and motivations for citizen action are often inextricably connected in middle-class practices and subjectivities, and they are often imbued with affective traces of aspiration and anxiety and the desire for a feeling of security or belonging. We suggest that an important outcome of affording the middle classes their due place in anthropological theories of capitalist relations will be to strengthen the foundation upon which anthropological studies of *all* class locations rest and to broaden our understanding of what counts as class politics.

There has long been an either-or debate about whether class is a material phenomenon (arising from a more or less Marxist understanding of socioeconomic relations of production) or simply a kind of associational category of people aligned around common sociopolitical goals. One argument holds that the very use of the word "class"—as opposed to, for example, "status group" or "habitus"—implies a materialist perspective: class is an idea associated with group experiences of socioeconomic difference.

All of the contributors to this volume share this basic understanding of class as a sociocultural phenomenon growing out of industrial relations of production and the modern state, at the same time incorporating notions such as status and habitus for the ways in which they are implicated in class relations, even if, as in the case of status, they are social phenomena not specific to capitalist relations of production.

This volume thus builds on the contributions to class analysis that have come from theorists who have been compelled—through empirical findings that combine historical perspective with ethnographic insight—to engage the writings of not only Marx but also Weber, Gramsci, Veblen, Bourdieu, Foucault, Lefebvre, Hartmann, and others. Their concepts of status, hegemony, conspicuous consumption, habitus, reproduction, discipline, and the production of space enable us to broaden our understanding of class relations, particularly the means through which people make meaning in their everyday lives, make do amid the conditions of possibility in which they live, become classed subjects, and ultimately influence the economic order of things. It is this attention to broad modes of capitalist regulation—still including analysis of the relationship between labor, capital, and the state but going far beyond—that is advanced by the scholarship in this volume. We view cultural logics, spatial practices, and affective states not simply as superstructural reflections of economic conditions; we understand them to be dynamics that can and often do have material effects on economic futures. That is, we see these material, affective, and symbolic dimensions of class to be dialectically intertwined in the production of class subjectivities and class relations.

Below, we identify more precisely the characteristic practices and subjectivities of middle classness, but for new students of the middle classes, we take a moment here to briefly highlight some of the key foundational works on the middle class. Written mainly by theorists outside anthropology, these texts focus largely on the location of the middle classes within relations of production. Although this theoretical lineage has been productive in our understanding of certain aspects of middle classness, its primacy has occluded the above-mentioned dimensions of class subjectivity that enable a broader understanding of how class works, and it has obscured the middle class in our theorizing of class politics.

A key collected volume on the middle class from the late 1970s was tellingly titled *Between Labor and Capital* (Walker 1979). This dual sense of class, with the primary site of class struggle as always already (and only) between the proletariat and the bourgeoisie, comes out of a long tradition of Marxist analysis in which the middle class was expected to "sink gradually into the proletariat," as Marx and Engels (1968[1848]:16) famously remarked in *The Communist Manifesto*. The middle class to which Marx and Engels were referring was the classic petty bourgeoisie, which included small producers, artisans, and farmers (Bottomore 1983:378). The proletarianization of the middle class would occur, Marx and Engels (1968[1848]:16) explained, "partly because their diminutive capital does not suffice for the scale on which Modern Industry is carried on, and is swamped in the competition with the large capitalists, partly because their specialized skill is rendered worthless by new means of production." Less often noted in discussions of Marx's limited engagement with the question of the middle class is that he did acknowledge, almost two decades later in *Theories of Surplus Value* (2000[1863]), the importance of the increasing middle class for the development of capitalism, particularly for the type of immaterial labor (what Marx referred to as "unproductive labor") necessary for capitalism to function (Urry 1973). Although neither Marx nor Engels made a distinction between different kinds of middle-class work, this latter discussion can be interpreted as Marx's recognition of the increasing numbers at that time of technical workers, clerical workers, managers, governmental officials, and teachers, among others (Bottomore 1983:378).

Despite the fact that this type of middle-class labor grew profoundly and became central to the workings of industrial capitalism, many strict Marxist theorists continued to omit the middle class from their theorizing, viewing it as an ideological illusion and thereby maintaining a polarized understanding of class relations. This failure to account for the "empirical evidence" of a large middle class in advanced capitalist societies led ultimately to what Erik Olin Wright (1989:3) described as the "'embarrassment' of the middle class" for Marxists. Attempts to rectify this lacuna by some Marxist theorists at first kept intact the notion of two primary classes, offering up the idea that the middle class was actually a segment of the other classes: either a "new petty bourgeoisie" (Poulantzas 1978) or a "new working class" (Mallet 1975), marking the distinction in the former through its mental (versus manual) labor and the latter through the proletarianization of mental labor that occurred in the years leading up to May 1968, which Mallet hoped would lead the "knowledge industry" to align against bourgeois class power.

This latter theoretical move was a great challenge to one of the central tenets of Marxist theory, which held that the proletariat was the *only* class with radical potential. Central to this rethinking was that the proletariat was no longer the only site for thinking through class politics. Wright's (1989) contribution to these discussions was to build on the work of the

Ehrenreichs (1979), who defined the new middle class *as a class*—the "professional managerial class"—with the potential to align with either the proletariat or the bourgeoisie because their material interests overlapped with both, echoing Gramsci's (1971) argument that the intellectual "ideas" of the middle classes could prove to be fruitful for the interests of *either* the proletariat or the bourgeoisie. Although Wright (1989:26) was ambivalent about whether this was a class unto itself, he saw that this was a group of people simultaneously located in various positions in class relations and thus positioned in contradictory locations within "exploitation relations." The broader implication of this theoretical shift, as Rouse (1995) has elaborated, is that cross-class coalitions—across *all* established lines of difference—are essential to undermining exploitation relations. Such an understanding of the middle classes broadens the parameters of who may qualify as a subject for a morally engaged anthropology.

This volume thus includes pieces that address the more entrenched structural lines of difference, such as gender, race, ethnicity, and religion, and other cultural meanings and distinctions marking class groups and their identifications. This perspective allows us to understand the broad spectrum of how people perceive themselves; make meaning in their everyday lives; make decisions about the types of jobs they hold, the products they consume, and the issues they decide are worth their political action; where they choose to live, relax, and shop; whom they choose as partners; how they raise their children; and when they make moral claims or demand ethical practices. As noted earlier, this broader understanding—beyond relations of production—is often deemed to transcend the boundaries of material concerns. This is why key theorists of the middle class who have, for example, included Weberian analyses of status in their understanding of the middle classes—like C. Wright Mills (1951), who coined the term "white-collar"—were regarded by some Marxists to have moved away from theorizing the role of material interests in the working of capital. Mills's work, in fact, provides an extremely important analysis of the material implications of middle-class status concerns. By revealing the means through which white-collar workers become consumed with status issues, such as their reputation in the office or their access to the boss, Mills demonstrates what leads some white-collar workers to focus little attention on their location in class relations and others to embrace white-collar unionism.

Following in the footsteps of Gramsci (1971), Mills (1951), the Ehrenreichs (1979), Wright (1989), and Rouse (1995), we take the question of whether middle classes are progressive or conservative, politically agentive or politically manipulated, as open to debate, but the debate itself highlights the fact that middle-class practices (not unlike working-class practices in the current political-economic climate; De Genova 2005) are often deeply contradictory. Regardless of whether one's interest in reading this book is a curiosity about middle-class lives or a desire to theorize middle classness or to critique the neoliberal capitalist globalization of our times, the necessary starting point is an understanding of people's everyday lives, including how they act, what they believe, what they say, and what they do not say. This is what historically minded ethnography provides and what this volume contributes. In order to embark upon this type of project, we must move beyond theories that were built on developments internal to particular countries—like most of those described in this section—and begin "to identify the historically specific character of the national/global dialectic" (Rouse 1995:396).

THE GLOBAL MIDDLE CLASSES: HISTORICIZING AND COMPARING THE "OLD" AND THE "NEW"

How are we to understand the differences and similarities among middle-class formations through time and across space? In this book, we argue that middle classes emerge under certain socioeconomic and historical conditions of possibility that allow us to conceptualize the middle class as a coherent category of social analysis. Yet, we also insist that the term's analytical coherence should not obscure the fact that, in actual practice, middle-class dynamics play out in potentially infinite ways. The multiplicity of middle classes documented in this book reminds us that class, despite its analytical value, is never, as E. P. Thompson (1978:147) argued, a "model" or "structure," but a lived experience, a "social process over time." As anthropologists, our job is to maintain a constant balance between the heuristic idea of class, as expressed in our theoretical conceptions, and the lived experience of class, as documented ethnographically in all of its multiplicity.

We foreground the middle class as a cultural and historical problem and explore what is at stake in how we theorize middle classness and its variations across time and space. Because the historical emergence of middle classes is tied to the history of capitalism, it is not surprising that class histories are subject to many of the same conceptual problems as the history of capitalism itself. Histories that understand capitalism to have "originated" in some time and place (typically, early modern Europe) and then spread globally also tend to impose the same teleological pattern onto the history of class. By this logic, capitalist class relations and formations believed to have arisen first in Europe are said to generate derivative echoes as Western capitalism "penetrates" and "modernizes" societies around the world. In this view, all middle classes share an originary moment and vary only to the degree of their distance downstream from the source of historical innovation in the West.

Drawing on the ideas of conditions of possibility, sociospatial interrelatedness, and scalar (rather than categorical or epochal) difference, Liechty (chapter 11, this volume) makes a case for a new reading of middle-class history that accounts for the emergence of middle classes through time and space without falling back on Eurocentric teleologies. Class is fundamentally a relational and interproductive phenomenon: class formations emerge only in relation to other classes, none more so than middle classes, which appear between—and in constitutive tension with—classes above and below. As capitalist economic logics have gradually encompassed more and more of market relations in regions around the world (a scalar rather than epochal process of transformation that is *not* driven by European capitalist penetration), new socioeconomic relations of production, exchange, and consumption also emerge, forming the necessary conditions of possibility for middle classes to materialize.

By this logic, middle classes and middle-class culture are the lived experience or manifestation of particular kinds of socioeconomic relations that arise within certain historical and spatial circumstances and are articulated in and through culturally specific parameters of gender, nation, race, caste, ethnicity, and empire. We can thus theorize the conditions of possibility of middle-class formation in a coherent way (that avoids Western teleologies) while acknowledging that both the conditions and the possibilities are local, highly variable, and nonderivative. For example, just because we see a concept such as respectability associated with middle classness across time and space—from Victorian England to contemporary Nepal (Liechty, chapter 11, this volume), Barbados (Freeman 2000, 2007, and chapter 4, this volume), and Egypt (Schielke, chapter 2, this volume)—does not mean that this class-encoded moral concern traveled by diffusion around the globe from nineteenth-century Britain. Our job as historically and geographically minded anthropologists is to always start with the premise that middle classes or middle-class practices are not real *because* they exist in theory but rather because people exist in classed ways that can be theorized (Wacquant 1991).

Central to this theorization is one of this volume's most important contributions, which is not just to document the emergence of "new middle classes" (which others have also done), but to examine how new and old middle classes coexist, often uneasily. Neoliberal policies have aimed not just at supercharging consumer cultures and organizing the consent and support of what David Harvey (2005:62) calls "traditional middle classes" for the neoliberal state, but also at spawning a host of new middle classes worldwide who are charged with the responsibility of being independent entrepreneurs and consumers, especially in the realm of services. If what Harvey calls the "traditional middle classes" emerged from the populist, modernist, bureaucratic, state-driven economic policies of mid-twentieth-century states (in capitalist countries, quasi-socialist states such as India or Egypt, and even socialist states such as Hungary; Fehérváry, chapter 5, this volume), the "new middle classes" are products of the post-1980 global neoliberal turn. Around the world, declining rates of accumulation during the 1970s triggered new policies of systematic deindustrialization in Western industrialized nations (that is, the "offshoring" of industrial labor) with a matched industrialization in nations such as India and China, along with the privatization of state functions (such as health, education, and security) around the globe. A host of nation-states packaged new economic policies in the ideological trappings of private property, entrepreneurship, and "personal responsibility" (read "personal accumulation and self-optimization"; Ong 2006). While real wages have fallen in the Western industrialized nations since the dawn of the neoliberal era in the 1980s (Harvey 2005:25), profit rates in certain economic sectors worldwide (notably, banking and finance) have soared. This has led, in turn, to the peculiar phenomenon in which, even as the traditional middle classes struggle to maintain their living standard (through longer hours and multiple wage earners), new (neoliberal) middle classes have emerged, with their members typically clustered around the new centers of global finance (Sassen's [2001] "global cities"), where they are best situated to feed off the "trickle-down" largesse of the (pre-2008?) neoliberal economic boom.

The anxious coexistence of various middle classes not just *between* nations and regions, but *within* them, is, both theoretically and ethnographically, one of the most important themes in this book. Ethnographically, around the world we see the tensions between these middle-class formations playing out in a fascinating array of moral politics, pitting against each other new and old economies, nationalists and trans- (or even post-) nationalists, religious conservatives and progressives, social collectivists and "self-made" entrepreneurs, and many others. Theoretically, these dual (dueling) middle classes represent different visions of the state, different modes of capitalist (re)production, and (perhaps most interestingly for anthropologists) different forms of subjectivity, imbricated within shifting fields of gender, race, ethnicity, and geography.

The contributors to this volume explore a range of middle-class sub-jectivities (often constructed in explicit opposition to *other* middle-class subjects), and are what these lived ways of being that need to guide our evolving (re)conceptualizations of the global middle classes. Rachel Heiman's work, for example, vividly illustrates tensions between "new" and "old" middle classes in the uneasy "McMansionization" of middle-class New Jersey residential suburbs outside New York City. Research in India (Srivastava, chapter 3), Egypt (Schielke, chapter 2), Hungary (Fehérváry, chapter 5), and China (Zhang, chapter 9) also points to similar and related tensions between "traditional" middle classes—often associated ideologi-cally with relatively collectivist, national modernization paradigms—and new neoliberal middle classes organized around ideologies of global "free trade," individual entrepreneurial success, and unabashed assertions of private property. This insight reminds us, crucially, that middle-class his-tory is ongoing, its lived embodiment continuing to evolve as its conditions of possibility continue to change across time and space, with elements of the "residual" and the "emergent" simultaneously in play (Williams 1977:121–27).

THE PROMOTION OF MIDDLE CLASSES: BOOSTER STATES AND THE COORDINATION OF CLASS CONTAINMENT

While keeping in focus different conditions of possibility in which middle classes emerge, grow, and contract, how can we conceptualize the relationship between states and middle classes, particularly the role of the state in the formation, management, and privileging of the middle classes? Addressing this question is one unavoidable challenge for students of the global middle classes. To begin, we need to acknowledge that the question of how states relate to classes has to do with how states relate to processes of modern capitalist industrial production. Of course, the existence of class groups *and* capitalism (as one form of market logic functioning among others) long predates the origins of the modern industrial capitalist state. When and how capitalist logic becomes the logic of the state is a question for historians, but, as Braudel (1977:64) argues, "capitalism only triumphs when it becomes identified with the state, when it is the state."

It is worth taking a moment here to remember that—from China and India to the Middle East and Europe—premodern states that depended on agrarian tax bases often harbored capitalist enclaves (typically, coastal trade centers). Relations between agrarian feudal elites and merchant capi-talist classes were often notoriously tense. Arguably, capitalism first "tri-umphed" over (or became) the state when and where weak or receding agrarian (land-based) states allowed coastal merchant enclaves to take affairs into their own hands, forming city-states in which capitalist values could be enshrined as the defining interests of the state itself. In Europe, this occurred famously in places such as fifteenth- and sixteenth-century Venice and Genoa and seventeenth-century Holland, following earlier but closely analogous, state-like capitalist merchant enclaves in the Indian Ocean such as Hormuz, Calicut, and Malacca (Chaudhuri 1985). Notably, it is in the earliest capitalist states that we see the earliest middle classes, complete with many of the same consumer practices, social preoccupations, and moral anxieties documented in this volume.[2]

Yet, to say that middle classes are associated with capitalist states is not to suggest that capitalist state power in some way *creates* middle classes. Rather, the "triumph" of capitalism within any state is one of the crucial conditions of possibility for middle-class subject formation, a process that contributors to this volume document as ongoing in, for example, postsocialist Europe (Fehérváry, chapter 5) and China (Zhang, chapter 9). It is *within* capitalist states—places where capitalist principles (such as private property), corporate rights, and moral values such as "individualism" and "equal rights" are enshrined in state law—that middle classes form in the context of larger relations of production, circulation, and consumption.[3]

Thus, middle classes may not be the *products* of capitalist states in any intentional way, but, as this volume makes clear, states have ever-increasing stakes in the promotion of middle classes and their class interests. It is here that we enter a rich and complex field of play in which capitalist states seek to manage classes and class relations in the interests of capital. At least since the rise of industrial capitalism, (capitalist) states have struggled to keep relations of production and consumption profitable and to maintain political stability, a particularly tricky ideological task for liberal democracies (Poulantzas 2000). The late twentieth-century neoliberal turn is only the most recent (and perhaps desperate) effort to protect rates of capital accumulation and to fend off political unrest, albeit with a much broader range of state players and state political structures. New middle classes have emerged and become more central to states' efforts to develop new markets through new forms of labor, to promote old and new forms of consumption, and to protect the interests of capital through new modes of security and surveillance, military involvement to secure resources and create markets, or the scaling back of resources earmarked for social welfare.

What is perhaps unique about the era of neoliberal globalization is the degree to which states now cooperatively *coordinate* the politics of class containment (Sharma and Gupta 2006). Vast multilateral "free trade"

16

agreements allow states to "free" the movement of goods and capital while regulating the movement of people, thereby creating new global patterns of labor differentiation and class spatialization (Liechty, chapter 11, this volume; Peebles 2011; Rouse 1995). Special "export production zones" in Mexico, India, China, and elsewhere allow robust consumer states with high labor costs to offshore the labor-intensive parts of their industrial work or, as in the case of China, to create spaces within the nation in which certain types of labor practices and trade policies are allowed that might not be acceptable elsewhere within its borders (Ong 2006). This set of conditions enables the free flow of underpriced consumer goods and services to the robust consumer states and to places like India and China with small but growing consumer bases. At the same time, many countries have little to export but labor, generating movement of all kinds, including rural workers flocking to national "special economic zones," formal state-to-state labor export-import schemes (for example, millions of Nepali labor migrants to various Persian Gulf states and Filipina maids to Taiwan and Europe), and flows of criminalized labor migrants across national borders (for example, between Mexico and the United States or between Zimbabwe and South Africa). Changes associated with neoliberalism suggest that the manipulation of transnational class relations is—more than ever—the business of the state (Ong 2006). To be left out of the neoliberal, nodal interstate system is to be essentially left out of the world economy, as Ferguson (2006:13) notes for much of Africa.

If the global regulation and interstate divvying up of class relations is one of the hallmarks of the neoliberal era, this is certainly not to say that capitalist states advocate an overt politics of class within their own populations. On the contrary, neoliberal states around the world typically delegitimize (or even actively suppress) class-based politics, with its revolutionary, Marxist implications. Indeed, states' promotion of middle classness, with the (false) notion that a majority of people belong to this category, is in part to dispel class tensions between working and capitalist classes. The trend is most starkly apparent in postsocialist states where talk of class struggle and workers' rights—until recently the very basis of the state's rhetorical legitimacy—is shelved, replaced by a new (neoliberal) gospel of individual prosperity (such as in Hungary [Fehérváry, chapter 5] and China [Zhang, chapter 9]). In the United States, anyone speaking of class (difference) is open to accusations of implying the (un-American) existence of inequality, promoting "failed socialism," or even "inciting class warfare." From the perspective of neoliberal statecraft, class is an idea—disruptive and destabilizing—whose time has (hopefully) passed.

Yet, even while rhetorics of class consciousness and struggle disappear from state discourse, talk of middle classes proliferates. Emptied of the otherwise contentious language of class, "middle-class" is cast as a benign category, free of implications of exploitation and social struggle, that neoliberal capitalist states can embrace. In the discourses of neoliberal states, middle classes are bastions of "democracy" and "equal opportunity" where ideologically individuated subjects exercise individual (consumer, "lifestyle") freedoms (as opposed to socialist politics that stress group activism and liberatory freedoms). Around the world, national middle classes have become the darlings of the state, identified as model subjects, their interests held up as the interests of the state.[4] Imagined as inclusive and open to any hard-working, deserving, "entrepreneurial" individual, the middle classes have become the (largely depoliticized) ideological and social construct upon which the neoliberal state rests its political legitimacy.

States have long worked to engineer social space according to their changing visions of national interests and ideal citizens. From boulevards constructed in rebellious Parisian neighborhoods, to the building of apartheid townships in South Africa, to bulldozing neighborhoods in U.S. cities for "urban renewal," states have long been deeply invested in creating spaces that (aim to) foster particular kinds of social relations, subjectivities, and practices. The global neoliberal shift toward privatized state functions and the exploding private capitalist development initiatives around the world might suggest an end to state involvement in social engineering. Yet, many have noted the irony that while neoliberal capitalism extols the virtue of "private initiative" and decries the inefficiencies of the bureaucratic state and "big government," as much as ever, states play pivotal roles in *enabling* the very "private" projects that claim to be self-made (often through "deregulation," banking "reform," tax policy, and so forth). Notable for this volume is the fact that much of this new (state-backed) private development is aimed squarely at, and expressly for, the middle classes. The vast new residential, leisure, and commercial developments springing up around the world, described extensively in this book (Srivastava, chapter 3, and Zhang, chapter 9) and elsewhere, graphically chart the rise of new (neoliberal) state practices that directly and indirectly promote the interests of the new, individuated, "self-made," entrepreneurial middle classes, or what Srivastava (chapter 3) calls ideal "consumer-citizens."

One of the key sociocultural phenomena associated with this state privileging of middle-class subjects (and their ubiquitous presence in state and public discourse and global media) is that "middle-class" has become not just an increasingly common category of self-identification, but—perhaps even more important—an *aspirational* category. As middle classness becomes a more and more emic concept (circulated in vernacular speech and made meaningful in local commercial and state rhetoric), middle-class membership becomes a powerful, life-altering goal for many of those poised on its margins, even for those living in states where middle-class booster-ism is not a primary ideological tactic. In chapter 2, Schielke describes the frustration and perpetually delayed gratifications of young Egyptians—in what he refers to as the "'lumpen' middle class"—who long for member-ship in the global middle and struggle to acquire consumer status markers that would allow them to create a version of middle-class domesticity. This middle-class aspiration is, we believe, one of the key political dynamics of contemporary states: by shifting the desires of marginalized groups *away from* liberatory politics (which would threaten the state's capitalist and, in some instances, repressive underpinnings) and *toward* relatively depoliti-cized aspirations for middle-class goods and lifestyles, states can contain discontent (including demands for public education, health care, infra-structure, and so forth) within the confines of never-ending private quests for the consumerist "good life." To aspire to or maintain middle classness is to "live in the future" (Schielke, chapter 2), with one's life oriented around longing, debt, and the struggle to secure that future. Of course, the 2011 developments in Egypt provide an important counterpoint: middle-class frustrations can also be precisely the impetus for revolutionary movements.

Contemporary states thus have deep interests in maintaining and privi-leging middle classes. Whether as a form of self-identification or aspiration, middle-class subjectivity shifts consumerist longing and political action away from social transformation (for the public good) to private trans-formation (for oneself, one's family, or one's small social group), vesting subjects in state commercial agendas (free trade, market access, privatiza-tion, individual responsibility, etc.) rather than in the protection and social welfare of the state. In some extreme cases, the new middle-class subject can even be politically valorized as embodying a new (neoliberal) freedom (usually vis-à-vis a demonized "old" socialist subject) in which individual entrepreneurship is cast as heroic resistance to the "failed economic poli-cies of the past."

Yet, this freedom and agency can be illusory for some and fleeting for others. In an era of globalized media—in which images of middle-class lifestyles and leisure move far more freely than do the marginalized peo-ple who long for them—mobility is a constant contradiction. Strategies of social mobility often require spatial mobility (often criminalized) across the very borders that neoliberal states construct to protect the interests of capital (and middle classes). Additionally, in the current neoliberal scramble for capital accumulation—in which many white-collar jobs now move around the globe as freely as has long been the case for manufacturing jobs—middle-class workers are increasingly aware of the temporality of their upward mobility. As Andrew Ross (2006) describes, young engineers in China are already actively optimizing their wages because they know that it is only a matter of time until another nation-state (such as Thailand or Vietnam) primes its policies and its citizens to offer a more affordable labor option for "offshore-able" middle-class jobs.

LONGING TO SECURE: MIDDLE-CLASS AFFECTS, LABORS, AND LONGINGS

Although the middle classes are clearly in a (relatively) privileged position in the economic order of things, all the chapters in this volume address—in one way or another—the feelings of insecurity that infuse middle-class subjectivities around the globe. This affective state of being, which includes a host of context-specific desires, aspirations, and anxieties, enables us to highlight the types of practices, spaces, and sentiments most associated with middle-class forms of (re)production, consumption, and citizenship. In calling attention to what we refer to as a "longing to secure," which is central to the ontology of middle-class subjects across cultural and national boundaries, one goal of this volume is to underscore the constant anxiety and work that go into the management of middle-class subjectivities. The affective and material contours of this work take many forms, through ever-evolving and newly articulated discursive and spatial strategies and disciplinary practices not only on the part of states but also via a host of key institutions, informal networks, and actors, including aspiring and middle-class subjects themselves (Foucault 1991). In light of the volatility now being experienced by most classed subjects, we suggest that the theorizing of middle-class subjectivities presented in this volume can prove fruitful for thinking through the ontology of all classed subjects in the current global economic climate.

When thinking about classed subjects, we have necessarily returned to classic theories of capitalism that have expanded the theoretical landscape well past the limits of structuralism in which subjects are, as Althusser remarked, mere "spectators...in *an authorless theater*" (Lipietz 1993:106). In particular, it is fruitful to first return to Gramsci's (1971) writings on Fordism, particularly the dialectic between contradictions in relations of production and the production of new subjectivities, or a "new man" in his words. Gramsci was fascinated with the Taylorist means of production being utilized in Ford's factories, particularly the moment when workers' bodies began to move in sync with machines, which in turn freed their minds for other thoughts. As workers started to realize that they were, in Taylor's words, "trained gorillas," they began to question their role in the means of production and to act as citizens in various ways to challenge those relations. Ford's solution was to offer higher wages to his workers, although he soon realized that increased wages brought a new contradiction to the fore: with more money, workers would be involved in leisure activities that might harm their ability to be stable, hard workers, such as drinking too much or spending too much time in the Ford cars that they were finally able to afford. To deal with this challenge, Ford sent sociologists and social workers to the homes of workers to do what Gramsci called a "psycho-physical" transformation, that is, to transform workers into subjects who were rationalized just like the means of production, including temperance in regard to drinking, desires in sexual relations, and ways of being "proper" U.S. citizens.

Gramsci's astute reading of this particular moment in capitalist relations offers a powerful reminder: new moments in capitalist modes of production are dialectically intertwined with new relations of production that involve new classed subjects, and grasping this dialectic means keeping in view people as workers, consumers, reproducers, and citizens. Gramsci's insights into the "psycho-physical" transformation of early twentieth-century working-class subjectivities also challenge us to think about analogous changes in modern classed subjects and how the middle classes might be a particularly fruitful site for theorizing the contemporary "hegemony of immaterial labor" (Hardt and Negri 2004) and what some see as the growing dominance of consumption over production as the defining force behind social class. Starting with the relationship between class subjectivity and labor, we quickly enter the domains and spaces of consumption, reproduction, and citizenship.

It is important to remember that, for Marx and in this example from Gramsci, labor is specifically located in formal relations of production (between the proletariat and the bourgeoisie) and specifically tied to the production of a physical commodity: labor becomes an expression of the commodification of the laborer himself (Marx 1961). Extending this understanding of labor's forms to include what some have defined as *immaterial* and, in particular, *affective* labor (Hardt and Negri 2000, 2004; Hochschild 1983; Lazzarato 1996; Mills 1951), we expand our understanding of not just what forms of commodities are being produced, but what kinds of experiences (from pleasure to alienation) and subjectivities lie at the heart of these modes of production, consumption, and exchange. Theorizing the U.S. middle class in the early 1950s, C. Wright Mills (1951:65) noted that "everything from managerial to teaching, office and sales work—involves putting subjectivity to work in jobs that are less about manipulating things and more about handling people and symbols." What was once a distinctive feature of middle-class labor now marks an ever-expanding field of labor across classes and has, concomitantly, become a central analytical question for scholars of all classes.

Expanding our understanding of labor to include affective labor allows us to more fully theorize the nature of class subjectivity. In the new economy, a variety of services, white- and pink-collar office work, and a widening field of entrepreneurial enterprises strain traditional Marxist notions of the commodity form and thereby what counts as labor and what we might consider a site and mode of production. By rethinking the commodity form in a range of "immaterial" and affective values—in domains such as elder, child, and health "care work"; aesthetic, therapeutic, psychological, and "pleasure" work; and many other services—we can see these forms of labor as new productive processes with new affects and subjectivities produced and consumed within them (Dill 1994; Heiman 2009; Hondagneu-Sotelo 2001; Padilla 2007; Parreñas 2001; Sherman 2007).

Significantly, this new, broadened understanding of labor stems from feminist readings of both the value produced and the skill involved in what had been invisible forms of labor. Drawing from C. Wright Mills, Arlie Hochschild (1983) drew our attention not just to the affective dimensions of exchange relations in the "personality market," but to the gendered labor processes entailed in emotion work (Weeks 2007).[5] Further, the manner in which class subjectivities are permeated by other social formations—not only gender but also ethnicity, race, and religion (De Genova 2005; Fernández-Kelly 1983; Freeman 2000; Ong 1987; Rofel 1999)—demonstrates how the types of labor performed transcend material relations and demand a dialectical class analysis that can account for ongoing transformations in reproduction/production and in production-exchange-consumption. In Barbados, for example, while sugar and manufacturing have declined as the nation's economic mainstays, the state and NGOs have actively promoted entrepreneurship and services as critical growth areas. For women entering the entrepreneurial arena, their business pursuits are tied to new desires in the realms of reproduction and consumption. Specifically, the neoliberal imperative for entrepreneurship is radically altering the structure of marriage and family life, creating new spaces for these newly middle-class subjects to enact their middle classness, such as family restaurants and summer camps for their children (see Freeman, chapter 4, this volume). This is but one example of the dialectical process whereby efforts to address the needs of the capitalist classes lead to new contradictions and a new set of "needs" that, in turn, reflect and produce new subjectivities and forms of alienation.

Attention to immaterial and affective labor is one way to keep labor in focus at a time when many have been inclined to see consumption as having trumped production and when "lifestyle" usurps "class" in the post-Fordist era (Featherstone 1991; Giddens 1991; Lash and Urry 1994). Moreover, as we argue here and as the example of Barbados demonstrates, we need to also make sure that our understanding of immaterial and affective labor includes *all* kinds of immaterial and affective labors. This means considering not only the effort that goes into the mustering of a warm smile on the part of a service worker but also the labor that goes into managing intimate relationships (Freeman, chapter 4) or aspirations for children (Katz, chapter 7, and Schielke, chapter 2), the labor that is required to travel across national borders to buy longed-for goods (Yeh, chapter 8), or the labor that is expended by anxious citizens trying to shape the physical and social terrain of their neighborhoods and communities (Fehérváry, chapter 5, Heiman, chapter 10, and Srivastava, chapter 3).

Like most aspects of middle classness, broadening our understanding of labor to highlight its immaterial and affective forms is not to suggest that these forms are exclusive to the middle classes or to middle classness per se. Rather, given the affective load of in-betweenness, or middleness, characteristic of middle-class life—the heightened anxieties, longings, and desires foregrounded in many of the ethnographic cases presented here—our attention is perhaps more finely tuned to the confluences of affect in middle-class subjectivities and practices. Nevertheless, analyzing relationships between affective and other forms of labor in the middle classes should also transform our understandings of labor dynamics in other classes, including the spheres of the middle classes that are becoming proletarianized or that are transitioning into the capitalist classes.

Along with this extension of the parameters of labor, we argue that a broadening of our understanding of consumption among the middle classes may have similarly illuminating implications for other classes. Consumption has been perhaps the single most recurring theme in scholarly works on middle classes. From early modern (McKendrick, Brewer, and Plumb 1982) to Victorian Britain (Campbell 1987) and the United States (Blumin 1989) to early twentieth-century Peru (Parker 1998) to contemporary Brazil (O'Dougherty 2002), India (Fernandes 2006), post-Soviet Russia

(Patico 2008), Africa (Burke 1996), and East Asia (Robison and Goodman 1996), historians and anthropologists have repeatedly linked middle-class formation with the emergence of consumer cultures. Likewise, every author in this volume (to a varying degree) portrays middle-class life as bound up in consumer practices whether in terms of debates over appropriate consumption, lives oriented around consumer desire, or consumerist projects of class distinction.

Yet, many of these same authors also argue that middle-class practices cannot simply be reduced to consumerism. Although there is almost universal agreement on the links between consumerism and middle-class practice and subjectivity, how consumption relates to labor (including new kinds of labor) in middle-class experience is both understudied and a matter of debate. Whether consumption is the defining theoretical characteristic of middle classness or one of several constitutive dynamics in middle-class life may depend on whether one takes a broad, *interclass* (relational) perspective or a more focused, *intraclass* point of view (and the two may not be mutually exclusive). Any system of interclass socioeconomic relations requires not only producers but also consumers. As the scale of production increases over time, the social location of consumption shifts and expands, as we are seeing most dramatically in China today.[6] Capitalist mass production requires mass consumption, and since the nineteenth century, Liechty (chapter 11) argues, the modern middle classes have emerged as the social location and mode of consumption of industrial capitalism. With the application of fossil fuels to industrial processes worldwide, the scale of production has exploded, requiring ever-greater scales of consumption—and ever-larger consumer classes—in order to maintain rates of return on capital investment. It is in this interclass, mutually constitutive context that consumerist middle classes have become not just more visible, but more and more crucial to the ongoing viability of global capitalism. As we have noted, this creates new tensions for states involved in this process. In Indonesia, for example, the dramatic rise in consumption among the middle classes led the state to fear that male state workers might escalate state corruption to support their wives' material desires. The state thus instituted training classes for the wives of state workers to teach them to be more modest in their material desires (Jones, chapter 6). States increasingly depend on consumerist middle classes, but along with this increased dependence come increased anxieties over the moral practices of consumption and increased state vigilance in managing middle-class consumerism.

Producing and nurturing middle classes have become central concerns of contemporary neoliberal capitalism nationally and globally because consumerist middle classes, along with entrepreneurial middle classes, have be-come so important for the future prospects of global capital accumulation. From a critical perspective, we have to recognize "entrepreneurship" as part of a broader neoliberal ideology that helps mask middle-class privilege, legitimates middle-class "success," justifies cuts in social services, and blames the poor for their poverty (Srivastava, chapter 3). Yet, it is now clear that neoliberal state ideologies that privilege entrepreneurial labor (through various subsidies and policy "reforms") in fact make possible new middle-class subject positions, new forms of immaterial and affective labor, and new patterns of class mobility, consumption, and capital accumulation (Freeman, chapter 4). State ideological practices have material outcomes through which middle classes serve as essential converters within capitalist relations of production, their entrepreneurial labor and consumption required for the transformation of commodity production into profits and for the capital accumulation of the capitalist classes. With so much of global economic "health" hinging on the unpredictable affective dynamics of middle-class consumers (consider the concept of "consumer confidence"), building consumer infrastructure, promoting middle-class buying power (consumer debt), and advancing middle-class freedoms (construed as consumer choice) and "security" (in gated communities) have become central goals of capitalist state politics from China to India to Europe to North America. Still open to debate is whether consumption by the middle classes alone is enough to satisfy the needs of global capital. As efforts in the United States during the Great Depression (Cohen 2003) and recent moves in China indicate (Wong 2010), in the face of global recession, nascent national middle classes may be too small, requiring states to recruit working-class consumers in their efforts to stave off recession and social unrest.

These efforts to promote consumption are inextricable from the development, management, and politics of a physical geography of consumption: sites *advancing* consumption (such as the offices of marketing firms), sites *for the labor of* consumption (malls), sites *of* consumption (homes), sites *about* consumption (mass media), and sites undergirding all four (public and private infrastructure). All of these spaces and places are critical when thinking about middle-class subjectivities. For example, if suburban shopping malls and gated communities are contemporary spatial manifestations of certain aspects of middle classness in particular contexts, they also are the reservoirs of middle-class (and other) anxieties, aspirations, and longings. Just as a conspicuously grand gate proposed by a new homeowner provoked the ire of a New Jersey zoning board for its challenge to the spatial codes of middle-class appropriateness set by long-standing residents (Heiman, chapter 10), so, too, are elements of interior home decor and modes of transportation scrutinized for their capacity to uphold expected markers of middle classness in liberalizing China, India, and Hungary (Zhang, chapter 9, Srivastava, chapter 3, and Fehérváry, chapter 5).

Spaces are critical for subject making not simply in terms of marking the physical spatialization of class—which proximities are afforded and which curtailed (Lefebvre 1991[1974])—but it is in those very spaces that classed subjects are made. All the places mentioned above are sites whose boundaries both reflect and actively produce class subjectivities and affects. Bourdieu (1977:90) notes, "The 'book' from which the children learn their vision of the world is read with the body, in and through movements and displacements which make the space within which they are enacted as much as they are made by it." We see this among certain middle-class segments in the United States as people channel their class anxieties into decisions about which schools their children should attend in order to acquire the right edge to eventually make it into a top university (Katz, chapter 7). We see this power of space vividly demonstrated, as well, in contemporary Tijuana, where having a visa to cross the border for shopping excursions into the United States not only marks one as a member of the Mexican middle class but also creates the conditions of possibility for becoming a middle-class subject (Yeh, chapter 8).

Not surprisingly, it is often in regard to space that we see the most pronounced presence of citizen action among the middle classes. Theorists who see middle-class politics as largely separate from interclass material relations (that is, consumption, production, reproduction, and circulation) often analyze it on its own terms, that is, outside an explicitly materialist worldview and without direct reference to its situatedness in larger capitalist relations. This view is often associated with the relatively leisured and educated people who, in early modern European history, pioneered a new "bourgeois public sphere" in which to rationally debate ideas and advance progressive causes (Habermas 1989). This is the approach taken by historians as diverse as Sanjay Joshi (2001), writing of an emerging middle class in nineteenth-century Lucknow, and Robert Johnston (2003), writing on "radical" middle-class progressivism in early twentieth-century Portland. In this book, we hold the question of middle-class politics in analytical tension. From residents welfare associations in India (Srivastava, chapter 3) to zoning debates in the United States (Heiman, chapter 10) to news reporting on party politics in Mexico (Yeh, chapter 8), middle-class politics may represent progressive political agency, even those inextricably bound up in, and therefore complicit with, the larger capitalist political economy. Politics, too, is a form of immaterial and affective labor with very real material effects.

CONCLUSION

At many moments in anthropology's history, the discipline has contributed in significant ways to class analysis. In these uncertain economic times, we strongly believe that too much is at stake not to contribute what we do best: provide close ethnographies of critical issues that push theories to account for the histories, intricacies, and nuances of everyday life. The contemporary moment calls not for a repudiation of class but rather a richer, more expansive framework in which "middle-class" is integral to the analysis. It is time for us to include people from *all* class positionings in our anthropological studies and, in so doing, to develop more nuanced accounts and theories of class itself.

What we are arguing for here is a framework for theorizing middle classness that is productive not only for anthropologists and others whose research seeks to tackle this set of questions head-on but also for those who have studied among the middle classes but have not analyzed the class dimensions of these groups per se. Even many participants in the advanced seminar that spawned this collection found that their work centrally engaged middle-class actors but their capacity to theorize the particularities of middle-class practices and subjectivities *as* class practices and subjectivities crystallized through our collective conversations. We hope that this volume provides the same rich experience for its readers.

The chapters that follow provide a supple understanding of class in which culture, consumption, and subjectivity are critical dimensions of class relations and of the project of class making, as are material and immaterial modes of production. It is this fascinating interweaving of desires and the creation of new "needs" that our volume brings to the fore. In so doing, it highlights the convergences and subtle redefinitions of labor and consumption as they unfold across processes of social reproduction, production, and citizenship. We hope to illuminate the means through which a person's identifications, habits, and affects have bearing on the workings of capitalism. Middle classness seems especially to demand this analysis, which ought to inspire a rereading of class more generally.

Acknowledgments

We are extremely grateful to everyone at SAR for their support of the advanced seminar, particularly the President's Council for its sponsorship, Nancy Owen Lewis for her masterful synchronization of our seminar sessions, Leslie Shipman for her warm and nourishing hospitality, and James Brooks for his immediate enthusiasm for our topic and continued confidence in its salience. We would also like to express our gratitude to Aihwa Ong for her involvement in the organization of the seminar and for her incisive comments during its discussions and to Hai Ren for the latter as well.

This introduction and the book as a whole are products of our collective debates and conversations at the seminar, as well as the discussions in the ensuing years with seminar participants and other colleagues who joined the book project. Collaborations can be challenging, and edited books often face delays and unexpected hitches. Our collaboration has been remarkable in both practical and intellectual ways. Despite having met only for the first time when we arrived in Santa Fe, we found that right from the start our weekly editorial meetings and collaborative writing process (courtesy of Skype) were intellectually invigorating and wonderfully generous. We have challenged and enriched one another's thinking in a process that has been an unexpected delight for the three of us (volume editors). We also want to express our appreciation to the two external reviewers for their extremely thoughtful and productive comments, Brooke Hansson for her extraordinarily careful readings and astute recommendations, Kriszti Fehérváry and Rihan Yeh for their close readings of the introduction in its final stages, Merryl Sloane for her meticulous and thoughtful copyediting, and Lynn Baca, Cynthia Dyer, Ellen Goldberg, and Lisa Pacheco at SAR Press for guiding us through the laborious process of review, revision, and production.

Notes

1. This is not to say that there has been no anthropological research with subjects from among the middle classes. There has been a long tradition of research among middle-class subjects with other theoretical questions in mind, as in gender studies (Ginsburg 1989; Martin 1987), colonial studies (Feldman 2008; Stoler 2002), science and technology studies (Gusterson 1996; Martin 1994; Rapp 2000; Zaloom 2006), linguistic anthropology (Mertz 2007; Ochs and Taylor 1995), urban anthropology (Low 2003), and visual anthropology (Mankekar 1999; Strassler 2010), for example.

2. See, for example, Schama 1987 on middle-class culture in seventeenth-century Holland.

3. Fehérváry (chapter 5, this volume) argues that in Hungary in the 1960s–80s the socialist state experimented with limited forms of private property, consumerism, and individualism in ways that fostered a "socialist middle stratum" that shared many cultural similarities with the experiences and conditions of middle classes elsewhere in Europe. Ong (2006:10) writes of China's use of zoning technologies in the 1980s and

1990s to create "economic and political zones that are marked off from the normative activity established elsewhere in the planned socialist environment."

4. Having lived through national election cycles in India and the United States in 2008, Liechty notes the comparable and striking, laser-like rhetorical and political focus on middle-class interests in both elections, in spite of the vast underclasses in each country.

5. And, as socialist feminist standpoint theorists have noted, these can be sites not only of exploitation but also of agency and transformation (Weeks 2007:237).

6. We could trace the consuming classes from prehistoric "chiefs," to medieval elites, to early modern urban bourgeoisie, to—with the advent of industrial capitalism—emergent middle classes. Although this wording suggests that these classes are related in terms of some unilinear historical process, these consumer formations (and, no doubt, many others) may be simultaneous and interrelated. What is more, there is no reason to believe that this sequence is not reversible, given that the scale of production (and therefore consumption) can as easily fall as rise.

2

Living in the Future Tense

*Aspiring for World and Class
in Provincial Egypt*

Samuli Schielke

As I am writing this, in early 2011, Egypt is in a state of transition following the January 25 revolution. The sense of boredom and frustration
that prevailed before 2011 has at least temporarily given way to an unpredictable mixture of pride, hope, and anxiety and an immense degree of
politicization. Many of the people whom I encountered during my research
were nihilistic about their country but have now become active in politics.
Where the transition will take Egypt is impossible to tell at this moment.
What can be said with certainty, however, is that the situation I describe in
this chapter has been one of the key grounds for the revolutionary uprising.
As Walter Armbrust (2011) pointed out in an early analysis, the January 25
revolution was directed against the humiliating and frustrating conditions
of life that had emerged through the entrenchment of neoliberal economics and politics since the 1970s, a process that generated tremendous expectations while keeping the means to realize them limited to a privileged
class. The Egyptian revolution has been a middle-class one insofar as it has
been carried by a deep frustration caused by the elusiveness of the promises
about a decent, comfortable, middle-class life. The success of Egypt's post-
revolutionary governments will be measured on their ability to make the
fulfillment of these promises less elusive.

Some of what is written in the present tense in the following pages
already belongs to the past. I have decided not to rewrite the chapter to

make it up-to-date. Things are still changing too quickly to do that. The reader should therefore bear in mind the historicity of this chapter, which is describing not a lasting condition but rather a unique moment in a changing world.

AT THE OUTSKIRTS OF THE WORLD

For several years, the Arabic satellite channel ART has broadcast all matches of the Champions League live. It was an instant success in Egypt, a country where association football (soccer) has long been extremely popular, where major matches of the national league sweep the streets empty as people gather in front of their televisions, and where football enthusiasts show an encyclopedic knowledge of the players and matches of European football competitions. The Champions League has successfully become a part of this culture of football, and when major teams meet, cafés and homes are full of enthusiastic fans rooting for their European teams. Teams with Egyptian players are always especially liked, but so are any other teams that have a record of playing well and winning.

Sa'îd, a football enthusiast from the village of Nazlat al-Rayyis in northern Egypt, who is wearing a Tottenham training suit, emphatically argues for the importance of football: "Here in the village, everyone is a football supporter. They support Egyptian teams, and everyone supports also European teams. I support Barcelona and Real Madrid in the Spanish league, Chelsea in the English league, Lyon in the French league, and so on."

Looking at the lively football fan culture in this village of fishermen and farmers, one has hardly the impression of a provincial existence. When the men (women never frequent cafés in the village) gather to watch a Champions League match, they consciously and enthusiastically participate in a global event that establishes a virtual, worldwide community of supporters. But after the match is over, things start to look different. Still wearing the training suits and T-shirts of their favorite clubs and national teams (next to Egypt, especially popular are Brazil, France, and Italy), still excited or disappointed about the match, the men have not forgotten that theirs is a less exciting, mostly disappointing share of the world. At another moment, when no football match is running, Sa'îd speaks in less enthusiastic tones:

> Here, there is no middle. There are only poor people, and those
> who are well-off are thieves. The country is divided between
> those who are honest and don't know how to steal and those
> who are thieves and well-off. You know why I come here to watch

football? I only watch football in order not to think. There are people who watch football because they really love it, but I just don't want to think. Just like people who take pills and hashish— if you talk to one, he is not there. He is happy and doesn't think about anything. And if his mother is sick or his family needs food, he doesn't care. He could only care if he had power over his situation. But you can only have power over your situation if you have money.

Even when interrupted by the intense concentration and excitement of a good football match, a much more prevalent mood among young men is a perpetual sense of boredom and frustration. Frustration (*ihbât*, in the sense of disappointed aspiration [*tumûh*], not in the Freudian sense of sexual frustration, which in Arabic would translate as *hirmân*, "deprivation") is a central topic when people tell about their life trajectories. It implies a sense of finding one's expectations unmet, one's plans obstructed, one's aspirations disappointed; every day is marked by boring stagnation as one looks forward to a better life but encounters only pressure (*daght*) and obstacles.

Why open an inquiry of middle-class aspirations with a story of people watching European football, when some of these people see themselves as just trying to escape from an oppressive reality? I want to look at the longing for a place in the middle of a society that takes as its point of reference a—real or imagined—standard of the First World (*al-ʿâlam al-awwal*). This is a highly ambiguous quest. It combines the compelling presence of a world of class and wealth, viewed through mediated images and ideal career trajectories, with a troubling absence of actual paths to success. The ambiguous nature of football fan culture well characterizes this mixture of presence and distance. The connection of the young men in the village to a wider world of possibilities through media and popular culture does not alleviate their boredom and frustration but actually intensifies it. As another young football enthusiast argues, "the more progress, the more boredom" (Schielke 2008b:258). In other words, the greater one's expectations, the deeper the sense of stagnation.

But where do the desire, despair, and pressure come from? Poverty and oppression alone fall short of explaining the situation. The previous generations hardly had a greater scope of freedom, and they were generally poorer. Sa'îd offers a clue, although he does so through a negation. He claims that in Egypt, there is no middle class, only rich and poor. This is a very common claim, yet it is hard to take at face value, given that a significant portion of Egyptians would describe themselves as "middle-class" in some sense. And Sa'îd has as his main aim to become a part of the middle class, to live a life that is characterized by comfort (*râha*) and respectability (*ihtirâm*). His claim about there being no middle class is the expression of a widely shared and powerful sense of aspiration, albeit a frustrated one. I will take a closer look at the nature of this aspiration, trying to understand what kind of an ideal of life it is directed at, what makes it so pressing, and why some solutions to pursuing this aspiration appear to be so powerful and compelling. With these questions, I foreground the issues of temporality and aspiration, which in my view are just as important as status and relative positionality when it comes to class and belonging. Rather than take the middle class as a given social formation, I look at it as a promise, a pressure, and a claim—an imagined site and a standard of normality and respectability that directs people's aspirations and trajectories.

The concepts of normality and respectability are associated with quite specific markers: higher education, a position as a civil servant or as a formal employee, a reasonable income, a house or an apartment of one's own, a classy interior, a marriage to a respectable family, command of English, possession of a range of goods, such as a computer, an automatic washing machine, or a private car, and, last but not least, a "refined" (*râqî*) habitus expressed in one's styles of dress, socialization, language, and religiosity. And yet "middle-class" is not simply a social formation that fulfills these markers. Instead, these markers communicate the possibilities of social status and, as such, are constantly in movement and notoriously relative (see Bourdieu 1984 ; Douglas and Isherwood 1979). Goods in Egypt, both conspicuous and inconspicuous, gain their value as markers through complex relationships that involve elite tastes, global fashions, mass production, installment plans, the art of necessity under conditions of poverty, and much more. What counts as higher education and refined habitus in one context can fall far short of the minimum in another. What appears as a powerful, high-status good can be quickly surpassed by new, more powerful goods. More than being clear criteria of middle classness, these are diffuse markers of aspiration.

Actual class distinctions in Egypt are highly complex, and there are different and at times incompatible articulations of "middleness," to which I will return below. Moreover, the aim to belong to an imagined middle of a society, a key component of which is the aspiration to a First World standard of living, has become shared by vastly more people than have the material and habitual means to achieve a middle-class existence (whatever its criteria may be). It is this global middle class *in spe*—real by virtue of the reality of people's aspirations, imagined by virtue of their unfulfilled nature—whose pressure and frustration I explore through the case of provincial Egypt.

What I am presenting is mainly a male perspective in a thoroughly patriarchal society where providing income and being in charge of a family are necessary conditions for being a "man" (*râgil*) in a social sense. It is therefore primarily (but not exclusively) men who are seen as responsible for generating the money necessary for social ascendance through, for example, migration. Middle-class aspiration among women in Egypt gets articulated differently, most notably via the centrality of marriage as a path of social mobility and the much greater concerns about reputation, styles of religiosity, and dress (see Schielke 2008a; cf. Jones, chapter 6, this volume). I do think, however, that it can be safely claimed that the overall pressure to advance and the search for "the good life" by belonging to an imaginary middle are shared by men and women alike. Although the trajectories involved are strongly gendered, there is a shared sense of what it means to live a good life as a respectable member of society.

I did fieldwork in Nazlat al-Rayyis, a large village of fishermen, farmers, and civil servants near the Mediterranean coast in the Nile delta,[1] and in the inland informal settlements of Alexandria, where workers and civil servants live physically near but in other respects rather far from the affluent Egyptians who inhabit the waterfront for two months every summer.[2] Although much research has been done about the dramatic inequalities of wealth and power in the city of Cairo (see, e.g., Abaza 2006; de Koning 2009; Kuppinger 2004; Singerman 2009; Singerman and Amar 2006), even that research, with its nearly exclusive focus on Cairo, is strongly part of the split that renders Cairo, along with the Red Sea and Mediterranean beach resorts and the waterfront of Alexandria, overly visible and "the provinces" (*al-muhâfazât*; also called "the regions," *al-aqâlîm*) nearly invisible (but see Hopkins and Saad 2004; Hopkins and Westergaard 1998; Weyland 1993; Zâyid 2005). My aim is not to do away with this centralist split; it, just like the global inequalities it partly reflects, is a fact of life, and an important one too. Instead, I try to look at it from the point of view of the aspirations of people who stand at the "outer" poor, or provincial, side of the class divide and look up with a mixture of admiration and frustration at the metropolitan centers of the nation and the world. These places are not the most marginalized in the political and economic map of Egypt (those are likely to be found in the south of the country). Still, those who live in them will always be reminded about their provincial status: aware of the world of possibilities accessible through media, fashion, and consumption, which appear at times within their grasp yet are mostly inaccessible.

MIDDLE CLASSES, OLD AND NEW

With some important exceptions (e.g., Abaza 2006; de Koning 2009; Singerman 2009; Sonbol 2000; Winegar 2006; Zâyid 2005), the issue of class has been rarely problematized in the more recent social scientific studies of Egypt and apparently much of the Middle East, where a strong focus on religion and political movements has often rendered class troublingly invisible. A part of the problem also lies in the elusive nature of class, especially middle classness.

The middle classes are called in Arabic *al-wasat*, "the middle," "the center," or *al-tabaqât al-wustâ* or *al-tabaqât al-mutawassita*, "the middle classes"—importantly in the plural—and one also hears the English term "middle class," which in its Egyptian usage refers mainly to the upper-middle class. It is an elusive category that includes various socioeconomic and symbolic positions, some of which lie extremely far apart, such as old artisan and merchant families; civil servants in the badly paid, wider ranks of the public sector and its privileged parts, such as the military, security, the oil industry, and the Suez Canal; employees in middle and upper positions in the private sector; shop owners and small- and middle-scale entrepreneurs; and wealthy land-owning farmers. Add to this the claim expressed by Sa'îd that, due to the growing inequality caused by economic liberalization, there is no middle class in Egypt (any more), and the confusion is perfect.

In the current age of global capitalism, there are several senses of middle classness (just as there are different senses of class in general, to which I will return). Here, I focus on two. One is the "new" middle class embodied by entrepreneurs and employees of private sector companies. They have global tastes and, increasingly, global standards of living and English private educations, are highly visible in both national and international media, and are often celebrated as the key to the progress of developing countries in becoming part of the First World. This "new" middle class is actually not entirely new. Although it partly draws upon the new wealth generated through the economic liberalization policies that began in the 1970s, it also partly represents a continuity of older middle classes and urban bourgeoisie who have been successful in tapping into new sources of income and status. The work of, among others, Leela Fernandes (2004) and Anouk de Koning (2009) has vividly shown the ways the "new" middle classes establish a normality of relative wealth, progress, and cosmopolitan belonging to the First World by systematically rendering invisible those who do not have access to this First World normality. This construction—often physically implemented through urban restructuring and other spatial regimes (Srivastava, chapter 3, and, Zhang, chapter 9, this volume)—of a

globally connected, upper-middle class not only excludes other, less affluent senses of middle-class aspiration but also implicitly denies their existence by relegating them to an invisible "outside." There, they appear as an
unstructured mass of annoying and dangerous riffraff. In the jargon of the
affluent Egyptians, that diffuse "outside" of the neat First World islands has
come to be referred to as *al-bî'a*, the vulgar environment (implying primarily the lower-middle classes, not the very poor), which has to be kept at a
safe distance (de Koning 2009 ; Sonbol 2000:201).

Whereas the upper, globally connected sense of middle classness
involves inclusion and versatility, with metropolitan tastes, language skills,
well-paid jobs, and global movement, another, sharply different sense of
middle-class belonging and aspiration has none of these. Grounded in the
tradition of the once new middle classes based on public sector jobs, Arabic
state education, and a strong modernist and nationalist sense of belonging
to an avant-garde of national culture (see Ryzova 2004, 2008), this latter
sense of middle classness is shared by a vastly greater number of Egyptians,
who enroll at state universities that provide low-quality education, aim for
badly paid public sector jobs that offer at least some sense of security, and
try to make ends meet by combining public and private sources of income.

Paradoxically, as this "lumpen" middle class—based on deteriorating
public sector jobs and state schooling—declines, it also grows and continues to exert attraction and the pressure to achieve. The established urban
families that once depended on government jobs in public education and
administration have in the meantime often moved up to the "new" middle
class of the private sector and the privileged parts of the public sector.
The government jobs that have been dramatically devalued in terms of
money and prestige appear now within reach of ever-larger parts of the
population. Rural farmers, fishermen, and craftsmen like Sa'îd now expect
either themselves or their children to also have their share of the modernist dream of education, a white-collar job, and relative comfort. This can
be best seen in the enormous emphasis on education, which has gained an
almost unquestioned dominance. Also, girls' education, once considered
a problem in many conservative milieus, is today generally considered a
necessary part of gaining any social status, especially on the marriage market. As the school system, too, deteriorates and the quality of education
appears more than questionable, parents are ready to spend a significant
part of their income on private tutoring, which has become an indispensable, albeit informal, part of the educational system. This highly paradoxical development is not restricted to Egypt but appears to be taking place
globally, making "middle-class" emerge as the social status aspiration of

FIGURE 2.1

Teachers and children during a break at a government school in Alexandria. Photo by S. Schielke.

ever-vaster populations, who thus come to claim a status and social position that may stand in dramatic contradiction to their material condition and the quality of their education (see, e.g., Liechty 2003; Freeman, chapter 4, this volume).

This is the sense of class and social status that most of the people I know either cultivate or strive for. Many of them are teachers, perhaps a characteristic profession of the class of underpaid civil servants. Although their income is low (with the exception of those who manage to mobilize large-scale private tutoring) and their social status has significantly declined, they are always careful to show themselves as modern, cultivated, and civilized in terms of dress, choice of jargon, preference for Salafi reformist or Islamist interpretations of Islam, and often a general display of intellectual superiority.

The class dimension of religion is an important element of this distinction. Although religious orientations are not automatically class dependent, subscribing to middle-class modernism is characteristically aligned with subscribing to reformist Islam, that is, an understanding of Islam as a clear set of rules rather than as a complex tradition of spiritual authority. Ever since its emergence in the nineteenth century, Islamic reformism in both its pietist and its Islamist activist variants has been centrally associated with urban middle classes with secular higher education who have worked to distinguish themselves from the more mystically oriented traditions of conservative rural and urban milieus. (Contrary to common assumptions in the Western media, militant Islamism is not a prerogative of the poor, but of students.) However, currently, the spread of Salafi and Islamist movements in all social milieus (including the elites) is turning reformist Islam from a distinctive marker of education into a prevailing common religious sense across class boundaries, with consequences that are yet to be seen (see Schielke 2006).

Only a short distance from the "popular" (*sha'bi*) classes where they often come from and whose more or less aspiring children they teach at government schools, civil servants possess a sense of belonging to a middle class that most importantly depends on a combination of a conscious display of modernism (most visibly expressed by the suits worn by civil servants at work) and attempts to acquire conspicuous consumer goods. The most desired of these is a private car, something that almost everybody in the upper-middle classes owns but that is still out of the reach of most teachers and other ordinary civil servants.[3]

For many decades during the royal and Nasserist periods, this "old" (back then, still new) variant was the hegemonic sense of middle classness: belonging to the progressive avant-garde of the nation and being distinct from the uneducated popular classes (who, in fact, could sometimes be wealthier than the middle-class civil servants—something that has become even more common in the wake of economic liberalization; Ryzova 2004, 2008). But, although the lower-middle class of teachers and other civil servants may appear national and conservative and the upper strata of private sector employees and privileged civil servants may seem cosmopolitan, this is so only in regard to their financial and educational capital (based on private education and good English skills). The world is equally a concern for all of them, albeit in changing ways and with different relationships to the nation. And if nationalism appears as the guiding value for all but a few elites in Egypt, the nation is continuously being thought of in terms of an indispensable relatedness to global standards of modernity, civilization, and sophistication (Winegar 2006:17–22).

This sense of middle classness, with its reliance on the public sector and strong commitment to nationalism, is also strongly related to an ideology of modernism. Modernism, in its Islamist and secularist varieties alike, has always been very much about how to match the metropolitan examples around the world—mainly, France in the early twentieth century, the United States since the 1970s, the Gulf states most recently. This is the class that once was seen as the "modernized" segment of Egypt and many other formerly colonized nations. Meanwhile, the aura of modernity of the old middle classes has become less bright, now that the new middle classes have occupied the privileged place of global connectedness, and the old middle class has become the most important milieu of Islamist movements (which are often mistakenly viewed as anti-modernist). And yet the old middle class continues to exert a strong pull, promising progress to all those sons and daughters of workers, farmers, small shopkeepers, and others who hope to take the step toward middle-class respectability and comfort.

The shift from the nationalist old to the neoliberal new middle class very much reflects the shift in the way Egypt is governed and represented by its political elites. The century-old image of the modernist and committed civil servant as the ideal citizen has not been abandoned, but it has been complemented and problematized by the image of the successful and self-reliant entrepreneur or private sector employee. Although these two images involve different markers of class and different senses of citizenship, they do share a history of nationalist modernism that is deeply involved in a constant comparison of Egypt with international standards of what it means to be a modern nation. The identification of the middle-class citizen with the nationalist project highlights a key temporal aspect of middle classness in its different formulations. The middle class, more than any other class, is oriented toward the future. It is less about being than it is about becoming, about aspiration to a place, so to speak, in the middle of the society as a respectable person in relative comfort and with an optimistic future. This becomes especially clear when we look at the expectations of those who can hardly claim belonging to the middle class by any definition but for whom a middle-class life nevertheless appears as the guiding aim of their trajectories and dreams.

FIGURE 2.2

Dining table used as a computer desk in a teacher's home in Alexandria. Photo by S. Schielke.

LOOKING TO THE OTHER SIDE

Sa'îd is a caterer for weddings, seasonal work of low status and unsteady and unreliable income. Most of his friends work as fishermen at nearby Lake Burullus. Others are teachers and civil servants. But they all have expectations for life that go much further. Their speech is saturated with the notion of advancement, be it in terms of money, social life, or politics. Advancement is also emphatically indicated in Sa'îd's apartment, to which he has recently moved with his wife. Usually a man's biggest investment in his lifetime, the apartment to which the new couple moves is a key site to display an image of the good life, even if it later may get worn down for lack of money for maintenance. It usually costs slightly more than people can actually afford, and the explosive cost of marriage and housing is a constant issue of lament and discussion among men. And yet it is rare to meet anyone who would be willing to compromise about the standards of

41

the marital apartment. With a television set, decorative Qur'anic verses on the walls, a guest room with sofas and a glass table, a European-style dining table, and a cupboard full of glasses and plates reserved for display, and a kitchen equipped with a refrigerator and modern household utensils, the apartment is not just about comfort. The functionality of many of these items lies less in their use value and more in their value as status goods. Appropriating a certain style is a tremendous concern for married couples furnishing apartments, and great effort and money are spent to acquire sofas, tables, silverware, glasses, and coffee sets whose primary function is to be shown rather than used. Items of more practical daily importance may be neglected if the couple is short of cash. Furnishing an apartment is first and foremost a conscious display of belonging and aspiration to a world of style, class, and wealth.[4]

The ubiquitous dining table is an interesting marker of this aspiration. Almost all Egyptians I know prefer to sit on the floor. The dining table remains largely unused, unsuited as it is for the Egyptian ways of sitting and eating. With the spread of private computers, it is sometimes turned into a computer table. Often, it simply stands empty. But whenever I, a rare European guest, have been invited to eat in Egyptian houses, the hosts have wanted to serve the food on the dining table. The same applies to other guests of honor, who are received with a formality that makes eating on the floor unsuitable and the dining table imperative. A friend of mine declined to sell his dining table in a difficult economic situation. Although to me it appeared to be a completely nonfunctional part of his apartment, for him it was too valuable to sell even when he was badly short of cash. The dining table is not primarily there for dining; it is there to show class, and class means, among other things, cosmopolitan styles in eating and housing.

I say "cosmopolitan" rather than "Western" styles because the world of affluence and advancement to which people so much want to belong includes different sites that cannot be understood separately and "the West" is only one of them. This aspiration for social advancement reflects a cosmopolitan way of looking at the world and positing oneself as potentially a part of it (see Graw n.d.; Marsden 2007, 2008; Pollock et al. 2002). The moments in which people compare their situation with other places and aspire to reach some of those standards are not so much related to a specific place, but more to a wider imagination of the world, primarily a First World world of possibilities. This is the world of wealthy Egyptians in the capital and in the holiday resorts, of the rich Arab oil-producing states, of Europe and the United States, of the interiors of soap operas and films. This world, in the diffuse and exciting sense of that vast conglomerate of places and possibilities that surround and influence us, is at once omnipresent and painfully absent in the experiences of young people from provincial Egypt. This world is seen in the Champions League, in the risks and prospects of migration, in the imitation of global styles and standards of housing and dress, and in countless other moments of everyday life. And in every one of those moments, it is also out of reach.

One of the most powerful expressions of the frustrating presence and absence of a life with higher standards is the constant comparison of "here" and "abroad" (*barra*) by people in provincial locations. "Here," there is nothing, no chances, no hope, whereas "abroad," chances are abundant and life meaningful. In this imagined political economy of time, in which the metropolises enjoy a time of meaning and progress while the global provinces are left with an empty, boring time full of nothing, migration appears as a solution over all others (Graw n.d.; Mains 2007). This is true in the eyes of Sa'îd and his friend Ibrâhîm, a man in his mid-twenties earning his money as a fisherman on nearby Lake Burullus and, like Sa'îd, a football enthusiast. They claim that boredom, a bad economic situation, and a general sense of pressure make migration inevitable. Said Sa'îd:

> Lack of work and the difficult economic situation make you bored. When you have money, you are not bored. When you have no money, you get bored because there is no chance of improvement. It stays like it is, or it gets even worse. You go to work if you have any, you go to the café, and every day is like the other. There is no hope of improvement. That's why everyone wants to get away. Either abroad or inside Egypt to Alexandria or Cairo. They want to go anywhere to have a chance of advancement.

The discussion then moves to the topic of illegal migration to Greece and Italy on fishermen's boats and the risk of death involved. Said Ibrâhîm:

> The people are so desperate that they are ready to take the risk of dying to cross the sea. Their boredom, their unemployment, their lack of hope has gotten them so far. And the political pressure gives an additional share. In Egypt we have the worst government in the world, the worst! It gives the people no chance but puts more pressure on them instead. It gets people so far that they, out of the emptiness [*farâgh*] they are in, are ready to take the risk of dying on the way to get across the sea.

To "get across the sea" is to get access to a better life.

I will return to the specific pressures and promises of migration, but for the moment, it is important to hold the image of being stuck in a provincial location and being forced to risk everything in pursuit of something that one imagines can be reached on the other side of the sea. The sea is a powerful geographical expression of a sensibility that characterizes the aspirations for a better life around the world. Geographic locations, as well as the obstacles that separate them, are invested with powerful expectations about the things they stand for. These locations stand for the economic, political, and personal possibilities that young people, mostly men, hope to realize in their lives. In this way, Italy, France, America, Saudi Arabia, the United Arab Emirates, and the socially exclusive locations of Egypt—the North Coast, Sharm al-Shaykh, al-Muhandisin, Nasr City, New Cairo—are constantly a part of people's lives in the village of Nazlat al-Rayyis, but in a frustrating, troubling way.

Mona Abaza (2006:51–52) points out that the countryside has been significantly transformed through the economic liberalization policies that began in the 1970s and that have gradually intensified ever since, mainly through cash-crop farming and labor migration to the Gulf states (see also Weyland 1993). Although the profits of this transformation have not been equally shared—tenant farmers, for example, have clearly been on the losing end of the transformation, as have many civil servants and the fishermen who provide the economic backbone of Nazlat al-Rayyis—there is no doubt that the countryside has experienced a tremendous influx of money, consumerism, and aspirations for a middle-class lifestyle since the 1970s. If, in the 1950s, peasants would enter the provincial city for an annual fair or religious festival with a sense of awe and intimidation (see Qâsim 1996[1969]), today people of rural origin self-consciously move between the village, provincial cities, the capital, and at times abroad and expect that the promises of progress and welfare, be these socialist or capitalist in nature, are theirs to share as well. And when they fail to get their share, they do not blame the promises. They blame corruption, nepotism, privatization of public enterprises, greedy elites, impenetrable class barriers, failing government, America, and the Jews. In terms of the real economic and social resources of advancement and wealth, Egypt is dramatically split between the wealthy center of Cairo (including Alexandria and the beach resorts) and the neglected and stagnating provinces. Yet, in terms of aspiration for a better life, Cairo is everywhere, and so is a First World standard of living, to which the affluent Cairenes have real access and which others believe should be their own too.

The dining tables and sofas purchased for marriage, the counterfeit sports gear worn by Sa'îd and his friends, the Western business suits worn by underpaid teachers and civil servants, the mobile phones, computers, and laptops brought home by migrants—all are significant markers of a lower-middle-class aspiration to live according to the standards of the world. Regardless of their often sharply felt shortcomings in terms of quality and status, these goods communicate a desire to belong to the same wider world to which both the inhabitants of the global metropoles and the affluent Egyptians are seen to belong.

This is the ground of the despair Ibrâhîm articulates: the frustrated aspiration to the kind of standard of living and civil rights he knows about, at times also encounters, but cannot reach in his own life. This "globalisation as absence" (Graw n.d.; see also Ferguson 2006) could easily be, and often is, framed as a situation between the Third World and the West, the poor and the rich. At least in Egypt, however, it is more complicated: "the world" includes not only Europe and the United States but also the Gulf states and the Egyptian upper classes. And the situation of many people who aspire to belong to that world is characterized not just by poverty, but, perhaps more urgently, by middle-class aspiration.

CLASS AS BELONGING AND LONGING

Amid such complex distinctions and distances, it is difficult to determine the place of "the middle." The world of the young upper-middle-class students and professionals in Cairo (see de Koning 2009) is so strikingly different from the world of the lower-middle-class students and civil servants in Egypt that it is questionable whether the notion of middle classness makes any sense at all. All Egyptians routinely speak about the middle classes, but people from the lower and upper strata often do not recognize the other strata as "middle." When Daniela Swarowsky and I were screening the first part of *Messages from Paradise* (Swarowsky and Schielke 2009) in Egypt, occasionally, some of the mainly intellectual or affluent middle-class viewers felt that we showed a marginal segment of poor villagers from the popular classes. This conclusion was striking, given that all of the people in the film were educated, some of them highly, and all had a firm modernist sense of middle-class distinction. But from the perspective of students at a private university, they appeared to be exotic and unspecific representatives of the mass of vulgar people somewhere out there on the margins.

What (or who), then, makes up the middle class? Is being middle-class something essentially characterized by aspiration, or is there a substantial middle class out there? Is the middle class a group of people or a structure of feeling? The answers are complex because there are different ways of belonging to and longing for class status simultaneously at work. Various kinds of people would describe themselves as "middle-class" in the aspirational sense of claiming to belong (or at least hoping to belong) to the middle ground of good and respectable people with a reasonable level of education and income. At the same time, they exercise a sharp and sensitive perception of class habitus that relies not on aspiration but rather on status. Fashionable dress and a good haircut are never enough to become refined, just as poverty will not stop a person from being recognized as an aristocrat. To clarify the relationship between aspiration and distinction, and the sense of the middle involved in these, it is important to look at the different ways in which a claim to being middle-class can be made.

First, there are at least two different senses of the middle. Following one sense, people claim to belong to a harmonious and quite wide middle of society, though this claim may be contradicted by the realities of their life. Following another sense, they cautiously assess their position as compared with people above and below them, working hard to distinguish themselves from those below and in an ambiguous manner at once criticizing and imitating those above. In the first sense, being middle-class is an imagined, stable position in the center of society, a very positive even if unrealized category, as expressed in the valorized connotations of the Arabic word *wasat* (middle, center). In the second sense, being middle-class is a precarious position in the actual social hierarchy, located in the more negative category of "in-between," as in the Egyptian Arabic expression *fi n-nuss* (halfway, in-between). In graphic terms, the middle in the first sense is located at the center of a circle, whereas the middle in the second sense is located between two fields in a vertical alignment. This also implies different, parallel senses of class. In the vertical alignment, class is habitus in Bourdieu's (1979) sense, a system and criterion of classification that can be very detailed and elaborate, especially when it comes to people who are seen to be immediately below or above oneself. Here, distinction becomes the key, and almost all people are acutely aware of their in-betweenness—possibly with the exception of people very high at the top and very deep on the bottom, although even they are likely to have some sense of inferiority and superiority, respectively. But in the sense of approaching the center of a circle, class is an aspirational category of belonging that is also expressed in attempts at acquiring means of distinction but which has an additional dimension: the hope or claim to belong to the "good, normal people." This is the middle not in the sense of being in-between, but in the sense of being in the center.

Second, the position from which one lays claim to middle-class belonging makes a difference. Given the complexities and contradictions of aspiration and distinction, the claim to belong to the good middle of the society requires different ways of dealing with contradictory reality. For the relatively well-off, neoliberal, new middle class, it is easy in material terms to perceive themselves as being part of the ordinary good people in the center of society. The material markers of the good life are largely available to them. At the same time, their small number vis-à-vis the less well-off majority of the population troubles their claim to being the good, normal people. The exceptional character (in quantitative terms relative to the society at large) of the upper-middle-class lifestyle necessitates elaborate policies of spatial, visual, and cultural exclusion to maintain the wildly inaccurate claim that the upper-middle classes make up as much as 80 percent of the population, an assertion that some upper-middle-class Egyptians have quite seriously tried to convince me about. In their turn, the less well-off, old middle class of civil servants, especially those who, like Sa'îd, possess no markers of distinction beyond aspiration itself, can more credibly claim to be the normal people. Yet, their material and cultural claims to constituting the (potential) middle are much more precarious, based as they are on low-quality public education, badly paid public sector jobs, and modest private wealth. Either way, the "normality" of a way of life is a normative claim, measured by its power in becoming a standard of aspiration and not by its statistical distribution.

To summarize a very complex matter, I argue that class in everyday practice cannot be reduced to any single criterion or perspective but consists of different elements that can have different significance. It is precisely this complexity that allows so many different people to lay claim to being middle class while at the same time they are acting in a highly stratified society of countless but nevertheless specific and recognizable classes (in Bourdieu's sense of classifications). For the people in provincial Egypt featured in this chapter, however, it is clear that the middle class is an aspirational category in a double sense. To be middle-class is to look forward to a better future and to work on the means of distinction and advancement to reach it. But for many people in Egypt, being middle-class is also a dream of social being that is highly attractive, compelling, and unfulfilled.

Does it make sense at all to speak about middle classes, given the ambiguity of the term and the complex stratifications of class in a society like Egypt? I think that in certain cases it probably does not. It does make sense, however, to speak about middle classness insofar as it is a powerful ideal that informs the ways in which people describe their society, their position in it, and their possible trajectories. Middle classness is a direction and a claim as much or even more than it is a place in society. In this sense, to claim to be part of or to speak in the name of the middle is also to take the moral high ground toward both the ignorant poor and the decadent rich.[5] This is one of the moments when the valorized position of the middle as the center of society (as opposed to its margins) is especially clear. But this moral high ground of critique is ambiguous. For one thing, the critique of the ignorant poor in the name of education and "consciousness" (wa'y)—a key term of intellectual distinction—is often articulated by people who, in terms of their material conditions, are only marginally different from the "ignorant" they criticize. More strikingly, the middle-class critique of the elites is mixed with admiration and imitation in an intricate way.

As I was taking a walk on the waterfront of Alexandria with my friend Mukhtar, a teacher whose modest income allows him housing only in the much cheaper and less valued inland part of the city, he pointed at a boy standing on the balcony of one of the high-rise buildings facing the sea. "Does he have more right to stand there than my son?" he asked bitterly. Talking about the seafront, he often expresses a moral critique of the wealthy who spend one month a year in an otherwise empty apartment, getting their money from questionable sources and spending their free time in establishments featuring alcohol and prostitutes. Thus, he echoes Sa'îd's comment that everybody in Egypt is either poor or a thief. But at the same time, Mukhtar makes it clear that he would very much want to live in one of these high-rises on the waterfront, that the standard of living and the lifestyle of the wealthy inspire the ways he tries to realize a modest success for his family. The ambiguous role of the wealthy in the middle-class aspirations of those who are barely making it is in many ways analogous to the paradoxical role of the United States in regard to Egyptian nationalism and modernity: in one instance, an enemy, a legitimate target of moral critique and opposition; in another instance, a standard of progress and the good life to be admired and imitated.

Looking at middle classness as a (moral) claim and at the denial of other people's claims implied in this claim, there is a risk of slipping into a comfortable position of moral judgment. In my own research, for example, I have long focused on the work of distinction and exclusion involved in asserting a middle-class status (Schielke 2006, 2008a). I think that I have had a point there, but in doing so, I may have unwittingly become part of a wider undercurrent in the social sciences in which the middle classes are somehow the most despised of all people. Whereas liberal political theory often celebrates the middle classes as the avant-garde of democracy and wealth, in more critical, social scientific works there is much less sympathy for (see, e.g., Bourdieu 1979) and sometimes even a kind of hatred of (see, e.g., Biehl, Good, and Kleinman 2007:11) the middle class, its ideals of the good life, its aesthetics, its attempts to move upward. This, I think, is problematic, even suspicious, given that most academics of our generation belong to the middle classes by any definition. The matter is more complex, less susceptible to such simple moral counter-hierarchies. Distinction implies aspiration, and exclusion implies belonging.

The "middle" in the middle classes denotes an aspiration for inclusion in the nation and the world, which is grounded in the awareness that there are others whose inclusion is more perfect and which is marked by attempts to distinguish oneself from the poor and the ignorant. "Middle" as a reality is forever elusive. But as a direction, an imagined site of good social normality (Fehérváry 2002 and chapter 5, this volume; Yeh, chapter 8, this volume), it is powerful.

PRESSING PROMISES

To understand exactly what kind of life is associated with that imagined middle and why that imagination is so forceful, almost inescapable, it is helpful to look at one of the most compelling paths to reach it: migration. The enormous urge toward migration, whatever the cost, among the less affluent middle classes and those aspiring to join them (as do Sa'îd and Ibrâhîm) is first and foremost an attempt to realize some of this, to become part of an imagined yet genuine middle.

Young men routinely state to me that the main—although not the only —reason to migrate is money. But "money" encodes a wider set of meanings; it is strongly associated with the quite specific things money is needed for, commonly expressed with the phrase "building a life." For a man, to build a life implies all the conventional responsibilities and assets that make a respectable man: marriage, an apartment or a house (a necessary precondition for marriage), and a reasonable standard of living. All of this, in the imaginary evoked by "money," is to take place in or near one's place of origin, be it in a new floor of one's parental house, a new house in the fields outside the village, or an apartment in a nearby city. Money evokes a sense of establishing oneself as a respected and wealthy man in the already existing web of family relations, moving upward but remaining connected, which significantly involves also willing financial assistance to less well-off relatives. Money evokes, in short, an ideal image of how advancement in a classed society should look. But although some money is earned even by the poor in Egypt, it is hardly ever enough to qualify as "money" in this sense of sufficient resources for social advancement. At the same time, money is absolutely indispensable in the informally privatized economy of the public sector, where clientelistic relations (*wasta*) and bribes are generally the only paths to good jobs. In this situation, where in order to move upward, one first needs to have money, migration appears as *the* path over all others to a middle-class existence.

In fact, most of the people who desperately desire to migrate are not living in utter deprivation. Those who most urgently aspire to a better life have usually already had some share of it. Even in a rural location like Nazlat al-Rayyis, there is some work, people have enough to eat, child mortality and illiteracy rates have significantly dropped, and the standard of housing has dramatically risen in a matter of a few decades.[6] And yet everybody complains about the unbearable economic pressure of rising prices, consumer debt, housing, marriage, education, and so on. Although material conditions may have improved, economic pressure appears to be only increasing.

By any standards, people in a village and in an urban "popular district" (*hayy sha'bi*) in Egypt have generally many more things than they did some decades ago. Yet, most of them are likely to complain that the economic situation has become much more difficult. The standard of living for most people has risen, but it is dramatically worse than that of the wealthier Egyptians living in the urban centers—a difference that people are acutely aware of. Most Egyptians can now buy many more things than they could twenty or fifty years ago, but buying these things is not something one chooses to do. In most cases, these are things one *must* buy—even if they may seem to be dispensable luxuries to an outsider. The unused dining tables, glasses, and coffee sets must be part of the apartment of a newlywed couple. Color television sets, mobile phones, and computers must be bought. Egyptians commonly find it strange that I do not have a car although I can afford one. If you can afford a car, you must buy one. Aspiration is not a choice. It is a necessity.

The same inevitable character also marks the necessity of migration, as Sa'îd and Ibrâhîm articulate. Mothers encourage sons to migrate to make money for marriage, which is getting more and more expensive partly due to the migrants who can outbid other men on the marriage market. Just as one is not free to wish to marry or not, one is not free to want to go abroad or not. There is very little choice. Migration is inevitable, and that is why the inability to migrate is such a disaster for young men. That is why knowing that one may die on the way may still be preferred to the social death of failing to meet one's obligations.

Herein lies the twist in the relation of migration and aspiration. Whereas aspiration is strongly related to an ideal of belonging to a wider world of class and style, migration does not usually have the direct aim of joining that world abroad to live in it in class and style. Instead, migration appears first and foremost as the path to realizing at home a life of class and style that may match that of the wider world. Migration is primarily (albeit not only) a strategy for being at home in the desired condition of wealth and respectability. It is about belonging to the wider world in the sense of class, not in the sense of geography. The question of migration thus becomes a question of the promises and pressures people face in looking forward to their trajectories at home. Where, then, lies the power of this pressure (*daght*)? What makes some things so inevitable?

This pressure depends not only on the limited means people have but also on, equally if not more importantly, their growing consumption. This is not to deny the enormous economic pressure people in a place like Nazlat al-Rayyis experience, and, like them, people in the cities and villages around the country hope to realize a better life for themselves and their children. But the pressure here is toward social ascendance more than struggle for survival. It is precisely the increase in consumption (and in the possibilities of consumption) that has brought along an increase in economic pressure. This can be best seen in the explosive increase of consumer and investment debt in Egypt. Small businessmen who in the past never took on debt now commonly finance their operations through credit. This is partly intentional, a policy strongly encouraged by international donor agencies, which promote debt as a form of empowerment (Elyachar 2005). Almost all consumer transactions beyond one's daily needs are financed by payment in installments. The system of *nuqta*, an exchange of loans paid in the form of wedding gifts, has rapidly expanded from a way to finance marriages into a much wider system of mutual credit. Every new television set and satellite dish, every new house and newly furnished apartment, even the new clothes people buy on the occasion of annual festivals are evidence of not only an increasing amount of consumption but also an increasing pressure of debt. Reliance on debt, in turn, is not just a matter of an acute lack of liquid funds, since the wealthy upper-middle classes also routinely depend on debt to live a lifestyle that suits their status. Rather, debt is a horizon of spending based not on what one has but on what one hopes to earn in the future.

This is not to say that people would not have gone into debt in the past as well. But what has changed, according to the accounts of small businessmen I know, is the reason to go into debt. In the past, people were compelled to borrow money mainly to overcome acute financial problems, and there was something dishonorable about borrowing money if one's finances were solid, except for very specific occasions such as weddings. Saving, not borrowing, was the ideal way to fund investments (such as building a house)—a view further supported by religious sensitivities regarding interest in particular and debt in general. Today, the pressure of investment and consumption has increased to a degree that it is nearly impossible to finance a home through savings, and debt as a way to deal with contingencies is giving way to aspirational debt, a permanent way of living on installment credit.

This pressure to live bigger than one can actually afford is a central feature of the sensibility of living on debt and aspiring for a better future. Consumer debt is a form of everyday financial discipline that is explicitly directed at the future (see Appadurai 1996:66–85). The prospect of being able to repay one's debt is dependent on the expectation of growth and advancement. A future built on debt entails fantastic promises and unbearable pressures.

Are there alternatives? Rather few, if any. Religion may appear a likely way out of the race of progress, and the tremendous wave of religiosity that has swept Egypt, a Muslim-majority country with a large Christian minority, could be taken as a sign of people searching for a nonmaterial steadiness. Yet, the way Egyptian Muslims approach their religion carries the same sense of future orientation, with a strong pressure to become even more pious, a cultivated anxiety about not being good enough, of perhaps falling short of God's grace (Schielke 2009). Religion is definitely expected to provide a nonmaterialistic counterbalance to a greedy world, but in practice, the idea of contentedness with the will of God is often overwhelmed by anxiety in spiritual, as well as in material, terms. This was bothering my friend Mustafa when we met in a café in downtown Alexandria. He had recently started his career as a salesman in an import-export company, and he was making good progress establishing business contacts. Still, he could sense nothing but pressure to get ahead:

> It's a strange thought I have had in the last few days. I think that
> qanâ'a [conviction, contentedness] is all a lie. Everybody talks
> about it, but nobody is really content. Sure, faith [îmân] should
> be about contentedness with what our Lord gives us. I'm sure that
> in the age of the Prophet, people were content. When you read
> the Qur'an, it praises the grain, the dates—but it doesn't talk
> about chicken or meat. In those days, people could be content

with the simple gift [*ni'ma*] our Lord gave them. But I don't see anybody today really having that. Everybody is under pressure, never content, always looking for something better. You can never stop and be happy with what you have reached. If I make 700 pounds [approx. US$150], I am already worried about where I can get more. The only way you can stop and be content is to surrender like a beggar, stretch out your hand, and let things happen to you.

Although Mustafa believes that there was a time when Muslims were able to be content with God's simple gifts, he does not see this happening around him, no matter how many religious phrases of patience and contentedness people may use. With this observation, he puts his finger on an important ambiguity of the Islamic revival that has found people searching for trust and guidance in a scripturalist reading of Islam: the Islamic revival preaches contentedness, but its emotional quality is marked by anxiety, a constant worry about one's share in the afterworld, a sense that one is never quite close enough to God. This anxious religious aspiration for contentedness shares a key sense of temporality with capitalist production and consumption. Both are based on the constant production of a sense of shortcoming, of an aspiration for a good life that is always only partly fulfilled, never to a complete degree of satisfaction.

CONCLUSION: LIVING IN THE FUTURE TENSE

What unites these moments of aspiration, frustration, migration, consumption, and credit is the temporality of the future (see also Koselleck 1989[1979]:349–75). Aspiring to inclusion in the world, to a place in the middle of the society, is in all its moments directed at things to come: money yet to be made abroad, installments yet to be paid, construction materials yet to be bought, houses yet to be built, a marriage yet to be arranged, wedding loans yet to be returned, children yet to be educated, private tutoring yet to be financed. Especially for those whose resources are limited, daily life becomes a breathless race to keep up with the demands of the future. The present is never good enough, and even if one may want to stop and be content, the pressure of debt and installments leaves little choice but to go on. Herein lies the troublesome ambivalence of aspiration for the imagined middle. Living in the future tense, one has the imagined good life always in sight but will never reach it, as in a famous Soviet joke from the age of the Cold War:

> Comrade Khrushchev has declared that communism is already
> visible on the horizon. Question: What is a horizon? Answer: An

imaginary line between earth and sky, which moves farther away
as one approaches it.

This perpetually unfulfilled nature of the aspiration for a better life
reflects great expectations and optimism but includes tremendous pressure
and frustration as a result. It is this pressure of which Ibrâhîm and Sa'îd
speak, one so strong that in order to have a chance in the struggle for social
advancement, young men are willing to risk death—especially when the
other alternative is the social death of failing to keep up with the pressure
of upward mobility.

In terms of the immediate trajectories, this struggle can be told as
a story of class aspiration. But I insist that we need to think about class
belonging in relation to global belonging. Since the colonial period and
even more so in our time of global consumer capitalism, aspiration and
social mobility cannot be accurately comprehended from an exclusively
national perspective. Class is not simply about social position in a given
society, but also a matter of positioning oneself in relation to the compelling and powerful metropolitan centers of the world, both near and far.
Following the same logic, the global is not an outside world of "flows" as
opposed to a static locality, but an ascribed quality of those things that
appear as metropolitan, powerful, and compelling. Both class and the
global are thus intimately related to normative expectations and claims
about the desirable conditions of life. Young Egyptians' aim to match the
national and global standards of the good life entails a global claim for
membership or, perhaps more accurately, equality (see Ferguson 2006).

For Sa'îd and Ibrâhîm, support of European football teams does make
them members of a real global community of fans. But they are only marginally part of the consumption that the whole contemporary industry of
football has been designed to facilitate. A televised match on an illegal
cable network and a counterfeit training suit are the best these men can
get. Connected to a global media event, they are highly aware of both
their belonging and their exclusion and the pressure created by the tension between the two. From their point of view, their experience is one of
always having to settle for the counterfeit instead of the authentic: a corrupt travesty of a modernist school curriculum, secondhand leftovers of
the metropolitan lifestyle of affluent Egyptians, Chinese imitations rather
than Japanese original products, the mediated image rather than the real
chances of America, and so on (Graw 2012). And they are acutely aware of a
constantly disappointing but still pressing and powerful promise of a world
of consumerist fulfillment just out of reach.

The problem is not that their belonging and longing are illusory because of their aspiration's imaginary nature. Belonging is always a work of imagination. The problem is more complex. Football fan culture presents one of the many little daily escapes in which people engage in order to find a way to live a dignified life under conditions of great pressure. But these little escapes also inform the desire to be part of a world of class and wealth. They, too, become part of a horizon of imagination and potential action where certain paths appear to be so overwhelmingly better than others that there is almost no choice. Herein lies the troubling ambiguity of imagination as a social practice: what offers itself as a possibility and a way out also becomes a source of anxiety and unbearable pressure, and vice versa.

Acknowledgments

This chapter is based on a paper that was presented at two workshops: "Migration at Home: Migratory Imaginations and Imaginary Cosmopolitanisms in Africa and Beyond" at Zentrum Moderner Orient (ZMO), Berlin, March 11–13, 2009, and "The Middle Classes: A Global Perspective" at the School for Advanced Research, Santa Fe, New Mexico, March 28–April 2, 2009. This chapter is strongly indebted to my shared work with Daniela Swarowsky on her documentary film project *Messages from Paradise,* which we shot in Egypt and with Egyptians in Austria (Swarowsky and Schielke 2009). Some of the interviews quoted here were originally conducted for the film, and many of the ideas were developed in our discussions during the production of the film and through feedback from the Egyptian audience that first saw it, in December 2008. Inspired to a high degree by this shared work, I owe many of this chapter's key ideas to Daniela, as well as to the many Egyptians who were willing to reflect with us about their own situation. I am also indebted to Mukhtar Shehata, Knut Graw, Jessica Winegar, and the participants at the two workshops at SAR and ZMO for their critical feedback and suggestions.

Notes

1. Fishing is the traditional economic backbone of the village due to its proximity to Lake Burullus. The public sector is a major employer because the village hosts a number of schools attended by children from the neighboring villages and hamlets.

2. Alexandria is split into two socially distinct parts: the more affluent and metropolitan seaside (*bahri*) and the poorer and provincial inland (*qibli*).

3. With the recent entry of cheap Chinese autos into the Egyptian market, the private car has now come within reach of a rapidly growing part of the population, and those who cannot yet afford one are learning models and prices by heart and discussing

the advances of different models with great enthusiasm. These displays of conspicuous consumption and modernism as markers of class belonging are also at work in China, where, as Li Zhang (chapter 9, this volume) illustrates, residential belonging has moved beyond the ability to afford real estate and relies more broadly on one's ability to afford a certain lifestyle, especially one that includes a private car.

4. Krisztina Fehérváry (chapter 5, this volume) identifies a comparable dynamic in regard to the family home in Hungary, where a new discourse of the normal is increasingly

reorganizing residential living.

5. Rihan Yeh (chapter 8, this volume) similarly explores the nuanced ways in which this

moral middleness is negotiated through a story of a *tijuanense* (Tijuana) resident who was able to overturn the decision of members of the elite in favor of a gentleman described as an "indigenous type." The subtext represents a moment in which a member of the middle class was able to wrest authority and power from the elite while speaking for a figure who was otherwise incapable of representing himself in public.

6. These assessments are all based on discussions with older people from the village.

3

National Identity, Bedrooms, and Kitchens

Gated Communities and New Narratives
of Space in India

Sanjay Srivastava

This chapter explores the relationship between new urban developments, discourses on the roles of the state and the market in contemporary
Indian life, new cultures of consumerism, and the making of "middle-class"
identities. I have placed the latter term in quotation marks in order to indicate its complex and shifting history in the Indian context; it is not something that is "out there," to be captured through quantifiable measures of
identity. In particular, the background to this discussion is that middle
classness is a moral and ethical claim to being a specific kind of person, a
claim that is made by diverse sections of the Indian population, covering
many income and wealth categories.[1] Beyond the claims of marketers and
advertisers, it is a significant category of self-definition.

The voluminous body of writing on the contexts of the Indian national
movement in the opening decades of the twentieth century constitutes the
earliest example of scholarly explorations of the making of middle-class
consciousness. During a slightly earlier period, the various "social reform"
movements of the nineteenth century were also significant sites of public
activity by the "educated classes" and provide another entry into the topic
(Shah 2004). In many cases, public agitation was carried out by associations
formed for the purpose of propagating reformist ideals. Hence, the idea of
an activist middle class as an agent of change was significant during both
the colonial (Joshi 2001) and postcolonial eras.

Scholarship on the more recent period has investigated the making of middle-class identities in the South Asian region through focusing upon the multiple processes and circuits of modernities. These have included the media and secular and religious nationalisms (Mankekar 1999; Rajagopal 2001), discourses and practices of consumerism (Liechty 2003; Mazzarella 2003; Rajagopal 1999), food (Appadurai 1988), the cultural politics of "tradition" (Greenough 1995), globalization and its impact on "lower middle-class" groups (Ganguly-Scrase and Scrase 2009), schooling and the postcolonial middle classes (Srivastava 1998), and identity politics in a time of economic reforms (Fernandes 2006). Other relevant studies include those of "educational reform" (Kamat 2002), "bourgeois environmentalism" (Baviskar 2002; Baviskar, Philip, and Sinha 2006), and middle-class "environmental activism" (Mawdsley 2004).

I will be extending the discussion in the works listed above in a particular direction, namely, the interweaving of the cultural politics of space and middle-class identities. Some scholarship on South Asia does address this aspect (see, for example, Brosius 2010; Fernandes 2006; Liechty 2003); however, it does not form the key focus of these works. This chapter builds upon perspectives on the meanings of space—especially new spaces in the urban environment—as crucibles of identity. I am not, however, concerned with accounting for the putative "fragmentation of social life" engendered by "new forms of urban property development" (Voyce 2007:2055). My key concern is the question of what cultural worlds result—and are invoked—through the changing relationships among the state, capital, ideas of citizenship, and consumer cultures as they inscribe urban landscapes with conspicuous territories of commerce, leisure, and residence.[2]

In an extraordinary range of large and small cities across India—and in an equally mind-boggling inventory of land under construction or where construction has been completed—there is an accumulating body of discourses and aspirations that gathers around gated residential enclaves, speaking the language of a "social" sphere that is produced and reproduced under tightly controlled conditions. The Lucknow-based Sahara Corporation, for example, has plans for the "world's largest chain of well-planned self sufficient high quality townships across 217 cities in the country"; it has already constructed the Amby Valley township near the Maharashtra city of Pune on ten thousand acres, described as "independent India's first planned, self contained, aspirational city remarkable for its unsurpassed grandeur and plush signature features."[3] In the Rajasthan township of Bhiwadi, some 60 kilometers from Delhi, no fewer than eleven real estate companies are reported to have launched gated residential projects in different price ranges, hoping to cash in on the proposed development of a number of "export processing zones" and "special economic zones" by large corporations, such as Reliance and Omaxe (www.indiarealitynews.com, accessed August 15, 2009). The Omaxe group also has residential projects in twenty-two cities across nine states in north and central India.[4]

The phenomenon of using gates to produce physically demarcated residential localities is not a new one in contemporary Delhi and other Indian cities. Residents welfare associations (RWAs) have been particularly active in installing and maintaining gates at key entry points into several of Delhi's residential "colonies." The gating of Delhi's residential localities began in the mid- to late 1980s (earlier than the late 1990s date suggested by Waldrop [2004]) and was carried out under the aegis of RWAs in different parts of the city. The gates were the earliest visible signs of the RWAs' increasingly public presence as a formal entity in urban affairs. The middle-class citizen marking out privileged, delimited, and "secure" spaces—where urban civil life and relationships could unfold—formed the raison d'être of RWA activity. Ostensibly based around the notion of collective action, RWAs, in effect, became the key vehicles for articulating an exclusionary urban politics of space. The result was the de facto privatization of public thoroughfares in residential localities by the installation of large iron gates at points where the internal streets of the neighborhood joined the external main roads. Across Delhi, these gates index a number of contexts: a lack of confidence in the state's ability to provide security, the strong sense of a middle class under threat from urban underclasses, and the overwhelming perception that such threats can be countered only through localized and locality-specific means that convert public thoroughfares into private and highly regulated spaces.

The trend in India of gating localities that had earlier been built as relatively open neighborhoods has—via the custom-built gated community—given way to stricter spatial expressions of community. Further, as I have noted elsewhere (Srivastava 2009), residents welfare associations and their involvement in a wide variety of urban governance issues—stimulated by the state through public-private partnership schemes such as Bhagidari in Delhi—have been a significant factor in producing citywide ideas about middle classness and the requirements of its nurture. Of course, as Kamath and Vijayabaskar (2009) point out, *all* residents welfare associations do not share a common set of concerns and interests with regard to urban issues, and these differ according to, for example, the socioeconomic characteristics of the localities represented. The significant aspect, however, is that while empirically there may not be a singular middle-class identity across Delhi, RWA activity itself is part of the process of *producing* the notion of a homogeneous middle class in the city. The RWAs are crucial to the processes of consolidating a common set of issues that are seen to affect all "middle-class" people and of producing consensus about middle classness. However, there is an important difference between the RWAs of the previously open localities that were subsequently gated, and those of (newer) gated communities that have always operated within walled spaces. The latter have far greater leeway in producing imaginaries of desirable publicness as compared with their older counterparts.

The transformation of vast tracts of land into walled enclaves that promise personal transformation through the occupation of specific spaces echoes developments in other parts of the world (see, for example, Caldeira 2000 on Brazil; Geniş 2007 on Turkey; and Pow 2007; Low 2003 on the United States and Zhang, chapter 9, this volume, on China), and I will outline the specificities of the local circumstances in the making of middle-class identities in India. In particular, I will explore the ways in which the gated condominiums of India establish their meanings through the simultaneous acts of fencing *and* establishing a connection with the worlds beyond the fences.[5] So, although there are similarities between gated communities in India and in other parts of the world, there are also key differences. Unlike São Paulo, for example, there are, thus far, no "fortified enclaves" in India that are "controlled by armed guards" (Caldeira 2000:258), though security is a key concern and part of a narrative that now engulfs the urban landscape. The following section explores this relationship between exclusion and desire in the making of contemporary Indian identities

DRAWING ROOMS, BEDROOMS, AND KITCHENS IN THE NATIONAL IMAGINATION

> *Living space crafted with utmost precision:* Imagine a drawing-dining room that is as vibrant as your evenings. Imagine bedrooms that provide blissful sleep. Imagine a kitchen that provides a playground for culinary delight. Imagine a life where aesthetics meets convenience. Imagine living in *Parsvnath Castle.* (Parsvnath Developers, www.parsvnath.com, accessed July 30, 2009)

There are many varied promises in the publicity material for the proposed Parsvnath Castle gated residential enclave in the Punjab industrial township of Rajpura (population approximately eighty-five thousand). As a great deal of scholarship has pointed out, narratives of space are produced out of the putative accomplishments of their past, the possibilities of their present, and the promises of their future (see, for example, Brosius 2010; Lefebvre 1991[1974]; Massey 1994; Soja 1989). Residential spaces are sites for enfolding current and future occupants into conversations about the possibilities of individual and collective transformations. The most significant shift in spatial narratives in India since the 1990s has been from imagining the nation as an affective site of belonging and being (see, for example, Jain 2007 ; Roy 2007), to envisioning drawing rooms, bedrooms, and kitchens as locales of identity. That is to say, if national spaces—the state-run educational system and factory towns, for example—were once the imagined spaces of personal and familial transformation, that role now appears to have passed to the more intimate localities of residence. As I discuss below, the postcolonial era in India has witnessed earlier periods when residential spaces *were* part of the state's imaginary of social life and change. Nowadays, however, the state loiters outside the home, and the relationship with it is of a different nature.

The mammoth transformations of space currently under way can be put alongside another, similar experiment during the mid-twentieth century, namely, the construction of "steel towns" by the postcolonial state. A comparison between contemporary—private—spatial transformations and mid-twentieth-century, state-sponsored ones points to significant shifts in the imagination that conjures the "ideal" citizen and "his" relationship to the state.

From the late 1950s, the Indian state undertook the construction of industrial townships in different—usually economically underdeveloped—areas of the country that were intended to be "exemplary national spaces of the new India" (Roy 2007:134). Located within the larger framework of centralized economic development (whose most public manifestation was the five-year plans for the economy), the townships were the state's attempts at postcolonial modernity in which the modern citizen would work and live in an environment that "proclaimed the birth of the sovereign nation" (2007:138). Hence, "apart from innovations in urban design" (2007:143), the thinking behind steel towns also addressed itself to the possibilities of engineering new "forms of subjectivities, practices, and social relations" (2007:143) that would distinguish these localities from the "backwardness" of their immediate environs and from the stasis afflicting national life: they were to be the specialized models of a new national culture. The townships of Rourkela (Orissa state), Bhillai (Madhya Pradesh), Durgapur (West Bengal), and Bokaro (Bihar) thus came into being. Of course, as

Roy points out, in subsequent years, the steel towns did not live up to the promise of sovereign modernity that was imposed upon them, but that is another story. Of greater relevance here are the unfolding narratives of citizenship, the state, and capital that link them to the contemporary spatial transformations of a similar—or greater—magnitude. Although both the steel towns and contemporary gated communities might be located within the discursive promise of a "new India," there are important differences in the nature of the new.

Most significantly, whereas the nationalist project of producing modern citizens related to external spaces—such as town planning, streetscapes, and the design of shopping spaces—that residents were expected to pass through, discourses of transformation surrounding the contemporary gated community shift the focus to internal spaces. Gated communities are presented as effecting transformations that significantly relate to the domestic aspects (kitchens, dining areas, bedrooms, etc.) of urban living. Intimate spaces are more directly addressed, locating the domestic sphere as the indispensable ground for the making of a global modernity. It is as if Indian *private* life must be aligned with global standards through *public* display of the spaces where this might happen. In this way, the public exhibition of intimate spaces indexes an era when *national* dreams of modernity no longer suffice to define Indianness. Gated enclaves posit a model of *postnational* citizenship that constitutes a particular gloss on the relationship between the state and its citizens against the backdrop of transnational consumerist modernity; the bedroom is a window to the world. The movement from postcolonial to postnational projects of citizenship also posits the journey from the "citizen-worker" (Roy 2007) to the consumer-citizen, from the spaces of national identity to those of suburban and domestic ones. Further, unlike in the steel towns, it is no longer the Indian state and foreign nation-states that manufacture the spatial transformations that are the putative sites of revolutions in personality and culture. Rather, it is the relationship between the state, citizens, and various forms of capital—national and global—that is seen to be fundamental to the task of remaking national life.

The emergence of the domestic sphere as the site of a new national (or, rather, in terms of this discussion, postnational) identity relates to newer models of family life. What is the family "type" that is being imagined through the focus upon domestic spaces as the new crucibles of national identity? Sociologist Patricia Uberoi's (2008) discussion of Indian bridal magazines provides a useful entry into this topic. The magazines Uberoi discusses were mostly launched in the mid-1990s and address an imagined high-income consumer, not unlike the occupants of an up-market gated community. The following quote from an editorial in the inaugural (1997) issue of *Bride and Home* magazine captures the social terrain that bridal magazines encounter and also allows us, via Uberoi's discussion, to think about the discourses of domesticity in the new context of consumer culture: "Arranging a wedding in India [the editorial says] has traditionally been a family affair, and so it should remain; but it is to offer choice that *Bride and Home* steps in and gives young couples a freedom to partake in the most important decision of their lives: marriage" (Uberoi 2008:239).

Indian bridal magazines such as *Bride and Home*, Uberoi (2008:245) says, seek to address young women through the neoliberal trope of "choice" in a social context "where descent, succession and inheritance are in the male line; post-marital residence is 'patrivirilocal'...and authority resides with the senior males of the family or lineage." And yet, within all of this is the idea that the "modern" form of marriage and domesticity—a modernity defined through association with consumer goods and services (including those of marriage planners)—is a key moment in the making of modern Indian identity. How, then, to address the tension between older (and very real) structures of power and the apparent promise of consumerism-led liberation? Here, Uberoi (2008:245) suggests, the domestic sphere becomes a site of "adjustment" to changes on a broader scale: it is a place "of the consolidation of this new, cosmopolitan culture of Indian kinship and marriage, that is self consciously both 'modern' and 'ethnic.'" There is little in what *Bride and Home* has to say about marriage that suggests that the new era of "choice" relates—in addition to buying goods—to "the freedom to choose the partner" (2008:241) . Applying this insight to the discussion of this chapter, we might say that contemporary domestic nationalism conjures a family type based on a couple whose modernity is based on their "freedom" to make choices about the goods they might consume rather than, say, "spousal choice" (2008:241) . That is to say, the emerging politics of domesticity—one that gathers around the spaces of the gated community, as well as the ideas of intimacy and marriage conjured by *Bride and Home*—consists of reformulations of older structures of power in a new era of consumerist modernity.

Let us now return to Parsvnath Castle in Punjab. The Castle is being built by the real estate company Parsvnath Developers, which in 2007 had residential projects in nineteen towns and cities of north India. It had also entered into an agreement with the Delhi Metro Rail Corporation—the government body in charge of constructing the light-rail system in the national capital—to "construct eight malls along the railway tracks...

in areas that are essentially occupied by the economically weaker sections of society" (www.parsvnath.com, accessed August 7, 2009). Whereas Parsvnath's "metro malls" hope to capitalize on the changing "shopping habits of Indian people," particularly the urban poor, Parsvnath Castle builds upon quite another history of space. With its "proximity to the erstwhile royal state of Patiala, Rajpura's royal alliance is an acknowledged fact," and "the Castle [has]…an inside loaded with royal luxuries" (www.parsvnath.com). In other parts of India, the patina of regional royalty for the newly enriched classes who can afford to invest in Parsvnath Castle competes with other—transnational—assurances of spatial distinction. In the city of Pune in western India, Panchshil Builders' Ssilver Woods condominium offers "extensive use of glass to accentuate the view, [and a] combination of style & comfort with innovative concepts like 'Island Kitchens,' 'Breakfast & Wine decks' and 'Central Conditioning'" (www.panchshil.com, accessed August 8, 2009).

One way of approaching the relationship between local and wider systems of prestige and distinctions is to think about the variety of civilizational debates that mark Indian consumerism. In one version, this presents as the strategy of maintaining Indianness while simultaneously "local" patterns of consumption, dress, worship, commensality, leisure, and partnering begin to overlap with perceived transnational or "Western" trends. A resolution to this "problem" of consumer culture is the ability to move between ("Western") hyper-consumption and Indian "traditions." So, for example, since the 1990s, a number of Hindi-language women's magazines have carried extremely explicit discussions of sexuality *along with* the usual articles about religious rituals and customs. This invokes a particular reader with the putative ability to move between transnationalism and localism. The magazines also seek to define an "authentic" Indian middle class that—unlike the Westernized middle classes—can "come back" to its Indian roots (see Srivastava 2007). The civilizational narrative that infuses the publicity material for Pune's Ssilver Woods condominiums reformulates the debate in the vocabulary of an increasingly confident Indian cosmopolitanism. It speaks of an Indian modernity whose "modernness" cannot solely derive from transnational logics of distinction; it must simultaneously be endorsed by *Indian* incarnations of globalism: "Every exquisite, east-west open apartment has something unique to offer.… And what adds a superlative grandeur to 'Ssilver Woods' is an exclusive touch by the multifaceted Shobha De, as all buildings flaunt a unique signature floor designed by her" (www.panchshil.com, accessed August 8, 2009). The model, journalist, author, and magazine editor Shobha De (b. 1948) is well known in India as a chronicler of upper-middle-class Indian life. She is also a significant choice as the "brand ambassador" for Ssilver Woods ("Ssilver" marks a distinction from just "Silver"). De's symbolic presence at Ssilver Woods might usefully be linked to the ways in which her writings articulate a civilizational debate that bears upon urban life, changing notions of the West, and the place of the Nehruvian high-art cultural sensitivity in postcolonial life.

First, De's writings articulate a vision of India that is strikingly different from the earlier nationalist ones, in which, in contrast to the Westernized city, the village was the symbolic site of "true" Indianness (Nandy 2001). For De, the city is the site of a new Indian—consumerism-led—renaissance. This echoes the discourses that gather around gated communities, ones that index transnational urbanism as both justification and style. Second, there is the cultural role of the "West" in De's writings. Within them, the West is just another place, "sketchy and unreal, more of a giant supermarket than a place of interest" (Dwyer 2000:124), not the site of an existential crisis, as might have been expressed in the writings of an earlier generation of privileged Indians or in the Indian English "art" novel. One of the most striking aspects of the naming of many early gated enclaves around the country—particularly in Gurgaon—was the almost exclusive recourse to upper-class English culture. It was as if the West that was most desirable was that which indexed the putatively precapitalist and uncommercialized lifestyle of the English aristocracy; Gurgaon is home to condominium enclaves with names such as Ridgewood, Princeton, Windsor, Hamilton, and Oakwood. But there has been a remarkable change in the pattern of naming newer developments. Gated enclaves currently under construction or recently completed carry names such as the Icon, the Aralias, Park View, City Park, Uniworld Resorts, Nirvana Country, the Verandahs, World Spa, Emerald Estate, and Gardens Galleria. The toponymic reinscription of older geographies of Englishness with newer ones that signpost more global senses of prestige, luxury, and cosmopolitanism may also tell us something about the changing nature of the "West" as an aspirational sign.[6] A clue to this is contained in the conversation I had with thirty-four-year-old Anita Kapoor (name changed), who lives in a DLF City gated community.

Anita and her husband, Deepak, lived for many years in North America and England, moving back to India in 2005. Deepak worked for a prominent American bank, heading a team of fifty Indians whose task it was to identify the possibilities of "outsourcing" the bank's activities to India. The couple would live for a month in India, then move for six months or so to New York, Brighton, Sydney, or wherever else the job demanded. Anita has a strong sense of her husband—and *India*—as being at the forefront of global change. I ask whether she has ever considered settling overseas. No, she says, never, because, "her life in Gurgaon is better than what might be 'there.'" "You know," she says, "most people who live in DLF have international experience. I went to a newly established furniture shop—made to look like IKEA—and asked them what it would cost to fit out our flat. The owner said around two crores [million]! They don't realize that most of us have international experience and have a good idea of what things cost!"

Although the majority of the residents of localities such as Ssilver Woods may not exactly share Anita's lifestyle or her husband's career path, what they do share is a gathering sense of self-confidence about the place of Indian culture and Indian achievements in the world. The new Indian middle classes, Anita seems to imply, are neither dazzled by ersatz Wests nor incapable of tabulating their "actual" value. It is in this context, rather than a context of an existential crisis of Indian selves, that Shobha De's representation of the West as a "giant supermarket" (Dwyer 2000:124) becomes important. De directly addresses an audience that senses the world—its pleasures, comforts, and hierarchies of prestige—through the apparently democratizing milieu of the marketplace, where Indian identities need not (any longer) struggle to resolve a crisis introduced by the encounter with the West. The West is just one way of making sense of the world, an idea that now exists *alongside* contemporary Indianness rather than as a threat to it.[7]

Finally, De's "signature" at Ssilver Woods also marks the consolidation of another aspect of the civilizational debate, one that questions the cultural hegemony of an older, "Westernized" middle class. This "intellectual elite" (Dwyer 2000:129) was both the vanguard of postcolonial cultural nationalism and the key ideologue of the state. It is, of course, too sweeping to say that newer fractions of the middle class do not share the "social" and aesthetic interests that marked the older "intellectual elite." However, it is significant that these concerns are expressed through different registers of political economy. The most salient aspects of this are the increasingly direct relationship with the *corporate* sector in order to achieve social objectives, and the consolidation of forms of cultural consumption other than those inspired by "high art" in the service of the nation. Hence, at the Windsor Garden (name changed) enclave in DLF City, the rainwater-harvesting scheme is sponsored by the Coca-Cola Company. The new practices of leisure at religious theme parks (Brosius 2010 ; Srivastava 2009), shopping malls (Voyce 2007), and multiplex cinemas (Viswanath 2007) also display this change in the patterns of middle-class cultural consumption: "Parsvnath Developers present yet another breathtaking landmark 'Parsvnath Pleasant' in Dharuhera.... Experience the unforgettable whiff of the countryside. Also witness its modern corporate feel with the state of the art plants set up here by big players like Sony and Hero Honda" (www. parsvnath.com, accessed August 20, 2009).

Gated communities such as Ssilver Woods do not constitute the dominant residential form in India. They are, however, the currently most visible expressions of people's aspirations: the desire for material well-being (for example, twenty-four-hour electricity and water supply), the changing relationship with the market and the state, and the desire for spaces that reflect transnational landscapes increasingly visited (and certainly viewed on television) by an expanding section of the population. One significant context of these transformations is the burgeoning role of the private sector in different aspects of urban life, and perceptions of the effectiveness of private capital in getting things done are crucial to the realignments among citizens, the state, and the market. Increasingly, domestic prosperity—measured through one's enhanced ability to take part in consumerism—is juxtaposed with the visible expansion of private sector activities in those public spheres that were earlier the domains of the state. For example, in 2009 the DLF Corporation won the bid to construct a light-rail system to cover certain areas of DLF City bypassed by the state-run Delhi Metro project, which links Gurgaon to Delhi (completed in 2010). In the public mind, the genesis of DLF's Rapid Metro Rail is an example of the paradigm of what might be called "efficient prosperity." The executive director of DLF Metro, the body formed to undertake the project, noted that he did not envisage the kinds of delays that affected the state-sponsored Metro project, which resulted from legal problems over acquiring land. "There won't be any such problems in Gurgaon," he noted. "Almost all the land where we will construct is owned by DLF" (Joseph 2009:2). Perhaps even more significant, the DLF Corporation has raised its own "police" force, called the Quick Response Team (QRT), which consists of men dressed in black who infrequently patrol the locality on motorbikes. Although the QRT's relationship with the official police force is unclear, its visible public presence—and the "Quick" in its title—adds to the luster of the private sector as an efficient overseer of both public projects and private property.

SPATIAL STRATEGIES: LOCALITY, COMMUNITY, AND *MOHULLA* IN DLF CITY

The Delhi Land and Finance (DLF) company (established 1946) was one of the earliest and most significant real estate companies in India. Its corporate history illuminates the complex relationships between the colonial and the postcolonial state and the making of "private" spaces and identities in India. In its early years, DLF expertly engaged with the monopolistic landholding powers of the state's Delhi Improvement Trust (established 1936) to establish a thriving and highly profitable real estate business in Delhi. The formation in 1957 of the postcolonial state's land monopoly, the Delhi Development Authority, led, however, to an abrupt end to DLF's business in Delhi. Regrouping under a different generation of leadership, since the late 1970s, DLF has been the most powerful and the largest agent of urban transformation in the national capital region, which lies immediately outside the borders of Delhi.

The most famous project of DLF is the 3,000-acre DLF City, located beyond Delhi's southern border in the Gurgaon district of the state of Haryana. Its "hyper-malls," gated residential communities, ultramodern bungalows, and corporate offices (occupied by, among others, call centers, BPOs [business process outsourcing], and prominent multinational corporations) speak of an urban transformation that is also the making of new ideas of the modern—middle-class—Indian self (Dupont 2005; King 2004). And, although detailed coverage of this topic is beyond the scope of this chapter, the role of the state in facilitating DLF's commercial activities in Haryana is an important backdrop to the present discussion. The state reclassified vast tracts of farmland as "non-agricultural" so that the company could acquire the land for its business (see Srivastava n.d. for more detail). The ethnographic vignettes that follow concentrate on DLF City, seeking to put flesh on the observations made so far regarding the cross-cutting realms of the market, the state, and middle-class identities.

"New" Performances of Space: Not like the *Mohulla*

During a conversation about life in DLF City and in older parts of Delhi, a resident of Windsor Garden said to me, "People want a 'community' here, but not like a mohulla, not like those older localities in Delhi." The idea of the mohulla—literally, "neighborhood," but a term that is frequently deployed to suggest an old locality, with village-like bonds and kin-like relationships among its residents—is an interesting counterpoint to the idea of urban spatial modernity. So, in the Istanbul *mahalle* (to use the local term) of Kuzguncuk, Mills (2007) says, the space of the neighborhood is created through processes of everyday surveillance that inscribe it with ideas of the familiar, the strange, threat, and security. Significantly, the net of surveillance is woven out of the watchfulness of "women who are continually *present at home*" (Mills 2007:343, emphasis added), who act as private sentinels.

What kind of neighborhood is Windsor Garden? For a start, unlike Kuzguncuk, it is the site of an extraordinary amount of comings and goings.

Many of the apartments are rented to employees of the several multinational corporations (MNCs) located in Gurgaon. Further, several flats have been bought by corporations to be used as short-term accommodations for visiting employees and guests. Given the substantial transitory population, the permanent and long-term residents of the complex cannot fall back on individual observations to keep track of strangers and possible threats from them. The complex swarms with affluent strangers. In addition, the constant movement serves to differentiate Windsor Garden from the older localities of Delhi: it is *intended* to be a new kind of space, comfortable with transitions. How are senses of community fostered under such conditions of dislocation? What characteristic acts here constitute "the task of producing locality" (Appadurai 1997:188)? And what anxieties and concerns underlie the making of a new community—and middle-class identity—in DLF City?

Let us begin with time. Certain diurnal rhythms typically structure life within and around Windsor Garden. These are connected to the political, material, and cultural economies of DLF City. Early mornings and late evenings offer the best vantage points for observing the cadences of space that mark DLF City with its own peculiar sense of locality. Between 5 a.m. and 7 a.m., the streets around Windsor Garden swarm with women and men who do not live within the gates: women walking briskly in groups and singly, clutching plastic bags, others riding in rickshaws, and men with small cloth bags, some containing food and others small implements. This crowd appears almost magically between the above hours, making its way toward the high-rises of the gated enclaves from the tight clusters of single- and double-story tenement housing that can be seen from the skyscrapers. They are the maids, servants, chauffeurs, and trades and other workers who reside in rented accommodations in some of the original villages that ring the condominium spaces. The women in rickshaws are maids being taken to work by their rickshaw-driver husbands. The workers—from Bihar, West Bengal, and, some say, Bangladesh—live in tiny, ill-lit rooms located in spaces with potholed roads, open drains, and a variety of small-scale industrial workshops. As they make their way to the gates—and the immaculately maintained premises—of the various residential enclaves, the women must produce identity cards, which are examined by the guards, whereas the men are allowed to pass without much fuss. By 7 a.m., the streets are empty of the women in cheap, shiny *saris* and the men in shiny trousers and shirts of fading color.

Another morning activity, given its origins in local material and cultural economies, is worth noting: the number of women driving around in cars far outweighs that of men. Most of the women drivers appear to be between twenty-five and forty years old. They are either driving to or returning from their morning activities: yoga classes run by individually contracted instructors, or calisthenics, aerobics, and other exercises that take place in a number of gymnasiums in the area. The ones most frequented are located in local shopping malls. A significant characteristic of the public spaces in DLF City is the presence of women. The regendering of public spaces—given their historically masculine nature—is an important aspect of the making of middle classness in DLF City. However, as I discuss below, the increased presence of "public" women appears to be accompanied by an increased emphasis on their "home duties."

The private guards who regulate the entry of maids (and visitors) to the complex also follow a routine. Every morning around seven o'clock, a supervisor arrives on a motorcycle to initiate a "changing of the guards" that begins with a military-style drill: those taking up duty for the day line up in formation, salute, and undergo inspection. Then, they disperse to their positions, relieving the night guards. Around the same time, many of the residents are being driven to offices since the business day, especially for those working in MNCs, begins early. There are also schoolchildren boarding buses—many of which sport "international" or "global" as part of the names of the institutions painted on their sides—to begin their day.

The quiet of the day changes in the evening to another set of rhythms that define space. Windsor Garden's park is filled with four types of residents: young children, teenagers in mixed groups, older women sitting together on park benches, and live-in maids shepherding infants. Office workers—both men and women (there is a high proportion of working women)—have not yet returned home, and the infants appear to be glad to be out of the house, being entertained by the maids. The maids who are daily—rather than live-in—workers make a quiet exit from the complex, their persons occasionally checked by the guards to make sure they are not carrying out any goods "illegally," and melt into the darkness.

These rhythms of space—and the making of locality—move along the contours of the postnational moment described earlier. They illustrate the processes through which quotidian life comes to be located within new contexts of work, leisure, and the valorization of the home as the site of consumerist cosmopolitanism. They also point to another significant aspect: the making of a community's life—one that is *not* like a mohulla—is increasingly enmeshed in a relationship with the corporate sector, diminishing the historically significant role of the state. Further, community life is also produced out of a postnational emphasis on the self and locality, where the techniques of both body and space are aligned to transnational flows that affect patterns of work, residence, and domesticity, as well as ideas about the cosmopolitan self.

Finally, in this context, the community life I have described is also based on changes in employment patterns that affect not only middle-class women but also poor women. "In the era of globalization," a report on urbanization and women's employment points out, "it has become commonplace to argue that trade openness in particular generates processes that encourage the increased employment of women" (Chandrasekhar and Ghosh 2007:1). However, as Chandrasekhar and Ghosh go on to suggest, rather than the much cited sectors of information technology and finance, "the greatest labour market dynamism has been evident in the realm of domestic labour" (2007:5). Indeed, women working as domestic servants—working for low wages under uncertain conditions—"account for more than 12 percent of all women workers in urban India" (2007:4). The women who each morning make their way to the gates of Windsor Garden and other such enclaves—to look after young children, cook, and clean—are participants in this "dynamic" labor market.

Commodity Cultures and the Making of Community

In addition to the above, other, more pointed rituals of space impart a specific sense of locality and speak to the notion of the consumer-citizen. The Hindu festival of Holi, which traditionally falls at the end of winter and involves the throwing of colored powder and water, is celebrated in many gated communities through activities organized by their residents welfare associations. In the public imagination, popular celebrations of Holi frequently figure as contexts of unruly behavior toward both women and "respectable" citizens (Cohen 1995). The 2009 Holi at Windsor Garden was an elaborate affair. A stage was set up on the main lawn, and it was surrounded by a large music system. Young men and women and middle-aged couples danced to Bollywood music being played by a disc jockey hired for the occasion. There was also a Bacardi bar that handed out free alcoholic drinks, as the RWA had secured sponsorship from the company, which had put up a number of its banners around the complex. A few weeks before Holi, the RWA had also organized a cricket tournament sponsored by a local car dealership (as the large banners installed for the duration of the tournament informed passersby).

The Janmasthami festival that celebrates the birth of the Hindu god Krishna is another popular event at Windsor Garden. Celebrated "on the eighth day of the waning half of the lunar month of *bhadrapad*" (Hawley

FIGURE 3.1
Holi in Windsor Garden, 2009. Photo by S. Srivastava.

and Goswami 1981:62), which falls during August and September, the festival has elaborate local roots that draw upon networks of kin, relationships in the neighborhood, and religious ties. So, in the north Indian city of Brindavan (where Krishna spent much of his childhood), Janmasthami celebrations involve a variety of priests, performing artists (who enact nativity plays), and lay worshippers, each of whom draws upon and contributes localized resources. Janmasthami celebrations at Brindavan (similar to those in other parts of India) are also organized around acts of commensality—feasts and fasts—that further institutionalize community bonds through residents' participation in a nonmonetized ritual activity (Hawley and Goswami 1981).

Since 2008, the festival at Windsor Garden has been organized by the International Society for Krishna Consciousness (ISKCON), founded in New York in 1966 by Srila Prabhupada. Members of ISKCON who live within the complex took an active part in convincing the RWA to allow the organization to take over the festival from residents. In 2008, the celebrations began with a *bhajan* (prayer song) by a group of ISKCON devotees who sat on a large stage that faced several rows of chairs. A powerful sound system ensured that the singing reached all parts of the complex. To the right of the stage was a large screen on which were projected swirling color images from a laptop. As the lead singer repeatedly requested that residents join the gathering, the crowd built to around a hundred, and a group of women, including one from a Windsor Garden family that belongs to ISKCON, began to dance in an empty space in front of the stage. It was an improvised performance that followed the ISKCON "street dance" pattern seen in many Western cities. The dancers exhorted others to join, and a few (all women) did so.

Then, two male ISKCON devotees joined the dance, but to the right of the stage, away from the women. They were joined by a few other male residents of the complex. While the women danced with gestures of bliss and devotion in front of the *jharokha* (a tableau depicting Krishna as child), the men—perhaps appropriately, given the association between masculinity and technology—danced in front of the laptop. Two specially attired girls came forward to dance to verses recited from the Gita, and an ISKCON devotee offered a discourse on the text. By then, the cinema screen was displaying graphics of flying machines, flaming arrows, a twirling globe, and psychedelic animation. The ceremony was building to a crescendo. The dancing women improvised and also did Indian dances such as the *garba* and *gidda* popularized by Bollywood. The ceremony concluded with an *arti* (lamp) ceremony and the cutting of a "Krishna birthday cake," which was then offered as *prasad* (sanctified food). The screen now showed scenes from U.S. cities where American *bhakts* (devotees) danced, sang, and spoke about their lives as "Krishna bhakts." The ceremony lasted some three hours, with the laptop uniting the Windsor Garden space with an American one. The "West" was in Windsor Garden via a confident cosmopolitanism that could include it in the broader tableau of Indian culture, a situation unmarked by anxiety and angst regarding "cultural imperialism." We ate our cake and dispersed.

The suffusion of local space with an easy familiarity with transnational cultures of commodities also happens in other, more obvious circumstances. One of the most common ways in which group interaction takes place is around a stall displaying the signs of consumer goods manufacturers. Every other week, a mobile van or a portable tent promoting a variety of goods can be found within Windsor Garden. In August 2009, the Honda company advertised its newly launched Jazz model by inviting residents to inspect the car, which had been parked next to an information booth. A young woman exhorted adults, "Come down and see for yourself," while

FIGURE 3.2

A promotional stand at Windsor Garden. Photo by S. Srivastava.

children took part in dancing competitions and were rewarded for composing ditties about the vehicle. Some months earlier, an electronic goods company had displayed its wares at the same spot.

The relationship with the market is, I suggest, fundamental to (but does not exhaust) the senses of space and community at Windsor Garden. It generates specific types of sociality: a space where men and women may dance together in public without the latter encountering the risks of the sexual economy of "fun" that is common in Holi celebrations (Cohen 1995); a "liberal" space where women may drink alcohol in public, a public that is created by the private that is liberated from the dangers and "backwardness" of the old; a sociality where female bodily expressions are a significant aspect of life within the gates (whether during Holi, Janmasthami, morning walks, or other rituals, the female body is allowed considerable play in the public spaces of the enclave); a space where children and adults sing, dance, and experience the physical sensuality of the commodities that come to them, transporting the aura of the showroom and becoming at one with their domestic lives.

Feminist writings on public spaces in India critically alert us to the gendered nature of such spaces and the restrictions upon the female body in such spaces (see, for example, Phadke 2007). Does the gated enclave, then, provide an alternative model of publicness with the apparent freedom of movement and participation in community life it seems to allow? This question might be more fully addressed through considering the kinds of activities the women of gated communities take part in. The cosmopolitanism of the new "arts" of the body—gym cultures, dancing in public alongside men, the exercise of running and walking, for example—are combined with "older" practices of religiosity, household duties, and participation in "women-oriented" customary rituals, which are also part of gated community life. As I have argued elsewhere (Srivastava 2007:chap. 8), this presents us with a situation in which "public women" are offered the "freedom" of public spaces (and activities) *in tandem* with the demonstrated ability to return to the "home." That is to say, unlike men, women's access to public spaces is tied to their commitment to the private sphere: they must be both "modern" and "traditional." This, too, is the politics of the national domestic.

Interior Decoration and Inner Lives

I have suggested that the consolidation of a relatively recent narrative of intimate and private spaces as the deus ex machina of personal transformation is part of the wider renegotiations of the relationship between the state, the market, and citizens. An ethnographic example may help to flesh out the story. Rina Khanna (name changed) is a trained architect who is in her mid-forties and lives in DLF City. She earlier worked with a large city firm but now concentrates on designing house interiors and has designed her own house. The Khanna residence has three levels of security: a guard, an electronic camera, and intercoms at the front gate and at the front door. The entrance lobby leads to a sitting area with a skylight, which is divided from a more formal room by an enormous glass window. An inner balcony looks down on the ground floor. Guests seated in the front room have an expansive view of the whole house through the glass window that apparently separates but also unites the different parts of the ground floor. In the basement are a well-equipped gym, a large office, a table tennis room, a library, and a fully equipped twelve-seat cinema. The theater is adorned with Bollywood and Hollywood movie posters, and a popcorn machine stands at the entrance.

The ground-floor sitting room has a well-stocked bar, and there is marble flooring throughout the house. Rina says she wanted an "open-plan house," since most of her visitors are "well known" to her. Because of that, she does not mind the fact that when people enter the house, they can see the dining area and the kitchen. "Most people," she says, "don't like that, as they have many visitors whom they don't know." She likes "clean lines" and cannot do designs that are very elaborate. She explains with distaste how another designer had planned a new apartment with a "glass wall behind the bed in the main bedroom, with shells and stars embedded in the glass!" In different ways, Rina establishes the distance from the mohulla that many others in DLF City also spoke about. Although the mohulla keeps watch on strangers, it is not unused to them, but at DLF City the processes of instituting locality and of becoming unused to strangers have happened at the same time: the gates and walls institutionalize unfamiliarity. Finally, in her comments on the shells and stars, Rina expresses horror at the possibility of the aesthetic of the mohulla reproducing itself at DLF City.

Rina often brings her clients to her house to show them the kind of designing she is comfortable with. She says that DLF City clients are much more "adventurous" and understand her ideas more easily than the clients she gets in Delhi: "In DLF, they've traveled around the world and are familiar with European designs, whereas my Delhi clients tend to be businesspeople who have recently made money but have no idea about design. However, the younger generation wants to redo the family home, as it no longer wants a traditional house." The most significant aspect of a "traditional" house, according to Rina, is that it is not open plan, because the family is not comfortable with outsiders being able to see, for example, the dining and other "private" areas. "So if my house [were] traditional," she says, "I would have built a buffer between the front door and the sitting areas and the dining areas that are visible." She points to a room upstairs where her daughter practices the piano: "Being an open-plan house, we can hear the piano all over the house. I always ask my clients, 'Are you really ready for an open-plan house, where you can see everything?' Many say no."

Rina provides an example in order to describe the nature of her design ideas. A client, a young man whose family lives in a joint-family dwelling in the West Delhi locality of Janakpuri, saw her house and said it was exactly how he wanted to redesign his own place. Currently, she says, his house is traditional: lots of ornate furniture, walls in different colors, and kitchens and toilets that have not been "updated." The client was getting married later that year and wanted the house to be ready by then. He also wanted a full-scale bar in the basement that had to look "commercial," "as if you have walked into a bar in a shopping center." He insisted, "It must not look like a home bar." He had also found Versace tiles and had told Rina, disarmingly, that he wanted them for "show-off" purposes. Once, when the client and his fiancée were visiting, Rina showed them a map of their present house, where she had marked out the "problem" areas. The couple responded that these were precisely the areas that they had heatedly argued over but "didn't have quite the words to express what they wanted." Upon seeing Rina's house, they had been able to put words to their desires. "So," Rina says, "I am building them a house with clean lines." Rina is like an agent of transformation: assisting, through providing a language and rationale, those at the threshold of mohulla life who are seeking to cross over to another locality, both symbolically and physically. However, she adds:

> I tell my customers that I no longer have the time or energy to work with carpenters and hence strongly recommend modular and pre-fabricated material. Who has the time to deal with labor and all its hassles? They simply have no respect for my time. Everything in my house is modular or prefabricated. I simply refuse to deal with labor any more. So if my clients want to do it, that's their hassle. Many of my friends are using modular material.

Her clients, Rina says, often go to the Chinese city of Guangzhou and buy *all* their interior decoration items from suppliers there:

> They pay 30 percent then and the rest on delivery. So they purchase furniture, taps [faucets], wooden railings for stairs, lighting fixtures, curtains...and European reproduction paintings. The entire house is fitted out with Guangzhou products. It's not very good quality, but the buyers are just as likely to replace it within the next five years, so they don't care.

The clean lines of the open-plan house that Rina speaks of and the insouciance with which the global marketplace is traversed for materials for the household—both cultural and functional—are the grounds for a vocabulary of spatial and personal transformations that is part of the new cultural confidence at DLF City. It is also, of course, part of the process of distancing oneself from local laboring classes; the new cosmopolitanism seeks to bypass as much as possible the "troublesome" aspects of local class relations through recourse to global consuming avenues that efface the visibility of relations of production.

Incomplete Transformations: Lives between the New and the Old

Intimations of change are, however, accompanied by anxieties of loss. I met Suresh and Meena Verma through interactions with Windsor Garden residents who are active in the workings of the residents welfare association. Meena is in charge of "social and cultural activities" and can be seen at almost all public events organized by the RWA. She is one of several women involved in the RWA, whereas the condominium association—which looks after the legal and financial affairs of the complex—has just one woman on its committee. Meena frequently notes that women residents do not play a part in the "really serious" affairs of the complex. Despite the large number of women at Windsor Garden with a variety of office experience, neither the RWA nor the condominium association has a woman in any of the key positions. The move away from patrilocal residence and hence from immediate contact with extended kin networks—particularly in-laws—has had an interesting impact on women's potential role in the administrative affairs of the community. In the absence of extended kin, who might help with the running of the household and the care of children, "working women" are expected to devote their after-office hours to the care of the household rather than take on administrative responsibility in either the RWA or the condominium association. Nucleation has had the effect of a more intensive focus on the household on the part of women, and their effective disassociation from a say in the organization and in the functioning of their immediate environment beyond the household.

The Vermas are in their early forties and have two teenage daughters. They are originally from two different small towns in the state of Rajasthan. Suresh's career has coincided with the opportunities that opened up in particular sectors of the Indian economy following economic liberalization in the early 1990s. He is an engineer and works for one of India's largest private telecommunication companies, Airtel. As Airtel's fixed-line, mobile phone, digital television, and Internet business has expanded, the Vermas have made their home in various Indian cities and towns experiencing high demand for telecommunication facilities. Before moving to Gurgaon, the Vermas lived in the Gujarat city of Ahmedabad. Meena says, "We had lived in flats in Ahmedabad, and the main difference is that there, people mixed much more than here. It's the same between Jodhpur [her Rajasthan hometown] and here: when I go back, it's like an old mohulla. Everyone invites you home, whereas here you have to make an appointment to visit. Once you close your door, that's it."

Spatial tumult—the making of new localities and the dismantling of older ones—is a frequent topic of discussion among residents of spaces that are its consequence. Suresh in particular reflected for a long time on the concept of a mohulla and how Windsor Garden differed from the kind of mohulla they were used to and how they missed that life: "Whenever I think about it, it really fascinates me.... Even now, when we take the children to visit our relatives in the mohulla where my parents lived, it's like nothing has changed.... People come rushing out to greet us, we drop into whichever house we want, we are offered food.... It's like going back to your family...[your] family home." Narratives of passage from the mohulla (mandated by different processes of contemporary capitalist transformations) to the gated community (created by a mixture of factors traceable to the same transformations) are also indications of multiple senses of belonging. These, in the tumult of dislocation and relocation, are enunciated through a logic of contradictions.

This nostalgia for the mohulla, a wistfulness for "authentic" locality, which also has echoes in other parts of the world (see, for example, Ghannam 2002 on Cairo's poorer residents), is a frequent topic of discussion. Meena talks of various sets of the elderly, "housewives," and so on, who are very active as social groupings within Windsor Garden. Many of these groups even travel together to other cities on holidays, reinforcing a sense of the togetherness that comes from collective interactions with "outsiders." Further, Suresh's employer, Airtel (which has purchased an African telecommunications network spread across fifteen countries), has been part of the remaking of senses of locality, whose key aspect is the deterritorialization of neighborhoods. And, finally, the freedom of public space—in the manner of the controlled publicness of Windsor Garden—that Meena currently enjoys would appear to be considerably greater than that which might have been available to her within the confines of the Jodhpur mohulla. The kin-like bonds of the traditional mohulla—with its invisible but palpable boundaries of being—have been exchanged for the apparent autonomy of the market. Yet, the mohulla arises as a trope of belonging—to a community, a morality, an ethic of caring, and procedures of contact—that both denies and sits alongside newer aspirations of locality and autonomy.

Neighborhood, Fear, Identity: Cracks in the Cosmopolitan Ideal

In communities designed to be self-contained territories, ethics of care and procedures of contact frequently exist alongside perceptions of threats from outsiders and demands for protection from them. In São Paulo, Caldeira (2000:257) says, "a widespread aesthetic of security shaped by the new model [i.e., "fortified enclaves"] simultaneously guides transformations of all types of housing and determines what confers the most prestige." "Urban fear," as Low (1997) has pointed out, is a significant narrative that circulates around gated enclaves in the United States. Davis speaks of the "obsession with physical security systems, and collaterally, with the architectural policing of social boundaries, [which] has become a zeitgeist of urban restructuring, a master narrative in the emerging built environment of the 1990s" (Davis 1992a:223). In other contexts, such as South Africa (Landman and Schönteich 2002) and China (Pow 2007; Zhang, chapter 9, this volume), the fear of the rural migrant or slum-dweller-turned-criminal is a frequently invoked reason for the "necessity" of gated communities.

In DLF City, there are local inflections of this global story. Threats against property and life are frequent refrains, but other aspects touch upon urban cultures of surveillance and policing and on national and global discourses of crime and terror. A significant aspect of the gated perceptions of the older communities of Gurgaon—its "unruly villagers" whose lands were bought by the real estate companies for their projects— concerns their supposedly backward nature and customs, which the thinking goes, spill over into criminality. Hence, the argument is usually framed in terms of a modernizing middle class encountering a backward rural population. There are, however, instances in which the peculiarities of the urban milieu make for a more complicated narrative of security, surveillance, locality, and identity.

On a cool October evening as I was driving out of Windsor Garden, I heard a commotion near the fence that separates the complex from its neighboring condominium, Buckingham Court (name changed). I stopped to inquire and saw that a boy, around sixteen or seventeen, had grabbed one of the security guards by the scruff of his neck and the latter was struggling to disentangle himself. Four or five other guards arrived, and I could now see that the boy had a companion, also around the same age. Soon, the two were surrounded by the guards. It transpired that the boys, not residents of the condominium, had been trying to put up posters for a street basketball tournament and had been asked by the original guard whether they had been given permission from the condominium authorities. The boys, who were from well-off families, had responded that they did not need permission and also that they were not willing to be questioned by the security guard. The latter sought to eject the outsiders from the premises, and matters came to a head when each threatened the other with violence. The boys dared the guards (for, by then, the other guards had joined the fray) to take physical action and warned them that should they raise their hands, they would be made to "disappear from this spot." By now, the condominium manager—an employee of the condominium association rather than a resident—had been called, but the boys were no more mindful of him. Then, one of the guards sought to lock the gate that might otherwise have allowed the boys to leave, and one of the latter grabbed him by his collar.

The commotion soon attracted residents on their evening stroll, and a sizable crowd gathered around the boys, the guards, and the gate that had been locked to prevent the former from "escaping." The boys continued to dare the guards to do their worst, until the head of the guards arrived, shouting obscenities in Hindi. He took out his mobile phone and announced loudly that he was calling the police and that they "would take care of it." The boys now looked petrified, and they begged for forgiveness: "Please think of our future. We didn't know we had to ask permission." The head guard was in full swing. "How dare these bastards come here! I'll show them!" he shouted. The boys cowered, the picture of abjection, the remaining basketball posters hanging limply from their hands.

The crowd of residents began to interrogate the boys: Who were they? Where had they come from? What were they doing there at this time of the evening? The boys looked increasingly desperate. Meanwhile, during the questioning, an adult drove into the Windsor Garden compound. He was the father of one of the boys. Apparently, the son had rung him on his mobile. The father leaned over the fence, standing on the Windsor Garden side, unable to join his son on the Buckingham Court side, where they had been apprehended, because of the locked connecting gate. The boys were now being asked to sign a piece of paper giving their personal details and to write that they were "sorry" for what they had done. The father pleaded with the crowd: "If they've done something wrong, punish them by all means, but treat them properly." A young Sikh man—a resident of Buckingham Court—had taken the lead by now and was doing most of the talking. He asked one of the guards to take down the father's car registration number ("I have six cars," the father snapped at the guard who asked for the registration). The father continued to berate the head guard for his rudeness to the boys. Finally, after the boys signed the apology document, the gate was opened and they were allowed to join the father. As they walked away, I could hear him shouting at them, "I should really beat the living daylights out of you in front of the entire crowd. The way you've lowered my dignity in front of these 'small' people [the guards]." As the crowd dispersed, one of the residents, an elderly man, said to me, "We can't be too careful. We had to do this. They could have been terrorists."

In the world of concerns about "safety" and "security," the making of middle-class spaces does not necessarily ensure the "dignity" of middle-class people. The implicit understanding that the middle classes share a common interest with respect to standing firm against urban terror breaks down in the face of an urban milieu in which "trust" circulates in ever-diminishing enclaves of sociality and interaction. The middle-class identity of the boys emboldened them to think it unnecessary to treat the guards with any respect; they were, no doubt, familiar with the marginal status of men who work in such positions. The police constable who might have arrived on the scene would have come from a similar background as the guards, but he would have had the might of the state to back him. On the one hand, the boys—having transgressed the inviolable cordon of security—were pitted against others of their own class, but on the other, they were responsible for the situation through their public demonstration of their class position: how dare the "lower-class" guards question middle-class people! This is another context in which broader narratives of "security" constitute local sites for the articulation of the contradictions of spaces such as DLF City. This example also demonstrates how class operates in contiguous and disjointed ways: aspirations to middle-class identity can sometimes be the site for the undermining of the benefits that are sought to be secured.

Although this has various dimensions, a group that perceives itself as under threat engenders ideas of locality and sociality through creating intricate networks along which conversations about crime, threat, and fear are generated. The web of interactions—among middle-class people—is also a way in which sustained engagement takes place among a homogeneous group, or a group that comes to be represented as homogeneous. In effect, then, and unlike Simmel's notion of urban engagement, these are ways of engaging with the city through face-to-face interactions rather than through the mask of "rationality" that allows for distanced engagement in an urban space (Sennett 2002). There is intense dialogue among neighbors that creates both the sense of neighborhoods within delimited spaces and the sense of similar neighborhoods across the city facing similar problems. The dialogue creates spaces where criminality, community, thick engagements, and urban performativity come together. People do not look away but find ways to peer into one anothers' eyes in order to find similarities in a heterogeneous urban environment. This, in turn, produces ideas about those who are different.

CONCLUSION

This chapter examines the various meanings of the term "middle-class" in India through exploring different contexts of transformation relating to residential spaces. While the discussion ranges across a number of geographic locations in India, it particularly focuses upon the gated residential enclaves of the privately developed DLF City in the Gurgaon region that borders Delhi. A key theme in the discussion is the shift from *postcolonial* to *postnational* notions of identity. The former term signified a context of identity in the period immediately following the colonial, when engagements with the West were marked by concerns and anxieties about "Westernization" and cultural domination. This was also an era of unquestioning allegiance to the ideologies of the state: the hyphen in "nation-state" was a bridge from one term to the other. The postnational moment of Indian identity describes, on the other hand, a situation that is marked by reformulations of the relationship between citizens, the state, and the West. It marks the emergence of a confident cosmopolitanism among the middle classes and a confidence about the place of "Indian culture" within transnational flows of ideas and culture. The background to the postnational era of Indian modernity is made up of a number of processes of transnational consumerist modernity. The chapter demonstrates the shift from the postcolonial to the postnational through a discussion that juxtaposes an instance of large-scale, state-sponsored, urban development in the form of the "steel city" factory towns of the 1950s and contemporary, privately financed urbanization in the form of gated residential communities.

The example of DLF City highlights the specific ways in which consumerist modernity is grounded in large-scale spatial transformations, such as gated communities, that are important sites of the making of middle-class identities. Gated communities index not only a turning away from the state but also a distancing from other, older ideas of the neighborhood, which I have glossed as the mohulla. These acts of distancing—from the state and from older forms of locality—are also the grounds for the emergence of the domestic sphere as the site of personal and social transformation. This is in contrast to the postcolonial moment, with its greater emphasis on the "national family" as the unit of transformative action. The consolidation of the domestic sphere as the site of new Indianness is, in turn, also the making of the consuming family and the institution of the new forms of locality that this family form is to occupy. The institution of the new cosmopolitanism of the postnationalist middle classes is not, however, a seamless process and is shadowed by constant threats to the cosmopolitan ideal. This exploration of contemporary spatial cosmopolitanism in India throws ethnographic light on the making of new class identities and on the changing relationships among citizens, the state, and the market in an era of consumerist modernity.

Acknowledgments

The author would like to thank Carla Freeman, Rachel Heiman, and Mark Liechty for their valuable suggestions on earlier versions of the chapter. Thanks particularly to Rachel for her assistance in various other ways. Comments by two anonymous reviewers are also gratefully acknowledged.

Notes

1. See Yeh and Jones (chapters 8 and 6, respectively, this volume) for additional discussions of the intersection between middle classness and morality and ethics.

2. Fehérváry and Zhang (chapters 5 and 9, respectively, this volume) also explore the changing relationship between the state, capital, consumption, residential spaces, and middle classness in Hungary (Fehérváry) and China (Zhang), where new forms of living offer a significant contrast to previously state-owned and labor-specific housing.

3. It is important to note that the word "aspirational" is here shorn of the pejorative taint that derives from the idea that the newly enriched classes aspire to possess the "tastes" (Bourdieu 1984) of older elites through purchasing the external trappings of such taste. The advertisement addresses the anxiety about the relationship between financial clout and cultural "refinement" by suggesting that the former constitutes a legitimate means of acquiring the latter.

4. A typical example is Omaxe Heights in Lucknow, which offers an "in-house club with swimming pool and wave pool, tennis court, basketball court, banquet/community hall, squash court, steam room, jacuzzi, gymnasium and television lounge."

5. Rachel Heiman (chapter 10, this volume) demonstrates how this process emerged without fully gated communities in the context of interclass struggle when just one gate was introduced into a previously open-plan community in the United States.

6. I am not suggesting that newer developments have completely abandoned the English naming practice, but there has been a substantial change in this regard.

7. Samuli Schielke (chapter 2, this volume) similarly recognizes that with the emerging wealth in Asia and the Gulf region, middle-class aspirations are no longer tied specifically to the West but are instead converging around a more global cosmopolitanism.

4

Neoliberal Respectability

Entrepreneurial Marriage, Affective Labor,
and a New Caribbean Middle Class

Carla Freeman

Middle classness is a terrain of ambivalence, both experientially and analytically. As "lifestyle" and consumption play a greater role in defining social identity, class is increasingly a process defined by consumer practices, goods, and services, that is, more by *how people live* than by *what they do* to make a living. Yet, as the state retreats from social welfare and as the cycle of retraining demanded by industry restructuring and retrenchments extends to white-collar fields, the emphasis on entrepreneurship—from micro-financing to medium-sized business enterprise—is expanding globally. This entrepreneurial imperative, I contend, urges us toward an analytical frame that reconnects productive and consumption-oriented class practices, as well as "public" and "private" life more generally. Today, the neoliberal mandate for flexibility in all realms of life—the capacity to constantly retool, retrain, and respond to the shifting tides of the global marketplace, the expectation that individuals will become "entrepreneurs of the self"—has come to embody many facets of middle-class experience within the global economy. Ethnographic perspectives on people's everyday lives within these conditions not only illustrate the changing landscapes of middle-class lifeways but also reveal a heightened *affective* economy—an intensified exchange and production of feelings—on which many of these transformations hinge (Freeman 2011).

One concept that seems to have encompassed middle classness across modern time and space, at least for the past hundred years, is *respectability*. For Mosse (1985b:4–5), the very definition of the middle classes of early modern Europe was rooted in the "ideal of respectability," a distinction "based as it was upon frugality, devotion to duty, and restraint of the passions,...superior to that of the 'lazy' lower classes and the profligate aristocracy." According to Skeggs (1997:1), writing about twentieth-century Britain, respectability continues to be "one of the most ubiquitous signifiers of class. It informs how we speak, who we speak to, how we classify others... and how we know who we are (or are not)." In the Caribbean, respectability is cast in the shadow of colonialism and carries a decidedly feminine aura. As Peter Wilson (1973:223–24) famously argued, "Respectability is the moral force behind the coercive power of colonialism and neocolonialism.... By and large...it is women who think and act in terms of respectability." In this chapter, respectability offers a critical lens not only on the historical and cultural particularities of middle classness but also on its gendered permutations as they unfold under conditions of contemporary neoliberalism.

This chapter is about a *new* middle class in the Caribbean whose significance, ironically, might be said to lie in its members' participation in some of the most familiar and traditional markers of middle-class culture: entrepreneurship and marriage. And yet, as I elaborate below, the local meanings of both entrepreneurship and marriage depart radically from the assumed European and American models. I discuss women entering the domain of an emerging entrepreneurial middle class on the island of Barbados, a former British colony known in the region, both proudly and disdainfully, for its heightened respectability and conservatism. Barbados is also known as the most "middle-class" and "developed" of all the Caribbean islands, perched proudly at the pinnacle of the UN's ranking of "developing" countries. I focus ethnographically upon contemporary transformations within a domain of life long held as a primary anchor of middle-class respectability in the Caribbean: marriage. However, by focusing upon women entrepreneurs and their contradictory relationship to traditional understandings of respectability, I want not only to spotlight a neglected middle-class subject but also to demonstrate some of the paradoxes and cultural specificities of the meanings of "middle-class" itself as it has operated in this part of the world and to connect these specificities to the expanding affective economy of neoliberalism.

Often portrayed as the quintessential neoliberal actor (Bourdieu 1998a; Harvey 2005), the entrepreneur in Barbados and the wider Afro-Caribbean has traditionally carried the contradictory associations of, on one hand, the privileged preserve of a powerful white elite and, on the other hand, a realm in which those without education or means (primarily the black majority, but poor whites as well) enact strategies for survival as a mechanism of last resort. The current attraction to entrepreneurship as a path to a middle-class livelihood and status thus embodies a host of new associations, many of them, as I have discussed elsewhere (Freeman 2007), steeped in a new discourse of economic and cultural neoliberalism.[1] In short, the growing entrepreneurial sector occupies a space of increasing political and personal optimism and has gained scholarly, as well as popular, attention. I examine some of the affective and intimate dimensions of entrepreneurialism that are, I argue, integral to the project of neoliberal self-making and the changing cultural economy.

Barbados currently embraces a neoliberal political economy signaled most powerfully by its support for the Caribbean Community Single Market and Economy, modeled on the European Union. The state offers competitive inducements to woo and retain offshore service industries and investments while grappling with the waning sugar industry and the precarious primacy of tourism as the island's economic backbone. Meanwhile, a subtle but striking self-consciousness is expressed in the island's newest national development plan: amid these challenging economic times, Barbadians must cultivate an explicitly "entrepreneurial culture," a "more open-minded, innovative, creative, entrepreneurial…outlook," and a "cooperative spirit in young people" (Government of Barbados 2007:180–83). The document makes clear that these are challenging and different times, times that call for decisive protection of certain core cultural values, times that necessitate certain innovations and changes. The strategic goals outlined in the plan are thus saturated in a familiar language of neoliberalism, including, in all respects, a purposeful and self-conscious articulation of a Barbadian "brand." In the broader cultural milieu, the influence of global capitalism and the attraction of American culture also signify new models of aspiration through the expansion of new niches of business enterprise, new quality standards, conditions of "fair competition," new scientific and technological capabilities and levels of productivity, and a new do-it-yourself ethic of "self-help" that cuts across both business and personal arenas.

Through ethnographic fieldwork and interviews conducted with 107 entrepreneurs (72 women and 35 men) between 1999 and 2008, I examined the growing appeal of entrepreneurship, its particular meanings and challenges for women and men, and its expansion not only as a newly defined path of upward mobility but also as a sign of Barbados's ever-deepening embeddedness within a global neoliberal cultural economy. The coupling of middle-class entrepreneurship with a new formulation of marriage among a notable proportion of those I studied brought into relief several intriguing convergences between the desires and practices of neoliberal self-making and a reformulation of the local cultural model of respectability, such that old-order patriarchal marriage and expectations for middle-class women's domesticity are being challenged. These relationships represent an ever-deepening neoliberalization of private and public realms of life in ways that illustrate a profound entanglement of not only work and family responsibilities but also the affects (care, love, pleasure, anxiety, and stress, to name a few) and affective labor that increasingly define middle-class life itself.

Through an examination of these interconnections, I propose that an emergent entrepreneurial middle class in contemporary Barbados offers a unique challenge to some of the long-standing scholarly and political ambivalences in anthropology and feminism toward the middle class. Although the overwhelming majority of these entrepreneurs are Afro-Barbadian (who are roughly 93 percent of the population at large), I also included a sample of twelve self-described white Barbadian women because they, more than any other group, have been held as the arbiters of middle-class respectability, despite the small white Barbadian proportion of the population (roughly 4 percent). Through ethnographic illustrations, this chapter demonstrates how the converging realms of neoliberal entrepreneurship (both self-owned business enterprise and self-mastery/making) and new desires and expectations surrounding intimacy and marriage express complex, changing articulations of affect, culture, and economy in the contemporary Caribbean and illuminate new dynamics of middle-class respectability.

THE ANXIOUS DOMAIN OF MIDDLE CLASSNESS IN CARIBBEAN ANTHROPOLOGY

Parsing today's emergent middle-class entrepreneur in the Afro-Caribbean, and Barbados in particular, highlights the cultural particularities of the seemingly ubiquitous signs of middle-class respectability and the neoliberal mantra of entrepreneurship. The ethnography of middle classes in "developing" and postcolonial societies is a relatively recent pursuit because of their contemporary visibility and for several reasons that are grounded in both disciplinary and regional traditions and anxieties. The Caribbean is no exception to this trend. As this volume illustrates, not only are historical and cultural particularities key to understanding the subtle nuances of contemporary middle classes around the world, but also the very capacity to theorize middle classness must heed epistemological particularities that are grounded in culture, time, and place.

One cannot begin a discussion of a new or an old middle class in Barbados without situating Caribbean anthropology and Caribbean social science generally in the strong analytical tradition of Marxist political economy (Freeman and Murdock 2001). For Caribbean social science, Marx's premise that the middle/unproductive petite bourgeoisie would ultimately become absorbed by either the capitalist class or the proletariat has fit well within the region's plantation economy framework for understanding the region's social, political, and economic structures. The history of class in Barbados is also unquestionably a history of race, a convergence portrayed most often by its pyramid structure: a small group of white plantation owners and a more recent business elite occupy the upper triangle; a thin middle layer is occupied by professionals, civil servants, and small business owners (who, in some parts of the region are also classified as racially mixed, "brown," or lighter-skinned blacks); and a vast majority forms the base, which is made up of poor and laboring descendants of African slaves. Barbara Christian has argued that these conditions are the key reason the Caribbean has produced so many scholars who have emphasized the primacy of class and maintained the Marxist tradition (e.g., C. L. R. James, Walter Rodney, and Eric Williams). James in particular articulated a commonly held antipathy toward and Marxist concern about the likely absorption of the West Indian middle classes into the bourgeoisie at the dawning of independence in the 1960s:

> They live entirely on the material plane.... They aim at nothing.... Are they capitalists? i.e., do they believe in capitalism, socialism, communism, anarchism, anything? Nobody knows.... The West Indian middle classes keep far from these questions. The job, the car, the fridge, the trip abroad, preferably under government auspices and at government expense, these seem to be the beginning and end of their preoccupations. (James 1962:124–26)

As within anthropology at large, then, the middle classes in the Caribbean have been viewed with suspicion and have presented a conundrum for social scientists.

If the Marxist paradigm of class struggle and the legacy of the Caribbean plantation structure has curtailed the study of the middle classes, an equally powerful gatekeeping paradigm has framed the region's cultural analysis of the middle class and of entrepreneurship more broadly. Polemically proposed by anthropologist Peter Wilson in the 1960s, the model of "respectability and reputation" contends that the Caribbean region can be broadly understood as steeped in the structures and ideologies of two competing but dialectically related value systems or cultural models. On one hand is respectability, the inescapable legacy of colonial dependence through which patterns of social hierarchy are upheld and reproduced. On the other hand is reputation, a set of oppositional responses to colonial domination and the elusiveness of respectability, through which people enact creative individualism and at the same time achieve a social leveling, or "communitas." Respectability, for Wilson, encoded a set of British colonially defined values and mores endorsed and practiced largely by the middle class, by women in particular and old or married men as well. Steeped in Victorian tradition, respectability sanctioned the nuclear patriarchal family over the "matrifocal" household, the more fluid "visiting union," or more casual sexual relations. Respectability enshrined the white Christian church over other, syncretic denominations. Ideals of respectable social order, propriety, monogamy, and domesticity are enacted through formal patriarchal marriage, the Anglican Church, the pursuit of higher education, and a secure place in the hierarchy of the civil service or the professions of law or medicine. The essence of reputation, by contrast, is rooted in African culture and expressed through an improvisational adaptability or flexibility associated primarily with a lower-class and masculine public sphere of performance and sociality. Reputation is performed in the public domain in such venues as the street corner, the political platform, the rum shop, the market, and the musical stage, where people flaunt qualities such as sexual prowess, verbal wit, musical flair, and economic flexibility and guile.

Whereas respectability in Barbados has historically been associated with both feminine domesticity and the orderly and colonial-infused hierarchical institutions of church, school, government, and patriarchal marriage, the qualities that Wilson describes as central to reputation can be thought of as the embodiment of an entrepreneurial esprit—always adaptive, self-defined, and resistant. The propensity for adaptability, innovation, and self-invention; a juggling of multiple occupations; and independent travel were long believed to be the necessary responses to Caribbean economic vulnerability, survival strategies more than lifeways to be sought or strived for. For Wilson, importantly, the reputation/respectability model was not a mere heuristic but offered a political agenda that sought to advance the cultural values of reputation over those of respectability as the way to combat a neocolonial order and beckon a more culturally authentic future for the Caribbean region. The tension between these value systems in the Caribbean fostered a culture of what Wilson (1973:58) called "crab antics" because their effect resembled a barrel full of crabs all trying to free themselves and, in the process of climbing out, each one yanking the one above back down.

The tension between reputation and respectability provides a valuable lens on today's entrepreneurial surge and for analyzing what it is to be middle class, for where entrepreneurship has historically been rooted in the tradition of reputation, it is the middle class—as a group, an identity, and a set of ideals—that is believed to form the very axis of respectability. Although many have critiqued this framework for its susceptibility to reductionist binaries, its resonance in the region's ethnographic corpus endures. Not only do most anthropologists working in the region take up or critique reputation/respectability in one manner or another, but also, I would go so far as to say, much of Caribbean ethnography itself privileges those domains of life and culture most squarely situated in the realm of reputation, interpreting respectability as a regrettable but enduring inheritance of British colonialism in the mindsets of women—especially those in the middle class (Abrahams 1983; Burton 1997; Cooper 1995; Wardle 2000).[2] As such, reputation has been examined ethnographically in the public spheres of the dance hall, the carnival, and the street corner as sites of cultural dynamism among the region's lower classes, whereas respectability, associated with formal marriage, the Anglican Church, the hierarchy of the civil service, and middle-class life, has received much less empirical focus. Respectability continues to signify a static, colonial yardstick upheld by a (feminine) middle class against the interests and authenticity of the majority.[3]

THE ANXIOUS DOMAIN OF THE MIDDLE CLASS IN POSTCOLONIAL FEMINISM

For postcolonial feminism, class—and the middle class in particular—has been a fraught subject with implications for the focus on "non-Western" and nonwhite middle classes. To understand this tension, it is important to highlight how early feminist efforts elided the experiences of women of color. Second-wave socialist feminism helped to illuminate the gendered specificity of class by broadening the lens of analysis beyond the shop floor and the waged economy to include the family and the private sphere as domains of labor and to reinterpret domestic relations as fundamental to class relations rather than outside them (Sacks 1989). Central to this feminist rethinking of class is the argument made several decades ago by Heidi Hartmann (1979) that understanding women's positions, experiences, and identities within any particular class is never simply a matter of their relationship to capital or the means of production and that their relationship to capital and to the means of production is never only or primarily economic. The so-called private sphere was a critical means of reproducing the capitalist order of things.

From the perspective of feminists of color, the waged-unwaged distinction between the public and private spheres was inadequate for many black, Latina, indigenous, and Asian women who engaged in both waged and unwaged labor in the domestic sphere. Black feminists in particular have questioned an assumed white middle class as the unmarked subject of social analysis, advocating in the 1980s and 1990s for feminist analysis to place the experiences of women of color at its center, rather than those of an assumed normative white middle-class woman (Collins 1992; Dill 1994; hooks 1984; Mohanty 1988). Thus, black, Third World, and postcolonial feminisms of today often define themselves against "middle-class feminism" (sometimes referred to as "second-wave," "liberal," or "white middle-class" feminism).

So persuasive have these critiques been that the very category of middle class has, outside the realm of work and family studies in the United States, been avoided in much recent feminist work. Because middle classness has been equated with white and Western and because the emphasis on axes of difference has been critical to feminist models of intersectionality, there has emerged a discursive logic in which lower-class women are frequently implicitly nonwhite and, in turn, middle-class women are implicitly white (Lacy 2007; Landry 1988; Patillo-McCoy 1999). In this distillation, the middle becomes an empty or problematic category that in many respects stands outside class analysis altogether, much as it did for Marx. bell hooks (2000:116–17) notes the political dangers of this flattening with regard to the poor, noting the pervasive public media portrayal of the "black face of poverty" despite the fact that the vast majority of America's poor, in sheer numbers, are white. Zora Neale Hurston (1950:954) remarked more than sixty years ago on the importance of documenting the middle-class African American experience, arguing that the upper class was "an interesting problem" to consider in contradistinction to the portrayal of poor black "folk" but that conspicuously absent was a "realistic story around a Negro insurance official, dentist, general practitioner, undertaker and the like." In this regard, more recent works about the black middle class in the United States (Lacy 2007; Landry 1988; Patillo-McCoy 1999) and in the Caribbean

(Freeman 2000, 2007; Thomas 2004), this chapter included, promise to complicate feminist intersectionality approaches and to add nuance to the particularities of middle class*ness* and middle class*es*.

NEOLIBERALISM AND THE NEW RESPECTABILITY OF ENTREPRENEURSHIP

My goal is to illustrate, through ethnographic cases of Barbadian women entrepreneurs, some of the complexities of gender, race, and culture that are inextricably tied to the "heroic neoliberal figure of the entrepreneur." In so doing, I demonstrate the cultural particularities of class as a prism that is always refracted through gender and race and sexuality.[4] In essence, the Caribbean framework of reputation/respectability constitutes a dynamic cultural logic of intersectionality in which race, class, and gender (as well as sexuality and religion) are intimately intertwined. I argue that the emergence of this new middle-class fraction demonstrates intriguing changes in the contours of respectability in a period of economic and cultural flux. The individuals I refer to as the "new entrepreneurial middle class" include those from lower-class family origins who have become upwardly mobile and those from middle-class origins who have moved horizontally into new domains of entrepreneurship.

These new middle-class entrepreneurs have departed from a long-standing Barbadian tradition in which upward mobility and middle-class status for the Afro-Barbadian majority have been associated with the pursuit of education, stable long-term employment, and a heavily bureaucratized public sector. There has long been a stigma associated with business as a "nonrespectable" or inaccessible path. Not only has business been viewed as the privileged preserve of a small, nepotistic, white elite (and, as some pointed out to me, the path for "dummies who couldn't advance at school"),[5] but also petty traders and higglers are well-established historical icons of reputation and the lower classes. The professional, educated black middle class has been a proud illustration of the fruits of free and universal education, whereas the business sector has been a resilient symbol of white economic domination within Barbadian society (Beckles 1989). Today's entrepreneurs—by eschewing higher education, leaving secure jobs in established public sector or private company domains, or entering into entrepreneurial endeavors that often depend upon global imports and exports and "foreign" management practices—represent both a changing social and racial landscape of the middle class in Barbados and a new and growing subject of neoliberalism: the global middle class*es*.

Entrepreneurship is a newly desired path to middle classness, but it is a sphere that, despite women's prominent history as economic actors, is symbolically fraught for women because of its links with "reputation." The association of entrepreneurship with "outside," the public sphere and the market, makes it a challenge for the maintenance of conventional middle-class feminine respectability, although women often bolster their claims to respectability via traditional markers—church, family, domesticity, formal marriage—which can offset the subtle reputational threats posed by their new entrepreneurial profile. However, the forms these traditional markers of respectability take under contemporary neoliberalism are notably different, and speak to the convergences of reputation and neoliberal flexibility and subjectivities, privileging emotion (love) and what women poignantly refer to as "partnership," an idiom that signals respectability's integral relationship to their entrepreneurial quests.

REMAKING RESPECTABILITY: PARTNERSHIP MARRIAGE AND MIDDLE-CLASS MATRIFOCALITY

Three adages about women are well known in the Afro-Caribbean and are explored richly in the region's social science literature: Caribbean women have always worked; work has never precluded motherhood in the Caribbean; motherhood often precedes marriage and even surpasses it in importance. In addition to these aspects of women's lives and Caribbean kinship, it is well understood that marriage has constituted one dimension of a set of respectable ideals but that its practice has been imbued with ambivalence and trepidation, as indicated by Merle Hodge's (2002:481) assertion that "marriage is regarded with a certain amount of reverence.... Yet many prefer to admire it from afar. To Caribbean women...its benefits seem dubious."

In light of these well-known patterns, I had every expectation of finding dynamic Barbadian women shouldering the double burdens (and pleasures) of family obligations, child rearing, and new entrepreneurial lives. I was less prepared for what appears to be a new discourse of intimate and emotional marital partnership and its central place within women's broader project of entrepreneurial self-making. I found, on one hand, a striking emphasis among entrepreneurial women on a new vision of marriage and, on the other, powerful illustrations of entrepreneurial women enacting what can best be described as matrifocal kinship and households, in which they are the self-described heads of their families and homes. I see both processes—the emergence of a new vision of marriage and the embrace of matrifocality within the entrepreneurial middle class—as articulations of neoliberal kinship and selfhood forged across the economic and affective domains of life. In these projects of entrepreneurial self-care and self-knowledge, the simultaneous compartmentalization of leisure, work, the social, the family, the couple, and the self *and* their increasing entanglements are all subject to regimes of flexibility and thus can be reconstituted and redefined. In short, marriage, like a business, becomes a project that demands adaptability, innovation, and sensitivity to external demands, creativity, and responsiveness. It becomes a site permeated by market relations and at the same time saturated by affects: hope, longing, intimacy, anxiety.

In the Caribbean, whereas matrifocality has always been imbued with such qualities as flexibility and creative resourcefulness (reputation), marriage has been construed as its antithesis: rigid, static, and foreign (respectability). Little has been said, however, about the powerful manner in which matrifocality operates in *middle-class* life. Instead, marriage has been seen as integral to "the rise to middle class status of coloured and black women in the post-emancipation period...as they [have] subjected themselves to the civilizing forces of Christianity and education and renounced concubinage" (Barrow 1996:181). Here, the equation of marriage with the moral benchmark of respectability and the codes of a foreign Victorian sensibility resurface as middle-class women attempt to distinguish themselves from the promiscuity and immorality of the lower classes. But, as Barrow and other contemporary social scientists have argued, these middle-class women have been "faced with their own husbands, fathers and sons, firmly embedded in Caribbean culture, for whom peer group popularity, non-domestic activity, marital segregation, concubinage and outside children [have] become a way of life" (1996:181).[6] In other words, where matrifocality has been reconsidered (and depathologized) as a central dimension of Caribbean creole culture *within the lower classes*, the legacy of Wilson's reputation/respectability model appears to have given solidity to marriage as a static patriarchal form and to matrifocality as a dynamic, albeit lower-class, one.[7] As we will see, the logic of respectability, as traditionally steeped in the moral order of patriarchy in the domestic arena and the church, is being refashioned in both private and public domains in ways that are giving rise to new gendered subjectivities via new middle-class practices and self-concepts.

A final dimension of the history of Caribbean kinship has a bearing on the contemporary entrepreneurial reworking of marriage and matrifocality and on the centrality of affect and of affective labor in middle-class life: an overriding emphasis on their different *economic* underpinnings and material effects. Economic security has long been understood to be the primary motivation for marriage. By the same token, matrifocality, with its serial relationships, visiting unions, and reliance on supportive networks of female kin, has been widely framed as an alternative economic survival mechanism steeped in a tradition of "cutting and contriving" a life. Questions of love, desire, and intimacy and the contemporary notion of partnership have been seldom addressed or analyzed, not only because of the way in which political-economic frameworks have dominated the scholarly inquiry but also because conjugal relations at large are emically described in an economic idiom.[8] As Barrow (1996:172) put it, "consensual sexual relations...are perceived and constructed as an exchange of male economic inputs for female sexual access.... Within the Caribbean family a man's most intensive and enduring *relationship* is the one he has with his mother."[9] I read the contemporary confluence of newly defined partnership marriages and what might be interpreted as the upward mobility of matrifocality as a rich social field in which interrelationships among gender, class, and race are being recast in both material and affective terms.[10] Not only was the proportion of married entrepreneurs in my research a striking inverse of the national profile, but also the particular manner of describing this new marital partnership ideal was especially evocative in the testimonies of women entrepreneurs.

New goals for partnership marriages, just like the entrepreneurial enterprises themselves, are described most often by entrepreneurs as individual quests for mutually fulfilling emotional and material relationships.[11] But these quests cannot be understood solely in individual terms. They also embody, at the community level, changing social and economic configurations of social ties and support and of historical arrangements of kin and the extended family network. At the national level, these partnerships and their emphasis on self-determination, mutual support, and nuclearization emerge in concert with mechanisms by which the state is gradually shrinking back from public service and social programs and defining an integrated, flexible, neoliberal nation. Finally, this notion of marriage as an intimate partnership, whether imagined, attempted, or realized, reflects and gives specific meaning to the rapid global circulation of "love marriage" or "companionate marriage" as an integral dimension of modernity itself (Hirsch and Wardlow 2006). Women raised in modest chattel houses, women who live in suburban "wall" houses, and those from the established corporate or plantation elite all articulate a remarkably shared vision for the new marital partnership. The cases I highlight here illustrate a striking convergence of young and middle-aged, white and black women's projects of entrepreneurial self-making under the rubric of contemporary neoliberalism.

For Barbadian women entrepreneurs, the expectation for a new kind of intimate partnership signifies, first, a dramatic generational break from the traditions of their parents and grandparents.[12] Women like Heather and Ashanti,[13] whose experiences I turn to now, spoke often and forcefully of the "traditional" patriarchal marriage system and the implicit counterpoint of matrifocality they associated with earlier generations of Afro-Barbadian women. The "traditions" that these women aimed to transcend echoed early ethnographers' depictions of the male breadwinner and patriarchal household in which husbands and wives shared little leisure time or emotional interaction. One went so far as to say that during his fieldwork in Jamaica in the 1950s, he heard no terms of endearment and sensed that husbands and wives were not especially fond of each other (Cohen 1956). The new partnership marriages were depicted by many of the women entrepreneurs in direct contrast to such portrayals.

Heather, a busy public figure whose work life includes not only an active consultancy business but also leadership on a number of prominent boards, articulated boldly how marriage and the nature of intimate relationships in Barbados are being radically challenged today. With emotion in her voice and expression, she described a dramatic difference between her own marriage and those of two previous generations in her family:

> For example, your grandparents would have tolerated…outside women…would have tolerated the occasional lash, would have tolerated drinking, would have tolerated nonparticipation in the upbringing of children. They tolerated a lot of things…because they didn't have any economic alternative. Then, the generation of my mother and father, their generation tolerated outside women. That generation did not tolerate the beating. But eventually the marriage would turn sour from this outside woman business, because they wanted more…the women wanted more fidelity. And gradually they would grow apart, but they would just keep the shell going because they [didn't] want anybody to know and, *hell no*, they [were] *not getting divorced*.… Many, many children of my generation grew up in that type of home, and the women in *my* age group [mid-forties] said *nobody* is doing that to me. I'm not tolerating it, and *if marriage is not producing for me what I feel it should, I am prepared to destroy it. I will break it, and I will move on* because I am not tolerating that kind of thing.… Those were the types of things that I said to myself…that as girls coming

along, we discussed.... *We're not doing what our mothers did....* If I have to get divorced and find somebody else, I will do that, but I am not prepared to tolerate someone who is not putting an effort into this marriage and that this marriage isn't producing the emotional satisfaction that I am looking for.[14]

Heather's delineation of what women have "tolerated" in the past suggests pragmatic changes such as general advancements in standards of living, the availability and successful enactment of family planning by more and more women, the increase in divorce, and along with these, changing codes of respectability. The "shell" of an empty marriage that women of her grandmother's generation frequently endured is a requirement of neither social convention nor economic survival for women like herself. Heather, like many women entrepreneurs, describes an intense desire for and wide-reaching efforts to achieve a more egalitarian and more emotionally satisfying partnership. Ashanti observed similar generational changes, especially among women in Barbados:

> All of a sudden, women have left the home. They're out in careers, they're building businesses, they're owning property. And all of a sudden, you're hearing that "men are in crisis."... Weren't we ever supposed to leave the home? Weren't we ever supposed to go and get an education? Weren't we ever supposed to do well? Weren't we ever supposed to...take the reins of our own existence in our hands, so to speak, and...guide ourselves, or were we always supposed to wait to be led?... The truth is that the men are the same spoilt brats they've always been. The difference is that women are not standing for it now!

The ideal of a partnership marriage as described by Ashanti and Heather is clearly valued both for its departure from the suffering (violence, infidelity, economic insecurity) endured by earlier women in their families and for the gift of affective exchange and intimate connection they eagerly seek. Heather said, "It's one of the things I [will] always be grateful for in my life...that I was able to love and be loved.... I bless God every day for him."

Heather describes her marriage and its complementary relationship to her thriving business enterprise and active political life through the use of a telling stage metaphor: "It's kind of like a singer and a manager.... He cannot sing, but he can do all the other things that help me and allow *me* to sing.... I am good at what I do.... It was only obvious that I would be playing this particular front role within the business...and my husband...does the support in terms of the administrative, financial management.... I really could not have done it without him." The music metaphor resurfaces: "I think it is Bette Midler that sang 'The Wind Beneath My Wings'? Nobody really sees the wind. They see the bird flying.... I realized that if ever I was going to succeed at what I was doing, I would need that wind beneath my wings." For Ashanti, whose husband is also an entrepreneur, this level of emotional backup is critical to her sense that theirs is a new kind of marriage: "Every single achievement I have, my husband is right there in my cheering section. I can hear his voice right there with me." The convergent demands of deeply personal and market-based stresses associated with the new entrepreneurial middle-class flexibility marks the manner in which affective desires and labors span the private and public spheres. In so doing, they also suggest that some of the central expectations and subtle codes of traditional middle-class respectability are changing.

NEOLIBERAL SOULMATES, PARENTS, SELVES

Middle-class entrepreneurial women's desires for a new kind of marriage not only hinge on the shifting emotional and material needs and new self-conscious understandings of their own identities as women, entrepreneurs, mothers, and so on, but also are formed in relation to a newly defined partner/husband who draws decidedly from but reconstitutes the old order of reputation and respectability. Today's idealized soulmate stands in contrast to the hegemonic masculinities of the breadwinning patriarch, "wutless [worthless] womanizer," or "soft," "namby pamby" (effeminate) man (Lewis 2003:109). Whereas "support" had long been women's key idiom of spousal love (i.e., emphasizing economic responsibility), "soulmate" and "partner" form the lexicon of today's marital ideal that speaks to new middle-class subjectivities. A good husband was described by most entrepreneurial women as a partner in all senses—emotional/intimate, sexual, and material/economic—and in all domains, private and public. Ashanti used such language to describe her unusual connection with her husband and its departure from what she saw as the negative conjugal models she had grown up with:

> We were in sync, we'd had the same kind of experience of life and the hurt and disappointment and all, and we connected.... His attitude was not to be coy and macho and all these things. [Growing up with hard times abroad] had left him with an outlook on life that I hadn't heard before.... He's very open. He's actually a very sensitive person, open with his feelings, which

is not something I'm used to…. He is very special because he doesn't think like your average Bajan man.

Ashanti described her husband as the embodiment of a new Barbadian (Bajan) masculinity, a departure from both the patriarchal stereotype of the authoritarian provider, who offers material support but finds companionship and camaraderie in the homosocial "outside," and the unreliable (reputation-oriented) man who can be counted on more for infidelity than intimacy.

For Heather, whose own business success has ensured the economic security of her household, love and emotional commitment are the core of her marriage, not the expectation of financial provision. In a gendered role reversal, Heather's husband performs some of the reproductive labor of emotional support and backup that women have long provided in subsidizing their husbands' formal economic activities in the public sphere (Hartmann 1979). Striking in her testimony is not just a determination to refuse the painful breaches that earlier generations of women in her family had to endure, but the tender intimacy and understanding that she shares with her husband:

> The thing about [him] is that he is emotionally sensitive to anything that is happening to me. And what that does, it means that if there is anything that is distressing me, he steps in and helps to bring me to a [new] perspective. He is not afraid of my emotions, which is unusual in men because most men feel overwhelmed by their women having emotions and they will abandon them in terms of…"Oh gosh, you upset? Let me go out… or let me whatever." Or they brush it off…. He never does that. It doesn't mean we don't have disagreements, or what have you, but they're never mean. We never say things to each other that afterward, you know, has stung anybody's skin. We've learned to be patient with each other…. We are soulmates.

For Heather, being "soulmates" is illustrated by a deep empathy and understanding, being "in sync" with her husband to such a degree that he knows, without needing the specific events or an explicit description, what she is feeling and also what might console and comfort her. Married more than eleven years, she described herself as "barren" when I asked about children. Although her face was visibly pained recounting her inability to have a child, she says, "My life is full…. I could not squeeze that [motherhood] into my life now." In a cultural context in which motherhood is prized above marriage and it is rare for women not to have or foster a child, regardless of marital status, the intense emotional intimacy she and her husband share is particularly striking.[15] In combination with the economic security provided by the business, the mutual commitment of energies and labors Heather and her husband channel toward the simultaneous cultivation of their entrepreneurial enterprise *and* their relationship realizes the dream that for many others remains a fantasy. The conditions of possibility for couples to enact these new intimate partnerships alongside their enterprises without the competing desires and demands of parenting bear further scrutiny. Just as we see some women enacting an upwardly mobile form of matrifocality when their expectations and hopes for intimacy and partnership are dashed, we may also be seeing a new articulation of childless coupling that stands in stark contrast with centuries of cultural tradition.

Heather recounted a recent experience that moved her visibly in her retelling and that encapsulated her partnership marriage and her husband's embodiment of a new Bajan masculinity. On her first trip to Europe, Heather had traveled to Paris for a series of business meetings. She was eager to do some shopping in between her formal appointments:

> It was the first time in my life I ever felt obese. I felt obese! To get anything above a size 10, you have to go to a specialty shop. You can't get a shoe size over a 7 or an 8. What is this? I was really frustrated...and it was more expensive. I had heard it was more expensive, so I had planned! I wanted to get one or two things...one or two really nice European suits, you know, but then the exchange rate with the U.S. was bad...so it meant that the money could not [stretch]. So, on Saturday, I'm walking and every time I find something...they don't have this size, and they don't have that, and they don't have the color.... And [my husband] had talked to me just before I was going...shopping. We'd talked on the phone, and I said, "Look, I'm just going," and he said, "Okay. I'll call you tomorrow morning." But that frustration set in on me...and I felt so, uhhhh.... He picked it up and my phone rang. "What's the problem?" Not "hello.".... He picked up my distress...and I said, "I'm just frustrated. I can't..." And he said [using a sweet diminutive of her name], "It's all right if you can't find anything. Just relax.... When you come back home later on, you could send to the States, or whatever, but don't [worry].... Instead of focusing on suits, find a couple of

blouses...or get a handbag, you know, any of those little things, but don't let yourself get stressed over it." I said, "Oh honey, thanks," and I put down the phone and I was, ohhhhhhhhhh, you know.... It's *amazing* how he does it.... So partnering for me, and that emotional satisfaction, is somebody who is willing to do that for me and somebody for whom I can do this [too].

Emotional support for women has traditionally been described as part of the wide range of Caribbean female alliances of kinship and friendship, and marriage has historically been equated with the desire for economic security. But among new middle-class entrepreneurs, such as Heather and Ashanti, such affective bonds are nurtured and desired between husband and wife. In their exchange, Heather's husband soothed her raw nerves and bolstered her self-confidence in ways that she noted are rare and treasured. The story is revealing both for its indication of a tender marital exchange and for the locus of despair. For Heather, the experience of foreign travel was anxiety producing and lonely, and soothing herself through consumption, in particular through fashionable European adornment, was seen as a reward for her hard-won entrepreneurial success and the daily stresses she endured. The disappointment of feeling "obese" and unsuited to the alluring and expensive European clothes and shoes was a reaction to the denial of an important dream of embodied middle-class entrepreneurial mastery. That this refusal was softened by her husband and by his fulfillment of a different middle-class entrepreneurial dream of intimacy and love is striking. Here, the compensatory affective support in one sphere (marriage) offset the affective longings denied in another (feeling beautiful and fashionable). The ideals of an intimate partnership and new modes of respectability are sought in a complex web of Barbadian social relations (motherhood/parenthood, the extended family, and traditionally gender-segregated social spheres), and such trade-offs are common along the rocky new path of entrepreneurial middle classness.

The quest for a marital soulmate should not be read outside or in lieu of the extended family, as some have suggested (and feared), or a full-scale realignment of gender. In most cases, the women most intent upon the new marital partnership (including those whose marriages failed) were also critically aware of their reliance upon the support and involvement (emotionally and in many other ways) of mothers, sisters, and other female kin and friends. However, the combination of new middle-class residential patterns (e.g., new suburban developments and a heavy reliance on cars for transportation) and the emergence of new modes of social life in which the couple has a new precedence sometimes stands in direct competition with the traditionally close proximity and involvement of extended kin networks. Equally, Ashanti's description of a "new Bajan" masculinity is intriguing in its signification of a new ideal, though not in any way a dominant reality. The mutual investment and concern shown by Heather's and Ashanti's husbands about both their businesses and their domestic lives are prized qualities of these new partnership marriages. Their husbands, entrepreneurs as well, provide emotional and other forms of support that these women see as critical to their entrepreneurial and emotional well-being and that present a new profile of emotionally attuned, sensitive masculinity fostered by partnership marriage and the neoliberal culture of entrepreneurship at large. However, just as the newly sought intimate dyad and the challenges to conventional gender ideologies are bound up in neoliberal ideals of affective individualism, self-mastery, and introspective selfhood, they also expose some of the illusory promises of independence and flexibility hailed by the same neoliberal mantra of entrepreneurialism.

Intriguingly, "flexibility" was the single most-cited explanation for women's attraction to entrepreneurship (Freeman 2007). The desire for flexibility is especially pronounced for mothers of young and school-age children. And yet, for these women especially, the challenges of juggling the multiple and shifting demands of an entrepreneurial life dramatically multiply. Not only are these women, like all entrepreneurs, navigating spheres of the market that involve the rough-and-tumble of customs officials, suppliers, and the port; the bureaucratic red tape of banks; and the slick domains of advertising and marketing; they are also increasingly propelled by a new self-help and parenting movement that calls for a host of additional resources and ways of being. As Cindi Katz (chapter 7, this volume) shows for the United States, the intensification of parenting and the deliberate cultivation of children today illustrate another sphere in which neoliberal subjects are being actively produced.

A new form of intensive parenting in Barbados, not just for children of the white elite, but for the growing black middle class, has begun to resemble similar patterns in Europe, Japan, and North America, with an expanding array of summer camps and extra lessons, swim programs, sailing, photography, pottery, and foreign languages. Whereas elite families have invested in piano, dance, and horseback-riding lessons for their children since the colonial days, the tremendous expansion of extracurricular activities geared specifically toward the cultivation of black and white middle-class children is notable. And although the presence of domestic servants has long been a staple of middle-class households in the West

Indies and grannies and other female kin have been traditionally integral to the care of children, the new hierarchy of service providers now includes cell-phone-toting, CPR-trained nannies with cars and university degrees, who are increasingly desired by working couples with children. Ashanti and her husband interviewed more than a dozen such candidates for a baby-sitter position)they have two school-age children). She noted her desire for a "well-spoken lady" who would bring out the best in her daughters, drive them safely to their activities, and stay on top of their homework. She expected that her relationships with her husband and children and also those sought in the marketplace (her employees, the nanny) would be steeped in caring exchanges and would include a host of new accoutrements signifying modern middle-class life (new technologies, an organized schedule of activities, a regular exercise routine, a healthy diet, etc.). The burdens and pleasures of their businesses, and life more generally, that women entrepreneurs desire to share with their partners/husbands are wide-ranging: managing budgets and employees, the rate of growth and debt, the care and transportation of children; meeting obligations within the extended family; and sharing quality time, leisure, and romantic intimacy.[16]

RECONSTITUTING PUBLIC AND PRIVATE

The expansion of affective labor as indispensable to more and more service enterprises in the marketplace is echoed across private life. It is both sought and produced within an affective economy that conjoins intimate and market relations, suggesting familial duty and love, material and emotional support. How these public and private labors converge and compete and how they are understood by social actors are critical questions for analyzing neoliberalism.[17]

For Ashanti, like most other women I interviewed, the planning of outings and special shared time is one aspect of the generalized emotional labor she continues to perform both in her domestic life and among her employees. "I have had to institute date by date just so that [I] and my husband can get out and go have dinner or see a movie or something like that." For those with children, the romantic couple is often subsumed by the larger domain of "the family." Many women in their forties shared sentiments about having had their youthful adventures and now prioritizing "quality family time" with their children, a phrase that is familiar to an American audience but that here represents a new generational concept. Indeed, this is one of many deceptively déjà vu examples of middle-class life that resonate so closely with American popular references that its particular meaning in Barbados could easily be missed. For Ashanti, who feels confident of the partnership she and her husband share as fellow entrepreneurs and as an intimate and domestic couple, having some separate time in which to enjoy different interests is a priority, so long as the needs of the children are met first. She explained:

> I spent so much of my twenties out everywhere, you know. To me now, life is at its best when I have a really good book or there is a really good movie on and I can just relax and be in my own space, and he is very much tuned in to me in that sense. So, you know, on a Friday night he might get the kids a pizza maybe and a movie...we get them settled, and he will help me with their [school] bags and get them to bed, their story time and all that. And once they've settled down, he [will] say to me, "Well, I'm going out," and that's fine, you know. Because he needs his space and a chance to unwind and if his thing is going out and catching a football game down at Bubba's [a local middle-class sports bar] or a boxing match or whatever, I don't mind. I'm not going to scream about it. You know, some women get really uptight about that, and they don't want them to leave the house unless they are going [too]. Maybe I'm silly, but I am just not going to worry.... I don't bother my head with it.

Ashanti's husband is intimately involved in the domestic sphere, participating in the rituals of children's baths, unpacking school bags, making Friday nights a special family movie night. All of this speaks to the close bond they share and to the challenges they are posing to traditionally gendered bifurcations of public and private spaces and traditional divisions of labor. These gestures go far beyond the basic provisioning of the household and even more dramatically transcend the absent or abusive male partners/fathers Ashanti witnessed in growing up and whom Heather talked about. Subtle and easily overlooked, these expectations and ways of understanding partnership, parenthood, and the affective underpinnings of these relationships have shifted the family onto a new field. New concepts of quality family time and date night have entered common parlance, and they are accompanied by notions of care and support that meld the structural, the economic, and the affective. And they signal the weighty desire and the onus of affect unfolding in public and private life.

It bears emphasizing that a woman's desire for a new partnership marriage entails not only private intimacy and support within the domain of her household and immediate family and the support and help of her partner in business, but also a greater participation *as a couple* in the public sphere. In essence, the new partnership marriage demands that new masculine subjectivities be cultivated in the traditional realms of reputation (rum shops, sports bars, and "outside") and also in the respectable domains of domesticity and marriage in a range of new public venues. This suggests that the public sphere of reputation is being reconstituted with newly respectable spaces for women, couples, and families to inhabit, including a new boardwalk on the island's south coast, where couples, friends, families, and individuals of all ages walk, jog, take in the coastal view, admire the sunset, stop into cafés, wine bars, and restaurants for a meal or drink together, or just enjoy some quiet contemplation.

Although Ashanti's husband still enjoys the homosocial world of the sports bar, his social life is not exclusively enacted with his male friends. Family time together at the beach, swimming and picnicking, suggests the enactment of a middle-class family that departs from most of these entrepreneurs' memories of their own childhood and from the portrayal of family life in the region's ethnographic corpus. Like several other entrepreneurs I met, Ashanti described enjoying mini-vacations at local hotels with her family, taking advantage of weekend-package deals designed exclusively for Bajans in the low tourist season. She mentioned a favorite new café where she goes for dinner with her husband while her sister watches their kids; she attends a new middle-class church actively geared toward family participation and offering special seminars on "spiritual" marriage and successful self-employment. These transformations signal a changing public sphere and a growing reliance on an expanding array of services specifically aimed toward busy middle-class lives—takeout food, global electronic media, entertainment and dining establishments, and new religious venues, to name just a few—which lie at the heart of the entrepreneurial sector in which many of these women's businesses can be found.

The gender-segregated (homosocial) social spheres that have characterized much of Barbadian life, where women, men, and children come together primarily in the context of family and sometimes at church-based gatherings, are being supplanted by new social domains. The new partnership marriage, then, increasingly demands that couples share not only feelings, worries, dreams, and responsibilities but also the pleasures of leisure time and the cultivation of a symbiotic couple and close family unit whose members relax together and have fun together. Here, the labor of planning and enacting these new activities and ways of relating mirrors the affective labor increasingly critical to their entrepreneurial enterprises.

These transformations are not always expressed without ambivalence, nor met with seamless success. For many women, the persistence of a West Indian tradition of separate gendered spheres of sociality and leisure, noted widely in classic ethnographies, as well as in some of the entrepreneurs' own testimonies, was a source of profound frustration. Entrepreneurial women across the age spectrum, especially those with young children, frequently complained that their own and their friends' husbands still believe themselves beyond reproach if they provide well for their children but show no other signs of emotional connection or a desire to share leisure time. The emerging resentment toward husbands who are admittedly "good providers" but who continue to prioritize segregated, gendered spheres of social life may not be surprising. It has been precisely the lack of basic provisioning and economic support that has caused women to complain about men as "marginal" partners and fathers throughout West Indian history (Miller 1991). However, among these contemporary middle-class couples, for women in particular, the grounds of conflict have shifted. Their desires are no longer primarily for basic economic support or even more equitable divisions of labor (although these remain points of contention) but increasingly revolve around more emotional aspects of relatedness and the willingness of men to shift at least some of their social and affective investments away from the traditional spheres of reputation. The idea that a "good husband" is now one who not only helps with the financial support of the household but is also an intimate partner and emotional confidant, a soulmate who shares leisure time, consults and worries about the rearing of children, and can be depended upon for mutual support, represents a significant redefinition and a radical generational departure in the minds of most of these entrepreneurs. The affective labors of the new partnership marriage and new middle-class household simultaneously mirror, draw from, and subsidize the growing expectations of affective labor in the formal entrepreneurial realms in which they invest so much of their working lives. And the prevalence of these expectations across all spheres of entrepreneurial life (including in the market and in private, to the extent such a boundary exists) suggests hope and renewal, as well as exhaustion (Freeman 2011).

FAILED PARTNERSHIPS AND THE LEGACIES OF MATRIFOCALITY AND PATRIARCHY

At the same time that entrepreneurial women are increasingly invested in new ideals of partnership marriage and the public and private couple and family, they are careful to maintain close ties of reciprocity and support with their networks of kin and close friends. Indeed, the quest for a new marital ideal simultaneously gives new middle-class expression to the tradition of matrifocality, for it is in women's relationships to one another (mothers, sisters, friends, and even the paid relationships with domestic workers) that the intimate partnerships, like the entrepreneurial businesses, are (invisibly) buffered. For many of my interviewees, cultivating their immediate nuclear families and marriages while at the same time maintaining involvement with extended kin so that they could also depend on them constituted yet another juggling act, another site requiring affective labor. On one hand, this might be read as a double standard: these women increasingly expect their husbands to forgo traditional homosocial commitments in favor of outings and emotional investment in the couple, and at the same time, they retain their webs of connection and obligation to female kin and friends. On the other hand, because these connections bring tangible support not just to the individual (emotional salve and companionship), but to the family unit, in the form of babysitting, meals, transportation, and a strongly held commitment to family itself, these relationships are seldom questioned. Here again we see the inextricable linkages and recursive articulations between the productive and reproductive spheres, between the public and the private, as the subsidies of affective labor offered by kin, for example, buoy women's entrepreneurial ventures and their private relationships as well. For the women whose business enterprises have brought about (or secured) their middle-class status, marriage ideally encompasses an elaborate matrix of mutual support and emotional connection that challenges the traditional contours of both domestic, private life and the public, social sphere.

The importance of the matrifocal legacy in Barbadian culture was made especially plain by those women whose desires and determination to achieve such ideals of emotional and practical support and connection were *not* fulfilled. This was painfully illustrated by at least four women entrepreneurs whose unraveling marriages I witnessed and was intimated by several whose life narratives alluded to significant spousal tensions and resentments.

Suzanne's "failed partnership" was evocative in several ways. The daughter of a white Barbadian family, her upbringing had the appearance of quintessential upper-middle-class respectability—her father was a businessman, and her mother, active in the parish church, was seemingly always available to her grandchildren and behind the scenes of her husband's company. Suzanne was educated at the same top public secondary school as many of the entrepreneurs I encountered from all racial and class backgrounds. She went to university in Canada, where she earned a degree in graphic design and business, then returned home and worked in a popular tourist restaurant. As a white woman in Barbados, many areas of work were off-limits for her, including the civil service and the professions: "How many white women do you see in government jobs or as doctors and lawyers? No way. We could never make it there, so if we want to stay in Barbados, business is the only way." After marrying the white Barbadian son of a small local hotelier, she had a baby and quit her job. Restless and lonely in their modest middle-class subdivision—in a pink "wall house" surrounded by a chain-link fence—she began a small design company from her living room. What began as a combined effort to "pay for nappies" and other growing expenses related to their new family life and to divert herself from the isolation of suburban motherhood has grown into a hugely successful enterprise in which she employs six people full-time and has recently won a foreign contract valued at half a million U.S. dollars.

Clearly, Suzanne benefited from the financial and other forms of support of her extended family, a signifier of the privilege of her white patriarchal family of origin that was unavailable to many of the black Barbadian women entrepreneurs: her father backed the bank loan for the US$20,000 she needed for equipment. His friendship with the bank's manager, no doubt, helped her application go through. But her dependence upon the support of her mother and sister for regular child care and school runs when meetings and travel kept her away from home was typical of both white and black women entrepreneurs, regardless of their class origins. Perhaps most significant of all, Suzanne's full-time nanny-housekeeper, a ubiquitous ingredient in black and white middle-class life, was, as she put it, her "lifeline." "I'd sooner give up my husband than my maid," she joked, noting, as did many of the middle-class women I met, that she could never live as I do in the States without a full-time "helper."

The joke, however, was more than a throwaway line. With her business's success and her nomination for the island's Entrepreneur of the Year award, her marriage progressively faltered: "He just couldn't handle the fact that I earned more and didn't need him in the same way." The story of her marriage's demise is poignantly echoed in the narratives of a striking number of women entrepreneurs I interviewed, both white and black. Four years after our first meeting, I returned to talk with Suzanne again and found that she had had an affair with a foreigner working on the island and had ended her ten-year marriage. She described with visible affection the ways in which her boyfriend's behavior had contradicted some of the "frustrating and selfish" qualities of her husband and "your typical Bajan man." But with her divorce, her economic circumstances were now more precarious, and her story had circulated widely through the island's rumor mill. As Jamaica Kincaid (1988:52) has noted of neighboring Antigua, "in a small place…the small event is isolated, blown up, turned over and over, and then absorbed into the everyday so that at any moment it can and will roll off the inhabitants of the small place's tongues." Suzanne's transgression of expected gender and race norms for proper middle-class womanhood had further ramifications beyond the gossip and social awkwardness among friends and family. For if neoliberalism is noted for the burden and, sometimes, the pleasurable expectation that individuals will reinvent themselves amid a rapidly changing marketplace of commodities, services, and renditions of the self, the fields upon which such reinventions can occur are not level. On a close-knit small island, crafting selves entails particular challenges for women, and these challenges remind us of the power of traditional mechanisms of patriarchal respectability to rear their many heads. So threatening to the social norm was her extramarital affair that Suzanne's husband managed to get immigration officials to revoke her boyfriend's work permit and "kick him off the island."

The combination of Suzanne's extended kin network of support, made up of her mother and sister; the paid help of a domestic worker; the financial backing of her father; and the emotional attunement of her boyfriend, which was similar to that of Heather's and Ashanti's "soulmate" husbands, offered her the means to break from her disappointing marriage. Although her marriage may have complied with the old-order patriarchal respectability, it lacked precisely the intimacy and close partnership she and other women so powerfully desire. Ashanti commented that many of her entrepreneurial friends' marriages had similarly "gone through the eddoes"— dissolved in a complex mix of financial and intimate struggles. At the same time, like Heather's childless partnership marriage, Suzanne's extramarital affair and later divorce can also be conceptualized as alternative models of middle-class womanhood today and as challenges to the old order's reputation/respectability distinction.

Cases of failed marriages like Suzanne's were in many ways as powerful an illustration of the stakes and entailments of the new partnership ideal— with its emphasis on shared entrepreneurial and affective labors and commitments—as those that appeared more successful. Formal marriage has long been associated with a white middle class and has been seen as an elite marker of respectability, but the patriarchal form of traditional marriage is being explicitly contested by both black and white Barbadian women. Underlying entrepreneurial women's expressed desire for romance, compassion, and an equal partnership is the knowledge that, if need be, they could support themselves and more than survive. Further, the powerful regional model of matrifocality as both a signifier of women's strength and flexibility and a practical locus of support from other kin, along with the critical figure of the paid domestic worker/nanny-housekeeper, offers an important alternative to formal marriage, not only for the poor but also increasingly for middle-class women. Economic security and middle-class status have become critical to these women's capacity to end their relationships without the fear of economic marginality.

Notably, race and ethnicity appear *not* to frame the changing contours of reputation and respectability as Wilson might have predicted. Black and white women echo the same marital partnership ideals and take parallel paths when their desires and efforts to achieve this partnership are dashed. Indeed, perhaps even more striking than the similarities in marital ideals expressed by these two groups of women were the shared patterns of the marital dissolution and matrifocal trajectories they pursued. Although divorce has long been understood to threaten a Caribbean woman's claims to middle-class respectability, their economic autonomy and the symbolic reservoir of matrifocality provide critical tools with which to mitigate losses for both black and white women in this new middle-class milieu. The neoliberal upward mobility of reputation has simultaneously recast respectability.

It is in this sense that the partnership marriage and matrifocality may be seen as two sides of a middle-class woman's coin, and on each side, the contours of respectability and reputation are being reworked. What we are witnessing is not just a matter of gradual creolization over time and a changing dialectic of reputation/respectability and matrifocality/marriage, but a decisive moment of economic and cultural transformation in which the logics of reputation and of matrifocality that were long understood to be oppositional cultural expressions to the hegemonic colonial and capitalist order are being profitably drawn upon in the reconfigurations of middle classness (Freeman 2007). Just as the public sphere of reputation is being redrawn (in part, by these very entrepreneurs' new businesses and new modes of livelihood) to include new venues and activities for women, couples, and families to enact new relationships, subjectivities, and ways of being in the world, so, too, are the contours and *feeling* of middle-class family life and marriage being reconstituted.

CONCLUSION

Read together, these brief narratives of women's entrée into entrepreneurship and middle-class marriage/matrifocality draw our attention to the complex articulations of class as a subjectivity forged in and through gender, race, and culture. As these women traverse the risky terrain of self- and market-oriented entrepreneurship through the neoliberal discourse of affect, they are in the process of redefining the meanings of and slippages between public and private life in Barbados. Their longings for self-realization, connection, and intimacy reflect new desires and new requirements for self-reflection (the inclination to probe "Who am I?" "What are my needs?" "What kind of woman, mother, lover, subject do I wish to be?"). Meanwhile, the convergent push and pull of their business enterprises and their efforts to become self-aware and adept entrepreneurs for themselves, their children, their families, and their intimate relations produces new stresses and strains. As entrepreneurs, they embody both owner and laborer, and the nature of their labor takes many hidden (and feminized) forms that closely resemble and sometimes compete with the affective labors of self-making and the crafting of kinship and intimacy. Indeed, these transformations signal both creative and alienating manifestations of the promise of neoliberal flexibility and seem to mark the very core of their middle classness in the contemporary moment.

These new entrepreneurs show us that understanding class in Barbados today cannot be reduced simply to the struggle between the planter/corporate elite and the laboring poor. Their narratives also support others' observations that, far from disappearing, new paths of middle-class possibility and the elusive idea of middle classness emerge as ever-powerful aspirational dreams. Ironically, perhaps, it may be through the contemporary melding of a conventional marker of middle-class respectability (marriage) with a pursuit more solidly part of oppositional reputation (entrepreneurship) that Barbadian women entrepreneurs not only are attempting to fulfill their own middle-class desires but also are taking active steps toward the fulfillment of Wilson's (1973:234) dream that "social separation of men and women must be narrowed and double standards dropped so that both sexes may come to participate simultaneously and reciprocally in a single value system." Through a new vision of intimate partnership, new gendered expressions of reputation/respectability, and new articulations of the market and the self, these entrepreneurs make plain that a growing affective milieu and, with it, expanding expectations for affective labor have become anchors of personal and public life. Together, these transformations invite

new analyses not just of middle classes around the world, but of the confluences and particularities of neoliberal subjectivities at large.

Acknowledgments

I thank my fellow editors, Rachel Heiman and Mark Liechty, for their close readings and excellent comments on this chapter. I thank Peggy Tally, Purnima Mankekar,
Cindi Katz, Anne Allison, Akhil Gupta, Robert Goddard, Jennifer Patico, and Joanna
Davidson for helping me think through the conceptual genealogy and current articulations of affective labor. And thank you to Jennifer Hirsch and Michael Peletz for their
insights and help on the discussion of marriage and love. I am indebted to Gul Ozyegin,
who has been my tireless interlocutor along all the intersecting lines of argument suggested here.

Notes

1. See also Cahn 2008.

2. In other parts of the world, scholars have highlighted the critical significance of
respectability as a medium through which local middle classes have attempted, however
precariously, to distinguish themselves and, in so doing, altered the borrowed Victori-
an/colonial models to suit the specific cultural milieu (Joshi 2001; Liechty 2003; Mosse
1985b; Walcott 2001). In the Caribbean, little of such dynamism is associated with this
central marker of middle classness.

3. Exceptions to this anthropological avoidance of the middle classes (and elites)
include Diane Austin's (1984) comparison of working- and middle-class communities
and the hegemonic force of education in class ideology and culture in urban Jamaica,
Lisa Douglass's (1992) ethnography of kinship, class, and gender within the "power
elite" of Jamaica, and Deborah Thomas's (2004) explication of the contemporary Jamaican formulation of nationalism she calls "modern blackness," which directly critiques
traditional creole notions of middle-class respectability.

4. The premise of heterosexual normativity in this discussion must be noted here.
Both marriage and the desire for the new intimate partnerships were talked about by
these entrepreneurs and figured prominently in popular romance literature from a
heterosexual perspective. However, it is notable that the few lesbians I did interview articulated a similar set of desires for sharing both intimacy and responsibilities (affection,
experiences, leisure, and economic responsibilities) in the domestic and nondomestic
arenas, although they did not make explicit their particular sexual identities when
discussing their desires for or enactments of these shared domestic arrangements.
For intriguing parallels of the partnership marriage as discussed here, but which center
on women's sexual and supportive relations with other women, see Wekker's (2006:440)

analysis of "mati work," in which women enjoy and prioritize this "thicker stream of exchanges and reciprocal obligations in their relationships with women." A fuller analysis of mati work might shed further light on the affective and other forms of labor in the new partnership marriages that make them both more onerous and more rewarding.

5. For discussions of race and class in the realm of business, see Barrow and Greene 1979; Beckles 1990; Karch 1985; Ryan and Barclay 1992.

6. Barrow acknowledges that Caribbean middle-class families have only recently become a focus for research. All family forms (common-law and visiting unions and marriage; "outside" and "legitimate" children) occur across the class and racial spectrum, but "the frequency…and associated meanings of these forms vary across the social hierarchy" (Barrow 1996:181; see also Smith 1996).

7. Rawwida Baksh-Soodeen (1998) makes the point that Caribbean kinship studies have focused so heavily on the Afro-Caribbean lower-class family and household that the diversity of Indo-Caribbean families and households has only quite recently begun to be explored.

8. See Hirsch and Wardlow 2006 for rich discussions of companionate marriage and love as they are taking shape in other parts of the world.

9. The belief that Caribbean people's primary affective ties are concentrated in the mother-child bond whereas the conjugal bond is casual and unstable is pervasive (de Zalduondo 1995:166).

10. As Sara Friedman (2005) observes, new articulations of intimacy and marriage form amid converging state interventions, changing market conditions, and increasing cultural "openness" in eastern Huj'an, China. Together, these changes foster new subjectivities and conceptions of intimacy, as well as of the state's power in monitoring borders, imposing taxes, and enforcing laws.

11. See Freeman 2011 for a fuller discussion.

12. A striking number of the entrepreneurs (both male and female) expressed that one of the deepest sources of determination to succeed in business was the need to prove their self-worth to an absent parent whose lack of support, love, and involvement in their lives had left lasting emotional scars. In this sense, the emphases by many on their efforts to distinguish both their entrepreneurial success and their very different expectations for marriage and parenting from the common patterns of their own childhood and of previous generations were notably intertwined.

13. All names are pseudonyms chosen by the individuals themselves. Some details of the entrepreneurs' profiles have been slightly changed or melded with those of others to protect their anonymity.

14. This comment was remarkably similar to that of a prominent and much older white male entrepreneur, describing his wife of more than thirty years. Heather's

narrative represents an intriguing gendered inversion of the invisible but indispensable wife/helpmate.

15. Inhorn (1994) discusses the emergence of new forms of loving companionate marriage when infertility deprives couples of a key marker of family or social success. As in Barbados, in Egypt, where womanhood is defined in large part via motherhood (albeit within marriage), she found that even when extended families urged men to divorce their wives in cases of infertility, some men and women forged close and protective marriage bonds in the absence of children.

16. Middle-class husbands in the United States are also reported to be doing more housework today than in the past; however, what appears to have changed less is the "invisible emotional labor" of planning, arranging family activities, maintaining social ties for the family, and so on, work that wives and mothers typically perform (Hochschild 1997). These are precisely the kinds of burdensome affective work and investment that women entrepreneurs mention when they speak about their desires for a partnership marriage and soulmate.

17. See Susan Gal's (2002) concept of the "fractal distinctions" of public-private, Hochschild's *The Commercialization of Intimate Life* (2003), and Kathi Weeks's (2007) discussion of work/life—all efforts to rethink the opposition of reproductive and productive labor under capitalism.

5

The Postsocialist Middle Classes and the New "Family House" in Hungary

Krisztina Fehérváry

Throughout the first decade after the fall of state socialism, Hungarian state television broadcast two series that portrayed strikingly different versions of respectable middle-class life. *Neighbors* (*Szomszédok*) was a serious teledrama focused on the lives of residents in a massive, modern apartment block. In contrast, *Family, Inc.* (*Família Kft.*) debuted as Hungary's first sitcom, complete with laugh track, and featured the lifestyle of an entrepreneurial family who lived in a large, detached family house. In this period of traumatic social, economic, and political transformation, these two shows embodied coexisting but competing conceptualizations of legitimate social orders through their portrayals of the subject populations and their material settings (not to mention the genres through which they were portrayed). The shows managed to top even *E.R.* and reruns of *Dallas* in prime-time ratings, meaning that large numbers of people in the country watched them on a regular basis.

Neighbors first aired in the waning period of state socialism and then turned into a show that explored how average people were experiencing the day-to-day tribulations of the regime change. The teledrama opened with a panoramic shot of a monolithic housing development on the outskirts of the metropolitan capital of Budapest, significantly, at dusk. It embraced the lives of those people who had constituted respectable society during the socialist era but whose status after the regime change had become precarious. Residents included doctors, educators, and bureaucrats still in state employ, service sector workers and struggling entrepreneurs, the elderly and retired, and young married couples still living with their parents. The show's scandals came in the form of extramarital affairs and the immoral habits of the new rich. In each episode, characters were portrayed as adhering to values they perceived to belong to a gentler past even as they tried to fit into a new order. In one, a man is drawn to the possibilities of connecting with the world via the Internet yet is unwilling to take on the moral burden of a loan for a new computer. In another, an elderly couple begin to renovate their apartment but argue over whether to follow the widespread practice of avoiding the 25 percent tax by having the painting done "without a receipt."

The sitcom *Family, Inc.* (*Família Kft.*) first aired in 1991, opening with a sunny shot of a large, moss-green house in the charming, historic town of Eger. The show depicted the antics of the extended entrepreneurial family who lived in the house and their friends and neighbors. By 1996, the show was watched by more than a quarter of the population every week, appealing in particular to younger generations with its upbeat focus and lack of moralizing or nostalgia for the past. The lead family prospered through entrepreneurial endeavors, worked hard but not too hard, and took part in a postsocialist good life: they had new cars, wore nice clothes, bought furniture and other consumer goods, and took vacations. Little if any reference was made to the socialist era spatially or temporally—except in the form of disparaging jokes. And any "problems" raised were on the order of debating what percentage of the time Hungarian men spend thinking about sex. The location shots provided backdrops of renovated historic streets and modern shopping areas the equal of any in Western Europe. Unlike *Neighbors'* focus on a community, the sitcom's name, *Family, Inc.*, echoed the paradigmatic social unit of bourgeois capitalism, the family, and at the same time embraced entrepreneurial endeavors by making the family "incorporated." Little mention was ever made of the family's background or connection to a historic bourgeoisie, despite the setting of the show in one of the most historic cities in the country. Disagreeable realities such as concrete-panel apartment buildings and run-down health facilities were literally cropped out of the picture, erasing evidence of the socialist past and constructing images of a postsocialist Hungarian middle class aligned with the modern, fashionable, and technologically sophisticated material worlds that circulated in the mass media. Notably, the show was financed through corporate sponsorships, and product placements were regularly worked into the scripts.[1]

Taken together, the two shows reproduced the symbolic dichotomy between the apartment building and the detached family house—housing forms that had long stood for the mutually constructing opposition between modernist communism and bourgeois capitalism and the social forms they valued: the social collective versus the insular, private family. The shifting values attributed to these housing forms after the fall of state socialism were nowhere as problematic as in the former socialist "new town" of Dunaújváros, where I did my fieldwork in the mid- to late 1990s.[2] This provincial town of about fifty-seven thousand people was built in the early 1950s on a plateau of agricultural fields above the Danube River as a model planned town adjacent to a new steel factory. It had borne the name Sztálinváros, or City of Stalin, until 1961, when it was renamed Dunaújváros, or New City on the Danube. The town's primary residential form was the apartment building, and 85 percent of the population continued to live in multi-story, concrete apartment blocks. A number of the city's workers lived in neighboring villages in traditional peasant houses or in more modernized houses self-built during the decades of state socialism and limited in size and style by state regulations, the available materials and paint, and the sophistication of labor.

By the mid-1990s, however, a new housing form was emerging on the outskirts of town and on the edges of nearby villages, a form made highly visible from a distance by its bright red tile roof. Distinctive architectural styles set these houses apart from the existing residences in the area. New housebuilders eschewed productive gardens and livestock pens and added elements signaling leisure-time activities: gazebos, lawns, decorative landscaping. A plethora of stylized media images of the single-family house with a red-tiled roof accompanied the emergence of these neighborhoods of new homes. Referred to by Hungarians as the "family house with garden" (*kertes családi ház*), the image was used in advertisements for everything from building materials to home insurance and the grand prize in product-related raffles.

In an interview, the local city planner explained to me that everyone in Dunaújváros with the means to do so was moving out of the town and into a family house. The emergence of such housing, she assumed, was a natural response to the new economic and political reforms of bourgeois capitalism, a continuation of long-term Hungarian practices and values, and a sign that Hungary belonged in Europe. Even to observers more critical than the city planner, the houses seemed to fit the dominant narrative of suburbanization as the housing form best suited to the middle classes. The overpowering image of oppressive urban public housing being replaced by private detached homes reinforced conventional understandings of a transition from state socialism to market capitalism, whereby socialist welfare and the collective values it stood for are replaced by neoliberal regimes that seek to produce self-governing, autonomous subjects.

Yet, the symbolic dichotomy between these two forms of housing smoothes over the vast differences within these housing forms as categories, the social statuses and lifestyles of the populations aligned with them, and the historic conditions and infrastructures in which they were built. Although Hungarians were well aware of suburban middle-class culture elsewhere, such a housing form and the conditions for its existence (utilities and paved roads, consumer services, private cars, and the notion of a commuting middle class) still had to be constructed for most of Hungary.[3] More important, much of the socialist era's professional, managerial, and white-collar classes living in the new town regarded these new buildings with a mixture of skepticism and distaste. In order to become accepted and valorized as an appropriate dwelling form for a modern and respectable middle class, this new family house had to overcome lingering associations with rural backwardness and worker/peasant lifestyles. It also had to overcome associations with the elaborate villas of corrupt, socialist era political elites and the new villas of equally corrupt, postsocialist economic elites (Czegledy 1998; see also Jones, chapter 6, and Zhang, chapter 9, this volume).

Such negative evaluations of existing family houses were compounded by pragmatic obstacles for building new ones. The fall of state socialism created highly unstable economic conditions. Private developers saw little promise in residential construction in provincial towns, and the new state could not afford to encourage such development by making guarantees to developers or by providing more than minimal economic assistance to families building their own homes. Nonetheless, by the end of the 1990s, the aspiring middle classes in Dunaújváros had recognized that such houses were becoming a defining element of middle-class belonging in the new order.

In this chapter, I chart the competing conceptualizations of the postsocialist "middle class" by attending to the ways it is both imagined and realized in particular material settings. These concepts are embedded in the paradigmatic settings of a number of possible middle classes and include the forms of dwellings, as well as furnishings. Although neoliberal politics and global economic processes factored heavily in the kinds of middle classes that were gradually emerging in Hungary, so, too, did the material forms and conditions through which they established themselves.[4] I argue that these material forms and conditions played a significant role in the

FIGURE 5.1
Panel-construction apartment buildings on the plateau behind old and new family housing in the village below, Dunaújváros, 1997. Photo by K. Fehérváry.

transformation of a socialist era, broad-based, consumer middle stratum into a much more narrowly defined, postsocialist middle class. Moreover, I show that the *particular* material and aesthetic forms of these new houses played a primary role in garnering them widespread acceptance. These houses distinguished themselves from their rural neighbors through a distinctive aesthetic drawing on new materials, new technologies, and new building methods. Housebuilders and their advocates were nonetheless able to align this new house form with values that had become materialized in their rural predecessors: the family houses built during the socialist era and the weekend cottages of the socialist middle stratum. New houses that were of markedly postsocialist construction and style also provided the space for realizing the norms and ideals of respectable middle-class life—ideals that had been impossible to realize during state socialism, given the space constraints of socialist-designed apartments. The costs of participation in this new house form excluded a large number of people who had considered themselves members of a respectable, socialist middle stratum, but they also offered those once excluded from such a stratum the possibility of admittance to an emerging middle class (cf. Freeman 2007). The new suburban house was thus a material form around and through which an otherwise diverse population began to coalesce and differentiate itself.

Private homeownership and social stratification through living space have long operated as markers of status, but beyond simply reflecting new social stratifications, chapters in this volume also show how these material forms are important as *constitutive* of the middle classes. In the ongoing development of suburbs in the United States (Heiman, chapter 10, this volume) and in the rise of a commercial real estate sector in contemporary China (Zhang, chapter 9, this volume), housing design and construction are done primarily by commercial developers, with varying degrees of involvement by the state—which might provide the necessary infrastructure, guarantee financing, or subsidize developers who target particular sectors of the population. In the Hungarian case, however, little new housing outside the metropolitan capital of Budapest was built by such schemes in the 1990s and 2000s. Just as during the socialist period, most new family houses have been designed and constructed piecemeal, each one the private project of an individual or a family, in a process called "self-build" or "auto-construction." Consequently, the role of this housing form in constituting a new middle class has been as much in the production process itself as in how it is consumed and appropriated. This process demands resources and labor, mobilizes contacts, draws upon and innovates architectural styles, and facilitates (or obstructs) bodily and social practices. It can thus provide us with a picture of the heterogeneous forces at play in how a provincial middle class in Hungary is emerging, smaller and differently constituted than the socialist middle stratum that preceded it.

As do other contributors to this volume, I understand the category of "middle class" to be shifting and ideologically loaded. On the one hand, it inscribes as its referent quite different assemblages of status, occupation, values, and material cultures in different places and times, and, on the other, it refers to a surprisingly stable set of characteristics and claims (respectability, normalcy, moderation) in nation-states with growing or already sizable spheres of commodified, mass-produced material goods and environments. The middle class so defined is not strictly limited to so-called capitalist economies and relations of production, though it is always seen as a category intrinsic to and comparable across nation-states. As I will demonstrate, many of the defining characteristics of the broad, postwar, American-consumer-based middle class can be found in socialist Hungary after the 1950s—despite strict limitations on private property ownership and wealth. A Hungarian postwar middle stratum was similarly defined by "possession" of one dwelling per family, perhaps a car and a vacation cottage, and goods (a refrigerator, a washing machine, a television, and so forth) that not only were symbolic of but also provided the conditions for modern respectable lifestyles. As the contributors to this volume show for their respective field sites, the "new" middle classes are both participants in and products of neoliberal global economic transformations. I see

FIGURE 5.2

New family house, featuring red-tile roofs, columns, and a round window, under construction on the edge of a village 12 kilometers outside Dunaújváros, 1997. Photo by K. Fehérváry.

such processes not as the inevitable outcome of a globalizing force called "capitalism," but as actively produced by economic interests and ideologies that are reconfiguring the role of states in regulating economic activities, especially relative to the growing power of other institutional and techno-logical actors, such as multinational corporations, international financial institutions, and computer-aided financial inventions such as derivatives markets. These new middle classes take on particular forms depending upon where they are located, a process partially determined by the need of middle classes to flag their participation in a global social order while establishing their legitimacy as distinctly national (Frykman and Löfgren 1987; Liechty 2003). This process is also partially determined by the shift-ing material conditions and infrastructures of a particular place—in other words, the histories of social orders as they are concretized in land use, buildings, and furnishings.

In the decade following Hungary's regime change, the transform-ing landscape was often narrated via a "discourse of the normal" that divided the material world between spaces and objects that conformed to Hungary's new geopolitical status, thus assisting in its integration into a European order, and those that remained largely unchanged, part of a discredited socialist past (Fehérváry 2002). Within this context, Hungarians aspiring to or identifying with middle-class status faced an imperative to adopt material signs of postsocialist status and to normalize them in everyday life, aligning themselves symbolically and discursively with the postsocialist order (cf. Rausing 1998). Just as consumer goods such as cell phones become essential markers of an individual's participation in a transformed geopolitical and economic order in public space, changes to domestic spaces proved to be equally important practices of personal and familial transformation.

Some middle-aged professionals considered moving to a family house. Others chose to move to better apartments within the city or embarked on renovations of their interior spaces. A few intrepid residents managed to blast through poured concrete walls in their apartments to create the coveted "American kitchen" (*amerikai konyha*), which is a kitchen open to the living area. Bathrooms were upgraded as space and ingenuity allowed, linoleum replaced with ceramic tile. Throughout the socialist-era buildings, uniform old front doors, often made of PVC, were replaced with wooden doors or personalized with brass door knockers or nameplates. These new construction and renovation projects, undertaken at a time of great economic uncertainty, were often achieved at an expense far beyond a family's means (Magyar Nemzet 1996). As with emerging middle classes in other peripheral nation-states, the material requirements for local middle-class belonging are often intertwined with the commodified images and consumer goods depicting middle-class respectability in a "First World" (Foster 2002; Liechty 2003; O'Dougherty 2002; Patico 2008; see also Schielke, chapter 2, this volume). Such materialities carry the promise of a set of benefits on a global scale: a full humanity conferred by coeval status with the West, moral legitimacy, respectability, local status, and a host of other materially enabled desires—many of them firmly grounded in a comfortable home. Since the imagined benefits of such material standards are immense, falling out of the middle class is no longer experienced solely in local terms. It is conceptualized as failing to claim membership in a First World translocal social order and thus risking the invisibility that accompanies Third World status (Foster 2002:133–35; Liechty 2003:138–41).

In the new formerly socialist town of Dunaújváros, these distinctions were felt particularly acutely. Residents were well aware that, to the rest of the country, their city was one of the "ugliest" in Hungary, an exemplar of Soviet city planning and modern architecture. Here, as elsewhere in the country, the transformations of the material environment according to postsocialist norms were central to the establishment of a collective and individual existence in a transformed present even as they were alarming signs of the disruption of a familiar social order and moral code. The material forms and aesthetics of new housing and furnishing styles became potent sites for negotiating class status and moral legitimacy.

FROM THE MIDDLE STRATUM TO A MIDDLE CLASS

Hungarian national politics after the fall of state socialism was dominated by a neoliberal ideology that greatly influenced the direction of sweeping institutional reforms. As with new governments across the region, Hungarian politicians considered the reestablishment of private property to be central to the political legitimacy of the new order, a position that was also required by international actors such as the IMF and the World Bank, which made the privatization of state firms a condition for granting loans (Verdery 2003:3). Privatization of state-owned housing in particular was seen as "essential to ending the dependency of citizen[s] on the state" (Ruble 1995:29). This ideological stance was somewhat misleading because in socialist Hungary, most housing was already in private ownership. Moreover, much of the apartment block housing constructed by the socialist state after the 1960s was owner occupied from the start: the state had quickly realized the financial liability of state-owned and state-maintained housing allocated to citizens for minimal rents and had shifted to property arrangements resembling co-operatives in the West. By 1980, more than 75 percent of the population lived in owner-occupied housing. After the regime change in 1991–92, most of the housing remaining in state control was quickly privatized. Relative to other cities, the socialist town of Dunaújváros had higher numbers of state-owned apartments at the end of the 1980s, but these were also quickly privatized after 1991, purchased at bargain prices by their occupants.

The instability of financial institutions prevented the new regime from doing more than rapidly divesting itself of state-owned property, such as privatizing apartments in housing blocks. Politicians discussed the importance of establishing some kind of mortgage system, but until the 2000s, inflation and economic insecurities limited the scope of these plans and thus the development of a real estate sector.[5] In metropolitan Budapest, private (often foreign) developers began to build multi-story "residential parks" and villa-style and lower-rise developments (Bodnár and Molnár 2010), targeting a population of expatriates and a new crop of Hungarian entrepreneurs and professionals often working for foreign companies. Dunaújváros and other small towns in the provinces were not an appealing prospect for real estate developers, particularly in the residential market. The primary form of new residential construction was therefore the time-honored practice of families building houses for themselves, either through exchanges of collective labor or through a newer system of piecemeal contracting.

An unopposed assumption in politics and the media was that Hungary's future as a democratic nation-state depended upon the emergence of a strong middle class based on private property. "The new middle class [in Eastern Europe]," Polish anthropologist Michal Buchowski (2008:49) has written, "is a concept influenced by teleological ideas of 'transformation,' and it plays an ideological role in the building of the new liberal political and ideological order." However, the size, character, and viability of this elusive middle class were bitterly contested. The term "middle class" (*középosztály*) was often used interchangeably with the term used during state socialism, "middle stratum" (*középréteg*) but also with the term "bourgeois citizenry" (*polgár*). Use of "middle class" was a new thing, because talking openly about class made explicit the new legitimacy of economic inequalities in a market democracy. People of all ages who imagined themselves to belong to some version of respectable society were careful to qualify their complaints about newly visible social inequalities with statements affirming their commitment to a market economy in principle (see Rivkin-Fish 2009 for similar sentiments in Russia). But a looming question was how a large population who understood themselves to be of a legitimate middle stratum—like the population featured in the show *Neighbors*—would fare in the new order.

THE SOCIALIST MIDDLE STRATUM

The considerable differences between these three terms warrant further explication. "Middle stratum" was coined by Hungarian sociologists in the 1960s to describe the middle layers of socialist society as they were defined by position, income, and modern consumer lifestyle—as well as to avoid reference to traditional class hierarchies and inherited status.[6] It is important to note that this middle stratum was not an epiphenomenon of a socialist organization of production, but an explicit goal of the state's modernizing projects (see also Betts 2010 for East Germany; Patterson 2001 for Yugoslavia). Even in the Stalinist 1950s, industrialization campaigns were paired with attempts to civilize "backward" populations into a modern, urban working class—in part through cultural programs (theater, classical music, literacy) but also through modern apartments, consumer goods, and new standards for hygiene. By the 1960s, communist bloc states began to take seriously the need to improve standards of living, in part to ameliorate social unrest but in part as an extension of the Cold War to the realm of consumer culture. In Hungary, the Kádár regime was unique in how far it was able to push market reforms within the framework of a planned economy. Material benefits for skilled labor, management, and white-collar workers and the profits generated by second-economy activities resulted in economic inequalities and the emergence of new systems of distinction (Róna-Tas 1997; S. Nagy 1987).

The socialist state's promotion of a modern, discerning consumerism and the cultivation of good taste contributed to the development of what Mark Liechty (2003) calls a normative "middle-class culture," in which respectability is tied to the acquisition of modern consumer goods and living environments. The material forms of these new living environments and their furnishings were to "transform" backward Hungarians into modern, socialist citizens. Thus, in political rhetoric, newspaper editorials, home decor magazines, women's journals, and film clips, the new urban apartment was privileged as the paradigmatic living environment of the "contemporary man." Tastemakers admonished the growing population moving into these small spaces to get rid of their beloved traditional furniture sets, now derided as dark and heavy, infused with the social hierarchies of the past, and completely inappropriate for modern apartments. These outdated furnishings were to be replaced with mass-produced, modern, multifunctional designs (or homemade versions of the same if they were unavailable in state shops), arranged according to an open plan (see fig. 5.3). Such a design would allow socialist citizens to divide small spaces into areas accommodating the needs of diverse individuals—an entertainment center for the man of the house, a sewing table for the wife/mother, and the all-important "child's corner" for the child, to develop a sense of having his or her own inviolate domain for toys and study (Bánk 1967). The superfluous spaces of a monofunctional bedroom and a family dining area were banished, replaced by pull-out sofas and spaces for informal meals in tiny kitchens. The institution of the large family meal was to be replaced with hot lunches in workplace cafeterias. At the same time, state home decor publications regularly portrayed members of a cultural intelligentsia (fine artists, writers, classical composers, theater directors, actors) as legitimately inhabiting a haute bourgeois, high-ceiling urban interior furnished with antiques, Persian rugs, and original works of art.

By the 1970s, a widening middle stratum had expectations for an urban apartment with modern appliances; occasional cultural outings and vacations; and a weekend cottage in the countryside. The state-run media explicitly encouraged comparison of this lifestyle, presented as a benefit of

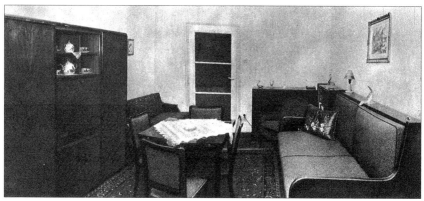

FIGURE 5.3

Before (photo, bottom*) and after (artist's rendering,* top*) of a room transformed into a "modern"
apartment. Lakáskultúra 3 (1967). Reprinted by permission of the Széchényi National Library,
Budapest.*

living in a socialist state, to that of average citizens in the First World. In
fact, although forms and timing differed, there were many parallels in the
kinds of societal transformations taking place in the Euro-American West
and in socialist Hungary, particularly the extension of middle-class living
standards to a far greater percentage of the population. Whereas cookie-
cutter suburban houses with lawns were a symbol of postwar prosperity in
the United States, even for the average worker (Jackson 1985; May 1988),
in Hungary, the ideal modern lifestyle consisted of the stimulation of the
city in an urban apartment during the work week, balanced by a weekend
relaxing in the fresh air and quiet of a rural cottage with garden.[7] This

middle-stratum culture, moreover, was discursively positioned between an uncouth proletariat, backward peasants, and poor Roma, on the one hand, and the remnants of an old-fashioned bourgeoisie or déclassé gentry, on the other (cf. Frykman and Löfgren 1987; Liechty 2003).

The economic crises and market reforms of the 1980s meant that many Hungarians were moonlighting in second-economy jobs just to maintain their standard of living. Thus, as members of the socialist middle stratum increasingly defined their harried experience of modern daily life as "abnormal," they idealized the lifestyles they imagined their counterparts in Western Europe and the United States enjoyed—somewhat ironically, given that neoliberal reforms were having similar effects on middle-class life there. The conditions for a "normal" life and personhood, including such transcendent values as family harmony and self-realization, were understood to reside in material worlds as they existed in "normal" parts of the world. With the end of state socialism and the obstacles it presented, members of the socialist middle stratum fully expected to constitute the new Hungarian middle class and finally be able to realize lifestyles commensurate to their professional positions. Instead, like the residents in *Neighbors*, most found themselves struggling to keep up their social status in the face of economic and institutional upheaval (Berdahl 1999; Fehérváry 2002; Patico 2008).

THE HISTORIC BOURGEOISIE, OR POLGÁR

References to the polgár were openly made in politics only after 1989; indeed, the term for the historic middle class became part of the name of the dominant conservative nationalist party of the 1990s and 2000s (Fidesz: Magyar Polgári Szovetség). The Hungarian *polgár* was closer to the German *burgher*, a combination of "bourgeois" and "citizen," than to the French *bourgeoisie*. Although the state-socialist regime had somewhat successfully disrupted the material basis for traditional class hierarchies, it had been less successful in discrediting them as cultural categories. The significance of the term *polgár* after socialism also stemmed from how it had been developed as part of an oppositional discourse during the socialist era.

An urban bourgeoisie had never been the symbolic embodiment of Hungarian national values and culture, because it had been associated with "foreign" elements in Budapest, primarily of German and Jewish origins, who engaged in capitalist enterprise in the late nineteenth and early twentieth centuries. Instead, the site of an authentic Hungarian nation had in the past been the land, associated with an autonomous peasantry and gentry values. Nonetheless, in the late 1970s, a dissident intelligentsia revived and revalued the bourgeois category. Drawing in part on Habermas's *The Structural Transformation of the Public Sphere*, translated into Hungarian in 1971, writers such as György Konrád (1984) proposed that a sphere of autonomy from the state—a kind of anti-political civil society—might be developed based on second-economy activities. Thus, identifying oneself as part of the bourgeoisie strangely became a form of resistance. I was startled to hear, for instance, a Hungarian avant-garde documentary film-maker in Chicago in the early 1990s, dressed from head to toe in black, announce that he was "proud to be bourgeois!" As sociologist Judit Bodnár (2007:142) has noted, "The ideological attack on the bourgeoisie effectively made anything 'bourgeois' an element of a desirable past." The domestic social relations and material trappings of this bourgeois, domestic, private sphere were a fundamental part of its idealization, particularly the interiors of sitting rooms, with their handcrafted furnishings, carpets, and art objects in rich, dark colors, and the enclosed spaces of gardens. The adjective "bourgeois" (*polgári*) in everyday parlance, as Bodnár (2007:142) sees it, "does not have much to do *with* the propertied bourgeoisie; rather, it is used as the incarnation of objects, lifestyles, manners, and arrangements that have been proven solid, efficient, and good. Its natural home is the bourgeois household with its interior dominated by traditional taste and propriety."

For some of the urban intelligentsia, the use of *polgár* referred to hopes for the revival of latent political and cultural dispositions as much as economic practices. "The polgár always meant more than money and property ownership," Zsuzsa Ferge (1997:19) has observed. "It also embodied culture and life-management (*életvitelt*)." For others, the notion of embourgeoisement (*polgárosodás*) was more often used to mean transforming the mentalities of the entire population: eradicating expectations of entitlement and dependence on the state, reforming slack work habits, and fostering risk taking, entrepreneurial activities, and civic responsibility (Szelényi et al. 1988). Unsurprisingly, the ascendance of this bourgeois category came with an open devaluation of socialist values and of the working class, a class increasingly associated with an unnatural form of government and with characteristics of dependency and lack of initiative. The socialist state participated in this shift in class values in the 1980s, not only through economic reforms but also by officially recognizing that a small-scale entrepreneurial stratum would "continue to contribute for some time to the life of socialist society."[8] The socialist state also threatened unemployment as a measure to "discipline" the working classes, who were depicted in the official media as lazy and shiftless.

THE MIDDLE CLASSES

For many Hungarians, particularly for an aspiring middle class in Dunaújváros, the celebration of a Hungarian bourgeoisie in the 1990s implied the privileging of those who could claim some form of polgár ancestry and thus the restoration of a form of social stratification that had been discredited for forty years. For the majority of the population who had no real claim to polgár status, as well as for many who did, contemporary models of middle-class life and ostensibly merit-based social structures to be found in the Euro-American West were far more appealing. Many were familiar with the American model from travel abroad, broadcast media, and books on the United States, many of which focused on the late nineteenth to mid-twentieth centuries. For example, a young convert to Mormonism wanted me to read a paperback bestseller by E. A. Jameson (1993[1920]) that cataloged the indigent beginnings and exploits of early industrial millionaires. Once-disparaged occupations such as "manager" and "entrepreneur" rapidly shifted in value from ambiguous to heroic, a trend mirroring the shift in value of business and sales occupations elsewhere in the world (see Freeman, chapter 4, this volume, for the Barbadian case). As we will see, the roles of the mass media and commercial venues in constructing these imaginings cannot be overstated.

MATERIALIZING THE MIDDLE CLASSES

Although there was little agreement as to what type of people constituted the new Hungarian middle class in the 1990s, images of the range of material trappings for this class were everywhere. Television shows, decorating magazines, and pull-out sections in newspapers continually exposed the population to new designs for housing, new concepts for interior decoration, and new ideas for renovation. Just as in the socialist period, people were attentive to the material settings of foreign movies and television shows. Although such settings were often extravagant even by Euro-American standards, their unmarked quality suggested to Hungarians that these represent a taken-for-granted standard of living for average, middle-class families.

Images of such material worlds came as much from Hungarian sources as from imports, as we have already seen in the examples of *Neighbors* and *Family, Inc.* Movies, television, print media, and commercial spaces constantly represented "appropriate" material environments for self-respecting Hungarian citizens. Furniture store displays, interior decorating shops, and Home Depot–style do-it-yourself stores did the same, reinforcing the notion that such upgrades to one's living space were necessary to mark one's place in the postsocialist order. One regularly featured style was the classic interior of the historic urban bourgeoisie, or polgár: spacious apartments filled with antique furnishings. The setting that was becoming equated with an urban, primarily male, professional class included high-tech modern decor and variations of IKEA products in apartments that could be situated in either older buildings or socialist era developments. Increasingly, the appropriate setting for an autonomous, entrepreneurial middle class was a family house with a bright red tile roof and a green garden.

THE TROUBLE WITH THE FAMILY HOUSE

The ideological power of this new suburban house form came as much from its symbolic opposition to the built environment of state socialism as from idealizations of Western models. In the simple aesthetic code of the postsocialist era, the values assigned to the two housing forms during state socialism were inverted. Housing developments were being equated with the past, with discredited ideals of collectivism, and, increasingly, with a denigrated urban proletariat—despite the preponderance of the former middle stratum still living in them. In contrast, the detached family house was acquiring new value as materializing the autonomy, property rights, and prestige of a new capitalist middle class (cf. Miller 1984 for England).

For Dunaújváros's former middle stratum of professionals, educators, civil servants, and skilled workers, such ideological rhetoric and accompanying commercial imagery did not align with their experience of single-family housing forms during the decades of state socialism. Urban apartment buildings, whatever their exact design, had been assumed to be the appropriate housing form in all iconographies of the socialist modern future. Apartments of roughly the same size had aligned well with socialist ideologies of egalitarianism and the development of a modern classless society. In contrast, the private family house had been politically condemned as a vestige of the past, conducive to private individualism, whether in the form of the backward peasant house or of the urban bourgeois villa. This political rhetoric was backed by policy; the socialist state's investment in infrastructure privileged the development of urban environments at the expense of the rural.

Despite this ideological and practical bias, the state not only permitted but also *planned* for families to build their own houses in order to ameliorate continuing housing shortages. As early as the 1950s, the state made provisions for single-family houses built by their future occupants. Even in the model socialist town of Dunaújváros, land for a "garden city" district was set aside for such housebuilders (Pittaway 2000). In the state's controversial fifteen-year housing plan of 1960, it projected that such self-built housing would have to account for a full 40 percent of the million units planned, since it could supply only 60 percent in the form of urban apartment buildings (Major and Osskó 1981; see also Molnár 2010). And, indeed, self-built housing surpassed these plans; by the 1980s, such housing had outstripped state construction in both quantity and quality (Hegedüs 1992).

The increasing prevalence of self-built, single-family houses did not, however, make them a symbol of middle-stratum respectability in Dunaújváros (Miskolczi 1980). Presocialist bourgeois villas were few, and the models for the self-built family house were split between the houses of the peasantry and worker-peasant classes, on the one hand, and the *kúria*, or manorial estate, on the other. Moreover, the differences between building a family house and acquiring an apartment contributed to how these two housing forms were evaluated. The self-build mode of house production was arduous and lengthy, lasting anywhere from two to ten years. The strain entailed risks to family relations and marriages. The challenge of obtaining materials was endless, and labor was extracted from extended family, from friends, and through a rural system of exchange for building houses, called *kaláka* (Sik 1988). The saying "to throw oneself into building" (*belevágni az építkezésbe*) acknowledged the Herculean challenges of do-it-yourself housing (Kenedi 1981). Severe housing shortages meant that for many Hungarians, particularly of the working classes, self-build was the only route to acquiring their own homes. The state encouraged such building through pronatalist policies, offering young couples building loans and outright grants for each child they promised to have, even as it did little to make the building itself any easier. In the 1970s, many such self-built village houses became spaces for profitable but low-status, second-economy activities such as raising livestock and growing produce. Thus, most homebuilders in the area were rural entrepreneurs and worker-peasants, those who had the contacts and the knowledge of village life to mobilize kaláka practices and who did not shy away from the dirt and the backbreaking labor involved.

In contrast, centrally located and state-owned apartments were among the most prestigious in the city, housing a greater number of professionals, many of whom had been lured to the provincial backwater by the promise of an apartment. Obtaining a state-owned apartment often involved a long wait, but once it was allocated, it came with low rents, free maintenance, and the option to bequeath the rights to the dwelling to one's offspring. Most of these apartments were built during the Stalinist period, and many

FIGURE 5.4

Self-built houses from the 1980s (left) with older peasant houses (right), 2000. This housing is a few streets over from an area of new suburban family houses in a village 20 kilometers from Dunaújváros. Photo by K. Fehérváry.

were of much higher quality than those built using concrete-panel technology after 1960. They had parquet floors, higher ceilings, and thicker walls. These apartments were exceedingly difficult to acquire, particularly as the state gradually phased out construction of state-owned apartments in favor of cooperative-style buildings requiring a substantial down payment.

Media representations of the new family house were set against a landscape where actual instantiations of such buildings in the 1990s were a novelty, a new residential housing form provoking both admiration and concern. Indeed, many of the socialist middle stratum in Dunaújváros, particularly those over forty, continued to respond to the family house phenomenon with ambivalence. For example, my interview with a sociologist at the local junior college suddenly turned personal because her disparaging comments about the family house form provoked a colleague sitting nearby whose family had just finished building one. Later and in private, the sociologist explained that her colleague was "the property-owning type...who lives to work on her house and garden." She contrasted this "type" of person with people like herself, who preferred living in an urban apartment during the week and using the weekends to do a little gardening in the fresh air of their cottage garden. Urban life, for her, was equated with a

FIGURE 5.5

A neighborhood of new family houses in a village outside Dunaújváros, 1998. The house on the right has a trendy thatched roof and utilizes curved forms in its more complex construction, whereas the house on the left is of the simpler construction typical of kaláka, or self-build—though it will eventually be distinguished by a decorative garden. Photo by K. Fehérváry.

desirable and morally imbued sociality: "I like social life, to visit friends for a quick coffee, or to pop downstairs to go shopping. I would feel isolated in a family house."

Resistance to the family house in the 1990s must be seen in the context of an older way of life being challenged by the emergence of postsocialist alternatives. The new socioeconomic order, it was becoming clear, might not honor claims to respectability based on profession or education, much less on older material indexes of modern life. And for a significant proportion of Dunaújváros's former middle stratum, a family house of any kind was simply out of reach. Until the 2000s, bank loans were difficult to obtain, even at the interest rates of 28–32 percent, and a mortgage system had not yet been developed. With the exception of new family grants, the government had frozen support for new housebuilding.[9] The price of building materials was skyrocketing, something prospective housebuilders tried to offset by buying bricks far in advance of the day they might actually use them.

Changes in modes of production were creating a marked distinction between housebuilders still using forms of kaláka and those using the newer contracted services—differences that were materialized in the resulting structures. Kaláka was on the decline because stonemasons, electricians,

KRISZTINA FEHÉRVÁRY

and plumbers were able to command high prices on an open market and neighbors and friends were less willing to lend their services. Kaláka was being replaced by a newer type of building called *önerő* (self-powered), which relied on the labor of immediate family, hired hands (often illegal Romanian Hungarian migrant workers), and professionals, as needed and to the extent of a family's financial means. Because such building methods used more skilled labor and could take advantage of new building materials and technologies, it produced a distinctive look that became the prototypical family house of the new middle class. These houses were in turn distinguished from the villa housing, which was contracted entirely to professionals.

LEGITIMIZING THE NEW FAMILY HOUSE FOR HUNGARY

For Laura, the thirty-six-year-old proprietor of a small private English-language school, living in a family house had been a long-standing dream. The daughter of a physician and a schoolteacher, she had always considered herself entitled to signs of prestigious distinction. Her new husband was a budding entrepreneur, first running a village disco bar and then opening a used "Western" goods store—supplied by Austrian Roma who picked through Viennese dumpsters. They both attributed the failure of their previous marriages to differences in social class made manifest in expectations for material standards of living (*igény*) and the drive to achieve such lifestyles. A family house was integral to their understanding of the social position they would occupy in the new Hungary, the appropriate material setting for two entrepreneurs in a newly European nation-state.

In 1994, they embarked on the building of a large detached family house on agricultural land at the outskirts of a nearby village. Like most Dunaújváros residents, they had lived their entire lives in urban apartments. Laura's childhood apartment had been relatively spacious, with an entryway, a main room with a balcony, one bedroom, a kitchen large enough for a small table and chairs, and a bathroom and WC. When she married her first husband, they moved into her grandmother's smaller one-bedroom apartment, furnished with antique Biedermeier furniture, including a sitting room set, shelving, and a wardrobe. (Her grandmother moved into Laura's father's apartment.) But the new house was set in a large enclosed garden and featured cathedral ceilings with an exposed second floor, three finished bedrooms, two and a half baths, a kitchen open to the living room, and a two-car garage. Small rooms were set aside for laundry and hobbies such as sewing. After they moved in, Laura's husband relegated her valuable antique furniture to the second floor, buying instead an inexpensive modern sofa set—a more tangible sign of their economic success in the present.

The new housebuilders of the early to mid-1990s, like Laura, represented a vanguard with a vision for middle-class life in Hungary. They signaled their difference from their peasant or working-class neighbors through the material forms of the house and the styles of life these represented. Nowhere to be seen were a multi-use garage, livestock pen, or productive garden—signs of a work ethic once seen as essential for rural respectability (Lampland 1995:316–23). Laura, for example, installed a rock garden, a goldfish pond, and a bricked-in patio, insisting on planting only flowers alongside a few herbs. "I've done enough hoeing in my life!" she said, referring to the long weekends she had spent—along with an entire generation of city dwellers with such gardens—planting, weeding, and then preserving the resulting fruits and vegetables for household consumption.

At the same time, proponents of the new suburban "family house with garden" drew upon continuities with both the weekend cottage *and* the self-built village house in constructing its legitimacy. These new family houses were aligned with the countryside as it was being revalued in opposition to the socialist city, an opposition that Raymond Williams (1973) demonstrates is transformed and deployed in times of change. Even though the political economy of building such houses had been fundamentally transformed, conservative proponents of the family house continued to draw on its associations with houses built through kaláka, or self-build. The private sphere of the home had been idealized as an island of autonomy and privacy from the socialist state—in the form of an urban apartment or a rural family house. As we have seen, a populist intelligentsia had looked to provincial peasant entrepreneurs to become a model for the new entrepreneurial classes; many of these writers lauded the human capacities mobilized by the privately owned materialities of a family house and its garden. For example, Sándor Kopátsy (1993) suggested that the family house inculcated a sense of self-sufficiency and pride and "everyday feelings of success and happiness" in seeing the fruits of one's labor on one's own property. These early advocates failed to recognize that the new kind of housebuilder had no interest in cultivating produce on his or her property, nor did he or she want to use his or her own labor to build his or her house. Even though many continued to expect the financial assistance and free labor of their extended family, they wanted to avoid the onerous obligations of community-building exchange as much as possible.

The new suburban house also took on the values once reserved for the weekend cottage, contrasting the fresh air and calming effects of being in "nature" with the pollution and hectic pace of modern city life. In Dunaújváros, with its high rates of childhood asthma, attributed to pollution from the steel mill, family houses in the country were seen as more healthful places to raise children and in general as more conducive to a balanced family life. The very term "family house" indexed its association with a wholesome, heteronormative married life with more than one child. Indeed, divorced or single mothers and single men understood themselves to be excluded from the family house, both as social norm and as practical possibility. The material environment of the family house was supposed to generate tasks inculcating healthy gender subjectivities, particularly for men. For decades, city apartments had been blamed for eliminating the adult male's role and space in the home. Household tasks and child care remained the responsibility of women, so the man's responsibilities were reduced to drilling holes for hanging pictures and maintaining the family car, if there was one. Masculine identity, it was assumed, was bolstered by the autonomy of a detached house, with its building projects and heavier garden work.

The new family house also provided the space for realizing widespread norms of respectable middle-class life, norms that had been fostered during the socialist period but were made untenable by the design and cramped spaces of socialist apartments. The new housing form included the expansion of the open plan and individualizing divisions of space. And it also accommodated new desires for spaces associated with modern lifestyles in the West, such as a dedicated master bedroom, bathrooms liberated from drying laundry, and, most of all, a large room open to the kitchen, in which the family could gather. Like the villas of the new economic elites (Czegledy 1998), many of these houses and their gardens fulfilled the spatial and representational requirements of business socializing.

Despite the diversity of these new houses, they shared an aesthetic that not only distinguished them from the older housing forms around them but also assisted in their construction as respectable *and* distinctly Hungarian. The new houses were larger than their rural predecessors and displayed clear signs of having been designed by a professional. Although most sported the bright red roofing tiles ubiquitously advertised by multinational firms, the houses themselves rarely echoed the white and rectilinear forms of these ads. Instead, they developed for the exterior an aesthetic that had emerged for interiors during the 1970s, one that transformed a socialist version of modernism with organic forms and materials.[10] Unlike postmodern forms in the West that featured fragmentation and renewed attention to facade, these housing forms reflected a particular disenchantment with the alternative modernity produced by the socialist state. In a condemnation of the straight line, the rectilinear form, and the standardization dictated by principles of efficiency, this aesthetic featured asymmetrical and rounded motifs, including undulating roofs, round columns, and arched windows. In opposition to the artificial, mass-produced materials favored by the socialist state, these houses made prominent use of natural materials, such as wood, stone, and even reed thatch. And in a rejection of the moralizing aestheticism of socialist modernism, this aesthetic promoted color, play, and fantasy. As we will see in the examples below, housebuilders had to negotiate carefully the variety of design elements available to them; they attempted to position themselves as part of this more exclusive middle class while marking their respectability through material signs of modesty and virtue.

Despite widespread mourning for the lost security offered by state socialism, discourses on new family houses and renovated interiors aligned with this critique of the socialist modernist project, including its attempts to dominate the natural world and its profound misunderstanding of the malleability of human nature. In this way, the material aesthetics of family houses reinforced acceptance of neoliberal ideologies even as they clashed with the lived experience of austerity measures, unemployment, radical income inequalities, and failing medical, education, and transportation systems. The values materialized in an anti-socialist aesthetics legitimated these new suburban house forms, along with the diverging fortunes they represented.

NEW MIDDLE-CLASS MATERIALITIES

By the mid- to late 1990s, anyone aspiring to new middle-class status had to face the often contentious question of whether to build a family house and, if so, what form the house would take and how to furnish it. New housebuilders now had enough examples of this type of housing to judge which forms and aesthetics were successful and which were not. The location of Laura's large house, for example, did not turn out to be an area particularly favored by other housebuilders of the new middle class. It was surrounded by plots set aside for young couples who were struggling to build themselves small houses of basic design through pronatalist building grants, laboring evenings and weekends at the building site. Instead of the middle-class suburban milieu Laura and her family had envisioned, they had to contend with the hostile stares of their new neighbors and eventually gave up trying to establish relations with them. Some of Laura's more ostentatious aesthetic choices, such as the goldfish pond, had misfired—at least in establishing a respectable modesty. At the same time, the scale of her aspirations might be reflected in the fact that she and her husband were more than pleased when friends from Germany referred to their place as the new village *kúria*, or manorial estate.

Two other families that initially rejected the idea of a family house during my fieldwork provide contrasting examples. Csilla, about thirty-four in 1996–97, was a director in the steel mill, and her parents had been unskilled factory workers. On some occasions, she was quite happy with her modern urban apartment, but she increasingly echoed widespread discourses in voicing her longings to move to the "peace and quiet" of the countryside, to "escape the [concrete] panel masses," which she found so claustrophobic. Her husband, János, was against the idea. His extended family had all lived in villages, and he wanted nothing to do with the labor, the flies, and the smells he associated with rural living. A factory driver and handball coach, he also assumed that a new family house was for the wealthy directors and simply inaccessible to someone of even Csilla's rank.

In another family, Margit, a lawyer in her late forties, resisted the emerging desire of her husband, Géza, for a house. For a time, both had been disdainful of conservative rhetoric that framed such houses as regenerating the extended family and presocialist values, and they instead regarded these as symbols of the nouveaux riches. Nonetheless, Géza's dissatisfaction with their panel-construction apartment grew, fueled by that of their eighteen-year-old son. Margit continued in her opposition, well understanding that the burdens of a house in the village—its isolation, the lack of services, and spotty public transportation—fall on the woman's shoulders. More important, she could not assimilate the family house into her identity as a member of an urban polgár intelligentsia.

By the end of the decade, however, both families had moved to such houses. In Csilla's case, János had been unwilling to help with the contracting necessary to build a new house, so she found an existing one for sale in a nearby village. It was built in the late 1980s in a neighborhood of similar houses, with several peasant houses nearby, but not far from a developing neighborhood of new family houses. They completely refurbished the interior, painted the exterior moss green, and installed a Finnish sauna. Although it was not what Csilla had hoped for, it was near the field where she had developed a passion for horseback riding. She made sure they got several dogs and a cat to provide their ten-year-old son—otherwise glued to the computer screen—with a "healthful" country experience. János began to spend far more time at home. For both, the form of their house provoked few anxieties about their class status; in fact, evidence of Csilla's ample salary spilled over into the driveway, where they parked their new Volvo.

With Margit's eventual blessing, Géza, who was an engineer at a division of the privatizing steel factory, had his dream house designed, and he himselfsupervised all aspects of the construction. In their new neighborhood of such houses, their neighbors included the star of the city's professional women's handball team, a former Communist Party secretary, and a truck driver. The house was equipped with the latest technologies, it was painted a dark watermelon pink, and the roof overhang was inlaid with wood. The interior was spacious and well appointed, but it made symbolic concessions to Margit's requirements for modesty and practicality. For example, it had no fireplace: "Who would clean it?" she asked. The large luxurious bathroom—modeled on one Margit had seen in a London hotel room—had a walk-in shower but no tub: "In this busy world, who has time to take baths?" Most strikingly, Margit's inherited polgári furnishings and art objects were stored out of sight, replaced in the open living area by leather sofas and a modern coffee table made of a slab of granite.

When I first visited the new house in 2000, Margit showed me around the growing neighborhood and commented that this was where Dunaújváros's middle class was moving, pointedly using the term for "middle class" (középosztály) rather than polgár. When I objected that this area was hardly for the average Hungarian, she conceded: "Yes, unfortunately, in Hungary the middle class is very small." As for her neighbors, she was dissatisfied with only two, making judgments about the residents based on their houses rather than on their professions. One had an oval-shaped roof that had apparently collapsed several times, a sign of the homeowner's irresponsibility and desire for extravagance beyond his abilities. The other had small statues of cherubs and fountains in the bricked-in front yard—a sure sign to her that the family was Roma.

CONCLUSION

The material requirements for the imagined standards of living of "First World" middle-class citizens have shaped the emergence of middle-class culture in Hungary, particularly in a suburban housing form unique in its materialization of contemporary ideals. However, in the new suburban family house, the incorporation of such standards is neither immediate nor unchallenged. The suburban family house in Hungary is not a form of enduring cultural value but has acquired newly invigorated value by virtue of its opposition to the ideology claimed for the state's socialist architecture (May 1988 ; Miller 1984). The family house, symbolically opposed to the socialist modern apartment blocks that came to stand for the collective, artificial uniformity, and forced egalitarianism of socialism and the working classes, now appears as the embodiment of the "natural" values of capitalism. Even though urban apartment blocks continue to house a wide spectrum of Hungarian society, including many who claim middle-class status, the new family house has successfully been aligned through discourse and material forms with the weekend cottage, contrasting the calming effects of nature with the invigorating (or nerve-wracking) effects of modern city life but also with the self-built family house of the rural entrepreneur. It thus appears to be both continuous and inevitable, coalescing into one form two values forged in opposition to state socialism: the romanticization of nature and the idealization of the private sphere (cf. Frykman and Löfgren 1987). The gradual triumph of this form has transformed local systems of value just as the form itself developed according to the aesthetic specificities of the Hungarian context. A socialist era middle stratum was gradually displaced not by a historic bourgeois middle class or its culture, but by a new entrepreneurial and professional middle class. In the process, the material form of the new family house not only has redefined the conditions for belonging to the ranks of respectable society but also has been instrumental in constituting and legitimating an emerging middle class.

Acknowledgments

I have accrued many debts in the process of writing this chapter and in related research. First and foremost, I want to thank the organizers of the SAR advanced seminar on the globalizing middle classes, the participants for the intellectually stimulating and enjoyable week we spent together in Santa Fe, and most important, the editors, Mark Liechty, Carla Freeman, and especially Rachel Heiman, for their masterful introduction to the book and their efforts in pulling it all together. I am also grateful to many generous colleagues and friends who commented on versions of this material presented at various workshops and conferences and, in particular, to the participants at the NSF/ University of Michigan "Workshop on the Cultural Politics of Globalization and Community in East Central Europe." Miranda Johnson, Lara Kusnetzky, Eric Karchmer, Jennie Burnett, and Laura Ring all provided valuable suggestions for this chapter. As always, my thanks go to Matthew Hull and Deborah Cornelius for their support and inspiration and to all the people in Dunaújváros who graciously welcomed me into their homes.

Notes

1. Both series ended in 1999. *Family, Inc.* could not compete with Western competitors on cable, but *Neighbors* has been rebroadcast a number of times since, suggesting that its themes still resonate with the considerable population that identifies with middle-class respectability but continues to live in panel-construction apartments.

2. The research for this chapter was conducted over twenty-two months in Budapest and Dunaújváros in 1996–97 and during shorter trips in 1994, 2000, 2004, and 2008. I lived in several areas of the town and in one of the suburbanizing villages, conducting interviews with building, design, and real estate professionals; civil servants; entrepreneurs; and a wide range of people who understood themselves to be deserving of a middle-class status. I conducted archival research at the city's land registry office, the steel mill museum, and the city museum. In 1997, I participated in a sociological survey, interviewing twenty-five families in four districts about their experience of the city. All told, I visited more than eighty apartments, houses, and weekend cottages. Funding for my fieldwork was provided by the Fulbright Commission (IIE) and the Social Science Research Council (IREX).

3. This kind of suburbanization did not begin until the late 1980s, even in the metropolitan capital city of Budapest, where it took off in the 1990s (see Valuch 2004:550). Precedents included the remnants of a turn-of-the-century bourgeois villa culture in larger cities and a middle-class "family house with garden" form built in the interwar period primarily in Budapest and its surrounding fringes; some versions of it could also be found in provincial towns, predominantly for "a lower middle class of office workers, artisans and skilled workers" (Kósa 2000:187).

4. By "material," I refer in part to economic base (the economic conditions that undergird class formation in a Marxist sense) and in part to symbolic indicators for the values and self-legitimizing practices of an emerging middle class. But I also want to draw attention to the more tangible "affordances and constraints" provided by the material (Tilley 2007:19), including existing and newly possible material forms, infrastructures, construction forms, and furnishings (Latour 2005 ; Miller 1987, 2005).

5. Even in Budapest, private self-built residential units made up the majority of new construction in the 1990s. In 2000, the state began to subsidize interest rates and then, in 2004, introduced new regulations allowing commercial banks to offer much cheaper mortgages to home buyers in foreign currency (Bodnár and Molnár 2010:797). Hungarians who took advantage of these mortgages were left holding inflated foreign currency debts after the economic crisis of 2008.

6. The appellation "middle stratum" was justified in a sense, given that the means

of production were largely controlled by the state, no segment of the population owned much capital, and the population enjoying this modern lifestyle included as many members of the skilled working class (predicted to become the universal class) as white-collar professionals and party elites.

7. Spending time at one's weekend or summer cottage was a widespread practice throughout the communist world (Caldwell 2011). Paulina Bren (2002) has analyzed the Czechoslovak state's support for the cottage as part of an effort to focus people's energies on small improvements rather than on politics, particularly after 1968.

8. Thirteenth Congress of the Hungarian Socialist Workers Party, as reported by the BBC, broadcast April 8, 1985.

9. The only financial incentive for building a house at this time was the price of land. Newly formed local governments, the result of radical decentralization, had few resources to apply to development. They tried to attract house builders by offering plots of land at discount rates, running rough roads to these plots, and promising to (eventually) provide running water and electricity.

10. A number of professional architects in the late 1960s began to design in opposition to what they saw as the abstract and dehumanizing effect of socialist modern architecture, becoming known as the organicist school. Their designs had some influence on vernacular tastes, but they were not widely known until the 1980s.

6

Women in the Middle

Femininity, Virtue, and Excess in Indonesian Discourses of Middle Classness

Carla Jones

Joking as we ran errands together one afternoon in Yogyakarta in 1997, my friend Ati casually revealed a fact that I would never have guessed after more than a year of friendship. Although, like most Javanese women, Ati managed her family's income and expenditures, her husband had expressly forbidden her from allowing her modest teacher's salary to enter their household, especially for buying food for their four children. This did not represent a hardship, as their income derived from a wide network of various joint and individual businesses and her salary was a nominal fraction of their total monthly resources. We chuckled together that day as we considered how contaminating Ati's husband considered her civil service income to be. Rather than a neutral "radical leveler" (Marx 1995:85), exchangeable for any good, money earned from a repressive and corrupt state could not be purified; instead, it contaminated and, crossing from the public into the private, generated existential angst in its recipients.

A decade later, sitting in a café in the capital city of Jakarta, thirty-three-year-old Santi, a divorced single mother and a key employee at a women's magazine, explained to me why she had recently chosen to adopt stylish Islamic dress. Santi was struggling to receive financial support for her seven-year-old son from her ex-husband and his family because they imagine her job as well paying and her requests for support as proof of her indulgent use of her salary for individual consumption. Santi explained that it was in part to find comfort for the pain of being criticized that she had become a more pious Muslim, relying on Allah for emotional support of her life choices, adopting more covered dress, and attending Qur'an study sessions in the evenings.

These examples reveal how anxieties about wealth have taken shape through anxieties about the feminine, the domestic, and consumption. Santi's in-laws consider her income earned from office work substantial yet unconnected to family. Ati's husband's concern about the taint of corruption and the effects of consumption, manifested in unusually direct instructions about their household and children, exemplifies how forms of feminine virtue, especially as linked to labors in the private sphere, have been at the center of national and personal anxieties about social difference in Indonesia since the 1990s. Indonesia has seen dramatic change during this period, including growth in the urban middle classes and the end of thirty-two years of authoritarian rule focused on national development (1965–98). A focus on progress continues in post-authoritarian Indonesia, but it now mixes with worries about social regress. Instead of explicit class affiliations, gender has long been a mode of identifying social difference, especially by the state and more recently by both progressive and conservative religious organizations, making performing and having correct femininity powerful. Despite the fact that the regime has been out of power for more than ten years and talk about class is more open, the gendered foundations remain, making women both the objects and subjects of debates on difference. Middle-class women are at the center of anxieties about how the rise of a public consumer culture threatens private morality, and they are positioned as both victims and agents of a new social landscape.

I situate this inquiry in two ways: geographically in the context of late twentieth- and early twenty-first-century urban Indonesia and intellectually in the lineage of feminist inquiry that asks how female labor can simultaneously be invisible and devalued even as feminine forms are iconic and visible. Based on more than a decade of relationships and fieldwork with families in Yogyakarta and Jakarta, the histories and accounts I provide suggest that it is impossible to think of the virtues, thrills, and concerns associated with being middle class in Indonesia without seeing those qualities take form in gendered ways. Putting gender on the same plane as something like class, which carries such a heavy but valued intellectual history, reveals not only the interconnectedness of class and gender but also the importance of gender as a constituting social process, a true intersection. Doing so can also illuminate the usefulness of class theory for scholarship on Indonesia and frame how Indonesian conceptions of middle classness might contribute to theories of gender and class.

Building on the questions of feminist scholars (e.g., Freeman 2001 and chapter 4, this volume; Lutz 1995;) who ask what grand theories look like when gender is placed in the center of the analytical frame, I argue that the middle-class project of transubstantiating money into morality, often through practices that reveal the relatedness of consumption and religion, is a form of labor that can be especially acute for feminine subjects, an effect that generates not only privilege but also anxiety. My analysis also intersects with feminist critiques of labor that have questioned the naturalization of domestic labor and femininity. Asking how consumption in the service of domesticity has been romanticized as the restorative solution to the alienating and extractive relations of capitalism yet still devalued as unproductive, feminist theories of labor have revealed how the work of reproduction and the private sphere rely on the unpaid but essential labor of subjects marked as feminine (Allison 1994; Collier and Yanagisako 1987; Di Leonardo 1987; Kurotani 2005). What kind of intellectual elisions occur when consumption and femininity are framed as aftereffects or secondary components of what consistently appear to be the primary processes at work: production and masculinity? Anxieties about this relationship take shape in a discourse on corruption, a condition to which women seem particularly susceptible. After corrupted income enters the space associated with feminine authority, the domestic sphere, it becomes even more intimate and invasive, a threat that is especially well resolved through religious piety.

Analyzing the relationship between femininity, consumption, and morality reveals how Indonesian public discourse on social difference, which has eschewed the language of class, has been reflected in the anthropological scholarship of the country. Anthropological scholarship on Indonesia has been less concerned with political economy than with symbolic analysis, especially Javanese ideologies of status. The anthropology of Indonesia has therefore overlapped with a broader anthropological indifference to considering middle classes as worthy or authentic subjects of analysis (cf. Heiman, Liechty, and Freeman, chapter 1, this volume), even as it has mirrored limitations in the political world in Indonesia, where the Suharto regime restricted Marxist critique. Rather than attempt to identify prior and discrete groups, celebrations of and anxieties about consumption in post-Suharto Indonesia suggest that it is more fruitful to ask about middle-class subjectivity than about class as a coherent category. Doing so potentially allows for two important effects. First, it reveals how official ideas about middle-class femininity, frugality, and propriety have been internalized beyond their institutional origins and can appear in forms of consumer discipline that are outside formal state organizations, even in contexts that appear antithetical to the state, such as Ati's husband's request that her civil service income not enter their household. Second, focusing on disciplinary discourses on conduct such as consumption and religion echoes Michel Foucault's argument that repressive regimes were not always most aggressively targeted at poorer classes. Rather, "the most rigorous techniques were formed and, more particularly, applied first, with the greatest intensity, in the economically privileged and politically dominant classes. The direction of consciences, self-examination, the entire long elaboration of the transgressions of the flesh…were all subtle procedures that could only have been accessible to small groups of people" (Foucault 1978:120).

Foucault's concern with the disciplinary nature of the care of the self is helpful in understanding how, even after the collapse of an authoritarian regime, public interest in and concerns about family life, gender, and consumption endure in unofficial, even explicitly anti-state arenas such as lifestyle. As I will show, gendered existential and corporeal anxieties about consumption and corruption intersect in the rise of new forms of corrective discipline and especially undergird the rising appeal of Islamic public culture. Echoing early European conceptions of consumption as wasteful and socially corrosive (rather than expressive and creative; Porter 1993), particularly when women engage in it (cf. De Grazia 1996; Rappaport 2001), Islamic public culture has become far more visible in urban Indonesia, rising out of a specifically middle-class youth critique of national morality in the 1990s and enjoying a unique moral stance, appearing to be outside, and the solution to, corruption and politics.

MISSING CLASS: THE INDONESIAN GAP

The Indonesian equivalent of "middle class," *kelas menengah*, is a loaded term. It tends to class up as much as the English term classes down in U.S. parlance, and it has resonances of wealth, newness, and even licentious freedom. For this reason as much as political risk, during the 1990s, families I knew who might qualify as middle-class or even upper-middle-class, according to government measures, would not identify as kelas menengah, for to do so would suggest arrogance and wealth. Those same families by the middle of the first decade of the twenty-first century were more comfortable identifying as kelas menengah, even if their material resources were not substantially greater than they had been a decade earlier. In light of the ambivalences surrounding how to talk about social difference, one of the prevailing concepts Indonesians use instead is the "gap," which refers to the inequality between the fabulously wealthy minority and the enduringly poor majority.[1]

Ati's ambivalence about the relationship between her income and her identity reflected this gap. Eschewing acclaim as a businesswoman in spite of the fact that her non-teaching work consumed much of her time and provided much of her family's income, she instead understood herself as neither kelas menengah nor wealthy, rather emphasizing her postgraduate degree and her husband's. Her sensitivity about the pollution of business overlapped with her husband's concern about the pollution of corrupt state employment in their parenting worries, which became apparent during a conversation with me about their then college-age daughter's current flame: "I don't really like Ully's boyfriend. He comes from a family of business-people. All they think about is money. Brother [her husband] and I would like her to find someone who values people, beauty, and humanity." Ati's primary perception of herself was firmly rooted in her identity as a person who values virtues outside the financial, and she was especially concerned to see those values reproduced in her daughter's dating choices. Ati's concerns echo Ariel Heryanto's (2003:29) explanation that, rather than see themselves as members of a class, middle-class Indonesians conceive of themselves as people who are "educated" or "developed" and thereby have to pursue a commitment to "truth, justice, ethics or beauty" while needing "to deny their privileged status, self-interest or desire for recognition, and occasionally misrecognition of their secret desire for power and wealth."

Ati's concerns parallel both analytic observations about Indonesian class history and political economic theory on class. Max Weber (1947:424) framed class formation as an effect of social processes such as religious piety and anxiety that, once combined with political institutions, turn status differences into rationalized, imprisoning relations of capitalism. Although much of the symbolic anthropology of Java benefited from a strong Weberian foundation, the approach focused more on interpretation than on social class.[2] In 1963, Hildred Geertz described a "metropolitan superculture" that included educated, artistic, and economically stable Indonesians for whom the national language, chosen in 1928 as part of the revolution against the Dutch, was a primary tongue. Geertz (1963:35–37) described this superculture as "still in the process of formation" but as mostly focused on cultural and political, rather than economic, characteristics. It emphasized a transnational awareness but a national consciousness, especially through employment in the civil service. Two years after Geertz's observation, Suharto began what would ultimately be three decades of authoritarian rule framed as anti-communist. Talk about class suggested a Marxist orientation that was almost instantly banned as part of a broader domination of political discourse. The site of the largest communist party in the world outside the socialist bloc in the early 1960s, the country was ravaged by anti-communist mass killings by the late 1960s, and the very term *kelas* (class) became imbued with strong leftist overtones. Henk Schulte Nordholt (2004:16) argues that the intellectual silences both within Indonesia and by foreign scholars have entrenched a lack of awareness of the demographic reality of changing Indonesian social and economic relations, calling for research on the new Indonesian middle classes as essential to "decolonizing Indonesian historiography," because they are "people without history" for whom the old colonial social categories no longer apply.

Rather than class, specific and historical ethnic conceptions of status have tended to be the mode of analyzing social difference, especially on Java. Status has been an illuminating analytic tool for interpreting the complex hierarchy of Javanese social relations, well outside the formal feudal settings of sultanates. From language to ideas about refinement, etiquette, comportment, conduct, and the relationship between money and power, status has been considered a more appropriate analytic tool than wealth. Ward Keeler (1990) has described status as the essential social differentiator in Java, resting on the linguistic and aesthetic enforcement of a Javanese hierarchy and especially privileging the nobility (*priyayi*). Indeed, the anthropology of Indonesia, especially in the scholarship of Clifford Geertz, influenced the discipline's turn toward symbolic and interpretive anthropology during the 1970s and 1980s, a turn that arguably reflected the concerns with status in the central Javanese communities he studied.[3]

But as much as Javanese ideas of status appear to deny desire for wealth, status still involves and produces assertions about the relationship between virtue and money, assertions that reveal how much this relationship rests on women's labor. Perhaps the most insightful and closest description of Javanese ambivalence about money is Suzanne Brenner's (1998) analysis of batik merchant households in Surakarta. Dependent upon female traders whose income required a public comfort with handling and managing money in the marketplace, merchant families engaged in a status-focused dialogue with dominant priyayi ideologies that denigrated the pursuit of wealth, justifying their wealth as the expression of a virtuous work ethic. Nonetheless, as Brenner describes, these women's income could not simply accrue as capital but had to be "domesticated" back into familial status through the purchase of goods associated with priyayi style, a process that ultimately bankrupted many of the families she knew. Brenner (1998:119) articulates the process she analyzed as intersecting with capitalist modes of production but as not directly capitalist; instead, it was a combination of Dutch colonial intervention in sultanate rule and Javanese conceptions of trade.

The more recent increase of multinational capital production and urban economic growth suggests that newer differentiations are amenable to a class analysis. In addition to national political control, Suharto's authoritarian techniques opened the country to international investment in private industry, which benefited from military suppression of organized labor in offshore, flexible, feminized, multinational manufacturing.[4] Although this combination of rule and recruitment relied on a mobile and rural population, a middle-income demographic segment also grew during that period, through both civil service and private entrepreneurship. Measuring that group and figuring out what to call it have become industries unto themselves in Indonesia since the 1990s. With just under 250 million people, Indonesia is the fourth largest country in the world and the largest majority Muslim country in the world. Determining how many of those people are "middle-class" is a matter of debate. Indonesian census data and the even more invested market-research industries estimate that a middle-income segment, based on monthly expenditures of approximately US$300, rose from roughly 19 percent of the population in the mid-1990s to 30 percent in 2009 (*Badan Pusat Statistik* 2008; Guharoy 2006:1, 2009).[5] For the first time in Indonesia's history, the International Monetary Fund in 2010 ranked the country as "middle-income" on the basis of US$3,000 per capita GDP, the growth of which was largely driven by household and personal consumption (60 percent of GDP, surpassing foreign direct investment; Deutsch 2011).

Economist Howard Dick (1990) has argued that the key factor uniting middle-class Indonesians is not income, or employment, or education, but consumption, through which middle-class Indonesians differentiate themselves from the communal consumption styles of the working classes by bounding and obscuring domestic spaces and the consumption that takes place in them.[6] James Siegel (2002:222) has argued that the reason Indonesians do not conceive of themselves as members of classes is the cultural history of Indonesian nationalism. Indonesians came to imagine themselves during the revolutionary decades of the early twentieth century as "a nation composed of kin," and this sense of familial nationalism has precluded other forms of collective consciousness, especially among the middle class and in contrast to the European bourgeoisie's formation through conflict with feudalism (Siegel 2002:209). Because the Indonesian middle class owes its existence to nationalist fervor and state employment, middle-class Indonesians have accepted the notion that enlightened leaders know best for the family, both personal and national, meaning that "class is largely the result of undesired distinctions within the body of the nation" (Siegel 1998:83). Siegel asserts that this devotion to a national unit of citizens related to one another as kin prevents middle-class Indonesians from recognizing the injuries of fellow citizens who seek independence from that family, such as separatist movements in East Timor and Aceh.

My friend Ati's dilemma regarding her husband's instructions about her salary illustrates some of the complexity about consumption in the post-Suharto period. Following Suharto's resignation and the gradual return of foreign investment to the country in the early 2000s, capital once again felt ubiquitous yet elusive, circulating easily yet mysterious in origin. This has generated a particular anxiety about corruption. Indonesia regularly ranks high on international watchdog lists measuring corruption (e.g., World Bank 2003). Corruption is cited, both within Indonesia and in the international finance world, as a key drag on Indonesia's economy. Understood as a uniquely Indonesian weakness for wealth and commodities that prevents citizens, especially civil servants, from being moral workers, corruption appears as consumer desire taken to its most culturally peculiar and pathological extreme.[7]

So serious is the existential bond between consumption and corruption that many middle-class Javanese I know take great care to avoid consuming goods that might contaminate them, for consumption in some ways entails corporeal absorption. An object that was bought with tainted resources, especially goods that touch the skin, such as clothing or food, can enter the body in ways that are disturbing and polluting, making Ati's work at home a task of purification (Douglas 2002[1966]). Although Ati's husband was not asserting that she herself was corrupt, her salary smacked to him of state money and therefore dirty money, which he did not want turned into any goods his children might consume. Ati's solution was to spend her salary in ways that did not technically enter or support the household and that essentially returned the money to the state, using it for their children's public school fees and uniforms.

Although the literature on Indonesia often elides the ambivalence of being middle class, its focus on nationalism as the defining event in Indonesian history reminds us of the significance of the notion of the family and potentially of the particular figures in that unit to discourses of difference. By suggesting that kin terms have become a key way to speak of classed distinctions does not mean, however, that gender is an Indonesian mystification of structural class differences, nor that talk about different femininities is code for speaking of differing class positions. Rather, the centrality of family, consumption, and gender to discourses of distinction makes it clear that social differences are conceived and constituted through these categories.

PRIVATIZING CONSUMPTION: HOMES AND BODIES

Indonesia's urban landscapes have been dramatically transformed since the 1990s. At first glance, Indonesian cities are replete with invitations to desire, with advertisements and malls populated with people who, themselves, consume. Upon closer inspection, this apparently unproblematic celebration of the joys of consumption is complex, suggesting ambivalence and critique about the relationship between consumption and morality. The highly visible consumption in many Asian capitals during the 1990s generated research on what was dubbed the "new rich" of Asia (Pinches 1999; Robison and Goodman 1996; Sen and Stivens 1998).[8] Much of this research conflated the more visible and even flamboyant displays of wealth, reminiscent of European nouveaux riches (or what have been called *orang kaya baru*, or OKB, literally, "new rich people" in Indonesian), with evidence of a more moderate, self-conscious, and anxious middle class (Barker et al. 2009).[9] Indeed, descriptions of OKB commonly start and stop with either residential aesthetics or women's dress, suggesting that the newer middle classes are recognizable by their lifestyle and the charged boundary between public and private spaces. The resistance I encountered among my friends to identify as kelas menengah was in part due to the overlap between OKB and middle classness and their avoidance of both wealth and new wealth.

Lifestyle has therefore become a telling measure not only of one's position in a social landscape but also of how one chooses to convey that position. Boundaries between the public and domestic spheres particularly illustrate Indonesians' hesitation to appear wealthy. Residential Indonesian terminology differentiates among the many meanings embedded in the single English word "private," including *pribadi* (personal), *keluarga* (family), *swasta* (private enterprise), and *rumah tangga* (household). The idea of the *rumah* (house) was thus in a dynamic relationship with the idea of the *jalan* (street) during the New Order, each defining the other. Boundaries around houses, especially the fortress-like layers of protection enjoyed by the very wealthy, contributed to "an aesthetic of security" (Caldeira 2000:191) in which ornate villas were concealed behind imposing, but undecorated, walls and gates, their public side contrasting sharply with elaborate decoration on the private side.

More modest, middle-class homes mirror some of these trends in both style and security. Especially during the upheaval of 1998–2000, anxieties about criminality and a concern that anger against the state would be expressed in violence against houses and citizens associated with the state found neighborhoods like Ati's especially locked down. Ati and her husband own a small home, to which they have added a second floor, in a neighborhood originally constructed for civil servants. All of the homes have seen investment and expansion since their construction in the 1970s, especially in their interiors. Communities such as theirs are not gated, and the homes open directly onto paved, narrow streets that do not comfortably accommodate cars. With little or no barrier or yard, houses in the neighborhood are nonetheless secured with multiple locks and managed through the day by one or two house staff.[10]

Ambivalences about consumption therefore especially focus on the borders between public and private and are emblematic of the classed and gendered unease surrounding consumption. Similar examples are available from other Asian contexts, suggesting regional parallels. Pei-Chia Lan (2006:188–90) argues that the transnational domestic labor force in Taipei explicitly remakes public spaces such as train stations into private zones of pleasure in response to its labor in the private sphere. Scholarship on China, a country that often figures as one of the most powerful and representative sites of Asian consumption, has also linked the rise of a consuming class to the rise of urban middle classes. Lisa Rofel (2007:123) describes the general commodification of social relations since the 1990s in China as creating new desiring subjects who consider consumption a liberating alternative to historical stresses of kinship, communalism, and politics. Similarly, Li Zhang (2008 and chapter 9, this volume) describes an ethical murkiness about the transformation of socialist economic relations as proscribing inquiry about production, thereby redirecting questions about individual income or employment into admiration of consumption.[11]

Visible wealth and collective worry about its potentially illicit sources in Indonesia have also transformed formerly status-based etiquette, making it appropriate, for example, for one woman to ask another about her new shoes or handbag, even to ask about the price she paid, but not to ask about how she paid for them. Ati's interaction with her husband over the use of her civil servant's salary underscores this separation even within the private sphere, as he never asks her precisely how her salary was ultimately used, instead trusting her to use it in ways that honored his request. The rise of feminine consumption to a central focus of public concern about social change has parallels in other historical and post-authoritarian contexts: whereas work had once directly defined the limits of consumption, new anxieties about corruption require obscuring the relationship between production and consumption.

The feminized home is hardly natural but demands regular reworking to sacralize the private as a correction to the ills of outside commerce or the taint of politics. Indonesia's most recent historical transformations echo the focus on the home in Victorian England in the face of industrialization and, more recently, the fascination with a "return" to the private sphere in postsocialist contexts (Gal and Kligman 2000). Although Indonesians identify their enthusiasm for consumption with the rise in corruption, that enthusiasm also indexes the thrill and risk entailed in linking the intimate to the economic, spheres that Viviana Zelizer (2005) describes as requiring each other even as they are imagined to be morally incompatible.

Mark Liechty (2003 and chapter 11, this volume) specifically links ambivalence to class formation, arguing that anxiety about respectability and appropriateness in Kathmandu, Nepal, can be interpreted as a cultural articulation of the middleness of being middle-class, a global phenomenon with local concerns. As a social group positioned between the poor and the very wealthy, the middle classes are aware of a precariousness, of possibly losing their status, and frame their position in the language of propriety and modernity rather than economic or structural privilege.[12] As a result, public spaces of consumption such as shopping zones come to be spaces of desire in which particular subjects, especially women, are framed as especially vulnerable. Building on Liechty's point, I argue that ambivalence is never only an expression of classed structural positioning but is also deeply, historically specific and gendered.

National debates about consumption in Indonesia link women's public mobility and visibility to selfish consumption while framing private and domestic invisibility as proper, familial consumption. We can see this in the form of three key gendered figures: the housewife, the career woman, and the fashionably pious woman. Domestic consumption was framed, especially during the Suharto years, as a moral and familial antidote to more public and spectacular celebrations of consumption. Domestic consumption was, ideally, to be managed and enacted by the figure of a frugal, full-time housewife, a primary marker of middle-class distinction during the Suharto New Order. Posed as the obvious counterpoint to a growing class of career women, the housewife was supposed to domesticate income through consuming for the family, and she was especially prominent during the 1980s and 1990s. However, the figure of the housewife also became linked to social and national decay, reframed as a woman who strained her income-earning husband through her feminine impulse to consume, generating a perceived growth in illicit consumption framed as corruption, particularly since Suharto's resignation in 1998. Female demands for consumer goods came to be seen as a driving force leading to increased male corruption. In the twenty-first century, a new figure has replaced the problematic image of the housewife: a woman who reclaims respectability through piety in the form of Islamic devotion. Notably, even this image of the pious woman has been tarnished. As a woman motivated simply by trends and the impulse to self-decorate, the fashionable, pious Muslim woman's claims to virtue through consumption are, themselves, now coming under critique. Through their appearances, their mobility, and their relationship to domestic consumption, figures of femininity are charged with the labor of consuming properly and, in so doing, maintaining their propriety and their families'.

This relationship between consumption and gender in Indonesia is a legacy of the gender categories and state development programs designed by the Suharto regime. Groups were structured to organize women's contributions to national development through generating correct family relations and domestic spaces, particularly through the modern figure of the housewife. By the 1970s, organizations such as Dharma Wanita (Women's Duty), for civil servants' wives, and Pembinaan Kesejahteraan Keluarga (Family Welfare Program), for female citizens in poor neighborhoods, modeled feminine citizenship through domestic frugality. These programs linked domesticity to broader national policies, especially the *azas kekeluargaan,* or the family principle, which framed the nation as a family and made the nuclear family, as the smallest unit of the nation, seem natural (Boellstorff 2005:189, 197; Shiraishi 1997). The *ibu rumah tangga* (literally, "mother of the household") was an explicitly modern figure whose contribution to the nation was through her scientific management of the family but whose appellation "mother" marked her actions as selfless and without expectation of public recognition (Djajadiningrat-Nieuwenhuis 1987:43).[13] Although women across the archipelago have long earned income outside the home and indeed have been primary household providers, the appellations of "career woman" and "housewife" reframed that history into apparently mutually exclusive moral categories (cf. Newberry 2006). The ideal housewife was a female citizen who gained her status in the national project through caring for the affective and physical needs of other citizens, specifically, her husband and children.

Not only did gendered state organizations summon a new category of modern femininity through domesticity, but also domesticity was explicitly linked to instruction and training on managing consumption. Dharma

Wanita and Pembinaan Kesejahteraan Keluarga held monthly meetings organized as classes in which domesticity was taught asan acquirable skill. Training for civil servants materialized the ties among the centralized authority, technocratic expertise, and social mobility similar to what Max Weber (1968:1002) described as bureaucracy's demand for cultivation, affecting "the most intimate aspects of personal culture." Particularly in Dharma Wanita, tied to the civil service that has been the historical foundation for an Indonesian middle class, sessions focused on cooking, fashion, and child rearing, all of which involved consumption, and the time preceding and following the meetings featured members selling goods such as makeup, handbags, or snacks to one another.

In this context, spaces outside the home, particularly those that involved consumption, became especially charged precisely at a time when many of the flagrant forms of development generated new public spaces of consumption throughout Indonesian cities. Lizzy Van Leeuwen (2008) has described the contemporary Indonesian middle class and its preferred public space of the mall, where, ideally, nothing detrimental to the political and social body might occur.[14] Yet, she also argues, that ideal exists precisely because malls are the spaces where so much more might occur. Rumors abound about how young women might find the excessive consumer desire of the stylish mall environment so powerful that they would engage in commodified sex in order to fund their shopping.[15] The proper feminine form and respectable, private, domestic spaces thus have become even more charged terrains for countering the thrills and ills of the public mall.

DISCIPLINING CONSUMPTION

The intersection of family, nation, and gender in Indonesian conceptions of distinction has generated corrective solutions that promise to resolve the excesses of feminine consumption through discipline. Two specific forms of correction have emerged in the twenty-first century: first, a structured government campaign, to manage corruption, that has identified mysterious sources of consumption as a threat to Indonesia's global success and, second, the rise of public forms of Islamic piety that can be understood as solutions to public anxieties about national immorality, especially in the form of corruption. Islamic piety and courses on consumption each address feminine subjects as the victims and the saviors of consumer excess, thereby reproducing both specifically middle-class ambivalences about consumption and Suharto era discourses on femininity as a learnable skill.

National campaigns and trials against corrupt officials became sensational fodder for the mass media after Suharto's resignation, in part because of greater press freedoms. Corruption exposés are now covered in far more detail and with greater public fascination than most soap operas, yet perhaps one of the more emblematic and consistent campaigns against corruption is not public. Modeled on the earlier training in Dharma Wanita, government programs specifically link corruption to feminine unruliness. Approximately every six months, training retreats are held in subregions for each crop of rising civil servants. When mid-level civil servants, assumed to be male, are identified as candidates for national-level positions, their wives are summoned to a week-long training session in which they are prepared for the responsibilities of being the wife of a high-ranking official whose increasing authority will put him in a position of temptation for bribes. My friend Dewi, who attended a training seminar before her husband's promotion to a national ministry, recounted to me that many of these women are educated and professional but that the content of the sessions focuses almost entirely on the feminine role in consumption as a mode of managing corruption. Wives are instructed to resist the temptation to go to the salon daily, or to wear diamonds during the day, or to discard clothing after one wearing. Instead, they are to see themselves as always under scrutiny and surveillance by the public and as the most important link in ensuring their husbands' professionalism. Instructions like these encourage a form of middle-class frugality against a backdrop that assumes that, without instruction, women will always favor excess. Further, the wives are taught to not ask their husbands for more money than they are usually allotted (which might encourage the husbands to engage in corruption), implying that men, rather than women, manage the household budget.

By stressing the management of domestic consumption and personal desire, the sessions emphasize that the work of the state is seen and represented by the public and private conduct of its civil servants and even their family members. Instructions on consumption address public conduct, such as reducing extravagant displays of wealth in social settings, and private conduct, such as managing household finances and even intimate dreams for goods. The sessions link social surfaces to the private in a way that builds on the Suharto era assertion that feminized consumption and domesticity are the backbone of healthy national development. Although these courses are linked to the civil service and therefore the continuation of these ideas may not be surprising in spite of the collapse of the Dharma Wanita program, similar ideas are expressed in fee-based seminars with names like Personal Development, which promise self-improvement through correct comportment, dress, and shopping techniques (Jones 2010a). Courses such as these have become ubiquitous and popular. For women who are not invited to participate or who can avoid the state programs, improving themselves through acquiring expertise on consumption and etiquette is still appealing, and it is often framed as "training" through acquiring self-confidence. Many of the students in fee-based femininity courses consider them more attractive than the state-sponsored programs on gendered conduct, even though the former require tuition and the latter are free, a choice that feels liberated and fashionable. The promise of female emancipation through consumption has, as Foucault (1978:7) has argued, come to have its own "market value," becoming a kind of commodity that sophisticated women would want to acquire. One reason for the ongoing appeal of commodified expertise for women, extolling the virtue of managed consumption and appropriateness, is the way in which it speaks to both the specific conditions of a post-authoritarian political context and the middle-class nature of the conditions these solutions might ameliorate. In other words, women are in the middle of a very middle-class dilemma.

A second form of correction to the anxieties of consumption in Indonesia links the familial and the ethical in the form of the pious woman, a phenomenon that is less formal yet much more visible than training retreats for the wives of rising civil servants. Especially striking is the figure of the fashionably pious woman, someone who has taken the call to correct excessive consumption through religion to the point that her motives are questionable as a form of vanity rather than virtue. Linking the solution to Indonesian political and economic corruption to eliminating moral corruption, Islamic piety has become even more publicly visible, especially in cities, than it was in the 1980s and 1990s. Although Islam has been a vibrant part of much of the Indonesian archipelago since the twelfth century (Ho 2006), since the late 1980s, it has experienced a new public prominence, taking a moral tone for the middle-class position between the working classes and the wealthy. Indeed, many scholars of the rise of Islamic piety in Indonesia assert that it has been a fundamentally middle-class phenomenon, appealing for its ability to critique a political and economic condition as an expression of a deeper moral condition (Brenner 1996; Hefner 2000; Smith-Hefner 2007). A number of area scholars link this boom to particularly Indonesian expressions of self-improvement (Gade 2004), corporatism (Fealy 2008; Hoesterey 2008), and neoliberalism (Rudnyckjy 2009), especially as a response to the Asian economic collapse that brought down the New Order.[16]

Based in large part on college campuses in the 1980s and 1990s, Islamic reformism blended the forced political silence under an authoritarian regime with a moral disdain for material excess and corruption

FIGURE 6.1

Chic, elaborate Islamic fashion by Indonesian designer Itang Yunasz. Copyright and permission, Noor *magazine, 2005.*

among elites and an anxiety about working-class women in the workforce.[17] A young male Islamic activist explained to me on a university campus in 1997 that undisciplined femininity made consumption an urgent target for social and religious reform: "All these young migrant workers who are wearing nice Nike tennis shoes, you do realize that they are also having 'free sex,' don't you?" (cf. Ong 1990). Islam became a safe and appealing space from which urban middle-class youth could propose an alternative, universal, and morally superior critique of their parents' generation while connecting to a global Islamic revival.

One of the most visible components of public piety has been the transformation of women's dress, especially the wearing of the headscarf, or *jilbab*, a move suggesting that tainted corruption, framed as consumer desire, could be corrected through alternative consumption, the purchase and use of pious goods. Women's Islamic dress was commodified very early in the piety movement, and by the mid-1980s, what appeared to be intentionally simple headscarves and solid pastel tunics and pants were in fact often imported (because of the rarity of such garb in the region) and therefore quite expensive.[18] Conversations with middle-aged women about that time involve little nostalgia, as it was difficult to find, afford, and wear Islamic dress. More recent versions of Islamic dress are far more elaborate, embracing prints, embroidery, and accessories. Particularly since the end of the New Order in 1998, the fashionably pious woman has thus become a problematic figure, emerging out of a moral critique of consumer culture but now dismissed for pursuing piety as a fashion statement rather than as a religious statement.

The personal and public appeal of enacting virtue through an Islamic identity has generated an impressive Islamic dress industry in Indonesia that now rivals the secular clothing market. This combination of decoration and ubiquity is in conversation with broader debates in Indonesia about the rise of public piety in the country, debates which posit that much of the public symbolism associated with piety is merely image (*imej*) rather than a reflection of deeper material and spiritual transformation (Jones 2010b). Women and women's dress figure centrally, suggesting that fashionably pious women are pursuing an impure and superficial goal of being fashionable rather than deeply, spiritually pure. Virtue, framed as both middle-class respectability and religiosity, has potently coalesced in the form of pious goods marketed especially to women. The figure of the fashionably pious woman has therefore generated a familiar middle-class concern—ambivalence—based on the possibility that the very practice that arose to quell anxiety about feminine consumption, Islamic piety, is now popular and flamboyant.

Fashionably pious women are aware of these critiques and defend their dress as religiously sincere. One Yogyakarta civil servant, Aeshya, who is known for her especially complex and stylish Islamic dress, said to me in

2008, "If you see these teenagers with the exaggerated, plain, oversized jilbabs that go to the knees, that are so out of date, we can respect them, but in my opinion, that is not genuine witnessing [*syiar*]. They make Islam look rigid, unfashionable, whereas in fact our God likes beauty." Although complaining about what she considers a pretentious version of Islamic dress that appears to critique the fashionable Islamic styles, Aeshya herself is the target of gossip because of her own dress.

Aeshya's pious style includes carefully chosen, complementary accents for each outfit, from the sequins on her jilbab, to the brooch at her throat, to the trim on her tunic. Her friends and colleagues describe the fun of seeing what she shows up wearing each morning, although some privately confided to me that they find her look déclassé. A colleague of hers described her reaction when they both attended a *pengajian* (religious study session) in which Aeshya had gone beyond her usual exuberance to coordinate an ensemble that included black-and-white diagonal-striped fabric adorned with red polka-dot embroidery, cutout work, red rickrack trim on her tunic and skirt hems, and a bright red headscarf with sequins and silk flowers at the ears. The final touch was a pair of matching red stilettos. Aeshya was proud of her coordinated outfit, but her colleague described the overall effect as dizzying and embarrassing, revealing the class tensions that can emerge in critiques of consumption, especially among women.

Moments of distinction (Bourdieu 1984) such as this also figure in other contexts in which the meaning of pious dress is up for debate. Taste, framed as modesty in a technical sense but also as a sense of elegance and simplicity, can become the terrain for sorting out the terms of piety, made all the more loaded, because until the twenty-first century, Islamic dress was synonymous with lack of taste, provinciality, or rejection of beauty. Ria, a fifty-year-old woman who has consciously resisted wearing Islamic dress on a daily basis but who is widely considered a religious role model, describes her frustration at comments when she does don it, especially for pengajian. She regularly finds herself the recipient of effusive, overly polite flattery about how much more beautiful she is when covered, comments she finds coercive and sexist because of what she considers underlying assumptions about an innate feminine desire to be desired. She responds by privately grumbling about how women who adopt pious dress are lazy about their personal appearance: "No wonder women want to wear *busana* Muslim. It lets them gain weight and just hide it under a larger, looser tunic. They don't have to exercise or be disciplined or take care of their hair. If my hair is graying, here, let's just throw on this *kerudung* [a looser headscarf associated with older women]." Ria's reference to lack of discipline is especially pointed, inverting a widespread assertion that one of the specific virtues of Islamic dress is its disciplining effects, nudging the wearer to become conscious of her interactions with the opposite sex and to be more vigilant about regular prayers. Suggesting that pious dress does not produce discipline is therefore a sharp criticism, although it was routed through the language of feminine appearance.

Tensions such as these underpin the growth of the Islamic fashion business, an industry that stands to gain from asserting that Islamic dress is a solution to broader social ills, yet this could also appear to be encouraging consumption. It is especially apparent in the content of Islamic fashion magazines in Indonesia, which mediate perceptions of Islamic fashion as comportment with ethical conduct but also as a legitimate space for delight and discovery. In one first-person account by a staff writer of *Noor* magazine, the author told of an encounter with an acquaintance at an Islamic fashion show (Lubis 2008). Knowing that the woman's husband had been convicted of corruption in the preceding year, she was surprised to see her friend decked out in a luxurious ensemble and sporting the latest imported handbag. The author proceeded to quote from verse 26 of Qur'an sura 17 against excess of all kinds, consumptive and abstemious, suggesting that true piety involves modest expectations, modest outlay, and concern for others. She concluded by reminding readers that even if one can afford branded fashions, it is not appropriate to choose to spend one's money in that way.

CONCLUSION

Consumption and femininity are closely linked components of classed subjectivities in contemporary Indonesian cultural politics. As specific as these examples have been to Indonesia, they overlap with experiences of middle classness elsewhere, suggesting that political economic analyses are useful for unpacking Indonesian history. As subjects of national progress or regress, positioned between poor and wealthy class segments, and as subjects who are ambivalent about their dreams, failures, and privileges, Indonesian middle classes are familiar. Their concerns with the contamination of a money economy coupled with economic fragility have generated discourses on discipline and virtue that have made Islamic consumption an especially appealing route in the twenty-first century.

These tensions are unique to recent Indonesian history, yet they also resonate with narratives about capitalism's corrosive effects, effects that seem to coalesce in the conduct of middle-class women and thereby place women doubly in the middle of the frame. Corporate and academic assumptions that consumption is naturally pleasurable, unproductive, or marginal erase the ways in which capitalist relations, including increasingly global and outsourced industries, rely on this erasure (Freeman 2000). In asking about the "proper labor of the consumer," Susan Stewart (1993:168) argues that "fashion and fad take places within the domain of the feminine not simply because they are emblematic of the trivial.... The conception of woman as consumer...functions to erase the true labor, the true productivity, of women. Yet this erasure forms the very possibility of exchange." Women's roles and the domestic sphere can thus have a double quality: malleable and available for public issues yet invisible as sources of productivity or contribution to the national project.

These examples also index anxieties about the relationship between money and morality, a relationship maintained at the boundary of the public and the private. Consumption, as a site of circulation across that boundary, has thus become a key site of concern, revealing a central component to our analyses of middle-class subjectivity: the fundamentally gendered nature of these anxieties. Indeed, ideas about Indonesian middle class-ness place women and consumption in the middle of these concerns, at the intersection of public concerns about the private costs of social change. Middle-class women are to perform restorative labor through correct consumption to correct the ills of a society affected by excessive consumption, a condition that is recognizable for its effects on women. Women emerge as both the signs of and the solutions for national progress, its victims and its saviors.

The labors of maintaining boundaries between production and consumption, private and public, secular and pious, may seem distinct, but they overlap in their reliance on notions of discipline and virtue and on their reliance on women to achieve and represent these boundaries. In Ati's case, her burden was to manage household consumption, like many Javanese women, but also to honor her husband's insistence that no goods purchased with her state-associated civil service income enter their home or contaminate their children. Proper private consumption therefore promised to domesticate the murky origins of income earned in the outer world of corrupted economic relations, transforming it into familial relations. As a result, feminine mobility and visibility have come to connote self-interested consumption and vanity, even when in the form of Islamic piety, whereas private, domestic, invisible consumption remains more respectable and self-sacrificing. These boundaries of visibility and invisibility further erase the labors of other classed and gendered individuals within households, such as maids, whose labor maintains the functioning of the home but is supervised by and credited to their employers.

The history, figures, and accounts I discuss here show that the work of linking consumption to feminine pleasure is always political and is a process that rests on irresolvable anxieties. In each of these brief examples, women's bodies and symbolic import, particularly through consumption, figure centrally, yet that centrality remains limited. Indonesian women are made available as symbols for public and especially religious debates, yet their responses to these debates are easily dismissed. Social differences produced through types of femininity have been in the middle of concerns about the costs of social change in Indonesia, making women ready symbols of proliferating desires and thereby increasing their share of the burden of proving middle-class respectability. Middle-class Indonesian women therefore are dealing with a social problem that simultaneously benefits and challenges them, dealing with anxieties that never disappear.

Acknowledgments

The insights in this essay are the result of several fieldwork periods, from 1995–2011. I am particularly grateful to the many families in Indonesia whose friendship was essential to these arguments. Carla Freeman, Rachel Heiman, and Mark Leichty provided generous critical comments for which I am grateful. Earlier research occurred during dissertation fieldwork, for which I wish to acknowledge the support of the following institutions: the University of North Carolina, Chapel Hill; the Fulbright Educational Foundation in Jakarta; the Pusat Penilitian Kebudayaan dan Perubahan Sosial of Gadjah Mada University; and the Lembaga Ilmu Pengetahuan Indonesia. Later research benefited from support from Emory University and the University of Colorado, particularly a CARTSS grant and Innovative Seed Grant.

Notes

1. A measure of how much more common the idea of the middle class has become since Suharto's resignation is evident in a comment by President Susilo Bambang Yudhoyono (2010) in which he argued that middle classes demand and produce democracy: "The middle class everywhere will grow.... As they grow in strength and confidence, sooner or later they are bound to seek greater transparency and accountability in the decisions that affect their lives."

2. James Peacock's (1968) analysis of working-class theater employed Weberian and psychological categories, and the influence of Weber, through Talcott Parsons, was an essential component of Clifford Geertz's strain of symbolic analysis of Javanese religion (1976) and agriculture (1963).

3. This is not to suggest that no political economic research was done in Indonesia, but that it was not the dominant strain of anthropological inquiry by foreign scholars. For example, Ann Stoler's (1985) *Capitalism and Confrontation in Sumatra's Plantation Belt, 1870–1979* explicitly analyzed the framing of white privilege and native labor as capitalist. A separate line of research focused on development; although it did not analyze the middle classes, it frequently researched poor women's informal economic activities (e.g., Manderson 1983; Papanek and Schwede 1988; Sullivan 1983).

4. Rates of employment outside the home have remained consistent, including the 38 percent of the civil service composed of women (Oey-Gardiner 2002:109). By the 1990s, images of the housewife were competing with a new figure, the career woman, or *wanita karir*. The representations of Indonesian women who work in white-collar employment, service industries, and other office settings associated with recent economic growth circulate differently than representations of other kinds of female laborers. Although related discourses elaborate the social costs of different types of feminine work, such as migrant domestic labor (Silvey 2004), factory production (Lindquist 2008; Wolf 1992), and sex work (Ford 2003), each of which has also contributed to Indonesian economic change, the figure of the wanita karir has a particular valence, in part because of her greater visibility. As office workers commute in and out of central Jakarta on public transportation, small groups of attractive women garbed in professional dress, carrying (often knockoff) designer accessories, and texting or calling on their cell phones become human signs of the broader pride and worry that the city evokes. Their mobility also seems to evoke two forms of lack of domestication: unsurveilled social contact and income that might be unconnected to family.

5. In addition to measures such as income and education, the special region of Yogyakarta measures population segments through the possession of key objects such as homes, cars, motorcycles, color TVs, and furniture such as sideboards.

6. Dick (1985:71) asserts that although there was considerable intellectual interest among Indonesianists in the developmental and modernizing promise of an urban middle class in the 1950s and 1960s, it dissipated with "a focus on the 'elite' [that] seems to have blinded social scientists to its middle-class nature."

7. Transforming access to the state into wealth has long been a trait associated with Indonesians seeking entry to the middle classes. Sociologist Justus M. van der Kroef described, in 1956, "a 'national' social class system…in its infancy" (138), which featured entrepreneurs and intelligentsia engaging in "unprecedented corruption and collusion" (143). Rumors about civil servants' corruption are partly based on two related facts: civil servants are paid very low salaries compared with private sector employees, and they face mandatory retirement at age fifty-five. The nationalist historical

explanation for low salaries suggests that civil service careers provide security and prestige. Attempts to reduce corruption by the current administration have partly focused on these problems, raising civil servant salaries by approximately 10 percent every year since 2005 and raising the retirement age for some categories of the civil service, including those in academia.

8. See also Samuli Schielke (chapter 2, this volume) for a discussion of the impact this emerging wealth in Asia is having on the class aspirations of Egyptians.

9. There are a number of terms for poverty in Indonesian parlance, including the direct *orang miskin* (literally, "poor person") and the more polite appellation *orang kecil*, or "little people," a term that captures the status-based quality of social differentiation.

10. Gated communities have become popular, promising safety and privacy. As families I know have become more affluent, they have chosen either to expand their homes or to simply buy new homes in gated communities. Also see Sanjay Srivastava (chapter 3, this volume) for a discussion of the rise of gated communities in India and Rachel Heiman (chapter 10, this volume) for an illustration of how even an ornamental gate in a previously nongated community can signal exclusion and inspire class-based anxieties.

11. In a related vein, William Mazzarella (2003) argues that Indian advertising executives called into being a desirable consumer category, the Indian middle class, through insisting on its Indian specificity.

12. Rihan Yeh (chapter 8, this volume) also explores the negotiation of and ambivalence around this middleness, in Tijuana, Mexico.

13. In a historical argument about English state formation as cultural revolution, Philip Corrigan and Derek Sayer (1985:4–6) argue that states gain authority through "moral regulation," which produces homogenizing effects, through minimizing social differences, such as class and gender, and individuating effects, and through naturalizing categories such as citizen, head of household, and, I might add, housewife.

14. Elizabeth Wilson (1992:101) argues that the one arena in which European women of the new bourgeoisie could be partly visible and, like men, enjoy the pleasures of looking and strolling was the department store, an environment that was "half-public, half-private," similar to the boulevard.

15. Mark Liechty (chapter 11, this volume) similarly notes such rumors surrounding female consumption in twenty-first-century Nepal, as well as nineteenth-century France.

16. Not all Indonesians agreed that religion was the best or only path for national transformation, but this moment did see the establishment of new Islamic political parties and social organizations. Individual Indonesians also found Islam an appealing

private remedy in a moment of national social upheaval. The rise of public piety has not been welcome by all citizens, however, and some have found the dissolution of the state's management of the press and political organizations to be an opportunity for establishing secular social justice movements, including those based on Marxist philosophy, which were outlawed under the Suharto regime. No Islamic political party has won a majority in a national election since Suharto's resignation.

17. Historically, much of the research on Islam in Indonesia has focused either on its syncretic quality or on global security and governance issues (Emmerson 2006; Liddle and Mujani 2007). Older research on class in Indonesia identified an explicitly Islamic middle class as a rural phenomenon. The urban middle classes were considered, at least by Indonesians, more syncretic if not secular in orientation and weak or apostate Muslims by their rural class counterparts (Abdurrachman 1990 ; Kuntowijoyo 1985). A publicly devout middle class in urban Java and other islands is indeed new, but it has become so prevalent since the 1990s that it is almost hard to remember a time when it was not.

18. The relationship between apparent asceticism and consumption echoes Max Weber's (1958:278) assertion that "asceticism is a bourgeois virtue."

7

Just Managing

American Middle-Class Parenthood in Insecure Times

Cindi Katz

Social reproduction is high-stakes drivel, childhood much the same. Unrecognized by most analysts of political economy and class formation, the material social practices associated with social reproduction in all their grind and glory are—like childhood itself—critical to making, maintaining, and any possibility for remaking social and political-economic life. In a time of economic crisis, the stakes are that much higher and can perhaps be felt most acutely around childhood or, more precisely, parenthood, since aspirations are commonly defined, managed, reached, and deferred in and through the family, among other sites. The time-spaces of middle-class everyday life intrigue me and are a way to get at its heart in every sense of the term. The generational and intergenerational strivings up and fallings down; the spatial expressions of class position, its protection through comportment, style, distance, and increasingly through bunkering, its imagined but fraught horizons—all suggest some of the ways the middle class is a "field of dreams" in always already turbulent times and heterogeneous spaces. At the heart of social reproduction, the family tenders a cluster of practices that reach toward and modulate possible futures for its members, defining as it mediates a battery of aspirations and scrambles to manage the risks associated with them.

This chapter is drawn from a book project on contemporary childhood in the United States. Shaped around the idea of "childhood as spectacle" (Katz 2008), my research traces some shifts in common understandings of children, childhood, and the means and spaces of child rearing. I examine the connections between them and some of the political-economic, social, and cultural transformations that began in the 1960s, crystallized throughout the 1970s, and continue to have resonance and repercussions today. Drawing on an archive that includes parents' blogs and websites; parenting books and magazines; marketing materials and data on surveillance technologies in homes and schools; discussions with childcare workers, teachers, and parents; and, most recently, the circulation and contradictory responses to the film *Race to Nowhere*, it is clear that contemporary childhood is a rich "transfer point" for relations of power, social life, and imagination (cf. Foucault 1978). Looking at what I call "childhood as spectacle" and the multiple figurations of the child it calls forth is a critical and illuminating way to grasp what is at stake as the geographic scale of social reproduction presses downward from the corporatist state to the household and individual, as it has since the 1980s in the United States. Under these conditions, the lives and well-being of some children (middle-class and wealthier children) have been fetishized; others—the vast majority of children—suffer the consequences of a disinvested public sphere and a radically reduced social wage. These effects will probably become more pronounced as the sense of precariousness stemming from the financial crises beginning in 2008 infiltrates everyday life more deeply and widely. Indeed, the present moment is both a ricochet and a reminder of the constellation of forces that spurred many of the shifts my broader project addresses, and it provides the context for my discussion here of the ways middle-class parenting in the contemporary United States has become a project.

SHIFTING GROUNDS OF U.S. CHILDHOOD

Significant shifts in the cultural forms and practices of U.S. childhood and parenthood can be pegged to some key social and political-economic changes that came to fruition in the 1970s. I will focus on three of them. First was the ontological insecurity provoked by the rattling of enduring relations of power and privilege, such as nation, class, gender, race, sexuality, and age, and spurred by social movements and world historical events as the long postwar economic boom sputtered out. The all too easy, hegemonic assumptions about the place of the United States in the world and the political-economic possibilities that came with it dimmed considerably as, among other things, the effects of the 1973 oil shocks, the U.S. defeat in Vietnam, Watergate, "stagflation," and the early moves of global economic restructuring came home. If these events precipitated something of a loss of innocence and dampened some of the bravado associated with U.S. exceptionalism, they also seemed to strengthen the undertow of anxiety about taken-for-granted privileges of middle-class life and about what the future held as its presumptions were buffeted by these shifts. Part of the response, particularly among the tenuously upwardly mobile "lower-middle class" or that fraction of the unionized working class that benefited from industrial Fordism and structural racism, was the election of Ronald Reagan in 1980; another was an incipient tendency to secure childhoods close to home. The latter brought with it a resentment-fueled loosening of commitments to social childhood in the form of tax revolts and antagonism toward social welfare, or in other words, the well-being of other people's children.

Second and not unrelated, the rise of neoliberal capitalist imperatives at once flattened the scales of social reproduction as it extended the reach of production and exchange globally. With Reagan affably at the helm, the new right was able to make good on a variety of seeds sown by its think tanks, policy makers, and pundits in the 1970s to promulgate a neoliberal agenda that advanced the global interests of big business while tapping into widespread and racialized economic resentments spurred in part by those very interests. Reagan's conservative moralism advanced policies intended to dismantle the welfare state (such as it was), drove tax rebellion, and expanded militarism and policing while claiming to shrink "big government." With these policies, responsibility for social reproduction increasingly was off-loaded from the institutions of the state and capital to the household and individual. Social and economic life became that much more precarious across the board as the divisions between rich and poor—people and nations—grew sharper and wider. As public education, government-provided social services, health care, child care, play environments, and open spaces deteriorated or evaporated almost completely, those with resources increasingly secured these things for their children privately, either with household labor or through purchase. Although the middle class was thus able to buffer some of the worst effects of the fading Keynesian state for themselves, their actions only made things worse for those who lacked the resources to mitigate the interconnected consequences of devolution and privatization.

Finally, third and not least, was the reworking of family forms and gender relations of production and reproduction, enabled in part by the availability of reliable new reproductive technologies, such as birth control pills and intrauterine devices, and by the increased presence of middle-class women in the labor force. These changes helped propel—and were sustained by—

the feminist movement that took root in the 1960s and came to fruition in the 1970s. Results of these shifts, among others, were a remarkable retreat from marriage among younger women and a postponement and marked reduction in childbearing in the early 1970s,[1] particularly among college-educated women. In tandem with these changes, more and more middle-class women, including women with children, were employed outside the home, out of necessity as much as desire in many cases. Among the eventual consequences of these circumstances were a backlash against what was seen as women's greater autonomy, imagined economic parity, and altered socio-economic roles; as well as a baby boomlet in the 1980s, when a rising number of older, more privileged, and more consciously intentional parents had children. Many of these parents were part of the so-called baby boom generation in the United States following World War II. Approximately 77.3 million Americans were born between 1946 and 1964 (Boomers Life 2008), constituting a demographic bulge with profound effects on the nation's culture and economy. The backlash and the boomlet are associated, particularly among middle-class people, with the preciousness around childhood that has become so palpable since the 1990s and with various subtle and not so subtle means of disciplining women, both of which are central to my concerns. Parenthood, among the middle classes at least, became a project.

SECURING CHILDHOOD, CHANNELING ANXIETY

Although these changes in childhood, parenthood, and the everyday lives of children and parents have become familiar, if not a cliché, in the United States—the focus of innumerable popular articles and books and much public and private hand-wringing—they are little theorized. My argument is that, in concerted and contradictory ways, the social, political, economic, and cultural shifts outlined here spurred many of the changes around children and childhood now common in middle-class family life and that understanding these shifts *as political* refocuses the problem away from individual issues of self-propelling anxiety, fear, or resentment to social concerns at the very heart of neoliberal global capitalism and the gendered social relations of heteronormativity. My goal, then, is not to write yet another piece on overstructured children, anxious parenting, children without childhoods, children as consumers, and so on, but rather to examine and theorize these concerns as part of a broader constellation of effects that reflect, make visible, and in varying ways contribute to the altered relations of production, reproduction, and power associated with neoliberal globalism, deteriorations in the social wage, and the uneven developments since the mid-1970s. These shifts have individually and in concert reconfigured social life and the "expectations of modernity" (*pace* Ferguson 1999) wherein the middle-class family is at once citadel—policed and policing the reproduction of its members and the broader social formations of which it is a part—and hothouse: grooming perfectly commodified children for niche marketing in the fragile realms of the future.

In other words, contemporary middle-class life in the United States is riddled with ontological insecurity provoked by political-economic upheavals, environmental crises, and profound changes in the social relations of production and reproduction, among other things.[2] This congeries of material social forms and practices haunts U.S. middle-class life, especially in the wake of the financial crises that surfaced in the late summer of 2008. The sense of economic precariousness has been heightened and made more sprawling in the wake of these crises, which continue to unfold, unraveling the economic stability and imagined futures of millions of U.S. households across class boundaries. Even middle-class households have experienced widespread job insecurity and loss, bank foreclosures, and homelessness. These changes fuse the global with the intimate and are likely having profound effects on family life, what it means to come of age, and the daily practices of parenthood and childhood (cf. Pratt and Rosner 2006). I will take up some of these concerns among middle-class households in the United States, looking in particular at the ways neoliberal restructuring infiltrates the affective labor associated with social reproduction and the formation of new laboring subjects. See Carla Jones (chapter 6, this volume) for a discussion of the ways neoliberal restructuring in Indonesia has brought about significant shifts in affective labor, particularly for women. Similarly, Carla Freeman (chapter 4, this volume) offers an account of changes in affective labor and marriage and in the formation of new laboring subjects in Barbados, also inspired by neoliberal economic shifts.

Anxiety about the future—or, more precisely, one's place in the future—is a commonplace of middle-class life (e.g., Bledstein and Johnston 2001; Liechty 2003 and chapter 11, this volume). Whereas others—many of them in this collection—have addressed this anxiety around questions of comportment, embodiment, taste, and material representations of self and status (compare, e.g., Bledstein and Johnston 2001; Bourdieu 1984; Fehérváry, chapter 5, and Heiman, chapter 10, this volume; Liechty 2003; Ortner 2003), I am interested in looking at how it is channeled and expressed through concerns about children and the nature of childhood and youth (cf. Currie 2005; Davidson 2008; Heiman 2009; Sammond 2005).

Contemporary middle-class anxiety about the future comes from a number of quarters, and I will attend in particular to three wellsprings of concern—political-economic, geopolitical, and environmental. Anxiety about the political-economic future is spurred, for example, as the grounds and promises of secure employment appear increasingly destabilized but work roles and rules and the social relations of production and reproduction stay largely as they were when their promises were different. The geopolitical future may also feel daunting to much of the U.S. middle class as long-held presumptions of hegemony and the privileges it assumes and affords face threats that reflect the porosity of national boundaries, encouraging not only broadened public support for U.S. state violence internally and externally, including fortressing at the national scale through such things as walling the U.S.-Mexico border and the projects of racial profiling that animate Arizona's new immigration law and other measures of border security, but also, at the domestic scale, security measures and neighborhood fortressing becoming more common in middle-class communities and homes (compare, e.g., Atkinson 2006; Atkinson and Blandy 2007; Katz 2001; Low 2003). Finally, deep anxiety is provoked around the environmental future. Looming issues such as global climate change, toxic wastes, or disasters such as the 2010 Gulf of Mexico oil spill and the earthquakes in Haiti and Japan (with the latter's devastating nuclear crisis) overwhelm and are experienced as beyond people's, governments', or corporations' capacity (or will) to control or ameliorate. These conditions and the understandable anxieties they provoke are managed in part by the domestic practices around social reproduction, particularly parenthood, and through a variety of affective and material practices around managing children's everyday lives, exposures, and aspirations (cf. Grewal 2006).

My concerns here dovetail with those of architectural theorist Beatriz Colomina, whose extraordinary book *Domesticity at War* (2007) argues that Cold War anxiety was channeled through the domestic sphere, wherein the ethos and fetishization of control over home and lawn, for example, were means of managing (and distracting from) a pervasive sense of threat. Colomina examines the ways that 1950s and later domestic architecture and household technologies absorbed and redeployed technologies developed for war, revealing their common origins and manufacturers, along with their uncannily allied concerns. Colomina's project, like mine, ties the manufacture of the threat by the state and capital to their interests in certain kinds of domestic development and, perhaps more significantly, to activities that would siphon social and political-economic concerns into the relatively benign but consuming (in every sense of the term) projects of home, garden, and family.

My project has parallels with Colomina's, and there is also a historic connection between the issues she addresses and those around children and childhood that concern me here. As is well known, the discipline associated with "better homes and gardens," as well as the tedium, if not tyranny, associated with the myths around controlling domestic details and its putative satisfactions, hit the skids in the 1960s–1970s. Betty Friedan's *The Feminine Mystique* (1963) acknowledged the frustrations associated with the quest for domestic perfection among middle-class women, tapping into a vein of dissatisfaction and anger that helped to propel the U.S. women's movement of the 1960s and 1970s. This dissatisfaction in part helped to fuel an incipient remaking of the heteronormative nuclear family with growing numbers of women entering the labor force, various attempts to change household dynamics, the postponement or rejection of marriage, and unprecedented divorce rates. If the myths and expectations of domestic perfection were busted with these changes, they seem to have reemerged a generation later around children and childhood. That is, anxiety around the political-economic, geopolitical, and environmental future did not recede— and may have been ratcheted up in the late twentieth century. But it was now relayed into securing children's futures and producing perfect childhoods in ways that resonate with the sorts of domestic control identified by Colomina (cf. Coontz 1992; May 2008).

These anxious strivings and affective relationships can be seen in the everyday practices of social reproduction in many contemporary middle-class households in the United States (compare, e.g., Coontz 1992; Lareau 2003). For example, a growing number of parents subscribe to various online services through their school districts, such as ParentConnect, PowerSchool, or Edline, which enable them to monitor daily their children's school experiences so that they are aware of homework assignments, skipped classes, grades, and the like, in real time without having to elicit this information from their children. With these services, which have grown exponentially in the twenty-first century to cover millions of students in thousands of school districts in the United States, parents—or in the words of Edline's pitch, "K-12 stakeholders"—feel a greater sense of control in assuring the competitive advantage of their children in college admissions and indicate that they are better able to keep on top of disciplining them (Banks 2007a, 2007b; Hoffman 2008).

While "student management systems" enable middle-class parents to monitor their children's every educational move in real time, other kinds of services are sought to enrich children's learning so as to better prepare them for the future. Evidence from parents' blogs and electronic networks in various parts of the United States, newspaper articles, program advertisements, and reports from those running childcare services indicates, for example, that language training is prominent among the enrichment activities contemporary middle-class parents seek for their children. Mandarin and Spanish are seen as particularly useful for success in the imagined future economy—although there was a telling tiff in one New York blog regarding one parent's claim that Spanish is a low-status language, perhaps of "political value in the U.S." but lacking in clout for the future, given that "Spanish speaking countries are not part of the world's economic powerhouses." Luckily, Mandarin immersion programs, some for children as young as two years old, are available in about half the states of the United States (http://miparentscouncil.org/us-schools), and dozens of summer camps in the United States and abroad offer Mandarin immersion or language training. Childcare staffing services report sharp increases in requests for Mandarin- or Spanish-speaking (or otherwise bilingual) babysitters and nannies in the hope of saturating the young children in their care with a second language. As non-English-speaking childcare workers develop English-language skills in preparation for employment, they are often surprised to discover their prospective employers insisting that they speak only their own language to their charges.

INVESTING IN CHILDREN

These sorts of material social practices are expressions of middle-class anxiety around the political-economic future. Part of my argument is that the commodification of children and their treatment as accumulation strategies are means by which parents manage this anxiety in what is experienced as a precarious world. Children have long been investments in the future, both familial and more expansive. In this way, children themselves can be understood as accumulation strategies or as commodities absorbing and embodying the energies and ideas of their parents and others whose labors—affective and material—consciously and unconsciously shape them as laboring subjects and social actors (cf. D. Harvey 1998; Sammond 2005). Well into the early decades of capitalist industrialization in the United States, children were an economic asset to their families' production and reproduction and helped secure the economic future of their parents and extended family (cf. Ryan 1981). In the Global North, more quickly among middle-class and wealthier families, children became more of a liability than an asset in the twentieth century as production moved away from the home, infant and child mortality declined, and the tasks and loci of reproducing a differentiated labor force became attenuated and varied, necessitating the development of more specialized institutions of formal education and training outside the home. This shift—with class variations—was essentially complete with the post–World War II baby boom generation.

By the middle of the twentieth century in the United States, the value of children had become more psychic than economic. Children, of course, were psychologically and emotionally important in earlier periods, but as the likelihood of their survival was increasingly assured and their employment relatively more expendable to their households, children became more "priceless" than valuable (Zelizer 1994). Without denying or diminishing the extraordinary and even transcendent experience of having and loving children, it is also the case that "pricelessness" smuggles with it an almost magical investment in the child as at once oneself and one's future. It also fosters a notion of childhood as a precious idyll and seems connected to the new modes of child rearing that became prominent in the United States in the 1950s with the extraordinary popularity of Dr. Benjamin Spock's advice manuals. He advocated a child-centered upbringing that claimed to trust parents' sense of things while constantly unsettling that trust by referring them to experts for all manner of developmental and day-to-day issues that might arise. Dr. Spock suggested seeing children as individuals with their own wills and desires. Of course, catering to these willful, desiring children and producing the loving attachments and ambience their healthy upbringing required intensified the expectations of "good" parenthood, by which he meant motherhood (cf. Douglas and Michaels 2004; Hays 1996).

If the combination of these shifts suggests a loosening of the relationship between work and U.S. middle-class childhood by the middle of the twentieth century, it remains that children are both an economic and psychic investment in the future (as well as good consumers in the present). This "investment" requires great quantities of emotional and reproductive labor, of love and care, as much as focused and diffuse attention to sharing knowledge of all kinds. In an illuminating study of child rearing across class, sociologist Annette Lareau (2003) coined the term "concerted cultivation" to describe middle-class child-rearing practices. In concerted cultivation, the domestic environment within and beyond the home is imagined and constructed as a context for learning that is essentially saturated with opportunities for cultural enrichment. Children's talents are cultivated; learning and development are consciously woven into the activities of everyday life; and chances for exposure to novelty, potential new interests, and rewarding experiences are sought out and seized upon in most middle-class households. These practices are all part of negotiating the field of dreams that is middle-class belonging and stability.

PARENTAL INVOLUTION

The social reproductive practices associated with the concerted cultivation of children are labors of love, but they are also an effective mode of disciplining parents. Their varying forms and contents create another potential terrain of comparison and competition, wherein the cultural forms and practices of class formation make a space of conformity, a space of social life in which middle-class parents cannot avoid participating if their children are to "stay in the game," even if—or especially when—the game is unclear (Liechty 2003; cf. Rouse 1995). As I will discuss below, these issues are crystallized in the 2010 documentary film *Race to Nowhere* and the talk-back sessions that have accompanied its screenings. Writing about the United Kingdom, Valerie Walkerdine and Helen Lucey (1989) take a dim view of these insistent practices of middle-class "domestic pedagogy." When every household routine is available to be turned into a learning situation, parents—particularly mothers—are expected to be ready and accessible for the always latent, teachable moment. Walkerdine and Lucey are astute in marking the disciplining aspects of the affective labor of producing children with the cognitive and communicative capacities associated with middle-class social formations (cf. Clough et al. 2007). Also, they are mindful not only of the sort of tyranny created for middle-class parents but also of how that style of parenting is a tyranny imposed upon working-class and poor households as the best mode for producing viable social subjects (Walkerdine and Lucey 1989; cf. Donzelot 1979; Lareau 2003; McDowell 2007).

It is common for parents and families to work hard to ensure that their children can "make it" in the future, all the more so with the unsure and seemingly shrinking employment prospects following the financial crisis that surfaced in 2008 (cf. Lareau 2003). The backbeat of anxiety about falling behind, which is a familiar rhythm of American middle-class life (Ehrenreich 1989; Newman 1999), quickened in the wake of the layoffs, foreclosures, business closings, and state budget shortfalls precipitated by the crisis, from which the middle class was far from immune. Indeed, one of the fallouts of the crisis, as various states have attempted to balance their budgets by undermining public unions and decimating state and municipal pension and benefits programs, is that one faction of the middle class is pitted against the other (cf. Lutrell 2011). If, in the best of circumstances, middle-class households tend to saturate their children with resources as both a conduit to opportunity and a bulwark against an uncertain future, it is likely that these practices will be stepped up as the anxiety that fuels them is exacerbated by the current political-economic circumstances. Under these conditions, familiar middle-class practices of child rearing, such as Lareau's "concerted cultivation" or sociologist Sharon Hays's "intensive mothering," can go into overdrive, as so much of the popular literature on parenting laments (Hays 1996; Lareau 2003; compare, e.g., Douglas and Michaels 2004; MacVean 2011; Warner 2005). Drawing on Clifford Geertz (1963), I call this congeries of practices "parental involution," that is, the embellishment and elaboration of parenting tasks and concerns that tend not only to absorb parents completely—if sometimes resentfully—but also to distract them, deflecting attention from the political-economic and other structural reasons for their insecurities. They instead take pains to outfit their children as ideal class subjects of the future who embody ever more elaborate, material social relations (cf. Sammond 2005:370).

Among the signs of parental involution are hothouse children and elders who hover so close that they have been dubbed "helicopter parents," along with the flow of material, affective, and psychodynamic resources that produce and enable them. These dynamics are witnessed routinely in the often stiff competition to get into schools that present themselves as conduits to success later in life and, at the other end of the spectrum, in the attenuation of formal education for more and more young people. In New York City—which may be the hyperventilating edge of such anxious routines and thus exposes a number of symptomatic practices—there is even competition among middle-class households for places in prestigious *pre*schools. Parents speak of "safety" preschools, which provide quality education and reasonably good access to prestigious private schools but where acceptance is less cutthroat. There are also "deans of admissions" for preschools and costly seminars or consultants to coach parents through the application process, including written profiles about their toddlers. There are regular stories of expectant parents registering their not yet born children on preschool waiting lists, and there was a front-page news story about an offer to upgrade a stock's rating as part of a parent's appeal for places in a prestigious Manhattan preschool for his toddler twins (Strom 2002).

These practices are repeated with greater intensity and pressure at each step along the way to postsecondary school, where the competition gets more intense each year. It is rarely remarked that this competition is in part an artifact of itself. When high school students routinely apply to more than a dozen universities, as many middle-class youth do, it produces a surfeit of applicants, resulting in lower rates of acceptance to any one place, which then exacerbates everyone's sense of competition further. The solution in most middle-class households has not been to back away from these behaviors but rather to tighten their frenzied embrace. And so we see students taking increasing numbers of Advanced Placement classes, parents writing their sons' and daughters' college application essays, and the growth of industries that prepare students not so much for college but for the testing and admissions procedures. Private preparatory classes for the standardized college entrance exams have become routine for middle-class kids, but many families now avail themselves of private consultants who charge exorbitant fees—$10,000 is not unusual—to coach parents and students through the admissions process, putting what used to be largely students' own responsibility into adult hands, parental or professional.

Parental involution is reflected in and is evident throughout the every-day practices associated with the "overscheduled child." By some accounts, homework has increased more than 50 percent since the mid-1980s, and school and extracurricular athletics have become less playful. School and after-school sports have become more competitive and strategic, taken on by many as a means to an end. Although sports scholarships for low-income students remain an important if problematic pathway to higher education, athletics and other after-school activities are increasingly engaged in as part of a strategic production of self among middle-class youth. Some parents even encourage their children to play sports that are less popular, such as lacrosse, or learn instruments that are less common, such as the oboe, because they imagine that these choices will help their children stand out. In a different register, Lareau (2003) notes that middle-class parents frequently commented on how the competitiveness of youth sports prepares children for succeeding in a competitive work environment. In another realm of disciplining or self-constituting, many middle-class children take two or more extracurricular classes or private lessons of some sort every week. As noted above, parents and others are increasingly advocating exposure to languages such as Mandarin, but children also take lessons in the arts, technology, and even finance and money management for their imagined cultural currency in the future (e.g., Martin 2002). A growing number of summer programs for teens and young adults offer young people from the Global North an opportunity to do service work in the Global South. Although these programs give young people a chance to visit another part of the world and volunteer their services, albeit for a substantial fee, virtually all concerned acknowledge that their popularity is linked to the ways they help burnish participating students' résumés.

So much enrichment can be exhausting to parents and children. Indeed, young people are increasingly diagnosed with a spectrum of psychological and physical problems, learning disabilities, and affective and cognitive disorders. Physicians, schools, and the popular media report "epidemics" of ADHD (attention-deficit/hyperactivity disorder), depression, bipolarity, eating disorders, and learning disabilities of all kinds among students, even at very young ages. As a result, there is a growing number of medicated children of all classes, another reflection of parental anxiety over every nuance of their children's well-being and their capacity to meet schools' and other institutions' benchmarks of achievement. Some diagnoses are strategic—another sort of management tool—as parents seek to have their children diagnosed with a mild learning disability so as to gain a bit more time to complete standardized tests and perhaps entitle them to other forms of assistance at school. The recourse to medication is, of course, part of a broader trend in the United States to medicate rather than treat psychological problems and advances the pharmaceuticalization of daily life.

CHILDREN AS ACCUMULATION STRATEGIES

All of these cultural forms and practices are intended to sharpen middle-class young people's competitive advantage, enhancing their value as accumulation strategies. But, given such relentlessness, these also affect children's identity formation and erode the intrinsic nature of childhood and its pleasures—the joy, for instance, of "doing nothing." Many middle-class American teens, for example, are increasingly strategic in the things they do, sometimes seeming to join activities or do things in a calculated, almost entrepreneurial, self-fashioning way as much as, if not more than, for the experience itself. The proliferation of programs to volunteer in other countries is part of this trend. But all of these middle-class practices of subject formation—whether on the part of parents, children, or others—hover alongside the figuration of the child "at risk" or as waste, which reminds us that access to the value accumulated in the middle-class child has become more precarious in recent years and encourages vigilance in its production and tending.

Even if, to a great extent, the "return" paid to parents is psychic, it remains that children are accumulation strategies. Although most middle-class families in the United States do not expect economic support from their children, the payoff comes to parents in multiple ways. There are the deep gratification, unparalleled pleasure, and profound joy in seeing one's children grow and succeed at what draws them. I do not want to diminish these emotions in any way or discount the time, love, and energy that foster them, but it remains important to attend to what else animates contemporary parenthood and its involution, including parents' satisfaction at fashioning a commodity of great value, their sense of accomplishment in reaching toward "perfection," and the narcissistic pleasure of their investment realized. But, as Marx reminds us, any commodity conceals the social relations that have gone into its production, and this is where a key project of middle-class parenting is exposed. Whether through the hard work of concerted cultivation or the more souped-up variety I am calling parental involution, middle-class parents are determined to pass on their class position to their children. Children as accumulation strategies are packed with resources that their parents imagine and hope will position them well in the market—cultural as much as political-economic—in which they come of age. My research suggests that the lure of this means of intergenerational capital accumulation is not only practically irresistible among contemporary middle-class parents in the United States but also intensified under conditions of ontological insecurity.

The production of and response to the 2010 film *Race to Nowhere* well illustrates this phenomenon and its often contradictory emotions and material social practices. *Race to Nowhere* is a powerful documentary produced and co-directed by Vicki Abeles, a former Wall Street lawyer and current San Francisco Bay area mother of three. The film is billed as a call to action against the anxious and harried conditions of young people's lives and the overheated educational and domestic environments associated with them. A first-time filmmaker, Abeles was inspired to make the film when she recognized that her child's panic attacks and stress-related illness were symptomatic of much broader problems around educational achievement and childhood success. Drawing on interviews with teachers, students, parents, and a range of professionals concerned with young people's well-being or educational practices, the film focuses on many of the concerns I have raised here but also takes on teen suicide, teacher despair and frustration, widespread cheating, the intensification of homework, the sprawl of high-stakes testing, kids' use of prescription and other drugs, children's and teens' anxiety, overwhelmed parents, and so on, as among the plagues of growing up in the educational environments spawned by the fear-mongering, "achievement-oriented" residues of a couple of key U.S. education policy documents: "A Nation at Risk," produced during the Reagan era, and George W. Bush's "No Child Left Behind." The film makes a strong if somewhat relentless case that childhood, family life, and education are being destroyed by these stressful practices, pinning most of the problem on the reduction of education to a bottomless pit of testing, teaching to the test, and endless assessments of "performance" and "achievement." The film takes pains to argue that "the dark side of America's achievement culture" —its tagline—affects all groups no matter what class or color, and surely it does, but Abeles concentrates on middle-class and privileged households struggling with and reproducing this culture.

Race to Nowhere is intended to spur a community-based but widespread response, and its mode of circulation is key to this prospect. Having failed to get a distributor, the canny Abeles determined to have community-sponsored screenings of the film nationwide over a six-month period. Circulating it through festivals, local theaters, schools, community organizations, and the like, and encouraging those hosting a screening to include a discussion afterward, Abeles and her collaborators sparked a national discussion and touched a raw nerve. The film's website offers access to various research documents that substantiate and extend its contentions and provides guidance for concerned parents, educators, and others to respond to and take action against the partially self-inflicted tyranny it portrays. "Unplugging" is a key metaphor in the film and the conversations around it.

I attended my first screening in Charlottesville, Virginia, and saw in microcosm all the issues the film raises and their near death-grip on people's imaginations and psyches. The raw nerve touched by the film is one of deep contradiction. When children are an accumulation strategy and the economic future feels so unyielding, the pressured practices scrutinized by Abeles may feel like lifelines. But children are never *just* accumulation strategies, so the affective experience of their striving is painful to witness and perpetrate—and yet parents do, all the time.

I am a veteran of events in the performance space of Charlottesville High School—school plays, concerts, graduations, and honors ceremonies. I almost always arrive with seconds to spare, my partner or I frantically parking the car, the other one running in to get seats. The evening of the *Race to Nowhere* screening was no different, but I had assumed that I would be one of only a few dozen people there—not many had purchased the $10 ticket online, and it was a cold Tuesday night. So I was shocked when the parking lot was absolutely packed in a way I had never seen it, forcing me to scramble to a whole other area of the school and park in one of the most distant spaces even there. Clearly, I had misread the situation. I got a seat near the back just as the film was starting. When the lights came up, I was not surprised to see that the middle-class audience was nearly all white, even though about 25 percent of Charlottesville is not, but I was surprised to see many high school students in attendance, many of whom expressed their concerns about too much homework, too much pressure, and too little downtime but also their reluctance "to be at a school that doesn't push" them, since that was "all [they'd] ever known."

A panel of three—the high school principal, an admissions officer at the University of Virginia, and a psychologist-educator from a local Montessori school—led the post-film discussion. The audience was clearly moved by the documentary and found much that resonated with their own experiences. From all over the auditorium, parents, teachers, and kids raised questions and comments in sync with the movie's clear message: "There's so much testing!" "Most of us are average," "We need to change the culture," "We need to change household practices," "Most successful people in this country did not go to prestigious schools," and so on. But the "dark side of America's achievement culture" is dialectically sutured to its bright side, and no doubt the audience for a film like *Race to Nowhere* spends a lot of time in its shadows. And so it started: "If we deemphasize Advanced Placement classes, how can we change the attitudes of kids so that they are not such high achievers or don't see themselves as losers if they take regular classes?" The principal was sympathetic to this parent's question but noted how much peer pressure there was to take the advanced classes. Although he and the psychologist encouraged parents, teachers, and counselors to help students be less (over)achievement oriented, the fact that most middle-class white students in the school had been "tracked" early in their careers into advanced and honors classes went unremarked. But just as the figure of the child as waste hovers around the child as accumulation strategy, so do those lesser educational tracks haunt the advanced ones. Among middle-class kids there is a lot of "peer pressure" not to be a "loser." And for these young people and their parents, the prize is to get into a good university, but also part of the pleasure is to study with kids like themselves. The admissions officer on hand did nothing to allay their concerns, though his tortured responses attempted it at every turn. When a middle-aged middle-school counselor, educated at a midwestern state university, asked why state schools "insisted on such high standards," the admissions officer responded with a question: "If the University of Virginia offered open enrollment, where would you put them?" Blaming high school students for applying to too many places—"We're the tail, not the dog"—he noted that universities "cannot change the culture" and emphasized that his school competes with the top private universities for "the best." When a parent asked how her son would look in the admissions process if he did not take a battery of Advanced Placement classes, the representative said he encouraged students to be well rounded and take other things, such as music and art. But then, unhelpfully, he added that "if they did not want to be a total 'grind'" (a student who studies all the time), his university and many others have arrangements with community colleges (two-year colleges open to almost all high school graduates) that can then funnel students to the better four-year schools. As an anxious murmur spread through the house, he somewhat lamely and unconvincingly added, "We like pointy students too." The race all of a sudden did not feel as if it were to nowhere. For middle-class households, it never really did—and never really can as long as parents are determined to pass on their class position.

Middle-class children in some deep sense know that they are accumulation strategies for their families and for themselves. In an ethnographic account of child rearing in a dozen American households in the mid-1990s, Annette Lareau (2003) makes a distinction between the cultural logic of middle-class parenting practices—what she calls concerted cultivation—and that of working-class and poor households, which she refers to as the "accomplishment of natural growth." She marks the different relationships these parenting styles have to children's time, language, experiences, institutional relationships, embodiment, routines, and so on, and notes that the practices she associates with concerted cultivation arose (in the 1980s–1990s) among middle-class parents who were generally brought up (in the 1950s–1960s) in the manner she associates with the accomplishment of natural growth. She suggests that some of this shift can be traced to the "rationalization" and commodification of modern life taking roost in the household but also makes a tantalizing association between these new practices and the insecurity of middle-class parents in the 1990s, who seem to be the first generation of Americans to imagine that their children's economic prospects might not be as good as their own. Concerted cultivation is intended to make their children more competitive as they come of age in insecure times.

My research on U.S. middle-class childhood in the twenty-first century picks up where Lareau left off. The fear of falling and failing seems even more palpable for this generation, their cultivation that much more concerted. Looking at some of the parenting practices associated with children as accumulation strategies, I have tried to analyze their entailments for subject formation, everyday life, and social reproduction and to understand the affective politics spurring and spurred by these intimate practices and the ways they rub against more global forces and help to manage anxiety about the future (cf. Freeman, chapter 4, and Heiman, chapter 10, this volume). It is my contention that the ontological insecurity and everyday anxiety stoked by contemporary political-economic, geopolitical, and environmental conditions are channeled into managing and framing childhood in ways that are materialized and expressed in the bodies and historical geographies of middle-class children in particular ways. As I hope I have made clear, U.S. childhood and the figurations of the child as accumulation strategy, commodity, and waste call forth particular modes of middle-class parenting that tend to concentrate parents' attention on their children in ways that discipline the parents and exhaust their resources and also sometimes come at great psychic, emotional, and physical cost to their children. At the same time, these practices also divert attention from social childhood—the well-being of everyone's children—as if no child could get ahead unless another was left behind.

I want to understand what drives these absorptions and draws middle-class parents away from a more political, collectively oriented response to contemporary currents of anxiety and what feels like a future with few guarantees. In other words, I want to think about how middle-class parents might not just unplug but instead be part of a political project that reimagines and expands the field of dreams that can be seen as defining middle-class experience. How might some of the vital concern and enormous effort that I have documented regarding the production of children as accumulation strategies—intended to conserve and expand household capital into the future—be rerouted so that such wealth is expanded and shared across households and class? How might the affective work of parents concerning their children's well-being and security over the life course and treating the future as something we make happen and habitable be redirected to a more social project, even under conditions of great uncertainty? Such a project might be better for the children who now absorb these efforts so singularly.

These sorts of concerns give childhood its resonance and make securing it so urgent. They open a great and important space for political organizing and for finding or making alternative routes to countering the sources of anxiety, insecurity, and fear that seem so prevalent in the present moment. As one fraction of the middle class squares off against another in the United States in the second decade of the twenty-first century, just managing one's own children's childhood seems besides the point, especially as the very grounds of that childhood are likely to be among the casualties of this squaring off. When public education, public sector workers' benefits, and children's health care get scripted as "entitlements," the middle class is in crisis. These disconcerting conditions present enormous political opportunities, to make and secure an expanded—and expanding—field of dreams.

Acknowledgments

Thank you to Carla Freeman, Rachel Heiman, and Mark Liechty for their acumen, encouragement, and inspiring suggestions and guidance all along the way. Special thanks to Rachel for inviting me to participate in the seminar, her humor, and her extraordinary—and much tested—patience and amazing knack for guilt-free cajoling. I learned a tremendous amount from my fellow seminarians, and thank them and the SAR staff for an amazing week with all kinds of delicious food for thought.

Notes

1. The U.S. birthrate bottomed out at fewer than 15 live births per thousand people in 1973. The birthrate did not start to go up again until 1977 and then increased slowly until 1991 when it reached 16.7. It has declined in the years since, hovering at just under 14 per thousand in the twenty-first century.

2. See Rachel Heiman (chapter 10, this volume) for a discussion of how these various socioeconomic shifts inspired class-based anxieties in an American suburb.

8

A Middle-Class Public at Mexico's Northern Border

Rihan Yeh

MIDDLENESS AT THE BORDER

In 1930, Robert Redfield wrote, "Mexico is in no small part modern.… In the more sophisticated villages of the north, in the middle classes of the cities everywhere, are to be found a people much like the masses in our own country. They not only can read, but they do read. The folk hear rumor; these people read the news" (Redfield 1930:3). His tone is cautious and didactic. It warns already: Mexico's modernity is not, in all eyes, assured. His U.S. readers ("*our* own country," he writes) might have thought that the distinctions he draws separated them from Mexico as a whole. They might, that is, have taken the U.S.-Mexico border itself as the line marking the split between modern and not. Redfield tries to resituate that line. But the border is always ready to reimpose itself as an insurmountable gulf separating Mexico from modernity, relegating its urban middle classes to irrelevance in a country pervaded by the dominant mark of the backward, the indigenous, the rural, the "folk," as Redfield calls them.

The issue of how to relate to the United States is a national preoccupation for Mexico, but in the northern border city of Tijuana, the problem is relentlessly literal. An integral part of the metropolitan constellation of southern California, Tijuana is nonetheless separated from it by one of the most fortified international boundaries in the world. A city of perhaps two million inhabitants, Tijuana began its exponential growth with the "vice industry" (Taylor 2002) of America's Prohibition. From gambling and prostitution to the violence of contemporary drug trafficking, Tijuana is apt to appear as a nightmare of modernization gone wrong. But though it may be "the most celebrated bastion of chaos on the border" (Urrea 1993:112), quite a different myth circulates locally: Tijuana as a city of opportunity, of upward mobility, of a modernity accessible here as it is not elsewhere in Mexico. In the context of what is often called Mexico's "neoliberal turn," this local myth takes on national resonances. Against the city's "black legend" of moral and social dissolution, those who have found some success here insist on Tijuana as the place where a new society can come into its own: a miniature Mexico of and for the middle class.

Warding off the same demons as Redfield did, those in Tijuana who aspire to middle-class, urban modernity (cf. Schielke, chapter 2, this volume) try to prove that if a good part of Mexico is not that, at least their city is. Their everyday relations with the United States are a crucial, but intensely ambiguous, part of their efforts to situate themselves on the right side of the divide between modern and not. A generation ago, it is said, "everyone" did his laundry and bought milk and eggs in the United States. Still today, with up to a two-hour wait at the port of entry—likely the most traversed in the world, with 110,000 crossings daily reported (Blum 2007)—people cross into the commercial cornucopia of southern California for innumerable reasons, not only for work, school, and shopping but also on errands as petty as picking up mail. In a 2000 study, Alegría (2009:86) calculated that 55 percent of Tijuana residents could cross the border legally. Besides U.S. citizens and permanent residents, many hold a Border Crossing Card, a ten-year visa that permits short expeditions to the United States (but not employment there). Legal, documented border crossing provides one of the most fundamental idioms of class distinction in Tijuana, and the way in which U.S. recognition thus underwrites middle-class status ratchets to unbearable tension the inherent contradictions of projects for an authentically *Mexican* modernity.

Suspended between the United States and "the poor,"[1] the masses of migrants constantly arriving from "the South," Tijuana reveals with particular clarity that the middleness of the middle class in a country like Mexico is a matter not merely of its position in the class structure of its "own" society, but of a delicately negotiated suspension between the national and the foreign, past and future, backwardness and modernity. The middle class has a special privilege and burden in mediating a modernity that seems always to come from "outside" (cf. Liechty 2003:61–86). It stands on the cusp; in this sense, the border is at the heart of what the middle class in the "developing" world is all about.[2] The vulnerabilities that so bedevil any attempt to be properly middle class in Tijuana, in the shadow of the U.S.-Mexico border, reflect far more general conundrums of middleness.

CLASSES AND PUBLICS

The binary oppositions Redfield (1930) traces are well known and by no means particular to Mexico. The last, though, stands out, and it is the opposition Redfield makes most emphatically, as if it somehow sums up and gives form to the others: "The folk hear rumor; these people read the news." That which is modern, urban, and middle-class in Mexico coheres, Redfield seems to suggest, in its news reading—in its formation, that is, as a public. In this chapter, I expand on this suggestion in order to examine the conundrums of middleness at the border. News reading and associated genres of informed "rational debate" appear as key to the performative processes by which a middle-class public takes shape in Tijuana.[3] Attention to the ethnographic details of how it does so, I argue, reveals some chronic contradictions in projects for middle-class collective being.

My approach to publics here is much indebted to Michael Warner's (2002:90) definition of them as, among other things, "the social space created by the reflexive circulation of discourse." *Circulation* should be understood to refer not to the physical movement of text artifacts, but to the semiotic processes of recognition and uptake by which certain forms come to be seen as in movement, as "the same" as others (cf. Lee and LiPuma 2002 ; Silverstein and Urban 1996). The practice of news reading, for example, involves the routine imagination of both the extent of distribution and the periodicity of publication (cf. Anderson 1983).

Through these processes of circulation, a sense of groupness, of collective subjectivity, may be evoked and inhabited on an everyday level: over my morning coffee, I join the "we" of the news-reading public.[4] The first-person plural is perhaps the most blatant form of the reflexivity Warner emphasizes, in which "we" doubles back upon itself to indicate "we who participate in communications such as the present one" (cf. Lee 1997; Urban 2001). Reflexivity is performative; it makes the group into a living, present reality. When Redfield, for example, addresses his readers as fellow Americans, he subtly includes them as part of "the masses in *our* own country." They are likely news readers themselves; undeniably, they read anthropological monographs, a not unrelated genre of realist reportage. As they recognize themselves in Redfield's casual representation, his text performatively constitutes them as a U.S. (modern, urban, middle-class) public.

Whether readers recognize themselves in a representation such as

Redfield's has much to do with their personal subjectivity, their "I" and how it can find a place in "we." To feel oneself part of and in turn to voice a middle-class "we," exposing oneself to the dangers of mis- or nonrecognition, depend not only on continual processes of recruitment to role in interaction, of negotiating the position from which one speaks (cf. Goffman 1979; Silverstein 2004), but also on one's broader fashioning as middle-class. Publics thus have everything to do with the institutions that form one as a subject over a lifetime of interpellation. In Tijuana, prime among these is the border and the U.S. visa as an emblem of status that sums up past achievements (education, property, employment, grooming, and self-presentation are all reviewed in the application interview) and enables future access to key arenas of consumption (goods are often prized for their U.S. provenance, though always with the nationalist caveat that the items in question are either not available or absurdly expensive in Tijuana). The formation of the middle class as a public is thus intimately tied to some very objective facts of life. But without a sense of how collective subjectivity is evoked in interaction, analysis of the middle class must remain at the level of statistical demarcations of socioeconomic difference or individual engagement with structural factors.

Studies of classes as publics of various sorts are in fact numerous, but despite increased concern in recent decades with the discursive processes that help constitute classes as social collectivities (Ortner 1998:3), the approach has not been clearly articulated as such.[5] Conversely, the question of socioeconomic class has not played a prominent part in discussions of publics, nor does it guide the broader, mostly politico-philosophical debates about the public sphere. It is worth recalling, then, that Jürgen Habermas (1989) in his foundational text argued that the bourgeois public sphere emerged in seventeenth-century Europe precisely as the network of institutions through which a new class consolidated itself. Through newspapers and novels, theaters and coffeehouses and salons, all conceived of as open, egalitarian spaces of rational debate, "public opinion" emerged as something weighty enough to impinge on state authority itself. Through the public sphere, the bourgeoisie was able to do just what Marx (1963[1852]:124) so famously claimed the small-holding peasants of France were incapable of: "enforc[e] their class interest in their own name." For a class to cohere as a group, it must be able, in effect, to say "we."

Tijuana's middle-class public is no bourgeois public sphere. But as a model, the bourgeois public sphere exerts a normative influence—in no small part, thanks to Habermas's work—on ideals of (neo)liberal democracy circulating in Mexico today.[6] In the following section, I sketch the diffuse complex of associations that, in Mexico, at once link the middle class with such ideals and interpellate a middle-class public. If news reading and (purportedly rational) debate appear as important ways to claim modernity, these practices are attributed much the same value that theorists like Habermas argue these had in the rise of the bourgeoisie and the birth of the modern nation-state. The Mexican middle class need not share any structural or sociological features with the old bourgeoisie to take up an ideology derived, in great part, from it. Supposedly, in contrast to aristocratic systems of fixed status, "anyone" can participate in rational debate. Those who do are the ones endowed with the promise of a new society, emerging precisely *between* elites and plebeians. Reason appears as a social leveler, the first principle of meritocracy, and full of democratic promise— with no regard for the fact that the performance of rational debate is saturated by power relations at several levels. These premises are fundamental to the articulation of a middle-class "we" in Mexico today and in Tijuana in particular.

To examine the middle class as a public highlights the formation of collective subjectivity as it is engaged and reproduced on the ground in a panoply of interrelated sites and genres running from the mass media to everyday conversation and back. I will first examine some mass-mediated discourses that speak to and evoke a middle-class "we" in Mexico, and then will compare these with the common representation of Tijuana as a middle-class city, as voiced to me in an interview. Finally, I will present two extended ethnographic examples, one highlighting the contradictions of Tijuana's middle-class "we" vis-à-vis "the poor" and the other its contradictions vis-à-vis the United States. In both cases, performances of rational debate appear at the crux of the articulation of a middle-class "we" and of the conundrums that assail it.

A MIDDLE-CLASS PUBLIC IN MEXICO

After a talk at the University of California, San Diego, Denise Dresser, a prominent Mexican political analyst and academic, fielded a question about what options Mexican voters have, given the dire panorama of "dysfunctional democracy" Dresser had painted.[7] In response, she focused on "what professional, educated middle classes can do." That is, she replaced "voters" with "middle classes." She concluded the question-and-answer session by declaring, "Revolutionary nationalism has run its course, and we're going to have to…create, build, aspire to a much more liberal country." By "revolutionary nationalism," she referred to the political system built in the wake of Mexico's 1910 revolution, which was of socialist bent but is often accused of institutionalizing cronyism and corporativism. The "we" of her address are the "professional, educated middle classes," including herself and her audience, for many in attendance were Mexican. Dresser evokes the middle class by positing its agency, almost automatically, as the one that will drive the making of a more modern Mexico.

As Claudio Lomnitz (2003:142) has noted, the Mexican middle class appears as the "avatar" of the national narrative, the forerunner of a "we" that seems always to be only just realizing itself. If in Latin America it represents a collective future to be aspired to, this is, Michael Jiménez (1999:217) points out, in no small part thanks to the social scientific literature that, over the past half century or more, has enshrined the middle classes as "the principal ideal object of historical change"—regardless of particular authors' optimism or pessimism as to the region's "progress" in this direction. Dresser's association of the middle class with the possibility of a "more liberal country" comes out of a robust literature.[8] However various and fragmented the middle classes might be objectively, this academic discourse has consistently projected onto them a "sense of themselves as the ballast of their nations, [having] corner [*sic*] on the respect for the rule of law and the devotion to the well-being of their fellow citizens" (Jiménez 1999:217). The middle class appears as the civic class, the law-abiding class, the class of the liberal democratic future.

These academic writings are authoritative texts; they bear a normative force, and their representations of the middle class are much more than projections. Not only individuals but also governments orient to such representations of the middle class as the emblem of modernity; if individuals aspire to middle-class status, nation-states aspire to join the ranks of the world's "middle-class societies." With powerful institutions impelling discourses of (neo)liberal democracy across the globe, academic texts emphasizing the middle classes' role in this (doubtless variegated) project have influence far beyond their own limited circulation. Dresser herself exemplifies a node through which political and social theory is transformed and retransmitted to a broader public—broader, even, than the UCSD talk would suggest. Recently, a colleague showed me an opinion piece by Dresser defending the right to free speech, forwarded by friends in a working-class neighborhood of Mexico City. However complex or even nebulous the links, everyday understandings in Mexico of the valence of "middle class" are not disconnected from academic social and political theory.

In late 2010, a book titled *Middle-Class: Poor No More, Not Yet Developed*

(De la Calle and Rubio 2010b) caused some stir in Mexico City intellectual circles.[9] The implicit noun modified by the adjectival title is Mexico itself; the authors argue that despite politicians' harping on the poverty-stricken masses, this discourse is out of touch with reality. Mexico, they claim, is now a country with a middle-class majority. In a magazine article published earlier in the year—part of a special issue on the middle classes—the same authors provide a slew of figures (mostly to do with consumption) to prove their point. They call the middle class "the essence of development" and declare that it "fits naturally" with democracy; they treat corporativism and citizenship as mutually exclusive, identifying the middle class with the latter. They conclude, "One might ask if Mexico has come of age in 200 years. The answer lies in its capacity to become a middle-class country" (De la Calle and Rubio 2010a).

The special magazine issue, the book (which sold out in Mexico City, booksellers told me, two or three months after its release), and the numerous reviews in major national dailies all linked together to interpellate a Mexican reading public that might well take up the arguments provided as vindicating the existence and strength of a national middle-class "we." This did happen. "We the middle class are the majority," wrote one reader in a comment appended to the online edition of a review.[10] The uses of the first-person plural in the online comments performatively clinched the reflexive underpinning of the articles as circulating texts; they prove the readers' uptake and their interpellation into a Mexican middle-class public.

Other readers, though, objected strongly to the book's argument. One called it "a marvel of propaganda," good material for the political "zombies" who insist, "You see, we did it, we're in the antechamber of the First World." Another accused a reviewer of being a "cheerleader," complete with "pom-poms" and a "little blue and white skirt"—a reference to the right-wing National Action Party (PAN)—shouting, "We's middle class!...Nothing's happening here!" The last remark implies that to call Mexico middle-class is a politically interested denial of poverty and inequality. As the one negative review I read put it, "those who sustain the argument about the 'middle-class' majority are critical of those who speak of Mexico as a country of poor people" (*Nexos* 2010). Two visions of the country, two projects for national becoming, are at stake in this debate on demographics: as Dresser put it, a "more liberal country" versus "revolutionary nationalism."

In Mexico, the ascendance of the middle class as a figure of national potential necessitates the decline of another: the *pueblo*, "the people," marked as a lower-class entity, which achieved status as the national subject proper, thanks to the 1910 revolution. With the revolution, the liberalism that had (however contradictorily) marked Mexico's nineteenth century (cf. Hale 1989) took a distinctly socialist turn—but soon ossified into a political system that is now frequently labeled a de facto dictatorship. The Party of the Institutionalized Revolution (PRI) was able to ensure its electoral victories at the federal level until 2000, when the right-wing PAN won the presidency for the first time.[11] Since 1940, the PRI had moved decisively to reconcile itself with the middle classes (Loaeza 1988:112), but the rhetoric of social revolution and of the pueblo as national subject remained the crux of state legitimacy. The PRI's name itself indicates this fact, as do the comments of certain participants in the debate on *Middle-Class: Poor No More, Not Yet Developed*, who feel themselves left out of the national project: "The Mexican political schema constructed in the PRI era," wrote one, "DOES NOT contemplate and NEVER contemplated the middle class." These readers, however, are not nearly as marginalized as they feel. Deriding one of the favorite themes of the first PAN presidency, a 2006 newspaper article declared sarcastically, "With the government of 'change,' all of Mexico belongs to the 'robust and thriving middle class'" (Fernández-Vega 2006). Official discourse is on their side. The pueblo does remain an important figure, but it has lost status with the "democratic transition" of 2000 as it had not in almost a century. Even in the midst of multiple crises and intense disillusionment, the middle class has found a new lease on its life as national subject. In Tijuana, the stakes of this shift are even higher. Baja California, a third of whose population resides in Tijuana, was the first state to vote the PAN into governorship back in 1989, and the party has remained in power there since. With 1989 as the herald of the 2000 "democratic transition," Tijuana as middle class could truly feel itself the avatar of the national narrative.

Of Brazil in the 1990s, Maureen O'Dougherty (2002) suggests that news of all sorts represented the middle class as the hardest hit by the economic crisis and that these representations interpellated a middle-class reading public as the subject of the crisis—and thus as the national subject itself. A slew of Mexican news articles seem to be doing something similar: "The Middle Class, The Most Damaged by the Economic Crisis" (Milenio 2009b); "Sacrificial Lamb: The Middle Class" (Milenio 2009a); "Building a Bigger Middle Class Is a Goal for Mexican Society" (Miranda 2009).[12] As William Mazzarella (2005:1) points out of India, such concern with the middle class must be taken seriously as a symptom of liberalization in its own right. Even and especially in the alarm over its demise, the middle class emerges as the site on which a whole narrative of modernization, of the happy development of constitutional democracy and a market economy, bears down and demands to be made a living reality.

The participants in the debate on *Middle-Class: Poor No More, Not Yet Developed* were not all sure, either, of the middle class's objective economic existence. But the debate nonetheless produced them as a middle-class public in an even deeper and more intuitive sense than the voicings of "we" mentioned earlier. One reader expressed this explicitly: "We are the ones who read newspapers, magazines…and expound our opinions here or in other media." The middle class, here, appears to have "corner" (as Jiménez [1999] puts it) not just on the rule of law or liberal democracy, but on one of its foundational pillars according to a tradition of political theory perhaps best exemplified by Habermas: rational, informed debate among the citizenry. The middle class, this reader insists, is synonymous with the news-reading public itself.

This representation of "we news readers" as the middle class itself went unchallenged by other readers. Whereas those who agreed with the book often used the first-person plural, those who objected did not: they did not voice any alternative collective subjectivity, whether of the middle class or the pueblo. In the broader national public sphere, the pueblo is not inert; it speaks for itself to dispute the middle class's status as the national subject. But despite all the argumentation, the debate over *Middle-Class* remains the sphere of appearance of a national middle-class "we," with all its (neo) liberal associations. If De la Calle and Rubio write of "*deliberative* liberal democracy" (2010a; my emphasis), their readers perform, in their online comments, their own deliberation. As they do so, they repeat a constitutive conundrum of rational debate as a figure of modern, democratic promise.

Habermas's elevation of the bourgeois public sphere as normative model rested on his interpretation of the role of argumentative reason in it. Though he recognized that the bourgeois public sphere was in fact highly exclusive (only educated, property-holding males need apply), he saw the value it accorded reason as an emancipatory potential that would slowly break down the boundaries of class and gender. Jodi Dean (2002), however, argues that the bourgeois public sphere's exclusion of the lower classes was constitutive—the public of rational debate *depends* on the figure of the masses who need others to think and speak for them. It must re-create them at every step.

The first conundrum that haunts the middle class is this simultaneous emphasis on equal status via rational debate and on denial that "the poor" could participate. The readers discussing *Middle-Class* repeat it in their

RIHAN YEH

attempts to speak *for* the poor, but always from a position as middle-class and hence properly versed in debate. Tijuana plays out this conundrum in intensified form. The border formalizes and polarizes the opposition between middle class and pueblo; here, the latter is all too often identified with the (illegal) labor migrant to the United States. As Tijuana tries to articulate itself as a city, it inscribes itself within the struggle between the middle class and the pueblo over which should be the legitimate national subject, a broad conflict over models for national becoming that would differently privilege various sectors of the population. It does so by trying to excise the pueblo from Tijuana proper, by refusing to acknowledge it as part of "us" at any level. This denied struggle sets the stage for the tensions implicit in the voicings of "we"—"we *tijuanenses*," "we Mexicans"—in the examples that follow.

THE PUBLICIST

When, in the midst of the 2006 electoral campaign, I walked into the PRI's Tijuana offices, the person on whom it fell to deal with me was the party's local publicist. A middle-aged woman, bright and candid in manner, she did not hesitate to grant me an interview on the spot. We began by talking about her work for the party (which had recently made a comeback in Tijuana). She explained that though the PRI sent campaign material from Mexico City, "the local reality in Tijuana is different," and she was obliged to adjust what was sent. "Not all the public is the same," she told me. "Before, it was conceived of as a mass. But it must be segmented." When I asked what the segments in Tijuana were, she answered, "First and foremost, those who have the least." They are the ones who come to the party offices and demand assistance. Never before in her life, she confided, had she seen so many poor people as in her year with the PRI. Before, when she worked for the PAN, she never saw them, for the poorest people in the PAN, she said, were of a "middle economic level." When I asked what she thought of the commonplace that Tijuana is a middle-class city, she agreed with it readily and tried to reconcile this with her earlier statement: "[The existence of the poor] is a reality we don't want to recognize. I didn't want to recognize it. [How curious] how we appropriate Tijuana and don't want to see what it was turning into."

The publicist's idea of her city, she says, has been changed by her experience with the PRI. And yet, even as she tells me that the public in Tijuana is now composed "first and foremost" of the poor, she reproduces the stereotype of Tijuana as middle-class. The "we" she voices herself as part of

198

refers clearly to a middle class understood as the city's original core, pre-dating the arrival of the poor.[13] "They" are not part of the city's true "we." This middle-class "we" becomes the very basis upon which she addresses me as anthropologist and outsider: not merely as employee of the PRI but as native tijuanense—"proudly tijuanense and proudly Mexican," as she put it—something the poor, always assumed to be migrants from the South, can never fully be part of.

The publicist's representation of Tijuana as middle-class reflects far more widely circulating discourses; her "we" appears as a local form of the Mexican middle-class public that took shape in the news readers' debate, repeating not only its stereotypes of party–class alignment but also its liberal aspirations for the nation. Her initial emphasis on "the poor" matches the stereotypes of PRI discourse that so many participants in the debate on *Middle-Class: Poor No More, Not Yet Developed* found outdated. As she speaks, though, the traction of this representation slips. In the very moment of its troubling, in the very moment that the publicist recognizes that her city is full of the poor, the middle-class "we" reemerges as the true Tijuana, in clear distinction from the PRI's constituency. At another point, the publicist explains to me, "It's a problem in our society that people seek paternal governments." She echoes the distaste for corporativism, a distasteassociated with "revolutionary nationalism" and the PRI, that the authors of *Middle-Class* emphasize as well. Since those who come to the PRI might be said to come seeking paternal favors, the publicist implies that authoritarianism is a "problem" created by the poor from the South. In the same gesture, she signals her own commitment to a more (neo)liberal vision of the self-reliant citizen, who eschews any form of vote buying and is not in need of social assistance.

While the publicist emphasized her nationalism, she also confessed that, married to a U.S. citizen, she now clamors to him, "Emigrate me already!" If the first conundrum of the middle-class "we" is its relation to the poor, the second is its relation to the United States. References to the United States were rife in the debate on *Middle-Class*. They revealed the United States as a benchmark of modernity and the source of a measuring gaze, but not the more pernicious tensions involved with engaging it. When, in San Diego, Dresser told her audience, "We're going to have to… build…a much more liberal country," she slid between addressing them as concerned *Mexican* citizens and as "you" citizens of a "functional democracy."[14] She thus sutured the Mexican middle-class "we" to an international world of opining citizens, the distinguished sort who would attend such an event as this one (a complimentary bottle of tequila on each table, a former U.S. ambassador introducing the talk). This suturing is both crucial to the middle class and deeply problematic.

Again, the middle class repeats in contemporary form a constitutive conundrum of the original bourgeois public sphere. Kant, one of its early theorists, portrays the enlightened citizen as formed in a transnational circulation of texts. The "public in the truest sense of the word" (Kant 1970:56) is a cosmopolitan reading public. But the impulse to move beyond national borders must be curbed, Kant writes, and reason put to the service of the nation-state. The tension between foreign and national is not always so easy to manage: rational debate should put one on a par with one's peers abroad, but in a world of radically unequal nation-states, such equality is never assured.

With a desire to emigrate, the publicist reproduces this tension at another level. It is just as routine, though, for Dresser, a professor in Mexico City. In her talk, Dresser spoke (like the publicist) of her nationalist pride —but the things she is proud of are all (she pointed out with a dry laugh) things tourists love. Her Canadian husband, in contrast, is proud of his country's profoundly democratic system. The solution for Dresser is to dedicate her professional life to making Mexico, in this, more like Canada. But the tension is the same as for the publicist with dreams of emigrating. At the border, the conflictual pull of the foreign is a quotidian reality not just for cosmopolitan subjects like Dresser but for a broad swath of the population. Tijuana's ability to imagine itself as middle-class may have even more to do with this fact than with its relative prosperity.

Analytic focus on the voicings of "we" the middle class brings out two quaverings of this "we," two conundrums of inclusion and exclusion that it fails to smooth over. First, the middle-class "we" hesitates in its relation to the poor. Beneath this hesitation lies a fear: "we" ourselves may be "poor," hopelessly unmodern, as revealed in the pun *clase media jodida*, "the half-screwed class." Second, "we" must live up to a standard imposed by the United States—but without running the risk of becoming a bit foreign ourselves (sometimes literally), we can never quite deal on an equal footing with our interlocutors abroad. In Tijuana, the middleness of the middle class is inseparable from the city's always unresolved suspension between "the South," aka the rest of Mexico (all too often the symbol of political, social, and economic backwardness), and the United States (the inevitable symbol of modernity). Thanks to its overdetermined middleness, Tijuana makes patent these two constitutive conundrums of the middle class as a public, which I take up in detail in the following two ethnographic examples.

THE PHOTOGRAPHY CONTEST: MIDDLE-CLASS
TIJUANA VIS-À-VIS THE SOUTH

Agnes was my hostess for a total of nearly two years between 2003 and 2007. She was born in 1927 into the extremely hierarchical world of the agricultural estates that lie along Mexico's border with Guatemala, on one of which her father had a well-paid position. Though she describes a privileged childhood, her father died when she was small, and Agnes spent her adolescence as a working girl in Mexico City (she mentions jobs as a seamstress and salesgirl). Her marriage to an editor brought another radical change: she describes a fully appointed home with servants. But before long, her husband sickened and lost his prestigious job; economic duress set in, and in 1972 the family moved to Tijuana. Soon after, Agnes was widowed and raised her four children as a single mother.

Agnes calls herself middle-class. In her reminiscences, though, she weaves together different idioms of distinction. She mentions her father's French citizenship and claims that his family once owned a silverware factory. She is critical of her mother's family but does not hesitate to tell me that they still own large estates in Guatemala. She is proud, too, of her Colombian husband's intellectual prowess and of his (now lost) papers proving descent from Spanish aristocracy. But she is intensely proud, too, of her ability to earn her living by working without shame and without putting on airs. She likes to tell of the velvet furniture in her childhood home, but she boasts just as much of how her most successful son (a corporate accountant) started off by mopping floors or how her husband, hit by hard times, was not afraid to roll up his sleeves and work as a mechanic.

When I asked Agnes the difference between Tijuana and her native city of Tapachula, on Mexico's southern border, she answered without hesitation: in Tijuana, "anyone" can have lunch at the country club; "anyone" can become a member. Surprised, I reminded her that the cost of membership was high: US$10,000, I had heard, astronomically beyond Agnes's means. That fact made no difference to her. In Tapachula, she explained, the club kept a list of names, and money could never buy one a place on it. "Middle-class" as Agnes uses the term and as it defines her means just this: not on the list in "the South" but admissible in Tijuana, if not without a fight. In the cleanness of this opposition, Agnes draws a swift, sure arc across her life, from South to North, closed to open, from the principle of birthright and blood to that of merit and money, from an oppressive hierarchy to the promise of mobility, and she amalgamates all the variety of her eighty years into a single term: *middle-class*.

I should have known, then, not to ask Agnes about Tijuana's "old family names," the founding fathers of local enterprise, the closest thing Tijuana has to an aristocracy. Evading my questions, she told the following story:

> Also, on another occasion, Gil [her son] had a heated argument. We had a friend, may he rest in peace, Castillo Luna. Dr. Castillo Luna. A very good doctor here in Tijuana. A very good friend of ours. And since he knew that Gil didn't work and all that, well, we'd go see him and he never charged us for it. He was a Masonic brother.[15]
>
> So then one day there was a photography exhibit and contest. And [the contestants] came from various parts of the republic. [Among them] there was a young guy, who came from I don't know where, but he was…indigenous type. Like, dark-skinned, hair sticking up like so, indigenous type. But Gil says he had very good photos and that, what with landscapes and things of that sort, he had very good photos.
>
> So the exhibit happened and all. And the judges came out. And among the judges was Castillo Luna. And then, well, they gave first place to a young guy from here in Tijuana, who didn't have good lighting in his photos, and some other little defects, right? And they give him the prize. And Gil asked to speak [*pidió la palabra*]. And he said that he didn't agree with that prize, because the judges didn't know what they were talking about.… "Let's see," he says, "they put Dr. Castillo Luna as judge, who is a great surgeon" (because for tonsils he was the marvel of the world), "a very good doctor. Very tijuanense, very much all that. But he doesn't know anything about photography."
>
> Because he [Gil] knew Castillo Luna for what he was, right? He'd chatted many times. He [Castillo Luna] was a historian, nothing more, because, well, he liked history a lot. And he ended up with books of Gil's, he did, because he died and we couldn't get them back.
>
> And then, uh, he [Gil] says, "And engineer *X*, and doctor *Y*…," he says, "may they tell me what they know about photography." And then a doctor said to him (also a Mason), he said, "Look here, kid. You don't know what you're talking about," and he [Gil] said, "Yes, I *do* know what I'm talking about because I *do*

know about photography."… And he started arguing with them. And, well, nothing to be done about it.

Gil's objection, Agnes claims, was "put up for debate," and the judges ended up giving the prize to the young, indigenous-type outsider. Gil told his mother later, "I recognized that the guy had better photos than I did." At this point, Agnes puts in his mouth the moral of the story: *hay que reconocer*. "One must recognize" merit; one must give credit where it has been won. Agnes would make this principle Tijuana's, defending the city from any revival of "acquired rights" (as the authors of *Middle-Class: Poor No More, Not Yet Developed* call them) and their ossification of status. With this principle, Agnes would distinguish her Tijuana from the South, from whence the young photographer came. If the judges represent Tijuana's elite, Agnes summarily introduces the South by means of its quintessential representative: an indigenous-type, dark-skinned young man. Where he comes from does not matter, only that he is recognizable precisely as a type. Contrary to all expectations, his photos are good, but the judges prefer a local competitor. Trampling merit, they follow (initially) the old aristocratic principle of status by birthright.

Agnes uses a formal phrase to describe Gil's request to speak: *pedir la palabra* is what one does in a chaired meeting or at town hall. It implies conventions of decorum, a whole set of formalities governing a particular speech genre. It evokes scenarios of democratic debate, in which citizens rise to speak their mind and rationally defend their propositions. Gil's argument with the judges was, for Agnes, a *discusión* in the literal sense of the word, a discussion in which status falls away and reason merges with rhetoric to prove which man is best.[16] Though Gil is clearly the hero of the day, he simply opens the space for true rational debate, the conclusion of which his reason merely foretold: "And it was put up for debate, and then, well…they gave the prize to the young guy."

"Look here, kid," the doctor says. "You don't know what you're talking about." Gil defends himself proudly: "Yes, I *do*." His position is informed. As a debate, this may sound infantile. And yet, by virtue of its lack of content, the exchange is a purer image of debate: there is nothing at stake beyond the issue of status by speech itself, the right to speak in a forum where speech effectively counts, and the possibility of having the photography contest be such a forum at all. Just as Castillo Luna is, above all, a figure representing Tijuana's elite and the "indigenous-type guy" represents the South, so Gil's *discusión* is emptied to leave an abstract image of rational debate.

Rational debate is at the heart of the representation of Tijuana that Agnes defends here. She describes how her son hijacked a public event by means of rational debate and, thanks to it, succeeded in leveling status distinctions there. Gil argues man to man with the elites, putting them to shame, and the indigenous-type fellow takes the prize. This possibility, she effectively claims, symbolizes Tijuana. The part that rational debate plays in the formation of Tijuana, as Agnes describes it, parallels the part it was supposed to play in the original bourgeois public sphere. Status falls away before the power of reason; interlocutors speak as equals and merit prevails. The old values of the aristocracy expire. But Tijuana as Agnes represents it echoes as well a basic conundrum of the bourgeois public sphere, which Dean (2002) points out: "we" only engage in rational debate because of the plebeian masses, who are unfit for enlightened discussion.

Though Gil appears to break into the closed circle of the elite, to wrest authority and power from them, he is able to do so only on the basis of his already established status in Tijuana: he is phenotypically white, raised there since early childhood, well spoken and well read despite his lack of formal education. Most important, he already has a relationship with the elite. In much the same way that Habermas (1989)postulated a public sphere of letters historically preceding the political public sphere, Gil's attack on the constituted authority of the judges was preceded by his exchange of books and his conversations about "history" with Castillo Luna. The indigenous-type man, in contrast, does not accede to Gil's circle. He remains mute and passive, incapable of representing himself in public. He is an accessory to the drama of the middle class's coming into its own, its necessary occasion—which is nonetheless summarily dispensed with.

Agnes narrates a public scene of rational debate as emblematic of Tijuana. She thus posits the city itself as a reflexive "we," a collective subject knit in "our" participation in such debate, and she stakes her own self-presentation before me, her U.S. anthropologist housemate, on this representation. Her life history, told in bits and pieces, makes clear that I am not the only audience for this performance—she has a perduring commitment to the values she lays out in this narrative, giving substance to what she calls "middle-class." Just as the category "middle class" so often serves to reconcile differences across a broad swath of the population, so it gives coherence and direction to Agnes's life of wild ups and downs. As she evokes Tijuana as a public of rational, egalitarian debate, as the teleological aim of her life history, however, she rearticulates in sublimated form a basic contradiction that haunts the utopian promise of the middle class as mainstay of liberal democracy.

THE BOARDROOM: MIDDLE-CLASS TIJUANA VIS-À-VIS THE NORTH

Asking about U.S. visas, I conducted a series of interviews in one of the transnational assembly plants for which the northern Mexican border is well known. Before my interview with the manager, he invited me into a boardroom to sit with him and four other men as they transferred files over their laptops. Only mildly occupied, the men had time for chitchat. This interaction and what the manager had to say about it afterward again show the importance of the idea of rational debate to Tijuana as middle class. As with Agnes, Tijuana's delicate middleness is at stake throughout, but here it is the contradictory relation of the middle-class "we" to the United States that is most evident—of course, the figure of the South necessarily plays a role.

The men began, courteously enough, with a topic that might well interest me: a *gringo*, an American, regularly sent down by the company's U.S. headquarters.[17] They recommended that I interview him. A good Spanish speaker, remarkably familiar with Mexican culture, he fulfills well (they seemed to judge) his formal role as cultural intermediary. I quote from my fieldnotes: "When we get, like, 'Fucking gringos!' he says to us, 'No, the thing is, it's like this, like that…'" The speaker paused. "And when they [the Americans at headquarters] get, like, 'Fucking Mexicans!' he also says to them, 'No, the thing is, it's like this…'"

The real inequality between interlocutors is, of course, the underlying theme of the anecdote: "Fucking gringos!" coming from the plant is in no way symmetrical to "Fucking Mexicans!" coming from corporate headquarters. But the anecdote sets up the two parties as equivalent. The dramatic pause between its two halves heightens the contrast between the expected asymmetry and the perfectly symmetrical punch line. In portraying both sides as equally reaching a breaking point, which is resolved in exactly the same way, the anecdote posits an equality free from the power differential not only between headquarters and plant but also between the United States and Mexico. Addressed to an American (me), it is a reminder of the equality of interlocutors under the principle of equal national sovereignties.

The gringo emerges, however, not just as mediator, but as defender of Mexican national sovereignty against *internal* assaults. The men recounted with delight an incident between a taxi driver and him: when the driver insisted on being paid in dollars, the gringo threw his pesos at him, shouting, "Mexican! You're in Mexico!" We may infer that the taxi driver recognized the nationalist accusation in the mouth of the gringo and was shamed into accepting payment in pesos. His countrymen in the boardroom, at any rate, laugh at him; he is shown up as a traitor.

However oddly, the authority of a Mexican nationalist discourse of equality is confirmed by the gringo's use of it. The men's convivial, in-group tone is subtly undone. They address me precisely as that most problematic of interlocutors: the American, the "they" who in some remote, offstage location explode, "Fucking Mexicans!"—all too quick to abuse a very real power that yet remains all too necessary in authorizing its own restraint. That is, the men end up invoking U.S. power and re-creating it in the interaction. This conundrum, the tension between egalitarian address and subtly resuscitated distinctions, was repeated as the discussion turned to regional differences and an explicit mobilization of debate among equals as a model for Mexico internally. One man, darker-skinned than the rest, informed the group, "In Mexico City, they really are spicy. Here, they aren't. There, they really are enchiladas. Here, your momma takes the seeds out, and there, they stuff more chilies in." With "your momma," this man addresses his fellows as native tijuanenses, people from "here," which at least two of them were. When the talk turned to soccer a moment later, this same man spoke with equal gusto as the sole defender of the Mexico City team.

With beaming smiles, the men exchanged insults. I was surprised to note that they universally addressed one another as *Ingeniero*, Engineer—a term they used frequently in this part of the conversation as they hammed up verbal flourishes of politesse before delivering their barbed puns and insults. The manager, sitting next to me, glanced at me more than once and, in a lull, after about fifteen minutes of banter, took it upon himself to do some explaining: "Here in the North, they don't come to blows over these things. It's pacific. Here, to each his own opinion, and talking and that's it." He made hand motions in the air, referring to their just enacted, egalitarian exchange of opinions, little motions in the direction of each participant. "But there in the stadium, with the beers and the heat…"

The exchange was clearly ludic, yet the manager reframed it as debate. The men's joking insults became "opinions" to which each was entitled; the speaking of one's mind appeared as a right to be respected. This type of interaction, he says, is characteristic of the North. The South, on the other hand, is represented by the stadium, where plebeian passions rise to blows. The feisty provocations of the dark-skinned man do not, however, represent an element of the stadium in the midst of rational debate. The North, with its emblematic mode of interaction, is more robust than that. The southerner here has already been reframed as northern. His contributions both provide the opportunity for and cinch the manager's claim as to the nature of the North and of the interaction. Like my own status as American, the color of his skin is a difference curiously both at issue and suppressed in the interaction. It *must* be there to be ignored. If the North is the place where all parts of the republic can represent themselves equally in the public space of free rational debate, if the North wins because it represents a future and a model for national being as a whole, this is only thanks—as in the photography contest—to the presence of the South, covertly summoned up in the interaction.

The exchange as a display of egalitarianism was anchored in the vocative *engineer*. All addressed the others as *ingenieros*; the term was a reminder of their equal status in the debate. It cleared a space within which "opinions" could be respected. In this space, the manager was willing to shed his status and assume equality with his subordinates—but this equality depended on the exclusivity of the boardroom. *Ingeniero* is also a reminder of relative status, of one's educational degree and of one's position in the plant, as in society. It is a reminder of those who are not present, who are not ingenieros, and who could not contribute so elegantly to the virtuosic tendering of "opinion." The exchange repeated, as Agnes did, the tension Dean points out in the original bourgeois public sphere between a utopian openness/egalitarianism and a de facto exclusivity. The man from the South is, before all else, an engineer like the rest of "us." But even within the boardroom, equality has its limits, for it was the manager's status that licensed the whole performance—which is why he retained the right of explaining it.

As rational debate, the banter in the boardroom may fall a bit short—as does Agnes's narrative of Gil's discusión. And yet—again, as with Agnes—it is held up in all seriousness as an image that typifies Tijuana and underlies social relations in the plant. In our interview later, the manager twice brought up the debate on soccer as an example of his personal ethos ("That's who I am") and a managerial style that, he claims, underpins daily interaction in the plant and, ultimately, productivity. "So if you treat your companions like people, I mean, or as equals? There won't be any problem. For example, in the discussion we had just now. The supervisor, a clerk from Materials, [the] coordinator, the plant manager. I mean, within the social structure in Mexico, 'No [way], how [could this be]?!'" The scandalized voice the manager mocks is that of the old, hierarchical Mexico he opposes himself to. He is able to create the boardroom as a new Mexico of equals because his status as manager allows him to impose his personal, tijuanense ethos. But he is not licensed as the manager by just U.S. headquarters. His status and the rational debate he animates as the essence of Tijuana are underwritten by the U.S. state in the form of his non-immigrant visa.

The manager has held a visa since early childhood. He reapplied as an adult: "I had no problem. The information you have to present is that you have to be economically solvent and that it's not your idea to have the visa to go work in the U.S." In Tijuana, the undocumented migrant to the United States is stereotypically southern; "we" tijuanenses are visa holders. Agnes and her children have had theirs since their arrival in Tijuana in the 1970s. Many still consider the migrant, much as the taxi driver desirous of dollars, to be degrading "us" both in real economic terms (this idea is, of course, erroneous) and in foreign eyes, and the manager has been described to me as "one of those who think you're betraying Mexico if you go work in the U.S." In our interview, he told me, "I prefer to be a first-rate citizen in my own country than to live better in another country where I won't be treated the same." With a salary twelve times higher than that of the line operators in his plant (also, stereotypically, migrants from the South), the manager could not very well live "better" in the United States. If he feels he is treated "the same" in Mexico, that is, in egalitarian fashion, this is only because he can accede to the sphere of "first-rate citizenship." Tijuana's middle-class, rationally debating public is composed of the "first-rate citizens" who know that they are such because the impossibility of their becoming "illegal aliens" in the United States has been embalmed for them in the form of a visa.

In the boardroom, the manager explained that baseball is the region's true sport. He traced a map in the air, signaling soccer and baseball states: "When I was little, soccer [he squinches his face, shaking his head]. We watched it on TV. Baseball we did follow, here in San Diego [he signals northward, casually], because of the Padres." His gestures in the air, dividing regions on an imaginary map of Mexico, parallel the ones he made earlier, signaling the participants in the debate: "to each his own opinion." "We" who first took shape as children, as a sports-viewing public, are precisely the ones to offer the possibility of seeing and representing as equal all those regional and personal differences that make up Mexico. This tijuanense "we" articulates itself through an attempt to instantiate rational debate among equals, the formation of "opinions" in a protected sphere of tolerance where status is shed. But this "we" is anchored in the last gesture of the manager's, pointing even farther north, across the border. It is the same gesture as that which evokes the gringo as authorizer of a Mexican nationalist discourse of equivalence; it is the same gesture as this entire performance before me as but another figure for the United States, from which recognition must always, in the end, be obtained. The collective subject, the "we" of rational debate, seeks to extend itself from Tijuana to all of

Mexico. But it appears deictically situated only between, on the one hand, a map on which "we" can be located and, on the other, the anchoring gesture, "here in San Diego."

CONCLUSION

Agnes and the manager are radically different, not only in age and income but also in personal and family histories. Yet, both make clear their allegiance to rational debate as a communicative genre that defines Tijuana, its forward-looking and progressive character, and its legitimate status as a horizon of future becoming for the nation as a whole. This representation of Tijuana finds its footing in multiple texts and images; backed by formal institutions, it is the dominant understanding of the city. A local newspaper, for instance, ran a full-page spread that declared, "To be of the border is to be open and frank, it is to look each other in the eye and converse, exchanging opinions and accepting dialogue."[18] The spread interpellated its readership as just the "open and frank" tijuanense public it described.

Tijuana's emphasis on "openness" and "dialogue" may be part of an older local ideology, inflected by Frederick Jackson Turner–style (1993) notions of the nineteenth-century western frontier as the cradle of U.S. democracy. Tijuana, too, conceives of itself as a frontier society of loosened boundaries, where hard work and merit rule supreme and everyone has a chance at prosperity. It is the "American dream" within Mexico. This local discourse resonates with a national shift toward the right, which gained even greater legitimacy with the "democratic transition" of 2000. Tijuana, with its overdetermined middleness, thus provides a privileged window on Mexico's turn to a new liberalism that would again relegate the pueblo to marginal status.

As Agnes and the manager represent Tijuana to me, they take up and rearticulate reflexive circulations of "rational debate," of the "open" exchange of "opinions," that draw the middle class together as a public and as a collective subject in Mexico. Our interactions are but moments in the circulation of an imaginary in which a prospering, visa-holding, comparatively white Tijuana can finally be the real Mexico. These representations are shot through with anxieties and contradictions borne of a middleness that is as much about nationality as class. The border, with its legal categories, only exaggerates the stakes of a national push toward a middle-class Mexico, as illustrated by Dresser or by the online news readers' debate, in which "we" likewise vacillate in "our" relation both to Mexico's poor and to the United States as an authorizing source of recognition.

Tijuana's middle-class public reformulates widespread discourses that tout the middle class as the hope for modernity. Agnes and the manager show Mexico's middle-class "we" in movement, localizing itself, calling itself "Tijuana," grounding itself in personal history and everyday interaction. In Tijuana, this "we" articulates itself by trying to instantiate communicative genres first given political weight in the bourgeois public sphere of seventeenth-century Europe. It treats rational debate as if it were capable on its own of breaking down old barriers of social distinction and creating a merit-based, democratic society of opportunity. The manager's version links freedom of expression and cross-class communication directly to economic profits and productivity—development, in the most neoliberal sense of the word. If the middle-class "we" echoes the ideology of the bourgeois public sphere, this should be no surprise. A strong, open, public sphere of debate is not often critically analyzed as part of contemporary (neo)liberalizing projects, but it is a cornerstone of them, as indicated, for example, by De la Calle and Rubio's (2010a) use of the phrase "deliberative liberal democracy." Rational debate thus appears as an imperative in its own right; Habermas's own writings have been influential in this regard, positing the old bourgeois public sphere as a model for contemporary societies. An intellectual history of his text's influence in Latin America would be of interest in understanding the extraordinary emphasis on "opinion" in a place like Tijuana and its connection to the figure of the middle class.

I have described two conundrums of the middle-class public in Tijuana and in Mexico generally: its relation to the poor or the pueblo and its relation to the United States. These echo conundrums of the bourgeois public sphere: its relation to the masses unprepared to participate in rational debate and to a foreign public of the enlightened. In contemporary Mexico, at the border in particular, these contradictions deepen as a middle-class "we" of rational debate is called on to mediate not just between elites and masses, but between the nation and the globe.

Egalitarian rational debate is shown up as a weapon of class distinction and, ultimately, exclusion: Tijuana's middle-class public subtly reproduces racialized and classed, regional and national differences. The display of egalitarian debate can take place only under certain conditions: the protected sphere of Agnes's dining room or the factory boardroom; my status as guest in these settings; the dark-skinned men's status as photographer or engineer. Neither do so-called reason or opinion stand on their own; they both depend on external recognition and authorization, in this case not that of the state to which a public sphere should ideally be oriented, but that of a foreign country. As the middle class tries to position itself at the vanguard of democratic openness and properly modern egalitarianism, it must ignore these contradictions.

Ethnographic focus on the reflexive circulations that undergird and reproduce a middle-class collective subject brings to light its self-contradictions: its use of egalitarian debate to exclude class others below it and its dependence on a foreign source of authority and recognition. Tijuana's middle-class public thus appears bound to a nest of binary distinctions—gringo versus mexicano, North versus South, white versus indigenous, patriot versus traitor, visa holder versus "illegal alien," middle class versus poor. All are articulated within the logic of "rational" and "free" public communication as a pillar of modern, liberal democracy—but this logic only tenuously holds together the principle of equal national sovereignties and that of equal parties to debate within the nation.

Acknowledgments

I thank the participants in the seminar that gave rise to this volume, above all, the editors, and Rachel Heiman in particular. Susan Gal gave comments on an early draft, as did participants in several workshops. The Center for U.S.-Mexican Studies at the University of California, San Diego, supported part of the research and writing. Alejandra Leal and Gabriela Zamorano gave crucial help with the final version.

Notes

1. I use "the poor" as a local category, as I do "the middle class."

2. As Olivia Ruiz felicitously titled her study of nearby Sonora, *Between Mexico and the United States: A Mexican Middle Class in the Middle* (1984). Schielke's (chapter 2, this volume) study of Egypt, across the sea from Europe, provides a striking comparison.

3. The quotation marks are meant to indicate that I am interested not in the rationality of debate per se, but in "rational debate" as a category of interaction, or a set of communicative genres, which people perform in different ways.

4. Following Benveniste (1971) on pronouns as the prime site of subjectivity in language, I sometimes use "we" as a shorthand for collective subjectivity, though this may actually be evoked by more subtle means.

5. Examples of works that approach classes as publics include E. P. Thompson's (1963) demonstration that the English working class was a reading public; Loaeza's (1988) study of how the Mexican middle class took shape as a specific political issue (education) was fought in the public sphere; and Liechty's (2003) study of the middle class in Nepal, which shows the intertextuality of major media forms not only with one another but also with urban public spaces.

6. An intellectual history tracing these connections is beyond the scope of this chapter. Suffice it to note Habermas's (1989:4) parallel argument: "The model of the

Hellenic public sphere…[has enjoyed]…a peculiarly normative power. Not the social formation of its base but the ideological template itself has preserved continuity over the centuries."

7. "The Need for Reform in Mexico," January 20, 2010, at the Institute of the Americas and the Center for U.S.-Mexican Studies at the University of California, San Diego (UCSD). A recording is available at http://usmex.ucsd.edu/assets/023/11118. mp3. The Institute of the Americas is an independent organization housed on UCSD's campus; its Tequila Talks series usually requires an entrance fee, though Dresser's did not. Thus, its public is somewhat exclusive and, though educated, not exactly academic.

8. John Johnson (1958) made the first extended argument on the central importance of the "middle sectors" for political change in Latin America. On the association between the middle class and democracy in Mexico, see Loaeza 1988.

9. Thanks to José Carlos Hesles for bringing this to my attention.

10. Reader comments are drawn from Aguilar Camín 2010 and *Nexos* 2010, though more articles were consulted.

11. See Gilbert 2007 for an account of the middle classes' (legendary) role in the electoral change.

12. Lomnitz (2003) builds on O'Dougherty (2002) in his analysis of Mexico City's reading middle-class public in the crisis of the 1980s.

13. Local wisdom has it that the 1980s were a watershed decade in which the poor began to arrive in massive numbers. Whether or not this is statistically true, lower-income residents had already been a palpable (and problematic, from the dominant perspective) presence for many decades.

14. "What I say in Mexico…is what every one of you would be saying here. It is what people say in a functional democracy." Earlier, though, Dresser implied that the United States is a *dys*functional democracy.

15. Agnes's husband was a Mason.

16. *Discusión* is usually better translated as "argument." I say "man" because of the public sphere's highly gendered nature. Rational debate in Mexico is very much (though not always) a male sport (cf. Piccato 2010).

17. *Gringo* connotes Anglo-American ethnicity; it is a standard analogue of *mexicano*.

18. *Frontera*, July 25, 2003.

9

Private Homes, Distinct Lifestyles

Performing a New Middle Class in China

Li Zhang

The post-Mao economic reform has brought about unprecedented wealth and remarkable economic growth, but the income gap has increased and social polarization has soared in this rapidly commercializing society. A small group of the newly rich—including private entrepreneurs, merchants, well-positioned government officials, and managers of large, profitable corporations—is taking an enormous share of the new wealth and cultivating a luxurious lifestyle beyond the reach of the majority of ordinary Chinese. At the same time, millions of rural migrant laborers, laid-off workers, and other disadvantaged citizens (*ruoshi qunti*) are struggling to make ends meet, a situation leading to widespread discontent and even public protests (see Lee 2000; Solinger 1999; Zhang 2001, 2002). Despite such rising social problems, neoliberal practices centered on the privatization of property and lifestyles are being increasingly naturalized and valorized in the urban public sphere. One of the most important changes in China's urban landscape, made possible by this privatization, is the formation of a new social stratum: the "new middle class" (*xin zhongchan jieceng*).[1]

The demise of the public housing regime and the rise of the commercial real estate industry have opened up new opportunities for urbanites to seek differentiated lifestyles, status recognition, and cultural orientations. Thus, reconfigurations of residential space have proved vital to the formation of a new urban middle-class culture. My central argument here is that private homeownership and the increasing stratification of living space are not merely expressions of class difference or an index of status but are the very means through which class-specific subjects and a new cultural milieu are being formed. Drawing from my long-term ethnographic fieldwork in the city of Kunming in southwestern China, I analyze this dual cultural process of space making and class making by examining how, on the one hand, self-conscious middle-class subjects and a distinct "class milieu" (*jie-ceng wenhua*) are being created under a new regime of property ownership and living and how, on the other hand, socioeconomic differences get spatialized and materialized through the remaking of urban communities.[2]

Rather than treat class as a given, fixed entity, I approach it as an ongoing process of "happening." As E. P. Thompson (1963:9) nicely put it, "I do not see class as a 'structure,' nor even as a 'category,' but as something which in fact happens (and can be shown to have happened) in human relationships." This approach is particularly important to my understanding of class making after Mao because, as a private real estate developer pointed out, "one may be able to see the emergence of social stratification based on people's economic status, but it is still very difficult to speak of any middle class because there has not emerged a distinct class culture shared by those who have accumulated certain material wealth. Class making after Mao is still in its very early, amorphous stages; this is going to be a very long and confusing process." Thus, it makes more sense to speak of the formation of middle-class subjects (often fragmented) than to assume a clearly identifiable class already in place (see also Schielke, chapter 2, this volume). It is this cultural process of making and happening, in which a group of people attempt to articulate their interests and stage their dispositions, that I hope to unravel.

What is central in the formation of middle-class subjects in China is the cultivation of a distinct cultural milieu based on taste, judgment, and the acquisition of cultural capital through consumption practices.[3] In this open, unstable process, competing claims for status are made through public performance of self-worth, and at the same time, what is considered suitable and proper is negotiated.[4] Class making thus takes place not only within the domain of relations of production but also outside it, namely, through the spheres of consumption, family, community, and lifestyle.[5] Although Marxist-inspired scholars have long recognized place as an important constituent of class, the emphasis has been on how the workplace serves as the primary arena for working-class politics. As a result, not enough consideration has been given to the cultural process that occurs within other social domains. The importance of community life in the formation of class is well illustrated by E. P. Thompson's seminal work, *The Making of the English Working Class* (1963), which delineates the everyday practices of the working class in their community, family, church, school, leisure, and consumption. For him, class is as much cultural as it is economic. Even though the situation of Thompson's (English working-class) subjects is very different from that of the middle-class Chinese I am writing about and even though his notion of class is deeply rooted in the fundamental conflict between capital and labor, I find his willingness to locate class politics in a much broader social and cultural realm and to treat it as a dynamic process extremely fruitful. This cultural and processual approach opens up a new space for rethinking class beyond economic terms and rigid structural divides.

I take a culturally oriented approach toward class here by focusing on two social spheres outside direct economic production—community making and consumption practice—in order to shed new light on the cultural formation of the new Chinese middle class.[6] Drawing on Pierre Bourdieu's theory of "habitus,"[7] I argue that the emerging forms of living and everyday consumption play a critical part in constituting the social dispositions of class-specific subjects, not merely in displaying their status.It is in this sense that I see lifestyle choices and consumption as productive forces. More specifically, my ethnographic account demonstrate, how commercialized real estate development and exclusionary residential spaces provide a tangible place where class-specific subjects and their cultural milieu are created, staged, and contested.[8] In delineating this mutually constitutive relationship among space, class, and consumption, I also consider how the rapidly expanding advertising of housing has become a vital engine in manufacturing and disseminating the dreams, tastes, dispositions, and images of the new middle class (see Baudrillard 1998).

In this chapter, I frequently use the Chinese term *jieceng* instead of *jieji* or the English words "class" and "status," for important reasons. Since the end of Mao's regime, Chinese people have largely avoided the term *jieji* in talking about social stratification because this concept was highly politicized and closely associated with the brutal and violent class struggle that caused pain and suffering for many under Mao. So *jieceng* is now commonly used to refer to socioeconomic differentiation. This vernacular term allows one to speak about various newly emerged socioeconomic differences without quickly resorting either to a set of preformulated, historically specific categories such as "capitalists" and "proletarians," largely determined by one's position in the relations of production, or to the Maoist conceptualization of class as a form of political consciousness. But at the same time, *jieceng* refers to more than just status. The term is deeply intertwined with one's ability to generate income and to consume. It is most commonly used by Chinese today to refer to an emerging social group called *zhongchan jieceng* (literally, "the middle, propertied stratum").[9] Although this group is still in a rudimentary stage of formation and thus lacks a shared identity, its members have begun to explore and cultivate a new culture of living as a way to articulate their economic and social location in society (see Tomba 2004). My intention in using the term *jieceng* (rather than "class" or "status") is *not* to erase politics and ideology from my account of the mounting socioeconomic differentiation in China, but to render a culturally and historically specific concept that mediates between the two distinct yet related analytical terms "class" and "status." The slippage between them is intentionally retained in the discourse of *jieceng*, which allows the simultaneous consideration of economic and cultural processes.[10]

In what follows, I first briefly trace the spatialization of jieceng as a result of the neoliberal move to privatize property ownership and lifestyle, and I analyze the role of real estate advertising in shaping the cultural meanings of the new zhongchan jieceng. I then turn to an ethnographic account of how different cultural milieus and class-specific subjects are cultivated within the stratified living space, by focusing on consumption practices and a sense of social insecurity (cf. Heiman, chapter 10, this volume). In the conclusion, I reflect on some implications of the rethinking of the cultural politics of class, space, and consumption at a time when certain neoliberal strategies are being utilized by the state to transform Chinese society, with often unexpected consequences.[11]

FROM *DANWEI* TO STRATIFIED LIVING SPACE

Under the socialist regime, the majority of urban Chinese could not own private property; instead, they lived in state-subsidized public housing allocated by their work units, or *danwei* (Lu and Perry 1997; Whyte and Parish 1984). In Kunming, a city of approximately three million residents and the capital of Yunnan province, residential communities prior to the housing reform were largely organized into two forms: (1) mixed, non-danwei-based neighborhoods, which were under the control of the municipal housing bureau and included mostly renters of diverse social backgrounds; and (2) danwei-based communities, which included relatively large housing compounds constructed, owned, and regulated by work units. In this kind of setting, the work unit acted not only as the de facto landlord and manager but also as the agent of direct state/party surveillance. This pervasive form of scrutiny deprived individuals of a sense of privacy, as any desire for privacy in this context could be easily interpreted as antisocial or suspicious. Prior to the reform, danwei, not specific street names and numbers, served as the most important spatial indicators for social mapping. Inequality in the public housing system was expressed mainly through the quality and size of apartments. Such differences were largely determined by the scale, strength, and status of work units and one's position within a given work unit, rather than by private wealth.

Such concepts as "poor working-class neighborhoods" or "upscale neighborhoods" were virtually nonexistent in most Chinese cities under socialism.[12] Then, in 1998 the State Council launched its reform to privatize public housing. Under the new policy, families were encouraged to buy their apartments from their work units at a discounted rate significantly below market value. Initially, many urban residents were skeptical about the privatization scheme. Their main concern was whether private homes would be protected by law; at that time, the constitution did not recognize private property ownership. Under these circumstances, the Chinese government launched several campaigns to assure its urban citizens that privatized housing would be treated as a form of commodity and be protected by the state. It urged people to abandon the welfare mentality and adopt a commodity-oriented perspective. One slogan put it this way: "Housing is no longer a welfare item; it is a commodity." By 2000 most danwei-based public housing had been privatized in Chinese cities.

There has also been rapid growth in the construction of new private homes that have little connection with the danwei system, which continues to exist today (Davis 2002; Fraser 2000). The real estate industry, centered on housing construction, has become the primary engine of economic growth in China. The emerging new communities (xiaoqu, literally, "small neighborhoods" or "small quarters") are rapidly transforming the Chinese urban landscape into a highly stratified and socially segregated environment marked by income. The new homes offer many choices in price, quality, style, service, and location for consumers in different socioeconomic positions. In Kunming today, the striking differences between the wealthy and lower-income neighborhoods can hardly be overlooked.[13] Lower-income housing consists mostly of matchbox-like apartments in buildings that are poorly constructed and poorly maintained. There is little public space between buildings, and there are virtually no green areas. The low-quality exterior paint is easily washed away by rain, making the surface of the buildings look like "crying faces with running tears," as one informant put it. By contrast, the commercially developed, upper- and middle-class neighborhoods feature a variety of architectural styles and high-quality construction materials and are spacious, clean, and well protected. The colors of these new buildings are bright and cheerful. There are plenty of well-kept lawns, flowers and other plants, and parking garages. Factors that further differentiate urban residential space today include property values, community services, and the social characteristics of the residents.

Who are the people inhabiting these private gated communities? How do they generate the wealth that supports this new lifestyle? During my fieldwork, one of the most difficult problems I encountered was the reluctance of gated community residents to talk about the source of their income or the nature of their business. In fact, it is a social taboo among the relatively wealthy people to ask how one generates income, because many business transactions take place outside the bounds of law and official rules (cf. Jones, chapter 6, this volume). My observation and interviews indicate that the majority of these residents fall into three categories: owners of private businesses of varying sizes, white-collar professionals with certain expertise (such as lawyers and doctors), and a managerial class working for private and state-owned enterprises. Even though they themselves are not government officials, they usually have close personal connections with officialdom through their business activities. City and provincial officials are offered heavily subsidized apartments in a special kind of community constructed by the government for them only.

In sum, the shift from danwei housing to a new stratified commercial housing regime is a radical change far beyond the spatial level. During this process, urban Chinese people are undergoing profound transformations in their everyday experiences and their cultural and ideological conceptions of status, privacy, and private property. Next, let us take a look at how mass advertising for new homes plays a critical role in creating new desires and understandings of modernity and middle-class lifestyles.

ADVERTISING JIECENG

Real estate developers in China not only manufacture homes but also construct and disseminate new notions of zhongchan jieceng (the middle propertied stratum) and a distinct set of ideas, values, and desires. Through the powerful tool of advertising, these widely circulated ideas and images become a primary source of social imagination through which the urban public comes to understand what "middle class" means and how its members should live. Advertisements for private housing frequently make explicit linkages between a particular lifestyle (embodied foremost in one's housing choices), a set of dispositions, and one's class location. In sum, they are not just selling the material product (houses) but are also selling the associated symbolic meanings and cultural packages. As a result, China's housing revolution has not only made possible a comfortable form of luxury living but also provided new meanings and spatial forms for a new social class (cf. Fehérváry, chapter 5, this volume).

Let us take a closer look at one such advertisement, published in a major newspaper in Yunnan province. Titled "Town Houses Are Really Coming!" this advertisement, taking up an entire page of the newspaper, was sponsored by a real estate corporation that was building a large residential community of four hundred new homes. The lower half of the page is a picture of a smiling young Chinese woman standing on the seashore, reaching for rose petals floating down from the sky. The caption below reads: "The platform of the middle class's top-quality life: Though not villas, the Sunshine Coast Town Houses are a special, tasteful living zone that specifically belongs to the city's middle class." The upper half of the page contains a carefully crafted narrative explaining what town houses are, where they come from, and what they stand for. Since most Chinese are unfamiliar with the history of the town house and its social index in the West, developers can easily manipulate the symbolic importance of this kind of housing. The opening section of the text identifies the town house as a preferred way of life for the new middle class: "In the year 2000 a brand new living space called the 'town house' ignited the buying zeal of China's middle class. From Beijing and Tianjin to Shanghai, Guangzhou, and Shenzhen, town houses have caught the eye of all urban middle-class people and become their top choice in reforming their lifestyles. Town houses signify the beginning of a truly new way of life in China." It further claims that "town houses are extremely popular in Europe and America, and are becoming the classic residential space for the middle class.... They can foster unprecedented 'community culture' and a strong sense of belonging among a distinct group of residents." Such claims suggest that if one can afford this type of home and lifestyle, one will automatically become part of China's new middle class, as well as of a privileged global middle class marked by Euro-American modernity. In many of the housing advertisements like this one, in addition to giving the properties foreign-flavored names, the "West" is frequently deployed as an explicit marker or a central trope for imagining a new modern cosmopolitan way of life.[14] The crux of this advertisement is that to buy a home is to buy class status and the new spatial form of the town house provides a pathway to the global middle classes.

What is so appealing about town houses to the Chinese is that they offer not only private property ownership but also extended private space (such as a small private garden) beyond the limits of the tiny danwei housing.

Developers can thus market town houses and their private gardens as a "perfect independent space that allows one to touch the sky and the earth"—a true pleasure of the new middle-class lifestyle. The connection between private space and personal freedom is important here. Owning one's own home, spatially and socially detached from the danwei and from the neighbors, is taken as a sign of true liberation because it enables one to break away from social constraints and organizational surveillance. Thus, this ad attempts to capitalize on this emerging popular desire to seek a new kind of privacy in the postsocialist period.

Some developers may not use the term *zhongchan jieceng* directly, but the message they attempt to send is loud and clear: buying a home or choosing a community is all about belonging to a class and enjoying exclusivity. For example, a promotional message for a newly constructed community was written on large banners that were hung over several major commercial streets: "For Urban Noble White Collars Only: A Social Circle of 500 White Collar People." In the Chinese context today, "white collar" refers to the relatively wealthy, who are not necessarily professionals. In another grand promotional campaign, launched by the developer of Sunshine Garden (Haoyuan), a massive new housing complex in the western suburb of Kunming, the advertisement, which reached almost every household in the city, highlights the centrality of community in the formation of a class milieu:

> Haoyuan is the noble residential community specifically designed for successful people and societal elites only. The current homeowners are all successful people, cultural celebrities, famous doctors, lawyers, artists, high-level intellectuals, and returned overseas Chinese. Haoyuan is the ideal living place for those who pursue high-class lifestyles and tastes and for those who seek success in their life. Remember the story of "Mother Meng Choosing Her Neighbors." Having a common living space shared by responsible, career-oriented societal elites is crucial for the creation of a first-rate cultural milieu and an opportunity for your further career success.

This narrative appropriates a well-known, age-old morality tale about how Mencius's mother moved three times until she finally found a decent neighborhood to ensure that her son would receive only positive influences from their neighbors. Her effort eventually paid off; Mencius later turned out to be one of the greatest men in Chinese history. This morally loaded story is used to convince today's home buyers that there is a proven linkage between one's living environment, class status, and future success. According to this cultural logic, residential communities are not simply a place to live; they provide the cultural milieu necessary for sustaining a distinct social group and the success of future generations.

Ironically, as I discovered during my fieldwork, a large portion of the residents in the luxury communities are not the so-called noble high class or cultural elite but instead are mostly private entrepreneurs and merchants who have accumulated quick personal wealth outside the state system. These people tend to be regarded by the society as having little cultural capital. But my point here is not that these advertisements make a false representation of the community; such housing advertisements, true or not, play a powerful part in reorienting the urban public's understanding of class by linking it directly to distinct community forms and consumer lifestyles. The insecurity resulting from one's lack of social status can reinforce the desire to turn toward the material index of class.

It is also important to point out that in the majority of the advertising brochures (if not newspaper ads), the issue of privacy is accentuated by highlighting the enhanced security force and the advanced surveillance technologies installed. Articulated in the language of family safety and crime prevention, the underlying message is that social exclusion can be effectively reinforced through such measures so that the gated space is accessible only to those who can afford it and property values are protected. This logic of surveillance is very different from the state surveillance that people experienced in the danwei under socialism. In what follows, I turn to an ethnographic account of the three kinds of communities into which the residents of Kunming are stratified.

"GARDENS" AND "VILLAS"

The newly constructed luxury neighborhoods for the zhongchan jie-ceng are commonly referred to as "gardens" (*yuan* or *huayuan*). Most of the housing consists of spacious condominiums in high-rises or multi-story structures in convenient prime downtown areas or the core urban districts (*shiqu*). There are also town houses and detached single-family homes, called *bieshu*, located in the developing suburbs. All of these are "commodity housing" (*shangpinfang*), which can be bought and sold freely by private individuals. Located in well-protected gated communities, each unit costs about half a million yuan or more, far beyond the reach of the majority of ordinary citizens. Some of the luxury single-family houses cost as much as two million yuan.

Jade Garden, located near Green Lake in Wuhua District, is one of the upscale gated communities that I visited frequently. Because it is near downtown, adjacent to a beautiful park, and located in the best school district, Jade Garden is one of the most expensive properties in the city. It consists of a high-rise tower and several large six-story buildings forming a completely enclosed residential compound of some two hundred units. The sale price per unit ranges from 600,000 to 800,000 yuan, depending on the view. Each unit measures roughly 150 square meters, which is considered spacious by Chinese standards. This complex is run by a private property management agency that is known for its high-quality customer service, modeled on that of its Hong Kong–based parent company. It has an indoor swimming pool, a gym, a clubhouse, and meticulously maintained landscaping.[15] Like most upscale compounds, this fortress-like complex is protected by surveillance cameras and private security guards. Residents use their keys to open three sets of gates: the large metal front gate (which is closed at night), the building unit gate, and the house door. During the daytime, the main gate is open, but the guard stops and questions anybody who does not appear to be a resident there. I was stopped twice and had to wait until the guard called my friends and confirmed that I was indeed their guest.

Mr. Zhou, who lives in Jade Garden, runs a specialty sports and leisure clothing business that is well known among middle-class families and expatriates looking for high-quality, Western-style clothing. Zhou, who is in his late thirties, graduated from a well-known college in 1987 but decided to give up his intellectual career for private business in 1991. He was able to pull together only several thousand yuan for the start-up, so in the beginning, the operation was small. He rented a stall of less than 10 square meters on a street near a local university. Four years later, the city government decided to widen several roads and thus demolished all the stalls and shops on them, including his. By then, he was already making good money and was able to rent a larger store on a main commercial street. Between 1995 and 1997, his business took off, and he made about one million yuan annually, which far exceeded what most people made at that time. He attributed his success to three things: knowing how to select high-quality products in classic leisure styles, offering superior customer service, and starting the business early. By the time I met him, his business had grown into a three-store chain operation with ten employees.

Zhou owns a spacious condo on the tenth floor with a sweeping view of Green Lake. I was greeted at the door by a young live-in nanny who did the cooking and cleaning and took care of his little boy, which is typical for a middle-class family in China. The furniture was good but not lavish. His

FIGURE 9.1

An upscale, gated condominium complex. Photo by L. Zhang.

family could easily live on the income generated from the clothing business, but his wife also wanted a career. She worked as a cashier at a major bank. I noticed a Bible on the coffee table and a statue of the Virgin Mary on the bookshelf—items not commonly found in Chinese homes. Zhou explained that informal Bible study groups are emerging among the urban middle class. The new private communities provide a safer space for religious activities because there is less direct governmental surveillance.

Although residents in the upscale neighborhoods have one thing in common—their wealth—their occupational and educational backgrounds are diverse, and they are not considered "elites" by the larger society. As merchants, entrepreneurs, or what David Goodman (1999) calls "owner-operators," they tend to be lumped into one of two categories: *zuo shengyi de* (businesspeople), as opposed to those working in the state sector, and *da laoban* (big bosses), as opposed to the wage laborers in the private sector. The secret of their success is that they started their businesses relatively early and thus were able to take advantage of the emerging private market for rapid capital accumulation before the competition intensified.

MIDDLE-STRATUM NEIGHBORHOODS

The middle-stratum neighborhoods (*zhongdang xiaoqu*) consist of commercially developed housing, but the ways in which the families obtain their homes vary and the social composition is complex. More than half the units are sold as straight commodity housing to private buyers at prices ranging from 200,000 to 400,000 yuan, depending on the size, quality, and location. The rest are bought in bulk by large danwei, which then sell them to their own employees at a subsidized rate (see Wang and Murie 1999a, 1999b; Zhang 1998). Danwei are able to negotiate a better price than is offered to individual buyers. Communities of this type are also gated and protected by security guards, but the controls are not as stringent. A well-dressed person with an urban professional appearance is likely to pass without being questioned by the guards. Catering to emerging middle-class families, this kind of neighborhood attracts firm managers, independent business owners, and highly specialized professionals and intellectuals who earn substantial incomes from sidelines.[16]

Ms. Tang lives with her husband and daughter in a 110-square-meter condo in Riverside Garden, a large, newly constructed residential community in the northern part of the city. This area used to be farmland but is now covered by new gated communities. Prior to purchasing this home, they lived for more than ten years in a small rundown apartment assigned by her work unit. After graduating from college in the late 1980s, Tang became a high school teacher, bringing in a monthly salary of about 1,500 yuan. Her husband first worked for a state enterprise and then "jumped into the sea of private business" and went to work for a small firm selling personal therapeutic equipment. He soon became the marketing manager of this national distributor's regional office, earning 5,000 to 10,000 yuan a month, depending on sales. By the time they purchased this apartment in 2001, they had saved enough cash for a large down payment (50 percent of the 200,000 yuan total) on a ten-year mortgage. Tang was very happy with the additional space and her new living environment. But she also felt isolated and disappointed in her neighbors, claiming, "They are not well educated and their *suzhi* [quality] is low."

GONGXIN NEIGHBORHOODS

Lower-income neighborhoods in China are usually called *gongxin jiecen xiaoqu*, which literarily means "salary/wage-based communities," because most residents there live on relatively fixed incomes (ranging from meager to moderate salaries or wages). There are varied types of housing, constructed under different conditions, and the body of residents is more diverse and belongs to the lower-middle class. A large proportion of such housing is developed by commercial real estate companies under direct contract with specific danwei, and there is also some lower-cost yet reasonably nice commodity housing priced at less than 200,000 yuan per unit. A second type of housing was created by the city and provincial governments to house relocated families being pushed out of the city core by several large-scale urban redevelopment projects in the 1990s (Zhang 2006). A third type of housing has been built under the state-promoted Stable Living Project (*anju gongcheng*), which gives developers special loans, tax breaks, and other benefits in order to keep the costs down and requires that these housing units be sold to qualified lower-income families at an affordable price.

Jiangan Xiaoqu is a large lower-income community located in the northern part of Kunming. Until the early 1990s, this entire area was farmland. The first several buildings were put up at that time by the Panlong District Real Estate Development Company for some three thousand relocated families driven out of the inner city. Later, this company constructed eight more apartment buildings for a nearby university. Jiangan residents are mostly factory workers, clerks, service sector workers, migrants, schoolteachers, and university professors and staff. There are also local farmers who were given replacement housing when their land was appropriated for development. Initially, the danwei assigned these housing units to their employees as part of their welfare allocation, but later, employees were asked to buy their homes from their danwei at extremely low cost. In recent years, social polarization within the community has deepened. Some residents were laid off by failing state enterprises, and others have gained more consuming power and are moving into better and larger commodity housing elsewhere, renting their Jiangan housing to migrants. Unlike the fortress-like upscale neighborhoods, Jiangan is more open and livelier, without walls and surveillance cameras. Every day, elderly men gather around small stone tables in open public areas to play chess and smoke pipes; retired women and men congregate to sing Chinese opera.

Theft, however, is a major problem in this rural-urban transitional zone because people of different kinds frequently flow in and out and the police are virtually absent; this area is not fully incorporated into any urban jurisdiction. Although the property management agency is supposed to take charge of public security and community services, its manager claims that to fulfill such responsibilities is impossible because of a lack of funding, and he has encountered strong resistance in his efforts to collect the regulation fees from the families. The security team is substantially

FIGURE 9.2

A lower-income housing compound protected by iron bars. Photo by L. Zhang.

understaffed and cannot afford any high-tech surveillance devices. Individual families are left to protect themselves by installing metal bars over their windows and balconies. Residents in the eight buildings initially owned by the university have organized mutual watch groups and installed metal

FIGURE 9.3
Social life and public space in a gongxin jieceng community. Photo by L. Zhang.

fences and gates around their buildings. These gates are locked between 11 p.m. and 6 a.m. but are wide open during the day.

Whereas urban residential communities have become more and more stratified along lines of personal wealth, it is far from clear whether people in the non-danwei-based neighborhoods share much in common. No longer "comrades" (*tongzhi*), residents in the new communities are merely "strangers" surrounded by walls and gates. Are they developing any sense of common social and cultural identification beyond material wealth? Can we speak of any identity of interests, habitus, and dispositions or even an emerging class consciousness among these strangers? Can shared spatial experience lead to a particular kind of class-specific subject?

CULTIVATING JIECENG AND RESPECT

One afternoon in the midst of a light summer rain, three of my former high school classmates picked me up in a silver Volkswagen Passat to go see a new upscale housing compound where the zhongchan jieceng live: Spring Fountain in the western suburb of Kunming. One of them, Ling, who had been recently promoted to the head of a local branch of a major bank, had just bought a home there. The condo Ling purchased was spacious, about 200 square meters, with three bedrooms, a large living room, a dining area, and two bathrooms. The Spring Fountain compound of 150 households is not considered large in comparison with other recent developments, but it is nicely designed with trees, grass, and other plants. The center of the compound features a goldfish pond, a Chinese-style pavilion, a miniature stone mountain, water lilies, and a fountain display accompanied by light Western music. These things are not merely an aesthetic veneer but are important in locating one's jieceng. Though impressed by the landscaping and generous living space, the other two friends began to feel uneasy. Both of them (and their spouses) worked for state entities, so they could not afford such a place. When I asked what they thought, one of them replied:

> Envy! I wish someday I can live in such a community and be part of this group! But if I rely on my salary, I will never be able to afford a place like this. Look at the environment here—plants, water, flowers, and music.... This is where human beings should live. My place has none of these but is surrounded by street noise, dust, and cooking smells from the street hawkers outside my window.

They then said in a semi-teasing tone that even though they still considered Ling a close friend, he really belonged to another jieceng now. Our other friend, a woman who worked in the provincial health education office, explained to me:

> Even though before I knew that [Ling] made good money, I still felt he was one of us because he lived in a community not so different from mine. We could go knock on his door whenever we wanted. But now things are different. Every time I [come] here, the security guards...stop and question me, especially because I do not drive a private car. I would not want to come to visit him here as often as I did before. It just makes me feel inferior and out of place.

Their sense of exclusion and uneasiness derived mainly from their inability to acquire a place that demands consuming power beyond their reach, a place that so tangibly demarcates socioeconomic differences through concrete spatial forms. Furthermore, through much enhanced surveillance devices (heavy metal gates, closed-circuit cameras, laser sensors, professional security guards, and so on), upscale communities have heightened their social isolation and segregation as they exclude unwanted intruders outright. Such exclusion is often justified by the fear of urban crime and by a neoliberal rationale that valorizes private property, personal wealth, and the pursuit of a privileged lifestyle at the expense of public space and social intermingling.[17] Through such highly visible spatial demarcation, it externalizes and foregrounds previously invisible or less pronounced socioeconomic differences. Community is thus deployed as an active element in structuring class differences.

Places like Spring Fountain are generally perceived by urbanites as *furen qu,* a place where wealthy people congregate, yet those living in these places sense a lack of any social and cultural cohesion among the residents. One question I asked my interviewees was, "Do you find anything in common with others living here?" Nearly all answered no or "not much." Many used the word *za* (diverse, mixed) to describe the social components of their community. Ling put it this way:

> People here have quite different social backgrounds and experiences. They are indeed a hodgepodge [*da zahui*]. The only thing they have in common is money and consuming power. But I guess a jieceng is much more than that. Perhaps after one or two decades of living together, these people will gradually form some sort of common lifestyle, tastes, and dispositions. But for now, I do not feel that I share much with my neighbors.

Residents in these communities tend to have a strong sense of privacy and rarely interact with one another. Among some thirty people I interviewed, only two said that they had visited their next-door neighbors once or twice, and then only to see the interior remodeling before the families moved in. The rest said that they never had visited. One elderly woman who lived with her well-to-do son's family told me that her son had specifically warned her not to invite neighbors in or to say much about his business because strangers are not trustworthy. I asked where they would seek help in case of an emergency. None of my interviewees mentioned neighbors. When I asked why, some said that it was because they had their own car and did not need others to help with transportation. In case of a medical emergency, they would rather call a fee-based ambulance service. Others said that they would rather hire a *baomu* (caregiver) to take care of a sick family member than ask for help from neighbors. One woman explained: "I do not even know my neighbors. On what basis do I ask for help?" She continued:

> We used to live in a danwei compound and knew almost every-
> one. We paid visits to neighbors and friends in our spare time.
> But since I moved into this new community, things have changed.
> I have not been to any neighbor's home so far. They would not
> invite you. At best, they say hello to you when running into you
> outside or playing with kids at the playground. I would not feel
> comfortable going to their home or chatting, as we really have
> little in common. After all, we are strangers to one another.

What we see here is a dual process at work: the spatial differentiation of people by community based on private wealth, and the atomization of individual families within each housing compound based on a heightened sense of privacy. However, the subjective experiences of this privacy are highly ambivalent and uneven. In some cases, it is cherished and celebrated as a sign of middle-class distinction; in other cases, it is seen as a moral loss and an erosion of social ties.

In upscale zhongchan jieceng communities, residents tend to engage in conspicuous consumption. The ability to consume the right kinds of things is taken not only as the measure of one's prestige (*zunrong*) and "face" (*mianzi*) but also as an indication of whether one deserves member-ship in a particular community. If one's consumption practices are not compatible with the kind of housing or community in which one lives, one would be seen as "out of place." Such social pressure does not emanate from any identifiable organization or set of written rules, yet it is pervasive and embedded in the everyday cultural milieu. Although homeownership and community choice constitute the core of this new consumer culture, realms such as private car ownership, interior design, children's schooling, leisure activities, clothing, food choices, and manners are also important spheres through which jieceng is performed and conceived. China's newly rich are getting ahead economically, but they share a gnawing sense of social insecurity and thus long for respect.

Ms. Liang and her husband had just bought a home in the luxury com-munity of Jade Garden. Though only a high school graduate, her husband was able to make a substantial living from his small-scale gasoline and industrial oil trading business. She explained how they had ended up here and her perception of the lifestyle suitable for a place like this:

> A few years ago, we had already saved enough money to buy a
> unit in another upscale [community], but we eventually decided

on a lower-level community. Why? Because even though we could afford the housing itself, we could not afford living there at that time. For example, when most families drive their private cars, I would be embarrassed if I had to ride my bike to work every day. Even taking a taxi is looked down upon there. If our neighbors [would] see my parents coming to visit me by bus, they [would] be laughed at too. Since my rich neighbors go to shop for shark fins and other expensive seafood every day, I cannot let them see me buying cabbage and turnips. All the families there seem to be competing with one another. If you do not have that kind of consuming power, you'd better not live there, because you will not fit in well.

By the time I interviewed her, her family was in a stronger financial situation, and thus she felt that they were ready to reside in an upper-level community and learn to live like their well-to-do neighbors. They bought a car and completely remodeled the entire house with gleaming redwood floors, marble tile, fancy lighting, modern kitchen appliances, and luxurious furniture. She stopped working outside the home in order to devote all her time to her husband and toddler, even though there was a full-time nanny. Her sense of readiness for membership in this community was closely tied to her family's ability to demonstrate a certain degree of consuming power in everyday life.

Like Liang, many zhongchan residents I met felt obliged to engage in the proper kind of consumption in order to validate their status and gain respect from their peers. But since everyone is learning to become a member of an emerging jieceng, what is considered proper and suitable is mutable and unclear. Often, there exist competing notions of suitable consumption, which generate anxiety among the residents. They watch and compare their own activities with their neighbors' in order to get a better sense of what and how to consume. For example, it has become popular to join an exclusive fee-based club (huisuo)—a new site of prestige that sets zhongchan families apart from the mass of others. Children have become another focal point for cultivating the consumption deemed necessary to become true members of the zhongchan jieceng class (see Katz, chapter 7, this volume). In Shanghai and other cities, for instance, the new middle-class parents have begun to send their children for expensive private training in golf, ballet, music, horseback riding, skiing, and polo, and even to finishing schools run by foreigners to learn how to become proper ladies and gentlemen (French 2006). I went once to a lavish, members-only golf club in Kunming with my friend Ling, the bank head, where he was teaching his twelve-year-old son to play golf.

Another distinct trend in consumption among the relatively well-to-do is the emergence of multiple sites catering to a small group of "leisure women." Although the majority of urban Chinese households today are two-income families, this is not always the case for the newly rich. Women in some well-to-do families have quit their jobs to stay home and thus have plenty of free time. Since their husbands are usually preoccupied by business and entertainment away from home, these lonely women seek out such leisure activities as hair styling, manicures, and facial treatments, which have flourished in the wealthy xiaoqu. One of the most popular activities in recent years for both men and women with disposable income is to frequent "foot-soaking entertainment centers" (*xijiao cheng*). These are small specialized salons where customers can soak their feet in a warm fluid brewed from Chinese medicinal herbs and then receive a long foot massage (see also Freeman, chapter 4, this volume). (Some of these are covert sites for sexual services catering to men.) Such salons tend to be concentrated in the new private neighborhoods, where the residents have the time and money to patronize them.

In sum, new consumption practices have come to play a crucial part in reshaping people's tastes and dispositions, creating a privileged lifestyle.[18] As my ethnographic account shows, zhongchan jieceng is not a static thing one possesses, nor is it predetermined by one's position in the social structure; it has to be constantly cultivated and performed through everyday consumption activities. To be able to consume certain commodities in certain ways is a key mechanism in the making of jieceng. In this particular context, homeownership and one's subsequent spatial location in the city have become the most significant components of social differentiation and subject formation in the reform era.

Why is consumption so important in cultivating and performing jieceng in China? This is partly due to the difficulty nowadays of pinpointing the exact sources of personal wealth or gauging someone's income simply by knowing his or her occupation. When the production of wealth has to be kept secret and is intentionally made opaque, then conspicuous material consumption serves as a viable way to assert and maintain one's status.[19] Another important factor to consider is the sense of social insecurity among the emerging upper and middle classes in their quest for propriety and respectability. The cultivation of habitus (or jieceng wenhua) through various consumption practices is a form of social experimentation in an uncertain cultural field and a strategy for getting ahead in an increasingly competitive society.

As socialism is profoundly transformed by privatization, market forces, and consumerism, class politics takes on a specific contour that requires a closer look at the interplay of property ownership, space making, and consumption practices. Whereas the shop-floor experience is central to the formation of a working-class identity and class consciousness among factory workers, state employees (now often laid off), and migrant workers (Lee 2002; Pun 2005), this is not the case for the emerging upper- and middle-class subjects. When spatially dispersed under the public housing regime, urbanites in China could not be easily identified as distinct social groups. But today, under the new commercialized property regime, individuals who have acquired personal wealth are able to converge in stratified private residential communities. Such emerging places offer a tangible location for a new jieceng to materialize through spatial exclusion, cultural differentiation, and private lifestyle practices. It is in this sense that residential space does not merely encode socioeconomic differences but plays an active role in the making of class and social performance.

As China increasingly embraces neoliberal reasoning and strategies, such reemerging class differentiation is portrayed as a natural and progressive move away from Maoist absolute egalitarianism. The sacredness of private property, the desire for privacy, and the possibility of pursuing personal freedom and happiness are deployed as the building blocks of a neoliberal way of life at the expense of equality, public space, and social responsibility for the poor. In this context, the political potential of the emerging middle class remains unclear. So far, there is little evidence to suggest the formation of a meaningful, independent political and civil space to counterbalance state power.[20]

The way jieceng is spatialized and performed in Chinese cities echoes a global trend toward the privatization of space, security, and lifestyle. Increasingly, upper- and middle-class families in North America and Latin America, for example, are drawn into what Teresa Caldeira (2000) calls "fortified enclaves"—privatized, enclosed, and monitored residential spaces—to pursue comfort, happiness, and security (see also Low 2003; McKenzie 1994). As people retreat behind gates, walls, security guards, and surveillance cameras, spatial segregation and social exclusion are intensified. Mike Davis (1992a:228) describes this kind of spatial politics and conflict, as expressed in Los Angeles, as a "new class war at the level of the built environment." Neil Smith (1996:47) calls such divided urban geography "the revanchist city," in which struggles between the middle classes and squatters and homeless people will only intensify. How the inherent tensions and contradictions in the increasingly polarized urban environment will play out in the Chinese context is not yet clear.

Acknowledgments

This is a slightly revised version of Li Zhang, "Private Homes, Distinct Lifestyles: Performing a New Middle Class," in *Privatizing China: Socialism from Afar*, edited by Li Zhang and Aihwa Ong (pp. 23–40). Copyright © 2008 by Cornell University. Used by permission of the publisher, Cornell University Press. Early versions of this chapter were presented at the 2004 annual meeting of the Asian Studies Association; the workshop "The Social, Cultural, and Political Implications of Privatization in the People's Republic of China," Shanghai, June 28–29, 2004; the Department of Anthropology and the Center for Asian Studies at the University of Wisconsin, Madison, September 2004; the conference "Class-ifying 'Asian Values': Culture, Morality, and the Politics of Being Middle Class in Asia," College of the Holy Cross, Worcester, Massachusetts, November 4–6, 2005; the "Modern China" seminar at Columbia University, October 5, 2006; and the workshop "Reclaiming Chinese Society: Politics of Redistribution, Recognition, and Representation" at the University of California, Berkeley, October 27–28, 2006. I thank Michael Burawoy, Mun Young Cho, Sara Friedman, Emily Honig, Rebecca Karl, Mark Miller, Kevin O'Brien, Aihwa Ong, Eileen Otis, Lisa Rofel, and the participants and audiences at these events for their helpful comments and conversations. The research was supported by the Wenner-Gren Foundation for Anthropological Research, the University of California President's Research Fellowship in the Humanities, the Davis Humanities Research Fellowship, the Institute of Governmental Affairs junior faculty research grant, and faculty research grants from the University of California at Davis.

Notes

1. The social stratum I describe here is new in the sense that it is a by-product of the privatization of homeownership, which was largely absent from the early 1950s to the late 1980s. This social group is not a structural continuation of the middle class that existed before the communist takeover.

2. My fieldwork was carried out during four summers from 2000 to 2003 with a total of approximately ten months of field research. Over the course of these four years, I interviewed about forty homeowners and management staff in several communities and maintained close ties with some of my informants. I also interviewed ten developers and local officials involved in the construction of new communities. Much time was also spent in daily observation of community life in ten housing compounds, with a particular focus on three of them.

3. I borrow this concept from Paul Willis (1977), even though it originally re-ferred to a set of distinct, localized cultural practices and beliefs associated with work-ing-class youth culture in a capitalist society he examined.

4. Such anxieties and instability in middle-class cultural practices have been dis-cussed by Barbara Ehrenreich (1989), Katherine S. Newman (1999), and Max Weber (1981).

5. Although Weber differentiates classes from status groups in that the former are largely defined in terms of production and the latter in terms of consumption, he also emphasizes that the two modes of group formation are closely linked through property ownership, which not only determines one's class situation but also serves as the pri-mary basis for differences in lifestyle (see Giddens 1981).

6. For a culturally oriented understanding of class making, see Liechty 2003 and Miller 1987, 1995.

7. Bourdieu (1984) treats habitus as a form of structuring structure, those ele-ments of culture that are anchored in and shape people's daily practices. Here, I do not intend to engage in the argument about whether consumption ultimately leads to emancipation or exploitation (see Davis 2005; Pun 2003). I simply want to emphasize the active role of consumption in shaping class and the often contradictory experiences it generates.

8. This is not to deny the social and economic differences that existed among urban Chinese under Mao. Yet, the existent living pattern based on *danwei* (work units) made it difficult for people with similar economic status to live together and cultivate a shared lifestyle, a habitus, and a sense of common identification as anything other than danwei comrades (see also Tomba 2005).

9. Goodman and Zang (2008) use the term "new rich" to describe a broad social group that has acquired a certain amount of wealth during the reform and that is iden-tified by Chinese loosely as part of the rising middle classes. They point out that "the new rich are not all by any means super rich," since this is a diverse social formation with its own hierarchies (2008:3). But even so, the Chinese middle classes do not repre-sent the considerably larger body of the population situated in the middle, as is the case in the United States or Canada.

10. I thank Rebecca Karl for her critical comments on my theoretical treatment of class and status. Although we do not fully agree on whether the use of the term *jieceng* can capture or depoliticize what is going on in Chinese society today, her engaging com-ments pushed me to think over this issue more carefully.

11. By "neoliberalism" I refer to the practices and thinking associated with the privatization of property and lifestyles and with the valorization of market forces, rather

than to a Foucauldian notion of neoliberalism as a form of governmentality and self-governing.

12. Shanghai presents an exception, for its residents have tended to maintain a strong consciousness of spatial inequality, partly owing to the city's colonial experiences (see Pan 2002).

13. The lower-income neighborhoods include mostly privatized danwei housing compounds and some newly developed, state-subsidized xiaoqu for teachers, other low-income families, and those who were forced out of the core city districts by urban renewal projects or commercial developments.

14. For more detailed discussion on the controversial use of Western modern images in new housing development, see Zhang 2010.

15. Most new commercially developed communities in China are now regulated by property management agencies and private security guards; they thus have little contact with residents committees (*juweihui*) and the local police. See Read 2000, 2003 for more details.

16. This is called *yingxing shouru* (invisible income), which often far exceeds the salary offered by one's work unit. It is nearly impossible to survey such incomes, for two reasons: they tend to fluctuate over time, and people are unwilling to divulge exactly how much invisible income they earn and the means by which they obtain it.

17. This is very similar to the situation discussed by Caldeira (2000) and Low (2001a, 2003).

18. Anthropological studies (see Freeman 2000 and Mills 1999, for example) have also demonstrated the centrality of consumption, not just production, in understanding the formation and transformation of the working-class identity and lifestyle in the era of globalization and capitalist restructuring.

19. The increased importance of consumption in post-Mao social life is clearly demonstrated by a series of studies in *The Consumer Revolution in Urban China* (Davis 2000).

20. Benjamin Read (2003) is optimistic about homeowners associations in China's new communities, seeing them as a possible force for democratizing the urban Chinese population. Yet, my own research indicates that these associations are often shortsighted, parochial, and short-lived.

10

Gate Expectations

Discursive Displacement of the "Old Middle Class" in an American Suburb

Rachel Heiman

In the United States, the dominant public discourse on middle class-ness tends to err on the side of homogenization, implying that *all* members of *the* middle class in the United States share a set of desires, needs, and expectations. When there is a move away from homogenizing language, it is typically through references to the "upper-middle class" or "lower-middle class," revealing the dominance of income-bracket logics of class in the United States, rather than an understanding of class locations as being produced within particular historical moments with their associated economic, cultural, political, and moral logics. Inspired by the language of "old middle class" and "new middle class" in places like Egypt (Schielke, chapter 2, this volume), India (Fernandes 2006; Srivastava, chapter 3, this volume), China (Zhang, chapter 9, this volume), and Hungary (Fehérváry, chapter 5, this volume), this chapter employs the productive analytical lens of "old" and "new" in the context of the United States and offers a way of thinking about tensions in sites of the middle classes by way of understanding the different historical moments of their emergence. Specifically, I provide a close discursive analysis of a zoning board debate in a suburban New Jersey town in the late 1990s that reveals the increasing discursive displacement of old middle-class approaches to the suburban landscape in the United States in favor of new middle-class neoliberal sensibilities. Although there have been middle classes in the United States since the late colonial period, for my purposes here, the "old middle class" comprises those who hold a liberal democratic understanding of land use, and the "new middle class" comprises those who have given up on those ideals in favor of unabashed claims to private property.

Frederick Law Olmsted, America's most influential landscape architect, is famous for his design of New York City's Central Park, but his most profound influence on the American landscape was arguably his vision for suburban land use. The landscape in the United States, he believed, should not be carved up with stone walls—aristocratic relics—to mark the edges of private property, as was prevalent in the English countryside that he visited in the mid-nineteenth century. Rather, he felt that the American landscape ought to exemplify the democratic ideal, no walls allowed and people living in houses with lawns that flowed together seamlessly, as if everyone lived together in one big park (Pollan 1991:58–61). When Olmsted designed Riverside, Illinois, one of the first planned suburban communities in the United States, the nation was just a few years from the end of its civil war and in much need of unifying ideals to create and build the "imagined community" (Anderson 1983) of an American public.

Olmsted continued his efforts during the late nineteenth century to limit walls, gates, and fences in the United States, although he conceded during the early years of private restrictive covenants that if a property owner felt the need for a gate or fence, it should be limited to a maximum height of 3 feet. People could see over this height, so the spirit of the democratic ideal of the shared lawn could still remain (Fogelson 2005:92). It was still several decades before the first municipal zoning codes came into effect and almost a century before the mass production of suburbs in the post–World War II period, but the idea of setting a maximum height of 3 feet for gates and fences along the front of one's property became a land-use habit and the starting point for land-use master plans in many suburban municipalities across the country.[1] It is important to keep in mind, however, that the United States was founded on a strong commitment to liberal democracy and its core Lockean (1980[1690]) ideals; this approach to the suburban landscape (versus public parks) may promote an *ideal* of shared community, but it masks the reality and exclusions of private property. It is this moral logic in regard to property that I refer to as that of the old middle class in the United States.

Many municipalities in the United States have over the years altered their zoning ordinances to allow gates and fences higher than 3 feet. There are several of these in New Jersey, though certain regions, most notably California, the Southwest, and the Southeast have been at the forefront in the growth of gates and gated communities, sometimes within municipalities but often on unincorporated land (Blakely and Snyder 1999; Low 2003). This dramatic move away from the ideal of the liberal democratic landscape—and toward an unapologetic claim to and marking of private property that I refer to as the moral logic of property of the new middle class—can be viewed as part of the larger trend of "neoliberalizing space" (Peck and Tickell 2002) in the United States since the late 1970s, which includes the intensification of gentrification (Smith 1996; Williams 1988), the expansion of private homeowner associations (McKenzie 1994; Ross 1999), the militarization of urban space (Davis 1992b), and the incursion of public-private partnerships into public domains of governance (Chesluk 2004; Lipsitz 2006).

This alarming trend toward what Evan McKenzie (1994) calls "privatopia" is quite revealing in regard to neoliberalizing space, and pronounced attention to the privatization of policies and services that used to be enforced and provided by municipal governments is well deserved. But when we view a time period through the lens of its characterization—such as "the neoliberal moment"—we run the risk of focusing predominantly on what is new or what has been exaggerated during that moment, failing to keep in view sites and strategies that appear to come from—or be relevant only in regard to—a previous historical moment. As Raymond Williams (1977:122) reminds us, "the residual, by definition, has been effectively formed in the past, but it is still active in the cultural process, not only and often not at all as an element of the past, but as an effective element of the present." As the zoning board debate that I examine in this chapter demonstrates, public zoning codes—although not as glaring as gates of steel or as convoluted as private covenants, conditions, and restrictions—continue to vigorously structure spatial relations and social milieus in the United States.[2] Despite the trend of moving away from municipal town halls toward private homeowner associations and gated communities, town halls and other sites of public governance continue to be key sites for struggles over land use and the built environment.[3] Debates within them provide a window onto local articulations of larger political-economic shifts and their associated cultural and moral logics, and the side of a debate onto which individuals fall does not necessarily map onto where they are located in income brackets, even if the increasing disparity in wealth in the United States is part of the conditions of possibility for these tensions.

GATE EXPECTATIONS

Tarragon Hills, a brand-new upscale subdivision of twenty-three custom homes ("No Two Homes Alike!" proclaimed the sales billboard) was constructed in Danboro, New Jersey, during the economic boom of the late 1990s.[4] Danboro had been a small farming community until the mid-1960s, when suburbanization began with the arrival of white-flight émigrés from the outer boroughs of New York City, particularly Brooklyn. The majority of the newcomers who flooded the town in the 1970s and early 1980s moved into moderately sized (by American standards) colonial-style homes, the size and style of houses that signified the suburban American dream in the early post-Fordist period. During the late 1980s, a few developments of larger colonial-style homes were built, but it was not until the economic boom of the late 1990s that a profound rupture in the architectural landscape of the town took place. Huge homes like those in Tarragon Hills were built adjacent to older subdivisions, mirroring the upscaling of the suburban American dream across the country. These new houses dwarfed their neighbors and produced jarring juxtapositions. When combined with increasing concerns about overcrowding—whether in regard to neverending traffic, overflowing public schools, or diminishing open space—these architectural shifts provoked class anxieties and roused uncertainties about the fiscal and discursive boundaries of inclusion and exclusion in the imagined future of the town. Like gentrification in urban areas, changes in the grandeur of suburban housing reflect a transformation of the class makeup of a town and reveal shifts in the larger class structure, the structuring of people's social locations, and moral discourses on private property.

The growing income divide between the middle and upper-middle classes in Danboro during the late 1990s (that is, the divide between those who could afford only moderately sized homes versus those who could afford any home in the town) was occurring within the U.S. middle classes as a whole as the income of the upper-middle class pulled significantly away from the rest of the middle class. This economic shift was part of a larger intensification of structural changes that had begun in the early 1970s. With the onset of broad-scale, global political-economic restructuring, the growth and stability of the U.S. middle class created in the post–World War II period proved to be relatively short-lived. The toll on the middle class was compounded by the rise of neoliberal approaches to social welfare, including declines in entitlements and safety nets for individual households (versus corporate entities), the privatization of various segments of the public sphere, and new modes of capital accumulation, including new techniques of optimization and an expanded ethos of consumerism matched by new

FIGURE 10.1

Completed homes in Tarragon Hills. Photo by R. Heiman.

means of acquiring credit (Harvey 1990, 2005; Katz, chapter 7, this volume; Ong 2006; Rouse 1995). These conditions, which in part created the economic crisis to follow, placed the burdens of everyday life increasingly on the backs of individual families and local communities. Although significant wealth was created during the economic booms of the 1980s and 1990s, it was acquired and distributed unequally. Some members of the middle class experienced downward mobility (Ehrenreich 1989, 2005; Newman 1988), whereas others, as in the town of Danboro, witnessed a considerable enlargement of the expanse separating the middle and upper-middle classes (Ortner 2003).

The Danboro residents who moved into the moderately sized homes in the 1970s and early 1980s were especially sensitive to these changes. They had considered their new homes at that time to be enormous, because they had grown up in the post–World War II period in apartments and two-family homes in working-class and lower-middle-class urban neighborhoods. During their childhoods, when many of their white peers moved to the suburbs, their less affluent families moved to the edges of Brooklyn, part of the inner-city white-flight migration (Rieder 1985). They spent their early adult years in the neighborhoods in which they had grown up, but when it was time to raise their own children, in the late 1970s, New York City had spiraled into a fiscal and racial crisis fueled by "urban renewal" policies that compounded, racialized, and spatialized the effects of industrial decline (Jackson 1985). Despite having adored their urban childhoods, a mix of urban fears, racial anxieties, pastoral yearnings, and class aspirations prompted them to take a financial leap and acquire a piece of the suburban American dream. They did so, however, just as the glory days of the middle classes were coming to a close in the United States, and "keeping up with the Joneses" was on the verge of transforming into "keeping up with the Dow Jones" (Folbre 1995).

By the late 1990s, when I conducted fieldwork in the town, Danboro real estate had seen many years of inflation due to being part of a metropolitan region experiencing pressure from new flows of capital and the people that came with it. Danboro is on the edge of commuting distance to New York City and has highly desired public schools. Most of the town's remaining farmland had been developed into subdivisions of huge homes like those in Tarragon Hills, further raising property values in the town. For some residents, especially retirees, it was a nice opportunity to cash out. For residents who moved unwillingly to more affordable towns at that time, the move was a form of displacement—an inflationary form of gentrification known as "capital valorization" (Smith 1996).[5] They had found that they no longer could afford their taxes, which in New Jersey are based heavily on property values. Those residents who could afford to stay and who wanted to do so, who are the focus of my discussion here, witnessed in their town the escalation of a new development in the spatialization of class in the United States: spatial segregation is no longer mapped simply according to where the working class, middle class, and elites live. The middle class and the upper-middle class are increasingly segregated into different spatial locations.

The lack of attention to the "residual" has kept out of view towns like Danboro in contemporary studies on middle-class residential areas in the United States, at least until the housing crash that began in 2008. This is likely because they appear at first glance to embody old middle-class ideals: places to which people move for open lawns, public schools, municipal recreation facilities, and town hall politics. Yet, when a town like Danboro is viewed ethnographically through the lens of historically minded critical geography, we are able to broaden our theorizing of the local articulation of political-economic and discursive shifts.[6] Our analyses shed light on what we are not able to see through income bracket logics: cracks in the processes of neoliberalizing space as old middle-class ideologies fight to survive within new middle-class logics of neoliberalism.

FIGURE 10.2
Proposed 6-foot-high gate.

Key sites for exploring these issues are disputes that pertain to land use (LiPuma and Meltzoff 1997). The particular debate that I focus on in this chapter occurred in Danboro during the winter of 1999.[7] A couple buying a home in Tarragon Hills decided that they wanted to build a large security gate across their driveway. The couple designed this particular gate so that it would both correspond to the style of their home and be consistent with the scale of the house. Accordingly, it was a big gate: the stanchions were sketched to be 8 feet long, and the gate was drawn to run 20 feet across the driveway and reach 6 feet high at its maximum points. However, a zoning ordinance in Danboro states that a gate in the front yard of a property can be no more than 3 feet high at its maximum point.[8] So the developers of Tarragon Hills had to submit an application to Danboro's Zoning Board of Adjustment to request a variance to build the couple their 6-foot-high security gate,[9] which would have been the first of its kind in Danboro, a town with no gated communities and only a few individual gates.[10]

The public hearing for this gate request became quite contentious and turned into a heated dispute that took people in the room by surprise. Gate requests are usually quick and easy since most people who submit an application to build an oversized gate or fence in the front of their property do so because they live on a main road and are concerned that their young children might climb over a 3-foot-high fence and get into harm's way. It rarely takes more than 20 minutes for the board to confirm that a safety issue really is at stake and to determine the additional height that it will allow. Yet, this gate request issue took far longer to resolve than anyone had expected, though I use the word "resolve" extremely lightly here. A vote among the board members ultimately finalized the variance that the board would allow. However, the highly antagonistic debate that night unearthed critical tensions that were illustrative of the shifting moral logics of property ownership in Danboro and comparable suburban communities during the late 1990s. Amid significant changes in the town's class structure, the proposed 6-foot-high gate—at once a mechanism for security and an object of class distinction (Bourdieu 1984)—acquired considerable semiotic force.[11] Its style and, particularly, its scale blurred the boundaries between security concerns, aesthetic desires, and social dividing lines, leading the variance request to become a request for far more than relief of the township's 3-foot-high ordinance. It became a challenge to the type of middle-class town long promoted and encouraged in Danboro and a sign to longer-term residents of the possibility of being locked outside the discursive or fiscal gates of their own town.

Through a close analysis of the zoning board debate that night, this chapter addresses a series of questions: What insights can be garnered about shifting middle-class configurations and social dividing lines in the United States through examining struggles over the built environment in suburbs like Danboro? What can we learn about middle-class space making by paying close attention to class anxieties, which hover at the edges of everyday life and shape discursive possibilities at often unexpected moments? Under what conditions—and through what processes—are racialized urban fears disentangled from trepidation about the security of the postwar American dream and aspirations, including the associated moral expectations in regard to community and property? And what is the historical significance of an effort to forestall the construction of this type of gate during a time when gates and gated communities were being built in record numbers across the United States, as well as in other countries with expanding middle classes?

FROM EXCLUSIONARY ZONING TO PROTECTIVE ZONING

Constance Perin (1977:179) has pointed out, "Developers and, often enough, their requests for variances and zoning amendments, light up for old-timers the early warning system of social shifts to come." The request for this gate was one such cautionary moment. An ordinance that sets a maximum height of 3 feet for a gate or a fence in the front of one's property implies hope on the part of the authors of the zoning code to preserve a bit of the pastoral amid suburban growth. Three feet of height is typically enough to keep small children and dogs *in* and stay within the spirit of community signified in the shared democratic lawn promulgated by Frederick Law Olmsted (Fogelson 2005 ; Pollan 1991). But a 6-foot-high gate like the one designed by the Tarragon Hills couple is much more about keeping people *out*, with an "aesthetics of security" (Caldeira 2000) that emulates the regal.

Zoning debates are particularly fruitful sites in which to explore discursive shifts; they offer a nexus through which to view the concerns of a particular historical moment, revealing the ways that public and private desires and anxieties merge and intersect with processes of space making. Since zoning is a means of demarcating boundaries of exclusion, in each historical moment we need to re-ask *what* land uses (and therefore *what kinds* of people or practices) are being excluded, and for what ends. Despite the democratic ideal that the shared lawn was meant to evoke, the building of the suburbs in the post–World War II period was intentionally exclusionary on the part of the U.S. federal government, whose policies explicitly stated that federally backed loans would not be granted for neighborhoods or towns with people of color (Cohen 2003; Jackson 1985). When these discriminatory policies were eventually revoked, towns turned to land-use rules as a strategy to keep out the working class and people of color and thus subdue (white, middle-class) fears of property value decline. Often referred to as "snob zoning" (Kirp, Dwyer, and Rosenthal 1995:61), these strategies included large-scale zoning plans to create residential districts (or entire towns) that excluded property owners from constructing multidwelling apartment buildings and from building on small lots (that is, what the working class and poor could afford). Given the racial politics of class in the United States, this enabled the exclusion of racialized others long after racial discrimination in housing deeds was deemed unconstitutional and racial bias in federal housing loans had ceased (Cohen 2003). These ordinances were crafted through making universal claims about the need to stem the "tide of suburban development," despite what were often exclusionary intents (Babcock and Bosselman 1973; Davidoff and Brooks 1976; Perin 1977; Toll 1969). This approach to negotiating social borders, which Richard Babcock (1966) refers to as the "zoning game," is an exemplary "liberal strategy of exclusion" (Mehta 1990).

Legal battles over zoning rules have always exposed the fundamental tension between private property and the public good, particularly who counts as the "public" and which "good" is at stake. This is not surprising, given the long-term, uneasy relationship between private property and the public good in a liberal democracy. John Locke's (1980[1690]:52) writings remind us, "The only way whereby any one…puts on the *bonds of civil society*, is by agreeing with other men to join and unite into a community for their comfortable, safe, and peaceable living one amongst another, in a secure enjoyment of their properties, and a greater security against any, that are not of it." Exclusionary zoning laws, a twentieth-century addition to the "bonds of civil society," clearly exhibit this spirit of dealing with those who are "not of it," who are kept outside the community in order to ensure its "security." Snob zoning continues to exist, albeit in more limited measure due to constitutional challenges (Duncan and Duncan 1997). Yet, what is often left out of commentaries on exclusionary possibilities enabled through ordinances is that zoning—like civil society itself—is also deemed necessary to curb the desires of fellow property owners (Frug 1999:145). In the late 1990s, neighbors from developments like Tarragon Hills risked pricing people out of their own town and taking away the "secure enjoyment of their properties." Suburban zoning laws in the late 1990s thus began to be used as a technology—through limiting the height of gates, for example—to restrain excessive optimization of property and to contain reminders of the changing moral logics of middle-class property ownership. This means of reining in the architectural accoutrements of neighbors from the new middle-class—what I call "protective zoning"—was a zoning game for the late 1990s neoliberal moment.

Before we turn to the details of the debate itself, there are a couple of issues to keep in mind. The first is that this type of gate was not outside the aesthetics held by many of the people in the town. Danboro is not an "old money" town where people (often elites) are modest in their display of wealth and where this type of gate would contrast with the low stone walls that dot the landscape. In fact, Danboro is somewhat infamous among its neighboring communities for being a town where there is extraordinary pressure to participate in an aesthetics of class display that is comparable to the style of this proposed gate. A few developments of large, ornate homes had already been built during the housing boom of the 1980s, but no one—until this request—had ever come to the zoning board seeking to build a 6-foot-high, ornamental security gate to go along with his huge home.

It is also important to keep in mind that in the late 1990s, when this debate occurred, the public discourse on the conditions of middle-class life in the United States was quite different from that ten years later during the economic crisis. During the late 1990s, the media were celebrating the economic boom as if it were benefiting everyone, with little attention to who was feeling the downside of its effects, financial or otherwise. It was still several years before the economic bubble would burst and several more before the housing bubble would burst and the media would begin to be flooded with a resounding critique of the "squeeze" on the middle class, the dramatic class divide, the over-mortgaging of daily lives, the freewheeling movement of capital into real estate and securities, and the threat that these conditions placed on people's abilities to remain in their homes and their hometowns. I emphasize this to get our heads back into the late 1990s, to be in that moment, since the reactions to the debate that night were, drawing on Gramsci's understanding of these terms, "common-sense," "spontaneous" responses to the spatialization of the class shifts during those years; that is, they were not, in Gramsci's (1971:198–99) words, "the result of any systematic educational activity on the part of an already conscious leading group, but...formed through everyday experience illuminated by 'common sense,' i.e., by the traditional popular conception of the world." There are now many "conscious leading groups" on these issues, but people's reactions that night were based on a "popular conception" of their town during a time when local spatial changes were challenging their sense of their community and its boundaries of inclusion and there was not yet a narrative in the public discourse that articulated these conditions in structural terms.

It is because of the unexpected and spontaneous nature of the reaction that I bring to life the majority of the debate, as if in real time. The board's final decision was not shaped simply by the semiotics of the proposed gate; it was the process of the debate itself—through narratives of legal argumentation, utterances of particular terms, and meaning making in the room in regard to publics—that shaped the outcome. My close reading demonstrates *how* this occurred by animating the micro-processes often erased in more macro-level accounts of "what happened" in legal and policy decisions (Hanson 2007). The tectonic shifts in the middle class affecting many residents in Danboro shaped how those on the zoning board and in the audience interpreted the strategic words being employed. Each word and phrase employed (and, at times, hurled as an epithet) during the debate could not, in Bakhtin's (1981:276) words, "fail to brush up against thousands of living dialogic threads, woven by socio-ideological consciousness around the given object of an utterance." Through a close discursive analysis of the micro-processes that shaped the outcome of the debate, my analysis disentangles the "dialogic threads" woven into the zoning board meeting, revealing how class anxieties became a powerful subtext in the discussion, which created the conditions of possibility for these anxieties to have a material effect on the built environment of the town.[12]

FROM PROTECTING THE PASTORAL IDEAL TO KEEPING OUT THE "REGAL"

Danboro's town hall sets a fitting scene for this debate, which reveals a shift from long-term ideas about protecting the democratic pastoral ideal to newfound efforts to keep out the regal. The building had been a working barn, and the exterior still reflected that, but the inside was retrofitted to look like a typical town hall. There was seating on a raised, semicircular platform in the front for board members, two tables nearby for lawyers and applicants, a podium for members of the public to share their thoughts, and rows of benches for the audience. The majority of town residents at the meeting of the zoning board that night were from a subdivision of moderately sized homes that backs up against a commercial park. There was a variance request on the agenda by the owners of a 4,000-square-foot entertainment complex, which is located in the commercial park. The owners wanted to offer teen dances in the facility, and some residents in the development were worried that these dances might attract teenagers from the neighboring town, which had a downtown neighborhood with many nonwhite, working-class residents. I took a seat near these people, since I, too, thought that this would be the most contested item on the agenda, sure to throw into relief the racial politics of class anxieties.

I ended up sitting next to an elderly man who was a volunteer for the Danboro Township Historic Commission. The commission sends a representative to all zoning meetings to keep a watchful eye on what needs to be protected, particularly the remaining buildings from Danboro's pastoral past. William Dobriner (1963) wrote about class tensions in what he called "reluctant suburbs," small towns that became suburbanized—reluctantly— during the postwar period. It is interesting to consider the rearticulation of those tensions in places like Danboro, which once were reluctant suburbs and may still be experienced as such by old-timers; in regard to the new huge homes, a new type of reluctance creates common ground between old-timers like the man from the commission and first-wave suburbanites. As this debate reveals, protecting the pastoral and excluding outsiders were no longer the only pressing concerns in towns like Danboro during the late 1990s. Apprehension about the influx of the regal took center stage and led to curious instances of bonding at the end of the night between this man and those from one of the many subdivisions that original residents like him had long bemoaned.[13]

ADDRESSING AN "UNDUE HARDSHIP" WITHOUT A "DETRIMENT" TO THE "PUBLIC GOOD"

The agenda for this meeting was—as usual—overburdened. The inexhaustible construction in Danboro during the late 1990s inundated the zoning board with requests of all kinds. In the spirit of moving as quickly as possible through the agenda, Joan,[14] the chairperson of the zoning board,

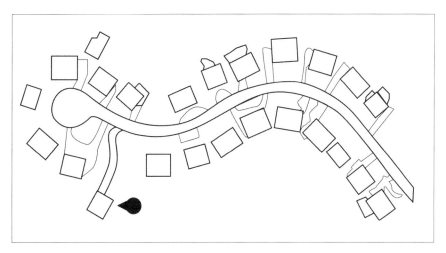

FIGURE 10.3
Flag lot.

decided to move the gate request earlier on the agenda. It was thought best to get the gate application out of the way before tackling other items on the agenda, like the teen dances, that were expected to require lengthier discussion. When the gate case was called, the lawyer and the developer from the corporation building Tarragon Hills approached the front of the room to present their case. In a confident and matter-of-fact tone, David, the lawyer, explained to the board that the lot in question was an "anomaly." All of the other houses in the subdivision were set back from the road at distances ranging from 40 to 90 feet, whereas this particular home—on a "flag lot"[15]—was set back more than 250 feet from the road, tucked away in the woods. The driveway—approximately 400 feet long—wound its way around trees before reaching the house in the rear of the lot. David explained that the gate being requested was for "security," the reasons for which the developer standing by his side would express to the board in a moment. He then emphasized, "There are certain circumstances being *unique* to the *shape* of the property that would warrant a relief." He also highlighted that they all (that is, he, the developer, and the prospective purchaser) felt that it could be done "without any *detriment* to any of the neighbors."

These last two statements, sprinkled with legalese, are particularly important when it comes to the zoning regulations at stake in this case. The Danboro Township Land Use Development Code states that the zoning board may grant a variance only "where, by reason of *exceptional* narrowness, shallowness or *shape of such property*, or by reason of exceptional topographic conditions, or by reason of other extraordinary and exceptional situation or condition of such piece of property, the strict application of any regulation…would result in peculiar and exceptional practical difficulties to, or exceptional and *undue hardship* upon, the developer of such property."[16] However, the code also states, "No variance or other relief may be granted under the provisions of this section unless such variance or other relief can be granted without *substantial detriment* to the *public good*."[17]

In light of the ambiguous meanings and protean implications of words and phrases like "hardship," "substantial detriment," and "public good," which depend heavily on the idiosyncrasies of local towns and the larger historical context, it is imperative that legal teams understand the particularities of place (in both space and time) when pleading their cases. It was at this point (and perhaps in this spirit) that David turned the microphone over to Jay, the developer. David explained to the board that Jay was best able to represent the prospective purchaser's concerns because he had been working directly with him on the concept plans for the property. But Jay was also a resident of the town, which was made known to all when he was sworn in and had to state his address.[18] It is a beneficial strategy for development corporations to have as their representative a hometown resident—someone who is both in the know and also known.

The atmosphere in the room shifted to a more relaxed and familiar tenor when Jay began his testimony. After restating the unique dimensions of the lot, he pointed out that as you drove through the development, it seemed as though the driveway was actually another entrance road. Although the driveway is "obviously narrower than a roadway," he acknowledges, "it's certainly striking as *not consistent* with the other homes." He explained that the lot had needed to be created in this fashion due to wetlands requirements.[19] During construction, he explained, the prospective purchaser had come to him with security concerns. The purchaser frequently traveled abroad for work, leaving his wife and children home alone for lengthy periods of time, and he was worried, Jay explained, that "somebody could—unannounced—come up the driveway." ("[Since the house] sits on its own away from all the other homes, it's really hard to see what's going on there.") The man wanted to find a way to enable his wife and children to control who came up to the house while he was away. The gate would have an electronic mechanism with a bell and an intercom system built into it. Jay explained that they all felt that this solution was "reasonable."

Jay then elaborated the prospective purchaser's concerns, particularly the possibility that some motorists might confuse the driveway with a roadway ("if they are *not familiar* with the neighborhood and they're *sightseeing* or they get lost or they make a turn—and there they are pulling up in front of this house, *who knows when or what time of night*"). Jay underscored that this made the man very uncomfortable. As Jay was saying this, a woman on the board nodded in agreement and murmured a quiet "yeah" under her breath. Perhaps it was her sympathetic body language and utterance that led Jay to feel that he could stop articulating his argument, or maybe he had planned to end his comments at that point. Regardless, he wrapped up his portion by pointing out that the 6-foot-high gate that they were requesting was only for the width of the driveway plus stanchions supporting it on either side.

David returned to the microphone, concluding their opening arguments by pointing out how the gate would accommodate necessary provisions, the first being the need for the fire and police departments to be able to get onto the property in the event of an emergency. He explained to the board that the motor of the gate would have a mechanism linking it to the alarm system in the house. Should the alarm go off, the gate would automatically open, thus providing for "the reverse side of the security, being able to gain access to the property." As a result, David emphasized, their request for this gate would not have any "negative impact," his language for what the zoning code refers to as a "detriment to the public good." He then addressed another potential negative impact on the community: the aesthetics of the gate. (Danboro's Land Use Code grants the zoning board the power to "promote a desirable visual environment"[20] and to "encourage good aesthetics.")[21] He assured the board that the gate would not be an "eyesore," for it would be set back approximately 25–30 feet from the curb line.

David seemed quite confident as he closed, casually remarking that this was all he had. His tone and comportment implied that he expected the board to move to a vote right away or, at most, to briefly ask a few clarifying questions. His apparent assurance was not surprising. Joan had moved their request up on the agenda because she thought that it would be quick. He and Jay had addressed the fundamental provisions in the zoning code, particularly the need for something "unique" about the property creating an "undue hardship." Jay's description of the prospective purchaser's worries was met with a sign of approval by a woman on the board, and they had acknowledged the limits of private property and the need to tend to local governance when they spoke to the accommodation of municipal services and policies, including police and fire department access and the zoning laws themselves. Additionally, they had tended to the "public good," which includes aesthetics that could "negatively impact" others if they create an "eyesore."

Despite their seemingly tight argument and the rapport that Jay apparently had with the board, the case that they constructed was resting on the shaky ground of class anxieties. When the question-and-answer period began, the foundation of their case was unearthed, its retaining walls were chipped away, and the very structure of their claims caved in. They may technically be in the business of constructing custom homes, but it also is reconstructing towns that have a "sense" about who they are and what they do not want to become. A commonsense reaction emerged from members of the board as the hearing continued, unexpectedly extending the debate and shifting its tone from cordial to contentious.

SIGHTSEERS, TRESPASSERS, AND SECURITY CONCERNS

As Joan began the inquiry, it immediately became clear that she was not convinced by their argument regarding security concerns. She asked, "Now, is this...gate connecting to any other fencing on the property?" Jay shook his head no as he responded, "It's strictly just to preclude anybody from coming up the driveway.... On one side of the property, at this point, it's heavily wooded, and people would not be able to get around. On the other side...there's another neighbor who has some landscaping, and you would not be able to get around that way." Joan had a look in her eye and clenched muscles around her eyes that indicated she was skeptical about something Jay was saying. "Let's just talk about this," she proposed. "You mentioned that...[with this] long driveway...[the purchaser is] concerned that maybe somebody would have thought this was a road [to] outside the development or into another area?" Jay nodded in agreement and added, "Somebody that wasn't familiar with it, looking at this long straight alleyway/roadway/driveway...would think that this was another road...to another section of the development, when in actuality, it leads directly to this gentleman's house." David jumped in: "If I can elaborate on that as well.... You get quite a few sightseers who like to drive around and just see homes.... The concern was that a sightseer will actually find his way down the driveway to see the home maybe a little bit better...and that will be a *trespass*." The gate would help "avoid any confusion that that was *private property* starting from the depression in the roadway where it meets the driveway." He then underscored, "That was *one* of his concerns, in addition to the security concern for his family."

It may have been the added tidbit thrown in about a "trespass" onto "private property," or maybe it was just general doubt, but Joan and other members of the board seemed to become more suspicious of the security claim. In a tone that revealed impatience, Joan reasoned, "Well, let's go on to the concern with safety. If the gate was attached to a fence that surrounded the property, we could talk about *security* because now we have a lock-in gate that's…surrounding the property." Becoming sarcastic, she added, "So you have a security compound, *if that's what you need in Danboro*. But what we have here is an *ornamental* gate to preclude somebody from driving up the driveway." Acting as if she were merely confused by their request, Joan asked in a playful, albeit reproachful, tone, "A sign at the bottom of the driveway wouldn't work the same…'No Road,' 'No Legal Access'? I mean, why…a large ornamental gate just to block the driveway?"

David calmly responded, "Clearly, if somebody wants to climb their way into the property, he can climb over a 6-foot-high or a 4-foot-high [gate]… for that matter. So it's not…the township does have a good police department." But he added, "The concern would be to preclude cars from being able to come through." Jay then jumped in: "The house itself is a very large home, and it does get a lot of *looks*.… People are driving up to it on a regular basis. People *we* don't know. And that's under construction. And they have *no problem* driving down a dirt driveway to go look at the house a little closer.… [The homeowner] feels that people [are] going to be continuously doing that, notwithstanding the fact that it's *private property*." As Jay uttered these words, people in the audience shifted in their seats and turned to catch their neighbor's eyes. There had already been skepticism on Joan's part about the need for extra height when Jay and David first mapped out their case. But at this point in the hearing, a profound rupture occurred. When pressed to clarify their request, the concerns that had been foregrounded in their opening arguments gave way. No longer was the main fear a scenario in which a unique and inconsistent driveway confused drivers who *inadvertently* found themselves at the secluded home. The issue was now trepidation about sightseers who *intentionally* committed a trespass and whose desire to look showed disregard for the nature of private property.

Jay, however, had made a strategic move when he emphatically called the sightseers "people *we* don't know." Like all members of the zoning board and most audience members that night, he, too, was a resident of Danboro. This underscoring was perhaps an attempt to clarify for everyone in the room that "sightseers" was meant to index a collective outsider; whether cars ended up on the doorstep of the prospective purchaser's home by way of intention or mishap, the sightseers were implied to be those outside the cozy comfort zone of Danboro's town hall.

At that moment, I presumed that Jay was referring to people who lived in the neighboring town, which had many nonwhite, working-class residents. Coded language—in which racialized, class-encoded Others are the referents—features prominently in the normative discourse in this white-flight town. Lawyers inevitably draw on ambiguous terms and phrases like these to plead their cases since biased racial sentiments cannot explicitly be articulated in public municipal forums. But utilizing the term "sightseers" ended up being a colossal miscalculation. For one thing, there was an awkward juxtaposition between the term "sightseers" and descriptions of when they were doing their looking; it is quite difficult to sightsee at night. But more significant, many people in Danboro like to go see new houses under construction and even get out of their cars to walk through the homes. The lawyer's and developer's use of "sightseers" was thus a bit "too close to home." There was a palpable feeling in the room at that moment, which remained tangible throughout the hearing, that it was not a common Other who would be excluded if the variance were granted for this gate. It was as if *they* (that is, current town residents) were the sightseers being indexed, as if the prospective purchaser was proposing a gate to keep *them* out. Was it possible that they were no longer part of the meaningful "we" in the town and that newcomers like the couple buying this house—with their moral logic of neoliberal privatopia—were a sign of what their town was becoming?

Objects being indexed by an utterance such as "sightseers" are, in Bakhtin's (1981:276) words, "overlain with qualifications, open to dispute, charged with value, already enveloped in an obscuring mist—or, on the contrary, by the 'light' of alien words that have already been spoken about it." The "obscuring mist" of class anxieties, combined with the alienating words being used to describe those who look, made it extremely difficult for the lawyer and the developer to appropriate "sightseer" for their own uses. "Many words stubbornly resist...; it is as if they put themselves in quotation marks against the will of the speaker" (1981:294).[22] Once "sightseers" was in quotation marks that night, the lawyer's and the developer's efforts to control its referent were futile. And when Jay said "people *we* don't know," maybe he *was* referring to residents of Danboro who were strangers to him, David, and the prospective purchaser. Was it possible that those who had moved to Danboro during the early years of suburbanization, with their old middle-class, liberal democratic understanding of private property, were now not unlike those targeted as undesirable in postwar exclusionary zoning practices, albeit now under the guise of sightseers who have no qualms about committing a trespass on private property and who thereby require gates to be kept out?

BARRICADES, STOCKADES, AND EXCLUSIONARY ORNAMENTALS

The tenor of the conversation continued to imply that something acutely was troubling about this variance request, as if the appeal for a 6-foot-high gate was asking far too much. This became particularly vivid during a linguistic tug-of-war regarding the ornamentation and aesthetics of the gate. As the discussion ensued, one of the board members interjected with an annoyed look on his face: "Let me...ask a question that will hopefully cut to the chase.... You testified that the purpose of erecting this ornamental fence is to [avoid] the cars driving down the driveway. Why do you need a 6-foot fence?... You have an ornamental light on both sides, and you have a very ornate ornamental on it in the center. If you cut those two lights out and you cut off the ornamental, you would be at 4 feet, which is 1 foot above the ordinance." The term "ornamental" can connote simple aesthetic additions but also can suggest superfluous embellishments. By foregrounding the excessive ornamental aspects of the gate, the functionality of the extra height that they were asking for fell by the wayside.

David responded by first acknowledging that the "ability to stop people from driving down the road would be accomplished even within the township's ordinance." However, he explained, the prospective purchaser came up with a design that would also "fit the home." He did have a "legitimate concern...[about] the ability of people to traverse on the property," but he also was concerned that the design of the gate be "consistent" with the home. David continued:

> If we were to build it at 3 feet, the *impact* would be the same, I would feel, as 6 feet.... It's just his way of beautifying the entrance to this home, in addition to providing his security concerns.... Whether we can stop the traffic with a 3-foot fence? I think clearly that's obvious we could. But...he wants to do more than just simply put up a, you know, a *simple* gate that's gonna just look as, as a *barricade*. He wants to do something that will also beautify and be consistent with what he is doing on the property and in the development itself.

What David was implying, whether or not intentionally, was that the maximum height that the township allowed—which had long been deemed appropriate for the town—imposed and maintained an unbecoming simplicity on a par with no-nonsense military structures.

Joan quickly seized upon David's choice of words, deftly inverting his

FIGURE 10.4

Typical stanchions. Photo by R. Heiman.

claims: "I understand that he wants to stop people from going into his driveway. But I think that the ultimate height of 6 feet is rather, um, *obtrusive* to the development when *nobody else* has something of this nature. It's gonna…almost appear as if there's a 6-foot *stockade* across his driveway." By suggesting that the proposed 6-foot-high gate would look like a "stockade," or a defensive fortification, Joan trumped David's claim that Danboro's 3-foot zoning code was promoting simple-looking barricades. But more important, her remarks underscored the key tension in the case. David said that the prospective purchasers wanted their gate to be "consistent" with their home and with the development. But the proposed 6-foot-high gate would be inconsistent with the development. Joan pointed out, "*Nobody else* has something of this nature." It also would be incompatible with the town because there were no other gates of its kind.

As the conversation continued, however, it seemed as if Jay and David were not clued into these implications of their request. When David readied himself to reply to Joan's allegation, he took a deep breath as if trying to control himself. After saying that he was going to "phrase this as intelligently" as he could (thus implying that the board was not getting *his* point), he tried to refute Joan's claim that *nobody else* had something of this nature, by pointing out that quite a few people in the development had stanchions that supported mailboxes, to "beautify their home" and to appear "consistent with the style of the home." But when he started his next sentence, Joan interrupted forcefully: "*No.* There are *no* mailboxes 6 feet high," after which she looked him squarely in the eye with a combat smile, as if to let him know that he was not getting away with such a claim. With a confident laugh, he acknowledged, "No, no, they're all about 3 feet high." He then explained that he was just trying to remind the board that the height of 6 feet represents the "tallest part of the ornamental section." Jay jumped into the conversation and in a semi-annoyed tone reminded the board that the gate would be barely visible: "If I can just make one comment. This is not being built right at the edge of the driveway where the roadway is. It's inset quite a bit.... If you drove straight through the neighborhood, this would not pop out at you. It's 25–30 feet in and off the road."

Joan snapped back, "*Again*, the fence doesn't have to be 6 feet high," and then voiced what was clearly on most people's minds, for there was a l ot of head nodding when she said, "It just appears that there isn't a valid reason other than they *like* it to be 6 feet high." David responded by asking her, "Is there a particular height that you would feel comfortable with, Madame Chairperson?" Before she had a chance to answer, another board member said, "I'm 6 [feet] 6 [inches], and I'm considered a pretty tall guy. This is a *tall* fence. Even though it's set back 20–30 feet, it's a mammoth-looking fence." He then said that he would recommend that it be no more than 4 feet at the highest point: "I think it would fit in nicer to the surrounding area."

Jay and David conferred for a moment, after which Jay returned to the stanchions issue. As he reminded the board that stanchions are built on many properties, Joan stopped him in the middle of his comments, speaking over him as she said, "So we really don't want to talk about this." Joan never explicitly stated what the "this" was that they did not want to talk about. Perhaps it was the fact that once the indexicality of "sightseers" had shifted, it no longer mattered whether other people had stanchions; whether the gate would be seen or how far back it was located; or whether it was the ornamentals or the gate itself causing the extra height. The bottom line was that "nobody else" in town had a 6-foot-high, regal-style gate to keep people *out.*

This important distinction—which matters deeply when powerful anxieties about exclusion and discursive displacement are at play—seemed to be lost on Jay and David. This was most evident when Jay retook the floor. In a conciliatory tone, he pointed out, "It's not a question of trying to negotiate with the board. At 3 feet, the concern is that it would be about waist high. It wouldn't accomplish any kind of grand entrance." When Jay uttered "grand entrance," many in the audience looked shocked. He was still trying to make that point? Apparently not sensing the sentiment in the room, Jay *did* negotiate: "Maybe the board would be inclined at 5 feet, to allow..." But before he had a chance to finish, Joan jumped in, sounding extremely irritated and tired, albeit willing to negotiate: "Personally, I would feel a lot better if it was no greater than 5 feet high.... And I think that's a compromise...that maybe we could live with." Jay tried to interject a comment, but Joan forcefully continued, "Personally, other than stopping somebody from going up the driveway, I see *no* security from this fence whatsoever. I can understand that the...purchaser is concerned with them thinking it's an access road.... But it's definitely not offering any security when you can just walk around it." Perhaps trying to cut their losses, David concluded, "With that, Madame Chairperson, we would like to amend our application before the board to...5 feet."

OPENING THE DOOR TO FUTURE FENCING

Joan paused for a moment, took a deep breath, and looked around the room. It was time to give the public an opportunity to share their thoughts. The one person who spoke lived right next door to the property in the same development and raised an issue that brought the predicament of exclusionary possibilities to another level. He explained that he was worried: "We might be talking about a fence around the property after this is constructed.... I wouldn't want to see even a 5-foot fence across the entire property to match a 5-foot gate." The board attorney pointed out to the man, "For your information, the application is just for the gate that has been discussed here. If they wanted to then put a 5-foot fence, they would have to come back in front of the board." The neighbor cut him off at the end, nervously explaining, "I understand that. However, if you allow construction of a 5-foot gate, I feel that it would open the door possibly to a fence that would match it, at the same height." The board attorney reiterated, "They would need to return to this board."

The attorney's comment clearly sidestepped the neighbor's fear of soon living next to a "security compound," as Joan had remarked earlier in the meeting. And the likelihood of this was made even more pronounced when David joined the discussion. He pointed out to the board that he and the neighbor, whom he referred to by name, "[knew] each other well enough": "And I think we still have a very good rapport." He then looked the man in the eye, said that he understood his concerns, but acknowledged: "Regrettably, the township's ordinance, as it's drafted now, would allow a fence in the front yard, a fence on the side yard, with restrictions as to height. And this relief, granted or not, would not preclude this particular resident, when he moves in, from making an application and fencing in his entire property. This particular section of the property, rather than having a 3-foot-high, would have a 5-foot-high [fence]." While claiming to understand the neighbor's concerns, David seemed not to appreciate the exclusionary semiotic effects of a 5-foot-high fence and what one property owner's approach to neoliberal self-optimization (Ong 2006) means to his neighbors. This was acutely evident when he added, "The extent of the impact, as I indicated earlier...is no negative impact on the community itself, *at all*. Whether he is going to actually [add] additional fencing, I can't intelligently comment."

Sounding increasingly frustrated with the direction of the conversation, David tried to bring the discussion back to security concerns and aesthetic possibilities. His approach, however, was strikingly confrontational: "I concur with your comments, Madame Chairperson, that if somebody wants to get in, a 3-foot-high fence is not going to stop them. Maybe the *dogs* on the other side of a 3-foot fence might.... The purpose here is just, in part, to beautify the entrance, to provide some security to preclude the cars from coming in. And we're hoping, with some compromise, we can accomplish both of those without having just a simple 3-foot-high stockade fence." There was a flabbergasted pause in the room when David finished speaking. As if an image of dogs being used to keep sightseers at bay was not provocation enough, he had uttered the words "simple" and "stockade" in a matter-of-fact tone, as if there was nothing divisive about them. Within this context, those words felt as hostile as the dogs, and the chasm between the parties' understandings in the debate felt as wide as the rift growing between the moral logics of private property of the "old" and "new" middle classes in the United States.

DESIRE, HARDSHIP, AND A "FEELING" OF SECURITY
After an awkward silence, Joan asked the board members to offer their thoughts in preparation for taking a vote. The first to speak proposed that the prospective purchaser get rid of "the lights and the swoop in the middle that's ornamental and just keep it to a *plain* 4-foot fence." He explained that this would still accomplish what the purchaser wanted to do, which was to prevent cars from entering the property. The next board member spoke

in a sympathetic tone, acknowledging that he understood "the prospective owner's desire to have this [gate] kind of be ornamental to go along with the type of house that he wants." He agreed that the main part of the fence should be 4 feet, but he felt that there should also be allowed a bit more height for some design. "We could probably make some sort of a design or something that's maybe half a foot higher or something in the middle to swoop it down that way." It is striking that the second board member used "we" in his statement. This inclusive pronoun was an implicit acknowledgment—despite all the concerns raised during the meeting—of the legitimacy of the couple's desire for a gate that was aesthetically and dimensionally consistent with their home. But since their home—like other new houses built in Danboro during those years—was out of scale with the moderately sized homes in town, the normative desire for consistency *within* properties competed with the desire for consistency *across* properties. The proposed gate semiotically teetered on this style-scale tension and, by default, on the tension between private property and the public good, which can include the feeling of being part of the meaningful, dominant "we" of the town.

The next board member's comments threw this predicament into relief: "I've heard *desire* on the part of the applicant to beautify the property, to present a fence that's consistent with the scale of the house. And I can understand that." But he reminded, "I think the charge we have is to try and find reasons consistent with the law to grant variances." The next board member underscored this point: "I think it's the obligation of this board to hear applicants who have a valid reason for *hardship.* I think you've come in and made a security statement at the beginning, but we've relented on that and it is an ornamental, decorative thing.... I don't feel that any *hardship* has been established, and I'm not in favor of anything higher than 3 feet, as the code so states." The final board member agreed that there were "limited reasons" to justify 6 feet or 5 feet. However, she was willing to compromise and grant a variance for 4 feet, with extra height for the "decorations."

Joan took another deep breath, looked around the room, and said that she had been listening carefully to everyone's comments. Although she agreed "as far as there being no proof to grant a variance," she thought that the applicant "offered somewhat his concern for people driving up what would appear to be a roadway...[or] an access road out...since the house [was] set back so much further than everybody else's house." Joan proposed that the gate be 3 feet high across, with an allowable extra foot for the lights and the decorative effect. "It'll give the contract purchaser of the house some *feeling* of security so that somebody's not driving up."

Joan's appreciation for the prospective purchasers' need for a "*feeling* of security" was also a significant acknowledgment—particularly right after the other board members' recognition of the couple's desire for the gate to be consistent with the house—that aesthetic desires do not necessarily trump security concerns. It is fully within normative sentiments in the United States, including Danboro, that the proposed gate could make the couple feel safer *because* of its grand aesthetics, even if it was not truly secure. The popularity of SUVs (Heiman 2000) and other efforts to consume a *feeling* of class security (Heiman 2009) are cases in point. Although "aesthetic desires" and "hardship" may have been opposed throughout the debate, their relationship, as this part of the meeting recognized, was clearly far more complex. This moment of empathy, however, was short-lived—and quickly eroded as the debate entered the final wrap-up and people in the audience started to get punchy.

MOCKING REGAL PRETENSIONS

Joan began to contemplate out loud the predicament that the couple would face if they had to stay within the limits of the ordinance: "There's no way to construct a fence…in any ornamental fashion…at 3 feet straight across.… If we give 'em an extra foot to put the lights on and to put that ornamental…*crown*…[it] might allow for what they want the fence to look like." The instant that "crown" came out of her mouth, several people in the audience began to laugh, and then a smirk formed on Joan's face. Wit—with the "lively current of unease powering [it]" (Warner 2002:103)—grants people another medium through which to critique, deflate, and defend against outside forces (Giddens 1979:72). This type of humor enabled a more pointed criticism of the exclusionary implications of the request through mocking its regal pretensions.

A few board members, however—regardless of the humorous tone in the room—continued to directly oppose the request, reiterating concerns that had been raised all evening: they had not heard any reason "under the law" for the gate to be higher than 3 feet; the application did not "meet the hardship [requirement] clearly set forth in the statute"; the request was "more of an aesthetic application"; and there was no other fencing like it in the neighborhood, so the gate would be a "detriment." And one board member reminded everyone that Danboro was "trying to avoid gates like in Roseburg," an affluent town that bordered Danboro and allowed 6-foot-high gates. This abrupt loss of appreciation for the couple's desire for aesthetic consistency underscored that consistency (in general) was a commonsense desire in the town but a stronger desire was for consistency *across* the town.

Joan then stated what everyone in the room was probably thinking: "On something that was very simple, it has turned into something that is not so simple!" She reminded everyone, "Let's keep in mind that 3 feet would be allowed anyway. So what we're talking about…is 1 foot for some ornamental crown on the top and two lights." She noted that, having been out to the property, there was "somewhat of an unusual circumstance" since the driveway did look like a street. She then asked for consensus from the board for 3 feet, with 1 extra foot allowed for the ornamentals, "keeping in mind that he could have a 3-foot stockade fence straight across the property, if he desired to do so." She then quickly rephrased this, pointing out that it would be "a 3-foot *fence* across the property. *Not stockade*": "I'm sorry. I didn't mean that. But it could *resemble* something that looks like that, if he wanted to do so!" There was more laughter in the room, during which a woman sitting near me, one of the residents who lived in the moderately sized homes behind the commercial park, joked that it could be a "picket fence!"

Joan then asked David, "Is this something you would compromise to… or is the applicant gonna just say forget it?" He replied, "The applicant will seek to get as much relief as I can from this board." He then turned and spoke in the direction of the board attorney, seemingly still not getting it:

> I believe our burden is not just a matter of establishing positive criteria that we have a special hardship, which I think has been established by the unique shape of the property and the concerns that are associated with the long driveway, which is *inconsistent* with everything else. More importantly…I don't think that there would be any impact on the community…. Quite the contrary, I think that the…3-foot-high straight run of the gate… would probably have a worse impact on the area than allowing them to do something a little more *elaborate*, that would allow them to *beautify the general area*.

The whole time he was speaking, most audience members seemed no longer to be listening. He may have continued to imagine that an "elaborate" gate would "beautify the general area," but most people in the room had long before agreed—through explicit statements, sidebar jokes, and knowing glances—that "beautifying" could be taken too far. If the proposed gate were allowed, it would require a redefinition of what was consistent and inconsistent in the town. Although developers attract buyers to subdivisions like Tarragon Hills by proclaiming that there are "No Two Homes Alike!" and operate under the principle that the optimization of a property necessarily benefits neighboring properties, uniqueness can be taken only so far until it becomes a detriment. The proposed gate would further upscale the town, possibly price more people out, and, perhaps just as important, create a relentless reminder to the old middle class of the radically altered middle-class playing field and its norms in regard to private property.

It was now time for Joan's final statement for the record in preparation for the board vote. She was particularly careful with her wording: "Taking into consideration the applicant's desire...to protect the driveway, which appears as a roadway because of the unusual shape of the property, the applicant has asked for a fence to be placed across the driveway. The fence is to be no more than 3 feet high with an extra foot allowed for lights on either end and an ornamental crown-shaped design in the middle. The lights will serve as, um, additional protection." When Joan mentioned the "ornamental crown-shaped design," there were bursts of giggles in the audience, and the woman who had made the "picket fence" comment murmured under her breath, "coat of arms." Several people in the audience laughed at her comment, during which the man from the historic commission leaned in her direction and joined the "collusive sideplay" (Goffman 1981) by asking, "Did they pick a color yet?" The woman turned her head in his direction, chuckling in confirmation as she caught his eye. People, like this elderly man, who had been living in Danboro since it was a farming community had long lamented suburbanites like this woman, who indexed the loss of Danboro's pastoral past. But through the new middle class in the town being articulated in bourgeois terms, these two groups appreciated their commonalities in this historical moment. With their shared concerns about the influx of the regal, a feeling of communitas emerged between them amid the mockery.[23]

While everyone in the audience was laughing and talking among themselves, Joan finished up her statement and took the vote. Each board member voted yes; Joan's suggestion of a 3-foot-high fence—with an allowable foot for the extras—had passed unanimously. A huge sense of relief swept through the room as everyone realized that this part of the hearing—which took more than an hour—was finally done. Danboro's old middle-class residents were able in that moment to feel like insiders—and not sightseers—in their own town. Amid this release, Joan thanked everybody for their efforts and then leaned over the table toward the audience and exclaimed (as if asking for forgiveness), "I thought this was going to be twenty minutes!"

CONCLUSION

The public hearing for this couple's proposed 6-foot-high, ornamental security gate became a forum for the subtextual display of class anxieties

Figure 10.5
The gate, as built. Photo by R. Heiman.

exacerbated during the economic boom years of the late 1990s. Jay and David—as representatives for the prospective purchasers—became signs of class transformations in the United States and their associated shifts in moral logics in regard to private property. This infused and doomed their legal strategy and persuasion tactics by evoking ever-present anxieties in the town. When these anxieties became dominant during the meeting, there was an irrevocable shift in the referent of "sightseers," pushing the prospective purchasers' security concerns and aesthetic desires out of the realm of the possible for most of the debate. There emerged a palpable feeling that the purchasers, David, and Jay—despite the fact that Jay himself was a long-time resident—were making an aesthetic request that was overstepping the boundaries of architectural (and thereby fiscal and discursive) inclusion and exclusion in the town. The decision not to grant the full 6 feet demonstrates an effort to temper the prevalence of neoliberal space making through the policing of aesthetic regimes. It is striking that when patriarchy was able to be deployed (that is, the fear of a wife being left alone at home while her husband is away) to justify the couple's class desires, the mobilization of racial anxieties through coded language was not able to overpower the subtextual class anxieties at play. This dynamic reveals the regulative relationship between the changing material conditions undergirding middle-class life, associated discursive logics in regard to private property, and middle-class citizens' action against neoliberal shifts, albeit through a commonsense reaction rather than politically organized efforts.

This commonsense reaction continued to be present in Danboro long after this debate. Several years later, I called the office of Danboro's Zoning Board of Adjustment to ask for clarification on a few issues. I explained to the woman who answered the phone that I had questions about having a 6-foot-high security gate across a driveway. In a panicked tone, she told me that I would need to speak with the clerk. Before I had the chance to explain why I was asking, she transferred me to the clerk, who immediately told me that Danboro did not allow 6-foot-high gates in the front of one's property. If I wanted to do so, she added somewhat hostilely, I would need to submit an application for a variance. When I had the chance to explain that I was asking for research purposes—and not as a resident looking to build such a structure—she seemed profoundly relieved. She rattled off the couple's street from the top of her head, asking whether it was *their* application that I was asking about. It was quite indicative of the significance of this request that, after several years, and hundreds of cases, that street (in a town with more than 750 streets) was still so present in her mind. Still present, too, was the feeling of being flabbergasted by the request, which came through when she informed me that no one had *ever* made *that* kind of request before them, nor had *anyone* done so since.

Granted, all applications for relief of zoning ordinances test the limits of a property owner's entitlement vis-à-vis the public good and a governing municipality. But the rupture during the public hearing for this proposed gate opened a window onto how this tension was articulated in cultural, moral, aesthetic, and visceral terms during the late 1990s. Those on the upwardly mobile side of the growing middle-class chasm who held a new middle-class sensibility could always afford to buy a home in the town. There was no way for a town to zone out the relatively rich. But through restricting the accoutrements allowed on properties, the zoning board could send the message to those who were considering buying homes in Danboro that Danboro wanted to stay a town that was at least trying to hold onto old middle-class logics of private property. It is my hope that reading this debate through the type of historical understanding that the phrases "old middle class" and "new middle class" enable—inspired by their productive analytical and political uses in places like India, China, Egypt, and Hungary—we can think in new ways about tensions over neoliberal shifts in the United States and what gets elided in a public discourse that insists on talking about either "*the* middle class" or its income-bracket parts, when the middle classes—and class in general—are far more complicated than that.

This zoning board hearing also reminds us to keep in focus exceptions to intentional efforts against neoliberalizing space. This debate was a spontaneous, commonsense reaction that closed the gate, so to speak, for the moment on neoliberal architectural space making in the town. It was not articulated through a counter-hegemonic narrative about spatialized class politics, unlike developed anti-gentrification movements (Smith 1996). Yet, its political-economic effect, through limiting the height of gates, was comparable to an ideological effort. It was an "agentive moment" (Daniel 1996) that proved contrary to Gramsci's (1971) expectation that common sense is, more often than not, a conservative cultural logic that needs to be transformed into coherent political consciousness for there to be political effects. In the late 1990s, a conservative reaction to gating was counter-hegemonic because the production of space was heading in the class-divisive direction of which Lefebvre (1991[1974]) had warned. Of course, had this debate taken place ten years later amid the economic crisis, perhaps this discussion would not have taken place on the level of the subtextual, since the structural conditions and moral logics that have shaped the landscapes of middle-class life have come to dominate the public discourse.

Despite suggestions that the economic crisis that began in 2008 could bring the end to neoliberalism and neoliberal space making and usher in a new New Deal or a neo-Keynesian era, the coming years likely will continue to witness the presence of neoliberal economic policies and practices, alongside postwar liberal logics. All scales of government—federal, state, and local—will continue to provide fruitful sites in which to unearth micro-processes of meaning making and to theorize how these anxieties, aesthetics, and moral logics shape the built form of everyday life.

Acknowledgments

The research for this chapter and its early stages of writing were funded by the Horace H. Rackham School of Graduate Studies, the Department of Anthropology, and the Program in Culture and Cognition at the University of Michigan. Subsequent writing support was provided by an Ethel-Jane Westfeldt Bunting summer fellowship at the School for Advanced Research, a visiting scholar position at the Russell Sage Foundation, and leave time from the New School. I thank all of these institutions for their incredible generosity. I also am grateful to the clerk and the officer of the Danboro Township Zoning Board of Adjustment for answering various zoning questions and for providing a copy of the sketch of the proposed gate. Earlier versions of this chapter were presented at the annual meetings of the American Anthropological Association, the Urban Studies Seminar at New York University, the "A Suburban World?" confer- ence of the Metropolitan Institute at Virginia Tech, the Department of Anthropology at the New School, and the Suburban Design Studio in the Urban Design Program at the City College of New York. For their thought-provoking questions and encouraging comments, I thank all audience members, panel discussants, and fellow panelists. I am particularly indebted to friends and colleagues who provided incredibly close read- ings and perceptive, fine-tuned commentary on this chapter in its various stages: Val Daniel, Ilana Feldman, Janet Finn, Bob Fishman, Carina Frantz, Pamila Gupta, Larry Hirschfeld, Mani Limbert, Brian Mooney, Gustav Peebles, Rashmi Sadana, Karen Stras- sler, and Aleksandra Wagner. It was through the SAR advanced seminar that this piece finally coalesced, and I owe many thanks to all of the seminar participants, especially Carla Freeman and Mark Liechty, and to the two anonymous reviewers.

Notes

1. There is a great likeness between restrictive covenants of the nineteenth cen- tury and contemporary public land-use zoning codes, because the latter were built on the tradition of the former. Property owners in the nineteenth century were on a "quest for [the] permanence" (Fogelson 2005) of property values in a time of volatile markets, industrial urbanism, land speculation, and the rise of "new money." Thus developed covenants and deed restrictions modeled on those in England from the eighteenth and nineteenth centuries amid the breakup of the commons (McKenzie 1994). Because mid-nineteenth-century subdivisions in the United States were prohibitive in cost to all but the elite, the main concern was the actions of one's class peers.

2. The continued importance of public governance is recognized in research on gentrification in urban cores, where city halls continue to be viewed as fundamental sites of struggle even as public-private partnerships proliferate. Although beyond the scope of the discussion here, it is also likely that comparable concerns about physical and discursive displacement will be (or already are) taking place within private home- owner associations, thus making homeowner association meetings an equally compel- ling ethnographic site for exploring these issues.

3. For a classic ethnography of the ways that broader forces of social change are struggled over in the context of municipal law, see Greenhouse, Yngvesson, and Engel 1994.

4. The town in which I conducted my fieldwork has been given a pseudonym.

5. Neil Smith (1996) explains that inflationary forms of gentrification can occur not only when developers optimize their profit on land that has not been previously devalorized but also when states loosen policies in regard to land use, as has been seen in many European nations. I would also add that capital valorization also occurs, as was

the case in Danboro in the late 1990s, when individual homeowners tear down their old homes and build bigger homes on their land.

6. Since the 1990s, there has been a surge of anthropological attention to the spatialization of political-economic shifts (e.g., Appadurai 1996; Caldeira 2000; Chesluk 2004; Ferguson and Gupta 2002; Guano 2002; Lipsitz 2006; Low 1996; Moore 1998; Ong 2006; Watts 1992). Aside from a few anthropologists who have done work on zoning, such as Constance Perin's (1977) work on suburban land use in the 1970s and Edward LiPuma and Sarah Keene Meltzoff's (1997) study of land-use planning in South Florida in the 1980s and early 1990s, the analysis of zoning has largely been the domain of planners, historians, geographers, and policy makers. Yet, with anthropology's increasing attention to technologies of space making as neoliberal strategies, zoning technologies have come to the fore as a key site of inquiry (Ong 2006).

7. Danboro Township Zoning Board of Adjustment, regular meeting, March 24, 1999.

8. Danboro Township Code, Land Use Development (1999), §84-58.A: "Fences hereafter erected, altered or reconstructed in any zone in the Township of Danboro shall be open fences not to exceed three (3) feet in height above ground level when located in a front yard area." In the code, gates are subsumed under the term "fences."

9. The Zoning Board of Adjustment is made up of citizens from the township who are appointed by the township's council. The zoning board hears requests on the part of individual homeowners and commercial applicants who want permission for a variance or an exception to (or an interpretation of) the township's Land Use Development Code. Individual homeowners can come before the zoning board without legal representation, but commercial applicants must have legal counsel. Because this couple was in the process of purchasing the property, the property was still under the ownership of the developer of Tarragon Hills.

10. The county of which Danboro is a part, and New Jersey in general, do not tend to hail gates and gated communities as treasures of their municipalities, unlike Los Angeles or São Paulo, for example.

11. My semiotic approach draws heavily on the writings of C. S. Peirce, particularly his attention to the iconic quality of signs and their relationship to subjectivity (Colapietro 1989; Peirce 1955).

12. What I am addressing here is what Bakhtin calls "heteroglossia," or the determination of meaning within the matrix of social and historical conditions at play. See Smith 2004 on the resonance between heteroglossia and Gramsci's notion of common sense. The dynamic that I am addressing here also resonates with Warner's (2002) discussion on publics, particularly the way that people can "know"—even if not

consciously—the moment in which they are no longer part of a "dominant public"; this type of momentary emergence of a counterpublic, even if in existence only for a brief time like this zoning board debate, can still be quite agentive. See also Yeh (chapter 8, this volume) on classes and publics.

13. See Hayden 2003:188–89 for a discussion of other reluctant suburbs in the "rural fringe."

14. All of the people described in this chapter have been given pseudonyms.

15. A flag lot is a piece of property with a narrow piece of land (the pole) that leads back to a rectangular-shaped section of the property (the flag). Such parcels also are referred to as "pork chop lots," a phrase suggestive of the process of carving up farmland into lots that look like pork chops. See Hayden 2004:78.

16. Danboro Township Code, Land Use Development (1999), §84-8B(2)(c), emphasis added.

17. Ibid., §84-8B(1), emphasis added.

18. Lawyers do not have to be sworn in to legal proceedings since they are considered officers of the court. Developers like Jay, on the other hand, need to go through the process of being sworn in like any other nonlawyer at a legal proceeding.

19. The wetlands requirements are part of the North American Wetlands Conservation Act. "Wetlands" (like "meadowlands") are swamps or floodplains that developers used to fill in to build residential and commercial properties. The conservation act made it illegal to do so, for environmental reasons (Rome 2001). Developers often create unusual parcels, like this flag lot, in order to maximize the development of their land.

20. Danboro Township Code, Land Use Development (1999), §84-1I.

21. Ibid., §84-2F.

22. See also Derrida 1988:18 on our inability to "govern the entire scene and system of an utterance."

23. Their brief connection could be the start of what Rouse (1995:361) calls "contingent coalitions" or "hybrid vehicles of collective agency that, while often dominated by segments of a single class, link people from a variety of positions." We often hear about such coalitions emerging during struggles against gentrification in urban neighborhoods. In suburban areas, burgeoning relations between old farming families and long-term suburbanites have developed into concerted efforts against neoliberal space making.

11

Middle-Class Déjà Vu

Conditions of Possibility, from Victorian England to Contemporary Kathmandu

Mark Liechty

While reading about middle classes cross-culturally and historically—from contemporary Brazil to mid-nineteenth-century France—I have often had a strange feeling of recognition, sensing in those distant places and times ways of life that are closely analogous to my middle-class experience and the middle-class milieu of Kathmandu, Nepal, which I have studied and written about for the past two decades. And indeed, in speaking with other historians and ethnographers of middle-class culture, I have learned that I am not alone in feeling these déjà vu moments in which I (like they) recognize what seem to be close similarities in the experiences of middle-class groups separated widely in space and time.

One such example concerns the explicitly locational language that I documented in my earlier work on the middle class in Kathmandu (Liechty 2003). There, I recorded an insistent middle-class discourse of middleness and a subjective experience of social betweenness. People continuously located themselves in a socio-moral middle ground while locating their class Others in morally compromised social locations "above" and "below" themselves. Intensely aware of class Others and forced to mingle with them on a daily basis, the middle class in Kathmandu in the 1990s was all about the discursive and performative production of middleness. Middle-class Nepalis anxiously walked a tightrope between the vulgarities above and below, carving out a middle ground of "suitable" behavior that avoided the immoral excesses of both modernity and tradition.

Of course, this highly moralistic locational discourse is not unique to late twentieth-century Nepal. In historian George Mosse's work on nineteenth-century European middle classes, he describes the "ideal of respectability" that characterized middle-class cultural life:

> The middle classes can only be partially defined by their economic activity and even by their hostility to the aristocracy and the lower classes alike. For side by side with their economic activity it was above all the ideal of respectability which came to characterize their style of life.... They perceived their way of life, based as it was upon frugality, devotion to duty, and restraint of the passions, as superior to that of the "lazy" lower classes and the profligate aristocracy. (Mosse 1985a:4–5)

The moral project of locating oneself between "the 'lazy' lower classes and the profligate aristocracy" would have been extremely familiar to Kathmandu's middle class in the 1990s, even though the cultural nuances of that project were very different from those of nineteenth-century Europe.

A recurring theme in the Kathmandu middle class's discursive project of mapping (im)morality onto other classes concerned accusations of sexual impropriety—prostitution—aimed mainly at the urban poor. Almost reflexively, people leveled accusations of prostitution against any "lower-class" woman who consumed "fashion" goods beyond her status. Asked why there had been a sudden increase in prostitution in the city, one middle-class woman explained, "It's just like that. The reason is fashion. They [lower-class women] need money for fashion. There are people who, needing money for fashion, will go and do this immediately" (Liechty 2003:78). Attitudes like this were common in middle-class Kathmandu, but what I have found in further comparative reading is that virtually the same attitudes are common within many other middle-class formations. For example, Joan Scott's (1999:135) historical study of French attitudes toward women's labor suggests that the Kathmandu "fashion prostitute" was alive and walking the streets of mid-nineteenth-century Paris. There, too, moralizing middle-class commentators reported that "the taste for luxury" had "corrupted" poor young women, leading them to "passion and vice," a conclusion easily warranted, given that they earned "wages insufficient to support the style of life they [led]" (cf. Jones, chapter 6, this volume). Elsewhere, I describe how several elements of Kathmandu's middle-class consumer culture bear remarkable similarities to analogous developments in other places and times (Liechty 2005).[1]

Part of what is unsettling about these uncanny flashes of recognition is that they force us to ask some very basic questions about just what we mean by "middle class" or the condition of "middle classness." What exactly is it that seems to resurface in diverse ethnographic and historical accounts of middle-class cultural formations? What is the nature of middle classness that seems to allow us to recognize its expression across huge spatial and temporal divides? Drawing on both theoretical perspectives and ethnographic material from Nepal, this chapter addresses these questions.

Fundamentally, these questions force us to grapple with how to conceptualize the relationships between particular forms of sociocultural life (namely, middle classness) and their locations in time and space. If "middle class" is going to be something more than a vague heuristic category, we need ways of locating and conceptualizing its occurrence both historically and geographically. As a Chicagoan with research interests in Kathmandu, how am I to make sense of the fact that there is a middle class in each place? Is it the *same* class or different? How should we conceptualize degrees of similitude? And, even more troubling, how am I to explain the déjà vu moments that seem to indicate close proximities between the elements of middle-class experience in contemporary Nepal discussed in this chapter and in, say, early twentieth-century Chicago, Victorian Britain, or nineteenth-century France? What can ethnographic perspectives from Nepal contribute to broader historical understandings of middle-class cultural processes? How can we think about seeming parallels across space and time without falling into the trap of historical derivativeness, thereby condemning locations like Kathmandu to following in Europe's teleological wake?

"REGULARITIES OF RESPONSE": THE CONDITIONS OF CLASS

To answer these questions, we need ways of understanding class and the emergence of class cultures that are able to recognize historical patterns—local and regional sequences of socioeconomic and cultural change—without postulating a universal (Eurocentric) narrative that claims a single originary experience for The West and a derivative experience for The Rest. In this chapter, I work with three key ideas that, when combined, form the basis for a nonreductive understanding of middle-class occurrence (history) and experience (culture). Together, these ideas contextualize the ethnographic material that follows by helping to frame trends in Kathmandu's local political and cultural economy within larger historical and spatial processes.

First is the idea of *conditions of possibility*. Rather than propose a single middle-class history—a unitary, linear, sequential narrative that all middle-class formations will necessarily trace and along which different middle-class experiences can be charted—I view middle classness as the historical manifestation of specific conditions of possibility. Middle classes across time and space appear not as repeated instantiations of structural laws of history, but rather through the convergence of socioeconomic forces in specific times and places that create the conditions under which middle-class cultural logics and subject positions become possible and instrumentally desirable for certain people. From this perspective, no middle-class experience is any less authentic (derivative) or more originary (the teleological source) than any other. No matter where, when sufficient socioeconomic conditions of possibility coalesce, middle-class formations (may) emerge in all of their local and regional specificity.

The idea of conditions of possibility appears in a number of sources (for example, Bourdieu 1998b:87), but I draw mainly from Foucault (1970:xxii), who argues that historically transformative ideas arise not simply from within the minds of creative individuals, but from the "epistemological fields," "modalities of order," or the worlds of logic, rationality, and common sense in which social groups live. As these fields of meaning and modes of social organization change, so do the ideas and experiences that become thinkable and possible. I want to push this concept further to suggest that we think of middle classes as social formations that emerge and develop historically within the context of certain conditions of possibility.

The other main inspiration for this conditions-of-possibility approach comes from the British cultural historian E. P. Thompson, who in the 1960s almost single-handedly brought class into the orbit of cultural analysis (see Thompson 1963). But, even more important, Thompson attempted to rescue class from its conceptual prison within social theory. Not unlike his colleague Raymond Williams (1977:129), who argued against "the mistake" of "taking terms of analysis as terms of substance," Thompson insisted that we understand class as a "*historical* category" (1978:147; his emphasis); class was not a "model" or "structure," not a "sociological or heuristic category," but a lived experience, a "social process over time."

By stressing an understanding of class as a historical process, Thompson makes two fundamental points. First, he insists that classes exist *only in relationship* with other classes. No class can ever arise or exist on its own but must, by definition, stand in continuous relations of mutual tension and interproductivity with other classes, against which it continually defines and defends its interests and identities as a group (Thompson 1963:9). This understanding of classes—including middle classes—as being *necessarily* relational (and therefore historically dynamic) is crucial because it forces us to be attuned to the question of how interclass relations change and how those relational changes affect the experiences and cultural lives of class subjects.

Thompson's second decisive point related to the idea of conditions of possibility is his insistence that we understand class not as a uniform transhistorical category, but instead as a complex, located, lived experience that, though always relational in its dynamic, in content will never be the same twice:

> We know about class because people have repeatedly behaved in class ways; these historical events disclose regularities of response to analogous situations...and of a culture with class notations which admits to trans-national comparisons. We theorize this evidence as a general theory of class and of class formation: we expect to find certain regularities, "stages" of development, etc.... But...it is only too often the case that the theory takes precedence over the historical evidence which it is intended to theorize. It is easy to suppose that class takes place, not as historical process, but inside our own heads.... Models or structures are theorized that are supposed to give us objective determinants of class. [Hence] once again, class as a historical category—the observation of behavior over time—has been expelled. (Thompson 1978:147)

Rather than understand class as a predetermined phenomenon or teleology (something that can be turned into a "general theory," complete with "'stages' of development, etc."), Thompson (1978:150; emphasis added) insists that the reality of any class formation consists in "how class *defines itself* as, in fact, it *eventuates.*" For Thompson, all classes and their histories are unique manifestations of local material and social conditions—the socioeconomic conditions of possibility. Yet, even though no class is "any truer or more real than any other" and none may make any "claim to universality," Thompson (1978:150) still holds that because people "repeatedly behave in class ways," if we undertake "transnational comparisons," we will be able to see certain "regularities of response to analogous situations." It is precisely these "regularities of response to analogous situations" that account for the déjà vu moments mentioned above. The point is that when we encounter these elements of regularity and analogy across a wide range of middle-class formations and cultures, we are encountering similar responses to similar conditions of possibility, not elements of structure in a unilinear history.

The second key idea that I will be working with is *interjacency*, building on Edward Soja's (1989:247) work in cultural geography. Interjacency points to the implications of how social groups (classes, racial or ethnic groups, genders) are organized in space and, in particular, how spatial organization manifests and reproduces power relations. As opposed to being simply *ad*jacent, the idea of *inter*jacency stresses the fact that social groups—whether physically intermingled or segregated—are never ontologically independent of one another but are, instead, always intereffective, interproductive, and mutually constitutive. Power itself is spatialized, and the ways that social groups are distributed in space (in ghettos and suburbs, in "free trade zones," and across militarized national borders) have everything to do with how power is (re)produced. The ways that social hierarchies are mapped onto geographic spaces are never coincidental but always (re)productive of the very conditions of social inequality. For my purposes, the idea of interjacency is crucial because it takes Thompson's insight into the relational ontology of class and literally locates it in space: a fundamental aspect of class relationality is the interproductive geographic distribution of class formations.

I consider the role of interjacency as one of the conditions of possibility of middle-class formation and historical transformation. Whereas Soja's focus is on neighborhood and region, I want to expand the logic of interjacency to consider how the ever-growing scale of sociospatial organization (specifically, of class groups) that we call "globalization" reproduces Soja's (1989:246) "instrumental nodal structures" and "essentially exploitative spatial divisions of labor," but on a global scale. The current global order produces an unprecedented level of class spatialization in which the interproductive interjacency of class communities occurs less and less *within* localities or even nations and more and more *across* national borders and even hemispheres.[2] Thus, the conditions of interjacency (the instrumental spatial organization of groups) are among the principal conditions of possibility within which middle classes form and transform.

The third key idea that I want to weave into this model concerns *scale*, particularly a scalar understanding of geographical and historical processes. A scalar approach offers a crucial corrective to many of our instinctive understandings of difference and change, understandings that impose rigid categorical divisions onto time and space at the expense of a realization of spatial and temporal simultaneity. As suggested above, I argue that there are patterns of interjacency (mutual intereffectiveness) between social groups at every level from the neighborhood to the global. The scale at which classes are organized interjacently changes over time (as they are integrated into larger and larger spheres of interproductivity), but these scales of organization coexist *simultaneously*, not sequentially or to the exclusion of other levels of organization. At different points in time, different scales of organization may form the dominant or relevant conditions of possibility around which class groups identify, but never to the exclusion of ongoing relations of interjacency (at other scales) that may disrupt or contradict the group's understanding of itself.

Just as a scalar understanding of spatial organization allows us to think of multiple processes coexisting simultaneously, not sequentially, the same goes for a scalar understanding of historical processes. Historians (and others) have tended to understand the past in terms of epochs: distinct historical periods separated by distinct transitions, the age-of-this followed by the age-of-that in the unilinear march of history. Most histories of capitalism are classic examples of this epochal logic, with generations of historians intent on finding the "origins of capitalism" or debating the periodization of the capitalist era. Lost in an epochal understanding of the history of capitalism is the ability to conceptualize how capitalism is able to exist simultaneously, not in sequence, with other forms of economic organization or logic. Drawing on Weber and Braudel, I take a scalar approach to historical processes, arguing that we have to see the "rise of capitalism" not as a matter of historical breaks, but as a slow process of scalar transition whereby capitalist market logics gradually encompass more and more of a region's relations of exchange. From this point of view, the dominance of capitalist market relations will rise or fall, but capitalism will always exist simultaneously with other market logics, against which it competes in a moral economy for hearts and minds. Crucially, it is this scalar interrelation of competing socioeconomic logics that forms one of the primary conditions of possibility within which middle-class formations may emerge.

MIDDLE-CLASS CONSUMERISM IN WORLD HISTORICAL TIME

One way to conceptualize middle classes and their comparative histories without lapsing into Eurocentric teleologies is by theorizing the relationships among class, consumerism, and capitalism in world historical time. This perspective is based on two main propositions: first, class is a material phenomenon linked to the history of capitalism, and, second, middle classes are intrinsically consumer formations. The very act of using the word "class" to account for middle-class phenomena locates us in some kind of materialist perspective. For people to constitute a middle class—as opposed to clusters of "status groups" (Weber) or "habitus" (Bourdieu)—implies that there is not only a middle *class* but also a *middle* class, situated between and in material relationship with at least two other classes. While acknowledging other perspectives, this chapter advances a materialist/consumerist interpretation of the middle classes because I believe that it offers an effective means of accounting for many of the cultural patterns we see associated with middle classes across time and space.

One place to start conceptualizing the middle class in world historical time is to consider the role of consumption in socioeconomic life. If middle classes are indeed *classes*, then at any given point in time or space, they must stand in relation to other classes within historically and geographically specific material conditions, such as modes—and relations—of production. Any economy is about circulation (the market processes that link production and consumption); therefore, middle classes will be emergent within the conditions of possibility constituted by both new and shifting modes and relations of production, circulation, and consumption.

Every mode of production also entails consumers and modes of consumption, or, as Althusser (1971:125) points out, the reproduction of any mode of production requires the reproduction of not only the means of production but also the "means of consumption." Within any system of market relations (relations of production, circulation, and consumption), as the scale of commodity production increases, the social location of consumption—the consuming class—shifts and expands. Thus, within regional systems of market relations, as modes of production change and more and more goods are launched into circulation, we see the composition of the consuming class shift from a small, luxury-consuming elite, to a larger urban bourgeoisie, to—under conditions of industrial capitalism—a modern middle class. Profitable mass production requires reliable means of mass consumption in the form of an established, large-scale consumer class. Around the world, we see the consumer mantle gradually shifting to new middle classes, along with the transformation of elements of earlier elite classes into new capitalist elites, the decline of landed forms of production and power, and the growth of landless, "free," wage-dependent working classes. Middle classes emerge within shifting systems of market relations (at every scale from the local to the regional to the global) as increasingly dominant capitalist modes and logics of production form new conditions of possibility within which people can pioneer new spaces of subjectivity built around consumerist socio-moral logics. Nowhere do middle classes eventuate in the same ways, but to the extent that people experience analogous class relations and behave in class ways (because of analogous social locations within material relations of production, circulation, and exchange), middle-class histories will always be particular manifestations of materially related conditions of possibility.

By emphasizing the central role of consumption in middle-class history, I do not mean to suggest that consumption is the only salient cultural dynamic at work in middle-class life. In terms of interclass relationality, modern middle classes stand primarily as consumers in larger capitalist relations of production. But when it comes to middle-class subjectivity—what it means to *live* and *be* middle-class—consumer desire and consumerist strategies of class distinction are only parts of a complex class experience. Tightly integrated with consumer ideologies are new ideologies of labor, and indeed middle-class modes of consumption are ideologically complicit with new middle-class modes of labor. It is no coincidence that around the world, middle classes couch their consumer privilege in ideological rhetorics of democratic, individual "achievement"[3]—as the result of either personal "entrepreneurial success" or (via "meritocratic" education) academically credentialed, salaried, "professional" employment. Middle-class consumption and labor are (clinically) codependent.

In fact, labor and consumption are ideologically integrated in ways that are perhaps unique to the middle classes. Elsewhere, I have argued that middle-class subjects—simultaneously sellers of labor and owners of capital (skills, education, achievements)[4]—might be said to embody, or combine within their own class-cultural practices, the mutually productive antagonisms between labor and capital that have historically been played out *between* the working and capitalist classes (Liechty 2003:18). This internalized class conflict may help explain the anxieties and contradictions so characteristic of middle-class life (and repeatedly conveyed throughout this volume). For example, it highlights the inherently tenuous nature of middle-class embodied capital, the achievements and credentials upon which middle-class subjects base their labor value and try to sell it in fickle, highly competitive markets. The fact that education itself, the classic mode of middle-class meritocratic validation, is essentially a consumer enterprise (with the most valuable credentials going to those who can invest the time and money to "achieve" them) points to the uneasy, smoke-and-mirrors foundations of middle-class privilege. It also underlines the ideological complicity of middle-class labor and consumption.

This internalized class struggle may also help explain why the middle classes have often been politically manipulable and ineffective (their motives dulled and allegiances split between their positions as laborers and as owners of capital). I believe that this embodied contradiction (in effect, being laboring capitalists) may also help to explain why middle classes have sometimes been characterized as politically progressive and even radical (Johnston 2003 ; Joshi 2001)[5] and at other times as being obsessed with consumption and a class politics aimed at protecting privilege—which is how I have characterized them (Liechty 2003). One view seems to capture a manifestation of the middle-class identification with, and as a seller of, labor; the other seems to reflect the middle class experience as owner of (tenuous, embodied) property. Either way, as Bourdieu (1998b:11) and Weber insisted, the middle classes are much more likely to exist as social networks bound together by complex webs of status competition and consumer lifestyles than as communities united around common economic or political objectives.

My point here is that middle-class subjectivity might usefully be thought of in terms of an inner class struggle through which people must reconcile, and try to integrate, the necessity to act simultaneously as consumers and laborers, owners and sellers, conservatives and progressives. As laboring capitalists, middle-class subjects embody the contradictions of capitalism; attempting to resolve the tensions between their conflicting class positions, their lives are shot through with the anxieties of maintaining (ideologically and economically) a tenuous class position. As I discuss below, part of *becoming* middle-class is learning to (or being forced to) embrace this form of subjectivity. Becoming middle-class means coming to terms with conflicted moral and material logics.[6] But how are we to understand this "becoming"? How are we to conceptualize the conditions of possibility under which middle classes emerge within the larger history of capitalism?

CAPITALISM IN WORLD HISTORICAL TIME: "RISE" VERSUS "SPREAD"

There is a crucial distinction between the rise and the spread of capitalism, and "capitalism" itself is a notoriously slippery concept. But to the extent that we agree that capitalism is a global, historical reality—an actual historical socioeconomic condition that can be objectively distinguished from other conditions—then it is going to have global, historical manifestations. The question of capitalism's *rise* or *spread* highlights the problem of the ontological status of capitalism: the conditions of its being or its reality as a phenomenon. In the spirit of Williams and Thompson, who cautioned against mistaking "terms of analysis" for "terms of substance," I want to argue that (as with class) the *reality* of capitalism lies in the specificities of its eventuation (its lived "substance"), not in any universal—typically Eurocentric—condition or experience (its analytical category). As a term of analysis, capitalism becomes an idealized category with a singular history, a history of origins and spread, a teleological narrative that becomes more real than the historical circumstances it is meant to describe.[7] But as a term of substance, capitalism is a process of eventuation that can occur only within specific social, cultural, and material conditions. Furthermore, there is no *thing* to "spread," no existential reality that can "move" through time and space. The reality of capitalism is always the reality of its local emergence—its "rise"—within shifting material conditions and in the face of competing socio-moral logics. The rise of capitalism in any time or place does not signal its "arrival" (as part of the quest-like "spread of global capitalism"), but shifts in the conditions of possibility brought about by changing patterns of socioeconomic relations (interjacency) at multiple scales of interaction. If the global history of capitalism is one of uneven and non-parallel development, this is not because of uneven spread, but because the very conditions of possibility within which people live are widely variable.

The move away from the History of Capitalism to histories of capitalisms is well under way in the growing historiography of "early modernity," a historical perspective that points to multiple emergences of regional capitalisms around the world from the sixteenth to the eighteenth centuries (Bose 1990; Ludden 2004; Pomeranz 2000). In the early modern world, South Asia was a leader in early capitalist market development, with manufacturing powers that not only surpassed Europe but indeed attracted Europeans like lesser moths to a greater flame (Chaudhuri 1985; Goody 1996; Parthasarathi 1998; Subrahmanyam 1996). The "early modern" thesis assists in the project of "provincializing Europe" (Chakrabarty 2000) by locating all capitalisms in a global context and situating European capitalism as one among many emergent variants on the global scene.

One important element of this perspective is that early modernity was a *world* phenomenon. From the sixteenth century onward, a truly global "world system" gradually emerged, linking earlier regional "world systems" (Abu-Lughod 1989) for the first time. Although commodities (and many other things)[8] had long circulated within local and regional commercial networks, once Europeans finally advanced to the point where they could directly access the ancient Indian Ocean luxury trade (with, fortuitously, New World wealth to finance this), commodity trading reached its greatest geographic extent. With increased scale and efficiency of production and transportation, over time, products that began as precious luxuries destined for elite consumption were transformed into mass market goods. By the nineteenth century, Caribbean sugar and Chinese tea had become the cheapest sources of calories and caffeine for the British industrial working classes (Mintz 1985), and cheap copper and machine-made textiles from Europe were putting the ancient Nepali copper-mining and weaving industries out of business (Liechty 1997).

But perhaps more important than the movement of goods was that these new circulations brought distant groups of people into new relations of class interjacency on a global scale. Increasing the distance of trade put more and more space between producers and consumers, and the increased volume of long-distance trade created distantly separated producing and consuming classes. Laboring classes (including slave labor) in one part of the world created (part of) the conditions of possibility for consuming classes elsewhere, and vice versa. Indian and Chinese textiles transformed emerging urban consumer cultures in places like London, and the massive surge in global silver circulation following Europe's entry into the Asian trading sphere not only expanded laboring classes across Asia (especially in the coastal textile-producing regions of South Asia and China) but also spurred similar transformations in Asian urban life. Although none of this eliminated *local* relations of interjacency, the point is that gradually expanding scales of trade (in terms of distance and volume) began to gradually transform the relations of interjacency between classes of producers and consumers on a *global* scale. Though it occurred at a glacial pace, processes of early modern "globalization" meant that, in many parts of the world, one's class Others—those to whom one was bound in mutually constitutive interjacency through patterns of circulation—were increasingly distant.

Crucially, "early modernity" does not signal an epochal shift but rather points to an era that saw the gradual expansion of capitalist market logics from *within* age-old local and regional systems of circulation. I have found Fernand Braudel's work to be very helpful in conceptualizing this process (most succinctly, Braudel 1977). Rather than search for the origins of capitalism or look to chart history in terms of shifts from one economic epoch to another, Braudel (1977:5) begins with the assumption that economic life is *always* a mixture of interacting market/exchange logics and practices ranging from subsistence production, to market exchange, to capitalist exchange (using wealth as capital). For Braudel, the fruitful question is not "When did capitalism begin?" because, he argues, capitalist market logic has likely existed, to at least some extent, practically everywhere and for a very long time.[9] Capitalism does not *start* somewhere and then *spread.* It is rather, in effect, always already there. The real historical question asks: "*Under what conditions* does capitalist market logic grow to encompass more and more of a community's or region's economic life?" This approach offers a profoundly different perspective on the growth of capitalism. Within any system of circulation, capitalist market logic stands in dynamic tension with other logics. When placed in the context of centuries of shifting relations of interjacency (at every level from local to global), these changes in the balance between different economic logics help turn capitalism into what Thompson called a "*historical* category" in all of its situated richness and specificity, instead of a rigid model all are condemned to follow. Globalized relations of interjacency brought about by, for example, British mercantilism and, eventually, colonial rule in South Asia mean that early modern capitalisms are often linked and therefore intereffective, but they are also particular expressions of related conditions of possibility.

This approach puts us in a much better position to understand the relationship between capitalism and class formation. From this perspective, local class cultures will be local manifestations of specific historical developments and shifting relations of class interjacency, not derivative repetitions of someone else's history. If classes are mutually constitutive within systems of production, circulation, and consumption, then as the volume and geographic scope of that circulation expands and as the conditions of possibility for the expansion of capitalist market logics develop, class histories become dynamically linked at larger and larger scales. If modern middle classes are (crucially but not simply) consumer classes that become possible (and necessary) under conditions of rising levels of capitalist production and larger scales of circulation, then we will see consumerist middle classes emerge within specific relations of interjacency. Like capitalism, middle-class culture or middle classness does not spread but grows organically from necessary but uniquely configured local conditions that situate places within larger and larger geographic and socioeconomic contexts.

Another of Braudel's key insights into economic life is his insistence that *exchange relations are always social relations* embedded in cultural/moral systems. For Braudel (1977:64–65), there is no economic exchange that is not simultaneously a moral exchange: different exchange systems rest upon different moral logics or "values." What is more, to the extent that different exchange logics coexist and compete within the same economic sphere (as Braudel suggests will always be the case), debates over the morality of exchange relations will be an inescapable part of *any* community's cultural and economic life. We have abundant documentation of the intense moral debates that accompanied the growing dominance of capitalist market logic in Europe in the early modern period (Tawney 1957[1926]; Thompson

1993; Weber 1958) and elsewhere more recently (N. Harvey 1998 ; Taussig 1980). In Kathmandu also, debates over the morality of consumption and exchange relations were a conspicuous feature of interclass negotiations when I conducted research there in the 1990s (Liechty 2003:chap. 4). And in North America and Western Europe, contemporary consumer concerns over things like "fair trade" and locally produced food illustrate how, even in "advanced" capitalist societies, consumers are still aware of the moral basis of production and exchange even after centuries of indoctrination about the value-neutral, "natural" laws of the "free market." My point is that the rise of capitalist market logic within any economic system is, itself, already a profoundly *cultural* phenomenon, a process that plays out in the lives of real people who wrestle with competing moral logics and economic imperatives as they come to embody new class subjectivities, middle and otherwise. The emergent class-cultural dynamics that accompany this "rise" are not epiphenomenal, but integral to larger historical processes.

COMPETING MARKET LOGICS AND MORAL ECONOMIES IN KATHMANDU

To illustrate some of these historical processes, I turn now to an ethnographic account that traces the socioeconomic, moral, and cultural transformations that have taken place in the Kathmandu valley.[10] In my 2003 book on middle-class culture in Kathmandu, I argued that, since the 1960s and more intensely during the 1980s and 1990s, the city saw the formation of a middle class that emerged from within the context of an earlier, essentially two-class social system of urban elites and merchant/agrarian commoners. A massive surge in cash flow (due to a huge influx of international "development" aid money, mass tourism, local manufacturing, and remittances from millions of Nepalis working abroad) formed part of the material conditions of possibility through which profound shifts in patterns of social interaction and exchange moralities occurred. Caste communities began to fragment as new consumerist middle-class neighborhoods sprouted on the outskirts of town. What I document in that book are the morally fraught and anxiety-inducing processes whereby a consciously "middling" social formation coalesced around newly possible consumer identities and practices of moral distancing, creating new forms of distinction that allowed them to construct themselves as a new sociocultural entity. I argued that a wide array of consumer subjectivities and "rational" (in the Weberian sense) behaviors was at the very heart of the new middle class's project of constituting itself as a "suitably modern" sociocultural formation. What I believe I encountered, and tried to capture ethnographically, is something of the cultural-historical moment in which a new middle-class socioeconomic formation struggled to make itself legible in local cultural terms within (globally) transforming local conditions of possibility.

Pramod was caught up in this larger process of middle-class emergence and the negotiation of new moral logics of exchange. I got to know him in the mid-1980s, and for several years, when in Nepal, I would spend part of almost every day sitting with Pramod in the tiny food and grain shop that he operated in Asan Tole, the market square at the center of the old city of Kathmandu, site of the ancient crossroads around which the city formed more than two thousand years ago. Pramod is from a Newar merchant caste, and the shop that he ran had been his family's business for as far back as anyone knew, several centuries, if not longer. Scattered around the Asan Tole area were literally dozens of shops almost identical to Pramod's, owned by members of the same caste, each selling more or less the same variety of grains, beans, and pulses and a few odds and ends like matches or eggs. Their tiny shops were no bigger than walk-in closets, with the walls and floors lined with bins.

Like Pramod's, these other shops had been there more or less forever: historical accounts show that this area was the city's principal grain market three hundred years ago and probably even long before that.[11] When I asked Pramod how all these shops survived selling virtually the same goods, at the same prices, all clustered right next to one another, he explained matter-of-factly that each shop owner sold goods to a set of customers, from various castes, who had been buying from his family for generations: his grandfather had sold rice and dal to his current customers' grandmothers. They had relationships with these families and exchanged ritual gifts and greetings on religious holidays throughout the year.

Getting to know Pramod and his business was a real education because it helped me understand why these old bazaar areas of Kathmandu worked. I had often wondered how merchants in the old city stayed in business when, at least traditionally, all the goldsmiths had their shops right next to one another and the same went for all the bangle sellers, all the cloth merchants, all the oil pressers, all the potters, and so on. I came to realize that, as with the grain merchants, each of these businesses had established service ties with a set of customary clients. By maintaining these ties across generations and by marking them in a variety of social and ritual ways, business relations were embedded in a moral economy of customary allegiance, caste interdependence, and community pricing. Profits were pegged to a merchant family's basic needs for social reproduction in the context of their caste and larger community.

That this system had persisted for centuries, if not millennia, amazed me, but in 1991 there were signs that the arrangement was under strain. No doubt, the system had weathered ups and downs before, but that year, Pramod confided that his grain shop was having real financial problems. When his father died a few years earlier, it had fallen to Pramod not just to support his mother and siblings but also (looking ahead) to get his sister married off. He described with obvious anxiety how weddings within his caste community were getting more and more expensive: newly available, imported consumer goods had escalated dowry demands, and wedding feasts now had to be fancy catered affairs. No longer could you offer the traditional Newar wedding fare: beaten rice and stewed meat served on leaf plates, with guests seated on the floor. Now, rather than use family labor, you had to hire expensive caterers and rent everything from table service to tents and folding chairs. Without a guarantee of this kind of wedding and a dowry of modern consumer goods, Pramod worried, many families would not agree to marry a son to his sister. Being unable to marry off his sister would be a terrible blow to his family's reputation within the caste community. Weddings had always entailed some borrowing for Newar merchants, but with the new consumerist demands, Pramod worried that he might never be able to repay the debt. The point is that the business that had kept Pramod's family securely within his caste's social life for centuries now seemed unable to meet the standards of new consumer demands.

On a later trip to Nepal, in 1996, I dropped in on Pramod's shop. His younger brother directed me to a dark back room where I found Pramod tinkering with what looked like antique machinery. It was a dilapidated knitting machine the size of a small car. Pramod explained that the family business was in terrible shape and losing money fast. A few months earlier, he had borrowed money from a relative to buy this machine. The hope was that he would be able to make and sell machine-knitted socks to support his family.

When I asked what had happened to the food and grain retailing business, Pramod told an interesting story. He described how, several years earlier, one of the neighboring shopkeepers—a man from the same caste as Pramod who also ran a tiny grain shop that had been in his family for ages—had borrowed some money and bought a small warehouse on the outskirts of town. Once he had his warehouse, instead of buying small amounts of rice, pulses, and wheat every couple of weeks to sell at his store, as he had done before, this man started buying large amounts from the state-run commodity-importing corporation. Because he was buying in large volume, he could buy the best-quality goods for lower prices. Pramod described how he and the other shopkeepers in the Asan Tole market realized that this one merchant was not only underselling them but also buying up all the top-quality products and leaving them the rest. To make matters worse, the man with the warehouse could hold goods until the market price went up and then make big profits, whereas his neighboring shopkeepers were forced to buy from wholesalers at inflated prices. With consumers feeling the pinch of inflation (brought about by greater levels of cash flow in the local economy), even Pramod's trusted old patrons sheepishly started to abandon him in their search for lower-priced goods.

By 2001 Pramod's shop was being run by his (still unmarried) sister, who sold some food items and cheap miscellaneous goods. Though she made almost no money, it was something for her to do. Pramod and his brother were working for low wages for a wealthy distant relative who ran an import business. (Another brother was working illegally in Malaysia and sending home irregular remittances.) It turned out that Pramod's sock-making machine could not compete with the cheap goods coming from India and China. Many of the old shops in Asan Tole were shuttered as Pramod's merchant caste fragmented in the face of a newly expanding moral economy of exchange—known as capitalism. Increasingly, those who were able to do so left their old caste occupations, invested in new explicitly capitalist trade and light manufacturing ventures, and moved out of the old caste neighborhoods as a new system of social stratification—known as class—reoriented their experience of everyday life in Kathmandu. Some moved to the new (mixed-caste) middle-class suburbs, but others, like the horrified Pramod, appeared poised to fall between the cracks into the expanding population of urban poor.

But this story of capitalist market disruption does not end here. When I visited Pramod in 2004, I found him back in his shop, with his sister married and prospects looking slightly less bleak. A couple of years earlier, Pramod and others like him had formed a retailers association that allowed them to buy goods as a block and to lobby the government for more favorable terms on import tariffs. Even more important, Pramod explained, government deregulation had encouraged numerous competing import wholesalers,[12] which meant that it was much more difficult for any single merchant to corner the local market, as had happened some years earlier. The plus side of this scenario was that the proverbial playing field was again relatively level. The downside, Pramod explained, was that his family's old customary client base was more or less gone; many of the old urban families had moved into more comfortable, middle-class suburbs, their former homes rented to poor rural migrants. With everyone now looking for the lowest possible price, merchants had to cut their profit margins razor thin. Pramod noted that his sales volume was high but there was little profit.

In 2008 I dropped in on Pramod's shop again, only to find his elderly mother presiding over the cash box. She greeted my surprised look with a laugh and pointed down the street, saying that Pramod was "at the other shop," which turned out to be just a few doors away. Pramod had rented a tiny storefront like his own from a cousin whose family had left the traditional caste business. Pramod explained that with two shops selling the same goods, he was able to trade at a higher volume, increase his local market share, and slightly improve his profits. The (to Westerners) familiar logic of "get big or get out" had arrived in Asan Tole. The problem was that this new strategy required that the two shops be staffed from morning to night, seven days a week. Hiring someone to work at the second shop would have eliminated any increased profit, so the work rotated between Pramod, his wife, and his mother. (Pramod's brother had by this time set up his own shop in one of the new middle-class suburbs.) Pramod seemed perpetually exhausted, but he was proud to be able to send his two daughters to decent schools.

Sitting in his shop in 2008, Pramod told me (in a tone of astonishment) that his merchandise now came from more than twenty different countries, including popcorn from Argentina, beans and peas from Canada, rice from Thailand, soybeans from Brazil, and corn oil from Malaysia. After a decade of Maoist civil war, Nepal's own agricultural production had slumped, not least because millions of rural Nepalis had fled the violence and gone abroad for work. Ironically, nowadays many of Pramod's customers use remittance money from around the world to purchase basic foodstuffs from around the world. Pramod has weathered the storm of local capitalist market transformation, but the current worldwide recession could bring this precarious (neoliberal) global system down like a house of cards: global dependencies create global vulnerabilities.

Although Pramod's story could seem like an isolated case in an inconsequential market in an out-of-the-way part of the world, that is part of my point in telling it. In spite of its seeming remoteness and insignificance, since the 1980s, Kathmandu's Asan Tole market has been encompassed by a capitalist market logic that, though not new in Nepal,[13] has greatly expanded in the past half century. Pramod's story is an almost textbook example of the introduction of a capitalist market sensibility into a noncapitalist economic niche. As such, it illustrates Braudel's (1977) main contention that what changes historically is not the presence or absence of capitalist market activity, but the extent to which that moral logic encompasses the totality of a community's economic life. Perhaps because they dealt in food items—

products heavily imbued with moral and religious qualities in Hindu society (Liechty 2005)—Pramod's caste's micro-economy was one of the last market segments forced to "adapt [its] manner of life to the conditions of capitalistic success...[or] go under" (Weber 1958:72).

What does Pramod's story have to do with theorizing the middle class? Pramod's caste community (of grain merchants) was among the last to be drawn into the consumerist moral politics of the growing class society. The moral and market logics of caste have now been almost totally transformed by the moral and market logics of class.[14] Pramod services a "rationalized"—and now globalized—market economy in which maximizing consumers have replaced the morality of caste-based exchange (based on notions of reciprocity and ritual hierarchies) with class-based exchange (founded on the morality of "free trade," market competition, and low prices). Pramod's story illustrates the process whereby the dominant logic governing a local economy shifts from what Braudel called simple market exchange (here, culturally articulated in customary caste-based relations) to a capitalist consumer logic in which all goods become freely traded commodities—"free," that is, from any meaning aside from price. The relationship between goods in the marketplace (reckoned in terms of price) has replaced the relationship between merchant and customer (reckoned in terms of customary moral reciprocities).

Have Pramod and his family "achieved" middle-class status? If not, then they are certainly aspirants: they are learning the rules, logics, and desires of middle classness and struggling to get a "feel for the game" (Bourdieu 1998b:77). Pramod's (forced?) embrace of rational, maximizing business logics suggests a shift toward a middle-class, entrepreneurial labor ethic, and his careful (and fiscally painful) investment in his children's education points to a new consumerist future orientation. Though I do not imply some crude shift from a "cyclical" to "linear" experience of time, it is true that the salience of the city's old ritual calendar—the annual cycle of religious festivals and caste-based feast days around which so much of Kathmandu's social and economic life revolved—is more and more eclipsed by a strategic logic of time tied to new periodicities and values, such as investment, risk, insurance, delayed gratification, and aspiration. Kathmandu's Newar businesspeople have, no doubt, always had an instrumental relationship with time, but the instrumentalities of time associated with the growing dominance of capitalist market logics place merchants in larger and more complicated chains of relations and dependencies that decrease the amount of control any individual has, raising both the anxieties and the stakes.

Pramod has clearly begun the shift toward a new form of middle-class subjectivity (with all its contradictions and anxieties), although "making it" into the local middle class may take generations. But if he and his children are *unable* to convert earlier forms of wealth (the assets and social capital of a caste-based market system) into new forms of middle-class capital (entrepreneurial skills, educational credentials, and so forth), then it is likely that they will slide into Kathmandu's growing class of "free laborers." Translating a middling *caste* status into a middling *class* status, while the socio-moral logics of the market shift beneath your feet, is a terrifying act of social navigation with terrible penalties for those who fail—and fall. It is the primal "fear of falling" (Ehrenreich 1989)—especially for one's children—that stokes the anxious, exhausting, entrepreneurial labor of marginal people like Pramod around the world.

THE SPATIALIZATION OF CLASS: FROM INTIMATE TO GLOBAL INTERJACENCY

One of the key shifts in Pramod's social existence in the past few decades has been his growing experience of (inter)dependency on globalized markets, a shift that has been realigning his social universe in relations of class interjacency at greater and greater scales. Although to this point I have focused mainly on the problem of locating the middle class in historical time, now I will turn to some thoughts on locating the experience of middle classness in space, with a more sustained focus on the experience and changing nature of class interjacency, or how the spatial organization of class groups affects the nature of their interproductivity.

One characteristic of middle-class life in Kathmandu during the 1980s and 1990s was the experience of what we might call intimate class interjacency. Though some spatial segregation was in place, to a considerable extent, urban Nepalis of all classes regularly shared public spaces and in very real ways competed to claim those spaces for their own class-based moral projects (Liechty 2003:255ff.). In this context of intimate interjacency, middle-class Nepalis engaged in a kind of continual moral locational discourse, repeatedly locating their class Others in morally compromised social locations "above" and "below." What is more, this inescapable public intermingling produced intense feelings of consumer anxiety among middle-class people as they struggled to walk the fine line of suitability between the vulgar poor and the vulgar rich. As a twenty-first-century Chicagoan, this experience of intense class interlocationality seems alien to me, but reading Chicago School sociology from the 1930s sparks a sense of déjà vu: at that time, Chicagoans too anxiously tried to maintain social distance in an urban class world of intense physical proximity (Hannerz 1980:63; Wirth 1938:12). This anxious middle-class experience of intimate class inter-jacency finds analogous expression in different times and places and suggests that similar configurations of class interjacency will result in similar class-cultural experiences and behaviors.

But what happens when different socioeconomic strata are no longer intimately interlocated, when different class formations come into increasingly less and less contact in physical space or in socially meaningful or consequential ways? As in many other U.S. cities, in the twentieth century, Chicagoland saw a steady process of sociospatial segregation, from the ghettoization of early immigrant/ethnic groups, to the production of racially segregated "projects" and slums, to the emergence of middle-class and elite suburbs—a process that Bullard, Grigsby, and Lee (1994) refer to as "residential apartheid." Similar processes are now also at work in Kathmandu as sprawling new middle-class residential suburbs spread out from the old, densely settled urban core, gradually creating more and more class-segregated urban communities.[15] Already in the early 1990s, commentators noted the imminent demise of Kathmandu's ancient, caste-based "urban instinct" in the face of a new, middle-class-driven "suburban instinct" (Dixit 1992).

How are we to understand these shifts in the spatial nature of class interjacency and the associated cultural practices whereby class groups naturalize their sociospatial locations? Each historical eventuation will be unique, but one pattern that seems to characterize a number of middle-class emergences concerns shifts in projects of class distancing. Whereas intimately interjacent middle classes first work to naturalize their class privileges in discourses of *moral* distance, that project of distancing eventually (perhaps even simultaneously) is transformed into a project of *spatial* distancing (as with the suburbanization of many of Pramod's old clients). In Kathmandu (and around the world) as middle classes use their consumer power to convert moral distance into spatial distance, they tend to reframe their moral politics. In some cases, this reframing is toward a more (neo)liberal ethic that embraces the supposedly value-neutral promises of an entrepreneurial, "free market" state economic agenda, as with India's "new middle class" (Fernandes 2006). In other cases, such as in North America, middle classes tend to "forget" socioeconomic difference or to depoliticize it by rendering difference as ethnic or cultural (from class politics to identity politics), thereby allowing them to imagine their society as egalitarian and classless. In either case, as Henri Lefebvre (1991[1974]:52) insists, middle classes increasingly embrace a discourse of political equality ("freedom," "rights") even while engaging in the active production, reproduction, and segregation of difference through spatial practices (cf. McCann 1999) such as the suburban residential "zoning games" described by Rachel Heiman (chapter 10, this volume). The existence of India's massive urban slums alongside posh, middle-class gated communities (Srivastava, chapter 3, this volume; Waldrop 2004) is strangely analogous to the parallel growth of prison populations and middle-class gated communities in the United States (Low 2001b). Both suggest new patterns of class interjacency—the "instrumental" and "essentially exploitative" spatial displacement of social difference (Soja 1989:246)—that verge on a new kind of middle-class culture of incarceration (voluntary and involuntary) and bear witness to the lengths that people will go to spatially segregate themselves from their class Others.[16]

If urban class segregation is one important measure of the growing spatial distancing between socioeconomic groups, the rise of neoliberal globalization has only amplified the effect, further distancing the relations of interjacency that link mutually productive class formations. Taking to the extreme a process that began in the early modern period, neoliberal globalization has increasingly divided the world into functionally interproductive class zones. After half a century of gains on the part of organized labor in the early twentieth century, the rise of conservative "free trade" economics in the 1970s and 1980s saw the growing export of Western capital and jobs to low-wage parts of the world. As millions of blue-collar, working-class jobs were "offshored," U.S. cities underwent major sociospatial transformations (Soja 1989). Once-vibrant working-class neighborhoods slid into poverty, their populations increasingly segregated along racial and ethnic lines. The vacuum left by the exodus of working-class jobs was quickly filled by a new sub-working class of un- or underemployed "flexible" laborers, including millions of new undocumented, criminalized, "illegal" migrants who now form huge pools of docile labor (legally unprotected, unrepresented, and often "invisible") in American cities (De Genova 2005). This influx of "illegal" Third World labor into the First allows the post-industrial service economy to feed at the same low-wage trough that industrial capital enjoys beyond the state's militarized borders (Harvey 2005).[17]

In terms of the modern Western experience of class interjacency, neoliberal globalization has meant an even greater distancing of the middle classes from their class Others. Fifty years ago, it was a novel experience for American consumers to acquire a product manufactured outside the

United States. Today, the United States' multi-billion-dollar annual trade deficits with China are evidence of the fact that it is almost impossible to buy American-made consumer goods. America's new role in the global economy is no longer producer-to-the-world, but consumer-of-the-world. With its working class exiled offshore and its underclass criminalized (evidenced in racially uneven incarceration and "illegal" immigrants) and spatially segregated, the huge American middle class can confidently shoulder its consumerist responsibility as the leading member of the world's middle classes, enjoying the "democracy of goods" at home and promoting "free trade" abroad. With its class Others largely out of sight and out of mind, middle-class Americans can happily embrace an ethic of "freedom and democratic equality" in which any mention of economic disparities invites accusations of being "anti-American" or inciting "class warfare."[18]

We need to understand these changes in the nature of class interjacency in terms of shifting conditions of possibility: shifts in capitalist circulation that occurred at increasing volume and scale for several centuries, culminating in crucial new forms of interstate relations that took shape in the middle decades of the twentieth century. As the era of European imperial domination began to wane and eventually collapse after two world wars, decolonization opened up new conditions of possibility out of which emerged new patterns of geostrategic organization. Among them was the emergence of what Kelly and Kaplan (2001:9) refer to as a new "world system of nation-states," formally egalitarian units arrayed in "democratic" international institutions (e.g., the United Nations) that cleared the way for ever-greater efficiencies and the rationalization of global capitalist market relations. With postcolonial states (as well as post- and neo-imperialist states) now formally equal and equally sovereign—each with its own (supposedly) independent "national economy" (Mitchell 2002)—new forms of "multilateral" (as opposed to colonial or binary) interstate relations were propounded in the form of agencies and treaty organizations (IMF, World Bank, GATT, WTO). All of these new multilateral entities had both political and economic powers through which they could uphold the dual ideologies (myths?) of "free nations" and "free trade" and impose uniform interstate property and contract laws. In the context of the Cold War, the United States (via the Truman Doctrine) took the lead in the global promotion of "freedom," offering "development" as the carrot (and military intervention as the stick) to bring reluctant nation-states into the freedom-loving and free-trading camp. As Kelly and Kaplan (2001:59) note, in the postcolonial era of freedom and national sovereignty, "only corporations, not nations, are free to pursue dreams of domination." In the postwar nation-state system, the domain of "economics" has been ideologically recast as a sphere separate from the powers whose interests it serves (Mitchell 2002:14).[19]

Although they do not use the term "interjacency," what scholars like Kelly, Kaplan, and Mitchell are talking about is how geopolitical shifts in the twentieth century created the conditions of possibility for new sociospatial organizations as class relations were mapped onto a world-scale "instrumental nodal structure" (Soja 1989:246). Half a century of neoliberal free-trade policies has produced a new global spatialization of relations of production, circulation, and exchange. To the extent that one's class Others have been offshored (or otherwise spatially segregated), one no longer has the sociospatial experience of intimate interjacency, which produces the intense discourses of socio-moral distancing that I documented in Kathmandu. Even Bourdieu's (1984:128–29; 1998b:5) famous maps of French "social space" from the 1960s and 1970s now seem out of date because of their prominent representation of working-class habitus in direct proximity to those of the middle and upper classes.[20] "Social space" (or class interjacency) in the neoliberal era needs to be charted less *within* national economies and more *across* global economic systems of production and consumption. To an unprecedented degree, neoliberal globalization produces a new *global* spatialization (and segregation) of class that increasingly neutralizes what were once visceral (and politically charged) *local* interclass relations. Class interjacencies that were once negotiated within local and national political structures are now the stuff of multilateral (GATT, WTO, NAFTA) deal making that effectively pairs off global blocks of producers (working classes) and consumers (middle classes) in the interests of global capitalist elites. States retain the important function of regulating exactly what is "free" to move within free-trade regimes by legitimating and protecting global capital transfers while also granting (or denying) citizenship and the rights to transnational movement (labor recruiting, "guest workers," "illegal immigration"). In this way, states more and more function to segregate mutually productive classes on a global scale by maintaining wage differentials across increasingly militarized national borders.

Where does Nepal fit into this new world of globalized class interjacencies? An extremely marginal player in a world economic system less characterized by capital "flows" and more by capital that "hops" between global financial centers (Ferguson 2006:37), Nepal's economy is largely a fly-over backwater. Although Nepal has been integrated into capitalist circulation for centuries (Liechty 1997), the scale of that integration has always been small, a condition that remains to this day as Nepal continues to have among the lowest GDPs and per capita incomes in the world.[21] From World War II to the 1980s, First World "development aid" largely funded Nepal's national economy, but since the end of the Cold War, Nepal's donors have increasingly focused less on aid and more on trade. Neoliberal doctrine has shifted the focus from national development (education, health, and so forth) to market development, "capacity building," and free trade. This means that Nepalis can now enjoy Argentine popcorn and Canadian beans (as in Pramod's shop), yet for large parts of Kathmandu's middle class (and even more for middle-class aspirants), access to this new consumer smorgasbord is possible only through remittances from family members abroad. With free trade but few jobs, international remittances now make up a huge but essentially invisible (because unmeasurable and unregulated) part of the national economy. Working through state-licensed labor-export businesses, millions of Nepalis toil in miserable, low-wage jobs in India, the Gulf states, Southeast Asia, and elsewhere, sending home the equivalent of billions of U.S. dollars per year. Among the most striking changes in the Kathmandu valley in the decade between 2000 and 2010 were massive suburban sprawl, numerous glitzy new shopping malls, and thousands of Western Union outlets.[22] Ironically, Nepal, too, has begun to offshore its working class, even if those drawn into global labor mobility are motivated by a desire to propel their own social mobility into the nascent Nepali middle class.[23] Global labor exports have created the conditions for a small Kathmandu-based middle class, which in turn coordinates, and feeds off, Nepal's position on the fringes of the neoliberal global economy.

CONCLUSION

Marx famously denied the historical significance of the industrial capitalist middle classes. Even Gramsci—who acknowledged the strategic political importance of the middle class—refused to characterize it as a potentially "hegemonic class." He argued that because the middle class is not involved in the key Marxist contradiction between labor (working class) and capital (capitalist class), it would not be a moving force in history (Mouffe 1979). Even if middle classes are unlikely to be hotbeds of historical and political dynamism, I argue that middle-class formations do play a key role in the cultural-historical processes whereby capitalisms (locally emergent patterns of capitalist market relations) play themselves out around the world. Middle classes emerge within the conditions of possibility formed by class interjacencies (sociospatial interproductivities) as changing modes and scales of production open up spaces for new consumer subjectivities and practices around which new middling classes constitute themselves in cultural life. Whether intimately interjacent or separated by continents (or national borders) from their interproductive class Others, middle classes everywhere stand between modern laboring classes and finance/capitalist classes as salaried or entrepreneurial consumers of capitalist production.

Middle classes first attempt to naturalize and protect their class privileges through discourses of moral distancing from their class Others, but as class spatial segregation grows, the middle classes increasingly embrace moral and political rhetorics of freedom, equality, and (in the neoliberal era) "free trade" while simultaneously reinforcing the spatial parameters of their own privilege. The gated communities and militarized (walled) borders of the United States, needed to protect the spaces of middle-class privilege, suggest that the possibilities of local and global class segregation may be reaching their limits.

Acknowledgments

Various incarnations of this chapter were presented at the University of Chicago, the University of Sussex, and Martin Chautari (Kathmandu). Special thanks to the SAR seminar participants (especially Rachel Heiman and Carla Freeman) and to Molly Doane and Paul Bick for their close readings, criticisms, and helpful suggestions. I have heeded most, but not all, of them and therefore am responsible for any remaining problems.

Notes

1. Just one example, continuing on the theme of prostitution: in Kathmandu in the early 1990s, hoping to attract middle-class men, prostitutes dressed in school uniforms and carried textbooks (Liechty 2005:15). Similarly, Timothy Gilfoyle (1992:285) notes that in early twentieth-century New York City, it was common for prostitutes to pose as school girls, wearing "juvenile attire" and carrying book satchels.

2. Schielke (chapter 2, this volume) captures this point nicely when he suggests that in Egypt, middle-class aspirations "are not so much related to a specific place, but more to a wider imagination of the world, primarily a First World world of possibilities" that includes the East and the West.

3. See Yeh (chapter 8, this volume) for a discussion of the middle classes as the arbiters of democracy and merit in Mexico.

4. Thus, the middle classes do not own the massive, capital-intensive means of production in the Marxist sense but *become* their own individual means of production.

5. This view of middle classes as politically progressive is often associated with a Habermasian logic whereby middle class (or bourgeoisie) is characterized as a relatively

leisured and educated class that, emerging in early modern European history, pioneers a new "bourgeois public sphere" in which to rationally debate ideas and advance progressive causes (Habermas 1989). This image of middle classes as a historical force for democratic, progressive action stands in contrast to perspectives (Weber, Bourdieu, Gramsci) that see middle classes in almost opposite terms—unlikely, or even unable, to mobilize coherent political action. But this progressive middle-class political stance would also fit into Lefebvre's (1991[1974]) characterization of middle-class practice (discussed further below) as being liberal and inclusive in its political rhetoric even while it actively pursues and protects its class privileges through segregating spatial practices. But even if we do not simply write off middle-class political progressivism as cynical rhetoric aimed at obscuring simultaneous projects of protecting class privilege (consumer property), Lefebvre's claims at least force us to acknowledge some deeply contradictory dimensions of middle-class life.

 6. For an expanded discussion of moral and material logics, see Carla Jones, chapter 6, this volume. Jones suggests that the middle-class project in Indonesia involves "transubstantiating money into morality, often through practices that reveal the relatedness of consumption and religion." The conflict of moral and material logics is particularly acute for women attempting to negotiate between expanding economic opportunities and persisting ideas regarding a woman's proper role in the home.

 7. This is the standard logic behind claims for the origins of capitalism in Europe and its spread around the world, a perspective critiqued by Blaut (1993) and Wolf (1982).

 8. Because my focus is on class and because class is (I am arguing) a social phenomenon related to modes—and relations—of production, circulation, and consumption, I am less concerned here with the circulation of noncommercial elements (people, knowledge, religions, technologies, etc.), even though these noncommercial circulations may be important aspects of the conditions of possibility from which new middle classes emerge.

 9. This is the same point that Weber (1958:xxxiii) makes in *The Protestant Ethic and the Spirit of Capitalism:* "Capitalism and capitalistic enterprises...have existed in all civilized countries of the earth...[including] China, India, Babylon, Egypt, Mediterranean antiquity, and the Middle Ages, as well as in modern times.... Capitalistic enterprise and the capitalist entrepreneur...are very old and were very widespread." In fact, Braudel's whole approach could be seen as an elaboration on earlier Weberian conceptualizations.

 10. In this short chapter, I can tell only a tiny part of this story. A fuller accounting would consider the slow expansion of capitalist market relations in the Himalayas over

previous centuries, the role of British colonialism in South Asia, the Nepali elite's extraordinary fixation on foreign consumer goods and its efforts to regulate consumption prior to 1951, Nepal's post-1951 liberal import policies, the rise of massive development aid and remittance economies, and so on. Elsewhere, I have sketched out these and other elements in what I consider to be the "prehistory" of middle-class formation in Nepal (Liechty 1997, 2003).

11. The square's ancient Annapurna Temple (dedicated to the goddess of grain and harvests) also suggests that the area has been a grain market for millennia.

12. These changes were due to neoliberal economic policies imposed on Nepal by the World Bank (cf. Rankin 2004).

13. Other segments of Kathmandu's economy, especially the merchant communities that have been involved in long-distance trade between Tibet and India, have operated around these capitalist principles for at least several centuries. See, for example, Tuladhar 2004.

14. It is crucial to understand that class logic does not *replace* caste relations but profoundly alters those relations, as I have documented in detail elsewhere (Liechty 2003, 2005).

15. See Li Zhang, chapter 9, this volume, for a discussion of this at work in China and Sanjay Srivastava, chapter 3, this volume, for a discussion of this at work in India.

16. Gated communities are now, also, increasingly common in Kathmandu's elite residential suburbs.

17. The growing prevalence of Third World (im)migrant labor in First World countries reminds us of how different systems of market relations can coexist interdependently even though spatially segregated across national borders. As Meillassoux (1972) noted and others have corroborated (Weyland 1993), the capitalist mode of production is often dependent on the coexistence of noncapitalist hinterlands—often rural subsistence-producing agricultural areas of the "Third World"—from which are extracted adult laborers and to which they are later expelled. In this way, the capitalist mode of production often avoids the cost of the social reproduction of the working class by offshoring the cost of producing and maintaining laborers before and after their period of peak laboring productivity.

18. Such as those leveled against John Edwards in the 2007 Democratic presidential primaries in the United States.

19. My thinking in this paragraph is heavily influenced by Kelly and Kaplan (2001) and Mitchell (2002). Mitchell (2002:7, 5) argues that global political and economic turmoil from the 1930s to the 1950s "transformed economics into a global form of knowledge" characterized not just by new geopolitical institutions but by "new forms of value,

new kinds of equivalence, new practices of calculation, [and] new relations between human agency and the nonhuman." In this world, a globalized capitalist class marshaled its powers through a depoliticized "rule of experts," who claimed state power in the name of "economic development."

20. In the United States, decades of conservative, anti-labor rhetoric have made the very idea of the working class vaguely sinister. Good Americans should be "hard-working" (wage-earning) but not "working class"—suggesting that consumption, not production, is (or should be) at the heart of our subjectivity. The middle class works to consume.

21. The World Bank and other analysts routinely rank Nepal behind countries such as Haiti, Mali, and Lesotho in a range of economic development standings. See http://siteresources.worldbank.org/DATASTATISTICS/Resources/GDP.pdf.

22. In 2008 I went to the Western Union desk at a major international bank in Kathmandu, intending to send money to India. But I was told that it was impossible. In Nepal, Western Union is set up only to receive money from abroad.

23. This is very similar to the Egyptian case described by Schielke (chapter 2, this volume), in which labor migration abroad is a strategy for local social mobility.

References

Abaza, Mona

2006   The Changing Consumer Cultures of Modern Egypt: Cairo's Urban Reshaping. Cairo: American University in Cairo Press.

Abdurrachman, Wahid

1990   Indonesia's Muslim Middle Class: An Imperative or a Choice? *In* The Politics of Middle Class Indonesia. Richard Tanter and Kenneth Young, eds. Pp. 22–24. Clayton, Victoria, Australia: Monash Papers on Southeast Asia.

Abrahams, R. D.

1983   The Man-of-Words in the West Indies: Performance and the Emergence of Creole Culture. Baltimore: Johns Hopkins University Press.

Abu-Lughod, Janet

1989   Before European Hegemony: The World System A.D. 1250–1350. Oxford: Oxford University Press.

Aguilar Camín, Héctor

2010   La sociedad invisible. Milenio, October 14. http://impreso.milenio.com/node/8848007 (accessed March 23, 2011).

Alegría, Tito

2009   Metrópolis transfronteriza: Revisión de la hipótesis y evidencias de Tijuana, México y San Diego, Estados Unidos. Mexico: El Colegio de la Frontera Norte.

Allison, Anne

1994   Nightwork: Sexuality, Pleasure, and Corporate Masculinity in a Tokyo Hostess Club. Chicago: University of Chicago Press.

Althusser, Louis

1971   Lenin and Philosophy and Other Essays. London: NLB.

REFERENCES

Anderson, Benedict

1983   Imagined Communities: Reflections on the Origin and Spread of Nationalism. London: Verso.

Anderson, Jenny

2010   Looking for Babysitters: Foreign Language a Must. New York Times, August 18. http://www.nytimes.com/2010/08/19/nyregion/19bilingual.html?_r=1&scp=1&sq=Anderson+bilingual&st=nyt (accessed April 2011).

Appadurai, Arjun

1986   Theory in Anthropology: Center and Periphery. Comparative Studies in Society and History 28(2):356–61.

1988   How to Make a National Cuisine: Cookbooks in Contemporary India. Comparative Studies in Society and History 30(1):3–24.

1996   Modernity at Large: Cultural Dimensions of Globalization. Minneapolis: University of Minnesota Press.

1997   Modernity at Large: Cultural Dimensions of Globalization. Delhi: Oxford University Press.

Armbrust, Walter

2011   The Revolution against Neoliberalism. Jadaliyya. http://www.jadaliyya.com/pages/index/717/the-revolution-against-neoliberalism (accessed March 23, 2011).

Atkinson, Rowland

2006   Padding the Bunker: Strategies of Middle-Class Disaffiliation and Colonisation in the City. Urban Studies 43(4):819–32.

Atkinson, Rowland, and Sarah Blandy

2007   Panic Rooms: The Rise of Defensive Homeownership. Housing Studies 22(4):443–58.

Austin, Diane

1984   Urban Life in Kingston, Jamaica: The Culture and Class Ideology of Two Neighborhoods. New York: Gordon and Breach.

Babcock, Richard F.

1966   The Zoning Game: Municipal Practices and Policies. Madison: University of Wisconsin Press.

Babcock, Richard F., and Fred P. Bosselman

1973   Exclusionary Zoning: Land Use Regulation and Housing in the 1970s. New York: Praeger.

Badan Pusat Statistik

2008   Indeks Pembangunan Manusia 1999–2005. Jakarta: BPS.

Bakhtin, M. M.

1981   The Dialogic Imagination: Four Essays. Michael Holquist, ed. Caryl Emerson and Michael Holquist, trans. Austin: University of Texas Press.

Baksh-Soodeen, Rawwida

1998   Issues of Difference in Contemporary Caribbean Feminism. Feminist Review 59:74–85.

Bánk, András

1967   A gyerek helye [The child's place]. Lakáskúltura 3:3–7.

Banks, Sandy

2007a   School's E-Monitoring Puts a Mother to the Test. Los Angeles Times, September 29. http://articles.latimes.com/2007/sep/29/local/me-banks29.

2007b   Report Card Has Mom Rethinking E-Snooping. Los Angeles Times, October 2. http://articles.latimes.com/2007/oct/02/local/me-banks2.

Barker, Joshua, and Johan Lindquist et al.

2009   Orang Kaya: Figures of Indonesian Modernity. Indonesia 87(April):35–72.

Barrow, Christine

1996   Family in the Caribbean: Themes and Perspectives. Kingston, Jamaica: Ian Randle Publishers.

Barrow, Christine, and J. Edward Greene

1979   Small Business in Barbados: A Case of Survival. Cave Hill, Barbados: University of the West Indies, Institute of Social and Economic Research, Eastern Caribbean.

Baudrillard, Jean

1998   The Consumer Society. London: Sage.

Baviskar, Amita

2002   The Politics of the City. Seminar: A Symposium of the Changing Contours of Indian Environmentalism 516:41–47.

Baviskar, Amita, Kavita Philip, and Subir Sinha

2006   Rethinking Indian Environmentalism: Industrial Pollution in Delhi and Fisheries in Kerala. In Forging Environmentalism: Justice, Livelihood, and Contested Environments. Joanne Bauer, ed. Pp. 189–256. New York: Sharpe.

Beckles, Hilary

1989   Corporate Power in Barbados: The Mutual Affair. Bridgetown: Caribbean Graphics.

1990   A History of Barbados: From Amerindian Settlement to Nation-State. Cambridge: Cambridge University Press.

Benveniste, Émile

1971   Subjectivity in Language. In Problems in General Linguistics. Mary Elizabeth Meek, trans. Pp. 223–30. Coral Gables: University of Miami Press.

Berdahl, Daphne

1999   Where the World Ended: Re-unification and Identity in the German Borderland. Los Angeles: University of California Press.

REFERENCES

Betts, Paul
2010   Within Walls: Private Life in the German Democratic Republic. Oxford: Oxford University Press.

Biehl, Joao, Byron Good, and Arthur Kleinman, eds.
2007   Subjectivity: Ethnographic Investigations. Berkeley: University of California Press.

Blakely, Edward James, and Mary Gail Snyder
1999   Fortress America: Gated Communities in the United States. Washington, DC: Brookings Institution Press.

Blaut, James M.
1993   The Colonizer's Model of the World: Geographical Diffusionism and Eurocentric History. London: Guilford.

Bledstein, B. J., and R. D. Johnston, eds.
2001   The Middling Sort: Explorations in the History of the American Middle Class. New York: Routledge.

Blum, Eric
2007   San Ysidro Seeks to Add Security, Reduce Wait Times. U.S. Customs and Border Protection Today, February–March. http://cbp.gov/xp/CustomsToday/2007/feb_mar/san_ysidro.xml (accessed September 2011).

Blumin, Stuart M.
1989   The Emergence of the Middle Class: Social Experience in the American City, 1760–1900. Cambridge: Cambridge University Press.

Bodnár, Judit
2007   Becoming Bourgeois: (Postsocialist) Utopias of Isolation and Civilization. *In* Evil Paradises: Dreamworlds of Neoliberalism. Mike Davis and Daniel Bertrand Monk, eds. Pp. 140–61. New York: New Press.

Bodnár, Judit, and Virág Molnár
2010   Reconfiguring Private and Public: State, Capital and New Housing Developments in Berlin and Budapest. Urban Studies 47(4):789–812.

Boellstorff, Tom
2005   The Gay Archipelago: Sexuality and Nation in Indonesia. Princeton: Princeton University Press.

Boomers Life
2008   Baby Boom Population - U.S. Census Bureau - USA and by State. http://www.boomerslife.org/baby_boom_population_us_census_bureau_by_state.htm (accessed March 4, 2012).

Bose, Sugata, ed.
1990   South Asia and World Capitalism. New Delhi: Oxford University Press.

Bottomore, Tom, ed.
1983   A Dictionary of Marxist Thought. Oxford: Blackwell.

Bourdieu, Pierre

1977   Outline of a Theory of Practice. Cambridge: Cambridge University Press.

1979   La distinction: Critique sociale du jugement. Paris: Minuit.

1984   Distinction: A Social Critique of the Judgment of Taste. Cambridge: Harvard
         University Press.

1998a   The essence of neoliberalism. Le Monde diplomatique.
         http://mondediplo.com/1998/12/08bourdieu.

1998b   Practical Reason. Stanford: Stanford University Press.

Braudel, Fernand

1977   Afterthoughts on Material Civilization and Capitalism. Patricia Ranum,
         trans. Baltimore: Johns Hopkins University Press.

Bren, Paulina

2002   Weekend Getaways: The Chata, the Tramp, and the Politics of Private Life
         in Post-1968 Czechoslovakia. *In* Socialist Spaces: Sites of Everyday Life in the
         Eastern Bloc. D. Crowley and S. E. Reid, eds. Pp. 123–40. Oxford: Berg.

Brenner, Suzanne

1996   Reconstructing Self and Society: Javanese Muslim Women and "the Veil."
         American Ethnologist 23(4):673–97.

1998   The Domestication of Desire: Women, Wealth and Modernity in Java.
         Princeton: Princeton University Press.

Brosius, Christiane

2010   India's Middle Class: New Forms of Urban Leisure, Consumption and
         Prosperity. New Delhi: Routledge.

Buchowski, Michal

2008   The Enigma of the Middle Class: A Case Study of Entrepreneurs in Poland.
         In Changing Economies and Changing Identities in Postsocialist Eastern
         Europe. Ingo W. Schroder and Asta Vonderau, eds. Pp. 47–74. Berlin: LIT.

Bullard, Robert D., J. Eugene Grigsby, and Charles Lee, eds.

1994   Residential Apartheid: The American Legacy. Los Angeles: CAAS
         Publications.

Burke, Timothy

1996   Lifeboy Men, Lux Women: Commodification, Consumption, and Cleanliness
         in Modern Zimbabwe. Durham: Duke University Press.

Burton, Richard D. E.

1997   Afro-Creole: Power, Opposition and Play in the Caribbean. Ithaca: Cornell
         University Press.

Cahn, Peter S.

2008   Consuming Class: Multilevel Marketers in Neoliberal Mexico. Cultural
         Anthropology 23(3):429–52.

Caldeira, Teresa P. R.

2000   City of Walls: Crime, Segregation, and Citizenship in São Paulo. Berkeley:
         University of California Press.

REFERENCES

Caldwell, Melissa

2011   Dacha Idylls: Living Organically in Russia's Countryside. Berkeley: University of California Press.

Campbell, Colin

1987   The Romantic Ethic and the Spirit of Modern Consumerism. Oxford: Basil Blackwell.

Chakrabarty, Dipesh

2000   Provincializing Europe: Postcolonial Thought and Historical Difference. Princeton: Princeton University Press.

Chandrasekhar, C. P., and Jayati Ghosh

2007   Women Workers in Urban India. www.macroscan.org (accessed December 12, 2008).

Chaudhuri, K. N.

1985   Trade and Civilization in the Indian Ocean: An Economic History from the Rise of Islam to 1750. Cambridge: Cambridge University Press.

Chesluk, Benjamin

2004   "Visible Signs of a City out of Control": Community Policing in New York City. Cultural Anthropology 19(2):250–75.

Clough, Patricia T., Greg Goldberg, Rachel Schiff, Aaron Weeks, and Craig Willse

2007   Notes Towards a Theory of Affect-Itself. Ephemera: Theory and Politics in Organization 7(1):60–77.

Cohen, Lawrence

1995   Holi in Banaras and the *Mahaland* of Modernity. GLQ 2:399–424.

Cohen, Lizabeth

2003   A Consumers' Republic: The Politics of Mass Consumption in Postwar America. New York: Vintage.

Cohen, Yehudi A.

1956   Structure and Function: Family Organization and Socialization in a Jamaican Community. American Anthropologist, n.s., 58(4):664–86.

Colapietro, Vincent Michael

1989   Peirce's Approach to the Self: A Semiotic Perspective on Human Subjectivity. Albany: State University of New York Press.

Collier, Jane, and Sylvia Yanagisako

1987   Introduction. *In* Gender and Kinship: Essays toward a Unified Analysis. Sylvia Yanagisako and Jane Collier, eds. Pp. 1–13. Palo Alto: Stanford University Press.

Collins, Patricia Hill

1992   Black Women and Motherhood. *In* Rethinking the Family: Some Feminist Questions. Rev. edition. Barrie Thorne, ed. Pp. 215–45. Boston: Northeastern University Press.

Colomina, Beatriz
2007   Domesticity at War. Cambridge: MIT Press.

Coontz, Stephanie
1992   The Way We Never Were: American Families and the Nostalgia Trap. New York: Basic.

Cooper, Carolyn
1995   Noises in the Blood: Orality, Gender, and the "Vulgar" Body of Jamaican Popular Culture. Durham: Duke University Press.

Corrigan, Philip, and Derek Sayer
1985   The Great Arch: English State Formation as Cultural Revolution. London: Blackwell.

Currie, Elliott
2005   The Road to Whatever: Middle-Class Culture and the Crisis of Adolescence. New York: Metropolitan.

Czegledy, André P.
1998   Villas of Wealth: A Historical Perspective on New Residences in Post-socialist Hungary. City and Society 10(1):245–68.

Daniel, E. Valentine
1996   Charred Lullabies: Chapters in an Anthropography of Violence. Princeton: Princeton University Press.

Davidoff, Paul, and Mary E. Brooks
1976   Zoning Out the Poor. In Suburbia: The American Dream and Dilemma. Philip C. Dolce, ed. Pp. 135–66. Garden City: Anchor.

Davidson, Elsa
2008   Marketing the Self: The Politics of Aspiration among Middle-Class Silicon Valley Youth. Environment and Planning A 40(12):2814–30.

Davis, Deborah
2002   When a House Becomes His Home. In Popular China: Unofficial Culture in a Globalizing Society. Perry Link, Richard Madsen, and Paul Pickowicz, eds. Pp. 231–50. Lanham: Rowman and Littlefield.
2005   Urban Consumer Culture. China Quarterly 183:692–709.

Davis, Deborah, ed.
2000   The Consumer Revolution in Urban China. Berkeley: University of California Press.

Davis, Mike
1992a   City of Quartz: Excavating the Future in Los Angeles. New York: Vintage.
1992b   Fortress Los Angeles: The Militarization of Urban Space. In Variations on a Theme Park: The New American City and the End of Public Space. Michael Sorkin, ed. Pp. 154–80. New York: Hill and Wang.

REFERENCES

Dean, Jodi

2002   Publicity's Secret: How Technoculture Capitalizes on Democracy. Ithaca: Cornell University Press.

De Genova, Nicholas

2005   Working the Boundaries: Race, Space, and "Illegality" in Mexican Chicago. Durham: Duke University Press.

De Grazia, Victoria

1996   Changing Consumption Regimes. *In* The Sex of Things: Gender and Consumption in Historical Perspective. Victoria De Grazia and Ellen Furlough, eds. Pp. 11–24. Berkeley: University of California Press.

de Koning, Anouk

2009   Global Dreams: Class, Gender, and Public Space in Cosmopolitan Cairo. Cairo: American University in Cairo Press.

De la Calle, Luis, and Luis Rubio

2010a   Clasemedieros. Nexos, May 1. http://www.nexos.com.mx/?P=leerarticulo& Article=73171 (accessed March 23, 2011).

2010b   Clasemediero: Pobre no más, desarrollado aún no. Mexico City: Centro de Investigación para el Desarrollo.

Derrida, Jacques

1988   Signature Event Context. *In* Limited Inc. Pp. 1–23. Evanston: Northwestern University Press.

Deutsch, Anthony

2011   Middle Income: Indonesia Promoted. Financial Times, February 7. http://blogs.ft.com/beyond-brics/2011/02/07/promotion-indonesia-becomes-middle-income (accessed April 1, 2011).

de Zalduondo, B.

1995   Meaning and Consequence in Sexual Economic Exchange: Gender, Poverty and Sexual Risk Behavior in Urban Haiti. *In* Conceiving Sexuality. Richard Parker and John Gagnon, eds. Pp. 157–80. New York: Routledge.

Dick, Howard

1985   The Rise of a Middle Class and the Changing Concept of Equity in Indonesia: An Interpretation. Indonesia 39(April):71–92.

1990   Further Reflections on the Middle Class. *In* The Politics of Middle-Class Indonesia. Richard Tanter and Kenneth Young, eds. Pp.63–70. Clayton, Victoria, Australia: Centre of Southeast Asian Studies, Monash University.

Di Leonardo, Micaela

1987   The Female World of Cards and Holidays: Women, Families, and the Work of Kinship. Signs: Journal of Women in Culture and Society 12(3):440–53.

Dill, Bonnie Thornton

1994   Across the Boundaries of Race and Class: An Exploration of Work and Family Among Black Female Domestic Servants. New York: Garland.

Dixit, Kanak
1992   Compact Development: Kathmandu Tried It First. Himal 5(1):39.

Djajadiningrat-Nieuwenhuis, Madelon
1987   Ibuism and Priyayization: Path to Power? *In* Indonesian Women in Focus: Past and Present Notions. Elsbeth Locher-Scholten and Anke Niehof, eds. Pp. 42–51. Dordrecht: Foris.

Dobriner, William Mann
1963   Class in Suburbia. Englewood Cliffs: Prentice Hall.

Donzelot, Jacques
1979   The Policing of Families. New York: Pantheon.

Douglas, Mary
2002[1966] Purity and Danger: An Analysis of Concepts of Pollution and Taboo. New York: Routledge.

Douglas, Mary, and Baron Isherwood
1979   The World of Goods. New York: Basic.

Douglas, Susan J., and Meredith W. Michaels
2004   The Mommy Myth: The Idealization of Motherhood and How It Has Undermined All Women. New York: Free Press.

Douglass, Lisa
1992   The Power of Sentiment: Love, Hierarchy, and the Jamaican Family Elite. Boulder: Westview.

Duncan, Nancy G., and James S. Duncan
1997   Deep Suburban Irony: The Perils of Democracy in Westchester County, New York. *In* Visions of Suburbia. Roger Silverstone, ed. Pp. 161–79. New York: Routledge.

Dupont, Véronique
2005   The Idea of a New Chic Delhi through Publicity Hype. *In* The Idea of Delhi. Romi Khosla, ed. Pp. 78–93. Mumbai: Marg.

Dwyer, Rachel
2000   All You Want Is Money, All You Need Is Love: Sexuality and Romance in Modern India. London: Cassell.

Ehrenreich, Barbara
1989   Fear of Falling: The Inner Life of the Middle Class. New York: Pantheon.
2005   Bait and Switch: The (Futile) Pursuit of the American Dream. New York: Metropolitan.

Ehrenreich, Barbara, and John Ehrenreich
1979   The Professional-Managerial Class. *In* Between Labor and Capital. Pat Walker, ed. Pp. 5–45. Boston: South End.

Elyachar, Julia
2005   Markets of Dispossession: NGOs, Economic Development, and the State in Cairo. Durham: Duke University Press.

REFERENCES

Emmerson, Donald
2006   One Nation under God? History, Faith and Identity in Indonesia. *In* Religion and Religiosity in the Philippines and Indonesia: Essays on State, Society, and Public Creeds. Theodore Friend, ed. Pp. 71–84. Washington, DC: Brookings Institution, School for Advanced International Studies.

Fardon, Richard
1990   Localizing Strategies: Regional Traditions of Ethnographic Writing. Washington, DC: Smithsonian Institution Press.

Fealy, Greg
2008   Consuming Islam: Commodified Religion and Aspirational Pietism in Contemporary Indonesia. *In* Expressing Islam: Religious Life and Politics in Indonesia. Greg Fealy and Sally White, eds. Pp. 15–39. Singapore: Institute of Southeast Asian Studies.

Featherstone, Mike
1991   Consumer Culture and Postmodernism. London: Sage.

Fehérváry, Krisztina
2002   American Kitchens, Luxury Bathrooms, and the Search for a "Normal" Life in Post-socialist Hungary. Ethnos 67(3):369–400.

Feldman, Ilana
2008   Governing Gaza: Bureaucracy, Authority, and the Work of Rule, 1917–1967. Durham: Duke University Press.

Ferge, Zsuzsa
1997   Polgárosodó Magyarország: Lefokozott szocialpolitika [Hungarian embourgeoisement: Decreasing welfare politics]. 168óra 31:18–19.

Ferguson, James
1999   Expectations of Modernity: Myths and Meanings of Urban Life on the Zambian Copperbelt. Los Angeles and Berkeley: University of California Press.
2006   Global Shadows: Africa in the Neoliberal World Order. Durham: Duke University Press.

Ferguson, James, and Akhil Gupta
2002   Spatializing States: Toward an Ethnography of Neoliberal Governmentality. American Ethnologist 29(4):981–1002.

Fernandes, Leela
2004   The Politics of Forgetting: Class Politics, State Power and the Restructuring of Urban Space in India. Urban Studies 41(12):2415–30.
2006   India's New Middle Class: Democratic Politics in an Era of Economic Reform. Minneapolis: University of Minnesota Press.

Fernández-Kelly, María Patricia
1983   For We Are Sold, I and My People: Women and Industry in Mexico's Frontier. Albany: State University of New York Press.

Fernández-Vega, Carlos
2006   Lavadora, pase de entrada a la clase media, según Fox. La Jornada, May 31.

Fogelson, Robert M.
2005   Bourgeois Nightmares: Suburbia, 1870–1930. New Haven: Yale University Press.

Folbre, Nancy, with Center for Popular Economics
1995   The New Field Guide to the U.S. Economy: A Compact and Irreverent Guide to Economic Life in America. New York: New Press.

Ford, Michele
2003   Beyond the Femina Fantasy: The Working-Class Woman in Indonesian Discourses of Women's Work. Review of Indonesian and Malaysian Affairs 37(2):83–113.

Foster, Robert J.
2002   Materializing the Nation: Commodities, Consumption and Media in Papua New Guinea. Bloomington: Indiana University Press.

Foucault, Michel
1970   The Order of Things. New York: Vintage.
1978   The History of Sexuality, vol. 1: An Introduction. New York: Random House.
1991   Governmentality. In The Foucault Effect: Studies in Governmentality. Graham Burchell, Colin Gordon, and Peter Miller, eds. Pp. 87–104. Chicago: University of Chicago Press.

Fraser, Davis
2000   Inventing Oasis: Luxury Housing Advertisements in Reconfiguring Domestic Space in Shanghai. In The Consumer Revolution in Urban China. Deborah Davis, ed. Pp. 25–53. Berkeley: University of California Press.

Freeman, Carla
2000   High Tech and High Heels: Women, Work, and Pink-Collar Identities in the Caribbean. Durham: Duke University Press.
2001   Is Local:Global as Feminine:Masculine? Rethinking the Gender of Globalization. Signs 26(4):1007–37.
2007   The "Reputation" of Neoliberalism. American Ethnologist 34(2):252–67.
2011   Embodying and Affecting Neoliberalism. In Companion to the Anthropology of Bodies/Embodiments. Francis Mascia-Lees, ed. Chap. 20. Malden: Wiley Blackwell.

Freeman, Carla, and Donna Murdock
2001   Enduring Traditions and New Directions in Feminist Ethnography in the Caribbean and Latin America. Feminist Studies 27:423–58.

French, Howard
2006   Chinese Children Learn Class, Minus the Struggle. New York Times, September 22.

REFERENCES

Friedan, Betty
1963   The Feminine Mystique. New York: Dell.

Friedman, Sara L.
2005   The Intimacy of State Power: Marriage, Liberation, and Socialist Subjects in Southeastern China. American Ethnologist 32(2):312–27.

Frug, Gerald E.
1999   City Making: Building Communities without Building Walls. Princeton: Princeton University Press.

Frykman, Jonas, and Orvar Löfgren
1987   Culture Builders: A Historical Anthropology of Middle Class Life. New Brunswick: Rutgers University Press.

Gade, Anna
2004   Perfection Makes Practice: Learning, Emotion, and the Recited Qur'an in Indonesia. Honolulu: University of Hawaii Press.

Gal, Susan
2002   A Semiotics of the Public/Private Distinction. Differences: A Journal of Feminist Cultural Studies 13(1):77–95.

Gal, Susan, and Gail Kligman
2000   The Politics of Gender after Socialism. Princeton: Princeton University Press.

Ganguly-Scrase, Ruchira, and Timothy Scrase
2009   Globalization and the Middle Classes in India: The Social and Cultural Impact of Neo-liberal Reforms. London: Routledge.

Geertz, Clifford
1963   Agricultural Involution: The Process of Ecological Change in Indonesia. Berkeley: University of California Press.
1976   The Religion of Java. Chicago: University of Chicago Press.

Geertz, Hildred
1963   Indonesian Cultures and Communities. *In* Indonesia. Ruth McVey, ed. New Haven: HRAF Yale University Press.

Geniş, Şerife
2007   Producing Elite Localities: The Rise of Gated Communities in Istanbul. Urban Studies 44(4):771–98.

Ghannam, Farha
2002   Remaking the Modern: Space, Relocation, and the Politics of Identity in a Global Cairo. Berkeley: University of California Press.

Giddens, Anthony
1979   Central Problems in Social Theory: Action, Structure, and Contradiction in Social Analysis. Berkeley: University of California Press.
1981   The Class Structure of the Advanced Societies. London: Hutchinson.
1991   Modernity and Self-Identity: Self and Society in the Late Modern Age. Stanford: Stanford University Press.

Gilbert, Dennis
2007   Mexico's Middle Class in the Neoliberal Era. Tucson: University of Arizona Press.

Gilfoyle, Timothy
1992   City of Eros: New York City, Prostitution, and the Commercialization of Sex, 1790–1920. New York: Norton.

Ginsburg, Faye
1989   Contested Lives: The Abortion Debate in an American Community. Berkeley: University of California Press.

Goffman, Erving
1979   Footing. Semiotica 25(1–2):1–29.
1981   Forms of Talk. Philadelphia: University of Pennsylvania Press.

Goodman, David
1999   The New Middle Class. *In* The Paradox of China's Post-Mao Reforms. Merle Goldman and Roderick MacFarquhar, eds. Pp. 241–61. Cambridge: Harvard University Press.

Goodman, David, and Xiaowei Zang
2008   The New Rich in China: The Dimensions of Social Change. *In* The New Rich in China: Future Rulers, Present Lives. David Goodman, ed. Pp. 1–20. London: Routledge.

Goody, Jack
1996   The East in the West. Cambridge: Cambridge University Press.

Government of Barbados
2007   National Strategic Plan 2006–2025. Research and Planning Unit, Economic Affairs Division, Ministry of Economic Affairs and Development, Bridgetown, Barbados.

Gramsci, Antonio
1971   Selections from the Prison Notebooks. Quintin Hoare and Geoffrey Nowell-Smith, eds. and trans. New York: International Publishers.

Graw, Knut
2012   On the Cause of Migration: Being and Nothingness in the African-European Borderzone. *In* The Global Horizon: Expectations of Migration in Africa and Beyond. Knut Graw and Samuli Schielke, eds. Leuven: Leuven University Press.
N.d.   Divination in the Age of Migration: Reflections on Globalization, Subjectivity and the Path of Travel in Senegal and Gambia.

Greenhouse, Carol J., Barbara Yngvesson, and David M. Engel
1994   Law and Community in Three American Towns. Ithaca: Cornell University Press.

REFERENCES

Greenough, Paul

1995   Nation, Economy, and Tradition Displayed: The Indian Crafts Museum, New Delhi. *In* Consuming Modernity: Public Culture in a South Asian World. Carol Breckenridge, ed. Pp. 216–48. Minneapolis: University of Minnesota Press.

Grewal, Inderpal

2006   "Security Moms" in the Early Twenty-first Century United States: The Gender of Security in Neoliberalism. The Global and the Intimate. WSQ (Women's Studies Quarterly) 34(1–2):25–39.

Guano, Emanuela

2002   Spectacles of Modernity: Transnational Imagination and Local Hegemonies in Neoliberal Buenos Aires. Cultural Anthropology 17(2):181–209.

2003   A Color for the Modern Nation: The Discourse on Education, Class, and Race in the Porteño Opposition to Neoliberalism. Journal of Latin American Anthropology 8(1):148–71.

Guharoy, Debnath

2006   Redefining Indonesia's Socio-economic Strata. Jakarta: Roy Morgan Research Reports.

2009   As Poverty Declines, "Upward Mobility" Is Being Redefined. Jakarta Post, September 8.

Gusterson, Hugh

1996   Nuclear Rites: A Weapons Laboratory at the End of the Cold War. Berkeley: University of California Press.

Habermas, Jürgen

1971   A társadalmi nyilvánosság szerkezetváltozása [The structural transformation of the public sphere]. Zoltán Endreffy, trans. Budapest: Gondolat Könyvkiadó.

1989   The Structural Transformation of the Public Sphere: An Inquiry into a Category of Bourgeois Society. Cambridge: MIT Press.

Hale, Charles

1989   The Transformation of Liberalism in Late Nineteenth-Century Mexico. Princeton: Princeton University Press.

Hannerz, Ulf

1980   Exploring the City: Inquiries toward an Urban Anthropology. New York: Columbia University Press.

Hanson, Paul W.

2007   Governmentality, Language Ideology, and the Production of Needs in Malagasy Conservation and Development. Cultural Anthropology 22(2):244–84.

Hardt, Michael, and Antonio Negri

2000   Empire. Cambridge: Harvard University Press.

2004 Multitude: War and Democracy in the Age of Empire. New York: Penguin.

Hartmann, Heidi I.
1979 The Unhappy Marriage of Marxism and Feminism: Towards a More Progressive Union. Capital and Class 3(2):1–33.

Harvey, David
1990 The Condition of Postmodernity: An Enquiry into the Origins of Cultural Change. Oxford: Blackwell.
1998 The Body as an Accumulation Strategy. Environment and Planning D: Society and Space 16(4):401–21.
2005 A Brief History of Neoliberalism. New York: Oxford University Press.

Harvey, Neil
1998 The Chiapas Rebellion: The Struggle for Land and Democracy. Durham: Duke University Press.

Hawley, J. S., and Shrivatsa Goswami
1981 At Play with Krishna: Pilgrimage Dramas from Brindavan. Princeton: Princeton University Press.

Hayden, Dolores
2003 Building Suburbia: Green Fields and Urban Growth, 1820–2000. New York: Vintage.
2004 A Field Guide to Sprawl. New York: Norton.

Hays, Sharon
1996 The Cultural Contradictions of Motherhood. New Haven: Yale University Press.

Hefner, Robert
2000 Civil Islam: Muslims and Democratization in Indonesia. Princeton: Princeton University Press.

Hegedüs, József
1992 Self-Help Housing in Hungary: The Changing Role of Private Housing Provision in Eastern Europe. In Beyond Self-Help Housing. Kosta Mathéy, ed. Pp. 217–31. Munich: Profil.

Heiman, Rachel
2000 Vehicles for Rugged Entitlement: Teenagers, Sport-Utility Vehicles, and the Suburban, Upper-Middle Class. New Jersey History 118(3–4):22–33.
2004 Driving after Class: Youth and the Cultural Politics of Suburban Life in the Boom Economy. Ph.D. dissertation, Department of Anthropology, University of Michigan.
2009 "At Risk" for Becoming Neoliberal Subjects: Rethinking the "Normal" Middle-Class Family. In Childhood, Youth, and Social Work in Transformation. Lynn Nybell, Jeffrey Shook, and Janet L. Finn, eds. Pp. 301–13. New York: Columbia University Press.

REFERENCES

Heryanto, Ariel

2003   Public Intellectuals, Media and Democratization: Cultural Politics of the Middle Classes in Indonesia. *In* Challenging Authoritarianism in Southeast Asia: Comparing Indonesia and Malaysia. Ariel Heryanto and Sumit Mandal, eds. Pp. 25–60. London: RoutledgeCurzon.

Hirsch, Jennifer S., and Holly Wardlow, eds.

2006   Modern Loves: The Anthropology of Romantic Courtship. Ann Arbor: University of Michigan Press.

Ho, Engseng

2006   The Graves of Tarim: Genealogy and Mobility across the Indian Ocean. Berkeley: University of California Press.

Hochschild, Arlie Russell

1983   The Managed Heart: The Commercialization of Human Feeling. Berkeley: University of California Press.

1997   The Time Bind: When Work Becomes Home and Home Becomes Work. New York: Metropolitan.

2003   The Commercialization of Intimate Life: Notes from Home and Work. Berkeley: University of California Press.

Hodge, Merle

2002   We Kind of Family. *In* Gendered Realities: Essays in Caribbean Feminist Thought. Patricia Mohammed, ed. Pp. 474–85. Mona, Jamaica: University of the West Indies Press.

Hoesterey, James

2008   Marketing Morality: The Rise, Fall and Rebranding of Aa Gym. *In* Expressing Islam: Religious Life and Politics in Indonesia. Greg Fealy and Sally White, eds. Pp. 95–112. Singapore: Institute of Southeast Asian Studies.

Hoffman, Jan

2008   I Know What You Did Last Math Class. New York Times, May 4. http://www.nytimes.com/2008/05/04/fashion/04edline.html?scp=1&sq=hoffman%20math%20class&st=cse (accessed April 2011).

Hondagneu-Sotelo, Pierette

2001   Doméstica: Immigrant Workers Cleaning and Caring in the Shadows of Affluence. Berkeley: University of California Press.

hooks, bell

1984   Feminist Theory. Boston: South End.

2000   Where We Stand: Class Matters. New York: Routledge.

Hopkins, Nicholas, and Reem Saad, eds.

2004   Upper Egypt: Identity and Change. Cairo: American University in Cairo Press.

Hopkins, Nicholas, and Kirsten Westergaard, eds.

1998   Directions of Change in Rural Egypt. Cairo: American University in Cairo Press.

Hurston, Zora Neale
1950   What White Publishers Won't Print. Negro Digest 8(April):85–9.

Inhorn, Marcia Claire
1994   Quest for Conception: Gender, Infertility, and Egyptian Medical Traditions. Philadelphia: University of Pennsylvania Press.

Jackson, Kenneth
1985   Crabgrass Frontier: The Suburbanization of the United States. New York: Oxford University Press.

Jain, Kajri
2007   Gods in the Bazaar: The Economies of Indian Calendar Art. Durham: Duke University Press.

James, C. L. R. [Cyril Lionel Robert]
1962   Party Politics in the West Indies. San Juan, Trinidad, West Indies: Vedic Enterprises.

Jameson, E. A.
1993[1920] Milliók a semmiből o [Millions out of nothing]. Budapest: Új Vénusz Lap-és Könyvkiadó.

Jiménez, Michael
1999   The Elision of the Middle Classes and Beyond: History, Politics, and Development Studies in Latin America's "Short Twentieth Century." *In* Colonial Legacies: The Problem of Persistence in Latin American History. Jeremy Adelman, ed. Pp. 207–28. New York: Routledge.

Johnson, John
1958   Political Change in Latin America: The Emergence of the Middle Sectors. Stanford: Stanford University Press.

Johnston, Robert D.
2003   The Radical Middle Class: Populist Democracy and the Question of Capitalism in Progressive Era Portland, Oregon. Princeton: Princeton University Press.

Jones, Carla
2010a   Better Women: The Cultural Politics of Gendered Expertise in Indonesia. American Anthropologist 112(2):270–82.
2010b   Materializing Piety: Gendered Anxieties about Faithful Consumption in Contemporary Urban Indonesia. American Ethnologist 37(4):617–37.

Joseph, Joel
2009   Hassle-Free Way for DLF Metro, Work to Finish before Deadline. Metronow, August 22.

Joshi, Sanjay
2001   Fractured Modernity: Making of a Middle Class in Colonial North India. Delhi: Oxford University Press.

REFERENCES

Kamat, Sangeeta
2002   Deconstructing the Rhetoric of Decentralization: The State in Education Reform. Current Issues in Comparative Education 2(2):110–19.

Kamath, Lalitha, and M. Vijayabaskar
2009   Limits and Possibilities of Middle Class Associations as Urban Collective Actors. Economic and Political Weekly 44(26–27):368–76.

Kant, Immanuel
1970   An Answer to the Question: "What Is Enlightenment?" In Kant: Political Writings. Hans Reiss, ed. Pp. 54–60. Cambridge: Cambridge University Press.

Karch, Cecilia A.
1985   Class Formation and Class and Race Relations in the West Indies, 1833–1876. In Middle Classes in Dependent Countries. Dale L. Johnson, ed. Pp. 107–36. Beverly Hills: Sage.

Katz, Cindi
2001   The State Goes Home: Local Hypervigilance and the Global Retreat from Social Reproduction. Social Justice 28(3):47–56.
2008   Childhood as Spectacle: Relays of Anxiety and the Reconfiguration of the Child. Cultural Geographies 15:5–17.

Keeler, Ward
1990   Speaking of Gender in Java. In Power and Difference: Gender in Island Southeast Asia. Jane Atkinson and Shelly Errington, eds. Pp. 127–52. Palo Alto: Stanford University Press.

Kelly, John, and Martha Kaplan
2001   Represented Communities: Fiji and World Decolonization. Chicago: University of Chicago Press.

Kenedi, János
1981   Do It Yourself: Hungary's Hidden Economy. London: Pluto.

Kincaid, Jamaica
1988   A Small Place. New York: Farrar, Straus and Giroux.

King, Anthony
2004   Spaces of Global Cultures: Architecture, Urbanism, Identity. London: Routledge.

Kirp, David L., John P. Dwyer, and Larry A. Rosenthal
1995   Our Town: Race, Housing, and the Soul of Suburbia. New Brunswick: Rutgers University Press.

Konrád, György
1984   Antipolitics. Richard E. Allen, trans. San Diego: Harcourt Brace Jovanovich.

Kopátsy, Sándor
1993   Az én házam az én váram [My house is my castle]. Családi Ház: Építkezôk, építtetôk, építészek, vállalkozók és reménykedôk lapja [Family House: The magazine for builders, engineers, architects, entrepreneurs and dreamers] 1:52.

Kósa, László

2000   The Age of Bourgeois Society, 1920–1948: Everyday Culture. *In* A Cultural History of Hungary in the Nineteenth and Twentieth Centuries. László Kósa, ed. Pp. 177–210. Budapest: Corvina / Osiris.

Koselleck, Reinhart

1989[1979] Vergangene Zukunft: Zur Semantik Geschichtlicher Zeiten. Frankfurt am Main: Suhrkamp.

Kuntowijoyo

1985   Muslim Kelas Menengah Indonesia Dalam Mencari Identitas [Indonesia's Muslim Middle Class Searches for Identity]. Prisma 11:35–51.

Kuppinger, Petra

2004   Exclusive Greenery: New Gated Communities in Cairo. City and Society 16(2):35–61.

Kurotani, Sawa

2005   Home Away from Home: Japanese Corporate Wives in the United States. Durham: Duke University Press.

Lacy, Karyn

2007   Blue-Chip Black: Race, Class and Status in the New Black Middle Class. Berkeley: University of California Press.

Lampland, Martha

1995   The Object of Labor: Commodification in Socialist Hungary. Chicago: University of Chicago Press.

Lan, Pei-Chia

2006   Global Cinderellas: Migrant Domestics and Newly Rich Employers in Taiwan. Durham: Duke University Press.

Landman, Karina, and Martin Schönteich

2002   Urban Fortresses: Gated Communities as a Reaction to Crime. African Security Review 11(4):71–85.

Landry, Bart

1988   The New Black Middle Class. Berkeley: University of California Press.

Lareau, Annette

2003   Unequal Childhoods: Class, Race, and Family Life. Berkeley: University of California Press.

Lash, Scott, and John Urry

1994   Economies of Signs and Space. London: Sage.

Latour, Bruno

2005   Reassembling the Social: An Introduction to Actor-Network-Theory. Oxford: Oxford University Press.

Lazzarato, Maurizio

1996   Immaterial Labor. *In* Radical Thought in Italy: A Potential Politics. Michael Hardt and Paulo Virno, eds. Pp. 133–47. Minneapolis: University of Minnesota Press.

REFERENCES

Lee, Benjamin

1997   Talking Heads: Language, Metalanguage, and the Semiotics of Subjectivity. Durham: Duke University Press.

Lee, Benjamin, and Greg LiPuma

2002   Cultures of Circulation: The Imaginations of Modernity. Public Culture 14(1):191–213.

Lee, Ching Kwan

2000   Pathways of Labor Insurgency. *In* Chinese Society: Change, Conflict and Resistance. Elizabeth Perry and Mark Selden, eds. Pp. 41–61. London: Routledge.

2002   From the Specter of Mao to the Spirit of the Law: Labor Insurgency in China. Theory and Society 31(April):189–228.

Lefebvre, Henri

1991[1974] The Production of Space. Donald Nicholson-Smith, trans. Oxford: Blackwell.

Lewis, Linden

2003   Caribbean Masculinity: Unpacking the Narrative. *In* The Culture of Gender and Sexuality in the Caribbean. Linden Lewis, ed. Pp. 94–128. Gainesville: University Press of Florida.

Liddle, William, and Saiful Mujani

2007   Leadership, Party and Religion: Explaining Voting Behavior in Indonesia. Comparative Political Studies 40(7):832–57.

Liechty, Mark

1997   Selective Exclusion: Foreigners, Foreign Goods, and Foreignness in Modern Nepali History. Studies in Nepali History and Society 2(1):5–68.

2003   Suitably Modern: Making Middle-Class Culture in a New Consumer Society. Princeton: Princeton University Press.

2005   Carnal Economies: The Commodification of Food and Sex in Kathmandu. Cultural Anthropology 20(1):1–38.

Lindquist, Johan

2008   Anxieties of Mobility: Migration and Tourism in the Indonesian Borderlands. Honolulu: University of Hawaii Press.

Lipietz, Alain

1993   From Althusserianism to "Regulation Theory." *In* The Althusserian Legacy. E. Ann Kaplan and Michael Sprinker, eds. Pp. 99–138. New York: Verso.

Lipsitz, George

2006   Learning from New Orleans: The Social Warrant of Hostile Privatism and Competitive Consumer Citizenship. Cultural Anthropology 21(3):451–68.

LiPuma, Edward, and Sarah Keene Meltzoff

1997   The Crosscurrents of Ethnicity and Class in the Construction of Public Policy. American Ethnologist 24(1):114–31.

Loaeza, Soledad

1988   Clases medias y política en México: La querella escolar, 1959–1963. Mexico: El Colegio de México.

Locke, John

1980[1690] Second Treatise of Government. C. B. Macpherson, ed. Indianapolis: Hackett.

Lomnitz, Claudio

2003   Times of Crisis: Historicity, Sacrifice, and the Spectacle of Debacle in Mexico City. Public Culture 15(1):127–47.

Low, Setha M.

1996   Spatializing Culture: The Social Production and Social Construction of Public Space in Costa Rica. American Ethnologist 23(4):861–79.

1997   Urban Fear: Building the Fortress City. City and Society 9(1):53–71.

2001a   The Edge and the Center: Gated Communities and the Discourse of Urban Fear. American Anthropologist 103(1):45–58.

2001b   The Secret, the Unspeakable, the Unsaid: Spatial, Discourse, and Political Economic Analysis. City and Society 13(1):161–65.

2003   Behind the Gates: Life, Security, and the Pursuit of Happiness in Fortress America. New York: Routledge.

Lu, Xiaobo, and Elizabeth J. Perry, eds.

1997   Danwei: The Changing Chinese Workplace in Historical and Comparative Perspective. Armonk, NY: Sharpe.

Lubis, Meita

2008   Shop 'till You Drop. Noor 3(March 7):92–93.

Ludden, David, ed.

2004   Capitalism in Asia. Ann Arbor: Association for Asian Studies.

Lutrell, Wendy

2011   On Carework. Paper presented at Researching Children, Global Childhoods and Education Conference, City University of New York, Graduate Center, March 24–26.

Lutz, Catherine

1995   The Gender of Theory. *In* Women Writing Culture. Ruth Behar and Deborah Gordon, eds. Pp. 249–66. Berkeley: University of California Press.

MacVean, Mary

2011   Parents Take a Deep Breath. Los Angeles Times, March 12. http://articles.latimes.com/2011/mar/12/home/la-hm-parent-anxiety-20110312 (accessed April 2011).

Magyar Nemzet

1996   Erejük felett építkeznek a családok: Kalákában egy négyzetméter negyven-egyezer forint [Families building above their powers: In self-build one meter squared is 40,000 forints]. October 15.

REFERENCES

Mains, Daniel

2007   Neoliberal Times: Progress, Boredom, and Shame among Young Men in Urban Ethiopia. American Ethnologist 34(4):659–73.

Major, Maté, and Judit Osskó

1981   Új építészet, új társadalom 1945–1978: Válogatás az elmúlt évtizedek építészeti vitáiból, dokumentumaiból [New architecture, new society 1945–1978]. Budapest: Corvina Kiadó.

Mallet, Serge

1975   Essays on the New Working Class. St. Louis: Telos.

Manderson, Lenore, ed.

1983   Women's Work and Women's Roles: Economics and Everyday Life in Indonesia, Malaysia and Singapore. Canberra: Australian National University.

Mankekar, Purnima

1999   Screening Culture, Viewing Politics: An Ethnography of Television, Womanhood and Nation in Postcolonial India. Durham: Duke University Press.

Marcus, George E., ed.

1983   Elites: Ethnographic Issues. Albuquerque: University of New Mexico Press.

Marcus, George E., and Peter Dobkin Hall

1991   Lives in Trust: The Fortunes of Dynastic Families in Late Twentieth Century America. Boulder: Westview.

Marsden, Magnus

2007   Cosmopolitanism on Pakistan's Frontier. ISIM Review 19:6–7.

2008   Muslim Cosmopolitans? Transnational Life in Northern Pakistan. Journal of Asian Studies 67(1):213–47.

Martin, Emily

1987   The Woman in the Body: A Cultural Analysis of Reproduction. Boston: Beacon.

1994   Flexible Bodies: The Role of Immunity in American Culture from the Days of Polio to the Age of AIDS. Boston: Beacon.

Martin, Randy

2002   Financialization of Daily Life. Philadelphia: Temple University Press.

Marx, Karl

1961   Economic and Philosophic Manuscripts of 1844. Moscow: Foreign Languages Publishing House.

1963[1852] The Eighteenth Brumaire of Louis Bonaparte. New York: International Publishers.

1995   Capital: An Abridged Edition. David McClellan, ed. Oxford: Oxford University Press.

2000[1863] Theories of Surplus Value. Amherst: Prometheus.

Marx, Karl, and Friedrich Engels
1968[1848] The Communist Manifesto. New York: Modern Reader.

Massey, Doreen
1994   Space, Place and Gender. Cambridge: Polity.

Mawdsley, Emma
2004   India's Middle Classes and the Environment. Development and Change 35(1):79–103.

May, Elaine Tyler
1988   Homeward Bound: American Families in the Cold War Era. New York: Basic.
2008   Homeward Bound: American Families in the Cold War Era. 2nd edition. New York: Basic.

Mazzarella, William
2003   Shoveling Smoke: Advertising and Globalization in Contemporary India. Durham: Duke University Press.
2005   Middle Class. *In* Keywords in South Asian Studies. Rachel Dwyer, ed. http://www.soas.ac.uk/southasianstudies/keywords.

McCann, Eugene J.
1999   Race, Protest, and Public Space: Contextualizing Lefebvre in the U.S. City. Antipode 31(2):163–84.

McDowell, Linda
2007   Spaces of the Home: Absence, Presence, New Connections and New Anxieties. Home Cultures 4(2):129–46.

McKendrick, Neil, John Brewer, and J. H. Plumb
1982   The Birth of Consumer Society: The Commercialization of Eighteenth Century England. London: Europa.

McKenzie, Evan
1994   Privatopia: Homeowner Associations and the Rise of Residential Private Government. New Haven: Yale University Press.

Mehta, Uday
1990   Liberal Strategies of Exclusion. Politics and Society 18:427–54.

Meillassoux, Claude
1972   From Reproduction to Production. Economy and Society 1(1):93–105.

Mertz, Elizabeth
2007   The Language of Law School: Learning to "Think" like a Lawyer. Oxford: Oxford University Press.

Milenio
2009a   Cordero sacrificado: Clase media. April 8.
2009b   La clase media, la más dañada por la crisis económica: Sedesol. July 14.

Miller, Daniel
1984   Modernism and Suburbia as Material Ideology. *In* Ideology, Power and Prehistory. Daniel Miller and Christopher Tilley, eds. Pp. 37–49. Cambridge: Cambridge University Press.

REFERENCES

1987   Material Culture and Mass Consumption. Oxford: Basil Blackwell.

1995   Consumption and Commodities. Annual Review of Anthropology 24:141–61.

2005   Introduction. *In* Materiality. Daniel Miller, ed. Pp. 1–50. Durham: Duke University Press.

Miller, Errol

1991   Men at Risk. Kingston: Jamaica Publishing House.

Mills, Amy

2007   Gender and *Mahalle* (Neighborhood) Space in Istanbul. Gender, Place and Culture 14(3):335–54.

Mills, C. Wright

1951   White Collar: The American Middle Classes. New York: Oxford University Press.

Mills, Mary Beth

1999   Thai Women in the Global Labor Force: Consuming Desires, Contested Selves. New Brunswick: Rutgers University Press.

Mintz, Sidney

1985   Sweetness and Power: The Place of Sugar in Modern History. New York: Penguin.

Miranda, Juan Carlos

2009   Construir una clase media más grande, reto para la sociedad mexicana: Nestlé. La Jornada, November 20.

Miskolczi, Miklós

1980   Város lesz, csakazértis… [There will be a city, despite it all…]. Budapest: Szépirodalmi Könyvkiadó.

Mitchell, Timothy

2002   Rule of Experts: Egypt, Techno-politics, Modernity. Berkeley: University of California Press.

Mohanty, Chandra Talpade

1988   Under Western Eyes: Feminist Scholarship and Colonial Discourses. Feminist Review 30(October 1):61–88.

Molnár, Virág

2010   In Search of the Ideal Socialist Home in Post-Stalinist Hungary: Prefabricated Mass Housing or Do-It-Yourself Family Home? Journal of Design History 23(1):61–81.

Moore, Donald S.

1998   Subaltern Struggles and the Politics of Place: Remapping Resistance in Zimbabwe's Eastern Highlands. Cultural Anthropology 13(3):344–81.

Mosse, George

1985a   Nationalism and Sexuality: Middle-Class Morality and Sexual Norms in Modern Europe. Madison: University of Wisconsin Press.

1985b   Nationalism and Sexuality: Respectability and Abnormal Behavior in Modern Europe. New York: Fertig.

Mouffe, Chantal

1979   Hegemony and Ideology in Gramsci. *In* Gramsci and Marxist Theory. Chantal Mouffe, ed. Pp. 168–204. London: Routledge and Kegan Paul.

Nader, Laura

1972   Up the Anthropologist: Perspectives Gained from Studying Up. *In* Reinventing Anthropology. Dell Hymes, ed. Pp. 284–311. New York: Pantheon.

Nandy, Ashis

2001   An Ambiguous Journey to the City: The Village and Other Odd Ruins of the Self in the Indian Imagination. New Delhi: Oxford University Press.

Newberry, Jan

2006   Back Door Java: State Formation and the Domestic in Working Class Java. Peterborough, ON: Broadview.

Newman, Katherine S.

1988   Falling from Grace: The Experience of Downward Mobility in the American Middle Class. New York: Vintage.

1993   Declining Fortunes: The Withering of the American Dream. New York: Basic Books.

1999   Falling from Grace: Downward Mobility in the Age of Affluence. Berkeley: University of California Press.

Nexos

2010   ¿Clases medias o clase media? October 22. http://redaccion.nexos.com.mx /?p=2139 (accessed March 23, 2011).

Ochs, Elinor, and Carolyn Taylor

1995   The "Father Knows Best" Dynamic in Dinnertime Narratives. *In* Gender Articulated: Language and the Socially Constructed Self. Kira Hall and Mary Bucholtz, eds. Pp. 97–120. New York: Routledge.

O'Dougherty, Maureen

2002   Consumption Intensified: The Politics of Middle-Class Daily Life in Brazil. Durham: Duke University Press.

Oey-Gardiner, Mayling

2002   And the Winner Is…Indonesian Women in Public Life. *In* Women in Indonesia: Gender, Equity and Development. Kathryn Robinson and Sharon Bessell, eds. Pp. 100–112. Singapore: Institute of Southeast Asian Studies.

Ong, Aihwa

1987   Spirits of Resistance and Capitalist Discipline: Factory Women in Malaysia. Albany: State University of New York Press.

1990   Japanese Factories, Malay Workers: Class and Sexual Metaphors in West Malaysia. *In* Power and Difference: Gender in Island Southeast Asia. Jane M. Atkinson and Shelly Errington, eds. Pp. 385–422. Palo Alto: Stanford University Press.

1998   Flexible Citizenship: The Cultural Logics of Transnationality. Durham: Duke University Press.

REFERENCES

2006   Neoliberalism as Exception: Mutations in Citizenship and Sovereignty. Durham: Duke University Press.

Ortner, Sherry B.

1998   Identities: The Hidden Life of Class. Journal of Anthropological Research 54(1):1–17.

2003   New Jersey Dreaming: Capital, Culture, and the Class of '58. Durham: Duke University Press.

Padilla, Mark

2007   Caribbean Pleasure Industry: Tourism, Sexuality, and AIDS in the Dominican Republic. Chicago: University of Chicago Press.

Pan, Tianshu

2002   Neighborhood Shanghai: Community Building in Five Mile Bridge. Ph.D. dissertation, Department of Anthropology, Harvard University.

Papanek, Hanna, and Laurel Schwede

1988   Women Are Good with Money: Earning and Managing in an Indonesian City. Economic and Political Weekly 23(44):73–84.

Parker, D. S.

1998   The Idea of the Middle Class: White Collar Workers and Peruvian Society, 1900–1950. University Park: Pennsylvania State University Press.

Parreñas, Rhacel Salazar

2001   Servants of Globalization: Women, Migration, and Domestic Work. Stanford: Stanford University Press.

Parthasarathi, Prasannan

1998   Rethinking Wages and Competitiveness in the 18th Century: Britain and South Asia. Past and Present 158:79–109.

Patico, Jennifer

2008   Consumption and Social Change in a Post-Soviet Middle Class. Stanford: Stanford University Press.

Patillo-McCoy, Mary

1999   Black Picket Fences: Privilege and Peril among the Black Middle Class. Chicago: University of Chicago Press.

Patterson, Patrick H.

2001   The New Class: Consumer Culture under Socialism and the Unmaking of the Yugoslav Dream, 1945–1991. Ph.D. dissertation, University of Michigan.

Peacock, James

1968   Rites of Modernization: Symbolic and Social Aspects of Indonesian Proletarian Drama. Chicago: University of Chicago Press.

Peck, Jamie, and Adam Tickell

2002   Neoliberalizing Space. Antipode 34(3):380–404.

Peebles, Gustav

2011   The Euro and Its Rivals: Currency and the Construction of a Transnational City. Bloomington: Indiana University Press.

Peirce, Charles S.

1955   Philosophical Writings of Peirce. Justis Buchler, ed. New York: Dover.

Perin, Constance

1977   Everything in Its Place: Social Order and Land Use in America. Princeton: Princeton University Press.

Phadke, Shilpa

2007   Dangerous Liaisons: Women and Men, Risk and Reputation in Mumbai. Economic and Political Weekly 43(17):1510–18.

Piccato, Pablo

2010   The Tyranny of Opinion: Honor in the Construction of the Mexican Public Sphere. Durham: Duke University Press.

Pinches, Michael, ed.

1999   Cultural Relations, Class and the New Rich: Culture and Privilege in Capitalist Asia. London: Routledge.

Pittaway, Mark

2000   Stalinism, Working-Class Housing and Individual Autonomy: The Encouragement of Private House Building in Hungary's Mining Areas, 1950–54. *In* Style and Socialism: Modernity and Material Culture in Post-war Eastern Europe. Susan E. Reid and David Crowley, eds. Pp. 49–64. Oxford: Berg.

Pollan, Michael

1991   Why Mow? *In* Second Nature: A Gardener's Education. Pp. 54–65. New York: Dell.

Pollock, Sheldon, Homi K. Bhabha, Carol A. Breckenridge, and Dipesh Chakrabarty, eds.

2002   Cosmopolitanism. Durham: Duke University Press.

Pomeranz, Kenneth

2000   The Great Divergence: Europe, China, and the Making of the Modern World Economy. Princeton: Princeton University Press.

Porter, Roy

1993   Consumption: Disease of the Consumer Society. *In* Consumption and the World of Goods. John Brewer and Roy Porter, eds. Pp. 58–84. London: Routledge.

Poulantzas, Nicos

1978   Classes in Contemporary Capitalism. David Fernbach, ed. London: Verso.

2000   State, Power, Socialism. London: Verso.

Pow, Choon-Piew

2007   Securing the "Civilised" Enclaves: Gated Communities and the Moral Geographies of Exclusion in (Post-)Socialist Shanghai. Urban Studies 44(8):1539–58.

REFERENCES

Pratt, Geraldine, and Victoria Rosner, eds.
2006   The Global and the Intimate. WSQ (Women's Studies Quarterly) 34(1–2).

Pun, Ngai
2003   Subsumption or Consumption? Cultural Anthropology 18(4):469–92.
2005   Made in China: Women Factory Workers in a Global Workplace. Durham: Duke University Press.

Qâsim, 'Abd al-Hakîm
1996[1969] Ayyâm al-insân as-sab'a. Cairo: al-Hay'a al-misrîya al-'âmma li-l-kitâb.

Rajagopal, Arvind
1999   Thinking about the New Indian Middle Class: Gender, Advertising and Politics in an Age of Globalisation. *In* Signpost: Gender Issues in Post-Independence India. Rajeshwari Sundar Rajan, ed. Pp. 57–99. Delhi: Kali for Women.
2001   Politics after Television: Hindu Nationalism and the Reshaping of the Public in India. Cambridge: Cambridge University Press.

Rankin, Katharine
2004   The Cultural Politics of Markets: Economic Liberalization and Social Change in Nepal. Toronto: University of Toronto Press.

Rapp, Rayna
2000   Testing Women, Testing the Fetus: The Social Impact of Amniocentesis in America. New York: Routledge.

Rappaport, Erika
2001   Shopping for Pleasure: Women in the Making of London's West End. Princeton: Princeton University Press.

Rausing, Sigrid
1998   Signs of the New Nation: Gift Exchange, Consumption and Aid on a Former Collective Farm in North-West Estonia. *In* Material Cultures: Why Some Things Matter. Daniel Miller, ed. Pp. 189–213. Chicago: University of Chicago Press.

Read, Benjamin L.
2000   Revitalizing the State's Urban "Nerve Tips." China Quarterly 163:806–20.
2003   Democratizing the Neighborhood? New Private Housing and Home-Owner Self-Organization in Urban China. China Journal 49:1–29.

Redfield, Robert
1930   Tepoztlan: A Mexican Village: A Study of Folk Life. Chicago: University of Chicago Press.

Rieder, Jonathan
1985   Canarsie: The Jews and Italians of Brooklyn against Liberalism. Cambridge: Harvard University Press.

Rivkin-Fish, Michele
2009   Tracing Landscapes of the Past in Class Subjectivity: Practices of Memory and Distinction in Marketizing Russia. American Ethnologist 36(1):79–85.

Robison, Richard, and David S. G. Goodman, eds.

1996   The New Rich in Asia: Mobile Phones, McDonalds, and Middle-Class Revolution. London: Routledge.

Rofel, Lisa

1999   Other Modernities: Gendered Yearnings in China after Socialism. Berkeley: University of California Press.

2007   Desiring China: Experiments in Neoliberalism, Sexuality, and Public Culture. Durham: Duke University Press.

Rome, Adam

2001   The Bulldozer in the Countryside: Suburban Sprawl and the Rise of American Environmentalism. Cambridge: Cambridge University Press.

Róna-Tas, Ákos

1997   The Great Surprise of the Small Transformation: The Demise of Communism and the Rise of the Private Sector in Hungary. Ann Arbor: University of Michigan Press.

Ross, Andrew

1999   The Celebration Chronicles: Life, Liberty and the Pursuit of Property Values in Disney's New Town. New York: Ballantine Books.

2006   Fast Boat to China: High-Tech Outsourcing and the Consequences of Free Trade: Lessons from Shanghai. New York: Vintage Books.

Rouse, Roger

1995   Thinking through Transnationalism: Notes on the Cultural Politics of Class Relations in the Contemporary United States. Public Culture 7(2):353–402.

Roy, Srirupa

2007   Beyond Belief: India and the Politics of Postcolonial Nationalism. Durham: Duke University Press.

Ruble, Blair A.

1995   Money Sings: The Changing Politics of Urban Space in Post-Soviet Yaroslavl. Cambridge: Woodrow Wilson Center / Cambridge University Press.

Rudnyckjy, Daromir

2009   Spiritual Economies: Islam and Neoliberalism in Contemporary Indonesia. Cultural Anthropology 24(1):104–41.

Ruiz, Olivia Teresa

1984   Between Mexico and the United States: A Mexican Middle Class in the Middle. Ph.D. dissertation, Department of Anthropology, University of California.

Ryan, Mary P.

1981   Cradle of the Middle Class: The Family in Oneida County, New York, 1790–1865. Cambridge: Cambridge University Press.

Ryan, Selwyn, and Louanne Barclay

1992   Sharks and Sardines: Blacks in Business in Trinidad and Tobago. St. Augustine, Trinidad and Tobago: Institute of Social and Economic Studies, University of the West Indies.

REFERENCES

Ryzova, Lucie

2004   L'effendiya ou la modernité contestée. Cairo: CEDEJ.

2008   Efendification: The Rise of Middle Class Culture in Modern Egypt. Ph.D. thesis, University of Oxford.

S. Nagy, Katalin

1987   Lakberendezési Szokások [Home Furnishing Customs]. Budapest: Magvet Kiadó.

Sacks, Karen Brodkin

1989   Toward a Unified Theory of Class, Race, and Gender. American Ethnologist 16(3):534–50.

Sammond, Nicholas

2005   Babes in Tomorrowland: Walt Disney and the Making of the American Child, 1930–1960. Durham: Duke University Press.

Sassen, Saskia

2001   The Global City. Princeton: Princeton University Press.

Schama, Simon

1987   The Embarrassment of Riches: An Interpretation of Dutch Culture in the Golden Age. New York: Knopf.

Scheper-Hughes, Nancy

1995   The Primacy of the Ethical: Propositions for a Militant Anthropology. Current Anthropology 36(3):409–20.

Schielke, Samuli

2006   Snacks and Saints: Mawlid Festivals and the Politics of Festivity, Piety and Modernity in Contemporary Egypt. Ph.D. thesis, University of Amsterdam.

2008a   Mystic States, Motherly Virtues: Female Participation and Leadership in an Egyptian Sufi Milieu. Journal for Islamic Studies (Capetown) 28:94–126.

2008b   Boredom and Despair in Rural Egypt. Contemporary Islam 2(3):251–70.

2009   Ambivalent Commitments: Troubles of Morality, Religiosity and Aspiration among Young Egyptians. Journal of Religion in Africa 39(2):158–85.

Schulte Nordholt, Henk

2004   De-colonising Indonesian Historiography. Lund, Sweden: Center for East and South-East Asian Studies, Lund University.

Scott, Joan Wallach

1999   Gender and the Politics of History. Rev. edition. New York: Columbia University Press.

Sen, Krishna, and Maila Stivens

1998   Introduction. In Gender and Power in Affluent Asia. Krishna Sen and Maila Stivens, eds. New York: Routledge.

Sennett, Richard

2002   Reflections on the Public Realm. In A Companion to the City. Sophie Watson and Gary Bridge, eds. Pp. 380–87. Oxford: Blackwell.

Shah, Ghanshyam

2004   Social Movements in India: A Review of Literature. New Delhi: Sage.

Sharma, Aradhana, and Akhil Gupta

2006   Introduction: Rethinking Theories of the State in the Age of Globalization. *In* The Anthropology of the State: A Reader. Aradhana Sharma and Akhil Gupta, eds. Pp. 1–41. Oxford: Blackwell.

Sherman, Rachel

2007   Class Acts: Service and Inequality in Luxury Hotels. Berkeley: University of California Press.

Shiraishi, Saya

1997   Young Heroes: The Indonesian Family in Politics. Ithaca: Cornell Southeast Asia Program.

Siegel, James

1998   Early Thoughts on the Violence of May 13 and 14, 1998, in Jakarta. Indonesia 66:75–109.

2002   The Idea of Indonesia Continues: The Middle Class Ignores Acehnese. Archipel 64(1):199–229.

Sik, Endre

1988   Reciprocal Exchange of Labour in Hungary. *In* On Work: Historical, Comparative and Theoretical Approaches. R. E. Pahl, ed. Pp. 527–47. Oxford: Blackwell.

Silverstein, Michael

2004   "Cultural" Concepts and the Language-Culture Nexus. Current Anthropology 45(5):621–52.

Silverstein, Michael, and Greg Urban

1996   The Natural History of Discourse. *In* Natural Histories of Discourse. Michael Silverstein and Greg Urban, eds. Chicago: University of Chicago Press.

Silvey, Rachel

2004   Transnational Domestication: Indonesian Domestic Workers in Saudi Arabia. Political Geography 23(4):245–64.

Singerman, Diane, ed.

2009   Cairo Contested: Governance, Urban Space, and Global Modernity. Cairo: American University in Cairo Press.

Singerman, Diane, and Paul Amar, eds.

2006   Cairo Cosmopolitan: Politics, Culture, and Urban Space in the New Globalized Middle East. Cairo: American University in Cairo Press.

Skeggs, Beverly

1997   Formations of Class and Gender. London: Sage.

Smith, Andrea L.

2004   Heteroglossia, "Common Sense," and Social Memory. American Ethnologist 31(2):251–69.

REFERENCES

Smith, Neil

1996   The New Urban Frontier: Gentrification and the Revanchist City. London: Routledge.

Smith-Hefner, Nancy

2007   Javanese Women and the Veil in Post-Suharto Indonesia. Journal of Asian Studies 66(2):389–420.

Soja, Edward W.

1989   Postmodern Geographies: The Reassertion of Space in Critical Social Theory. London: Verso.

Solinger, Dorothy

1999   Contesting Citizenship in Urban China: Peasant Migrants, the State, and the Logic of the Market. Berkeley: University of California Press.

Sonbol, Amira el-Azhary

2000   The New Mamluks: Egyptian Society and the Modern Feudalism. Syracuse: Syracuse University Press.

Srivastava, Sanjay

1998   Constructing Post-colonial India. National Character and the Doon School. London: Routledge.

2007   Passionate Modernity. Sexuality, Gender, Consumption, and Class in India. New Delhi: Routledge.

2009   Urban Spaces, Disney-Divinity and Moral Middle Classes in Delhi. Economic and Political Weekly 44(26):338–45.

N.d.   Urban Spaces, Post-nationalism and the Making of the Consumer-Citizen in India. *In* New Cultural Histories of India. Partha Chatterjee, Tapati Guha Thakurta, and Bodhsattava Kar, eds. New Delhi: Permanent Black.

Stephens, Sharon, ed.

1995   Children and the Politics of Culture. Princeton: Princeton University Press.

Stewart, Susan

1993   On Longing: Narratives of the Miniature, the Gigantic, the Souvenir, the Collection. Durham: Duke University Press.

Stoler, Ann Laura

1985   Capitalism and Confrontation in Sumatra's Plantation Belt, 1870–1979. New Haven: Yale University Press.

2002   Carnal Knowledge and Imperial Power: Race and the Intimate in Colonial Rule. Berkeley: University of California Press.

Strassler, Karen

2010   Refracted Visions: Popular Photography and National Modernity in Java. Durham: Duke University Press.

Strom, Stephanie

2002   Private Preschool Admissions: Grease and the City. New York Times, November 16.

Subrahmanyam, Sanjay, ed.

1996   Merchant Networks in the Early Modern World. Aldershot, England: Variorum.

Sullivan, Norma

1983   Indonesian Women in Development: State Theory and Urban Kampung Practice. *In* Women's Work and Women's Roles: Economics and Everyday Life in Indonesia, Malaysia and Singapore. L. Manderson, ed. Canberra: Australian National University Press.

Swarowsky, Daniela, and Samuli Schielke, dirs.

2009   Messages from Paradise #1: Egypt : Austria/About the Permanent Longing for Elsewhere. Documentary film. Austria, Egypt, and the Netherlands.

Szelényi, Ivan, with Robert Mancin, Pál Juhász, Bálint Magyar, and Bill Martin

1988   Socialist Entrepreneurs: Embourgeoisement in Rural Hungary. Madison: University of Wisconsin Press.

Taussig, Michael

1980   The Devil and Commodity Fetishism in South America. Chapel Hill: University of North Carolina Press.

Tawney, Richard H.

1957[1926] Religion and the Rise of Capitalism. New York: New American Library.

Taylor, Lawrence

2002   The Wild Frontier Moves South: U.S. Entrepreneurs and the Growth of Tijuana's Vice Industry, 1908–1935. Journal of San Diego History 48(3):204–29.

Thomas, Deborah

2004   Modern Blackness: Nationalism, Globalization, and the Politics of Culture in Jamaica. Durham: Duke University Press.

Thompson, E. P.

1963   The Making of the English Working Class. London: Gollancz.

1978   Eighteenth-Century English Society: Class Struggle without Class? Social History 3(2):133–65.

1993   Customs in Common. New York: Free Press.

Tilley, Christopher

2007   Materiality in Materials. Archaeological Dialogues 14(1):16–20.

Toll, Seymour I.

1969   Zoned American. New York: Grossman Publishers.

Tomba, Luigi

2004   Creating an Urban Middle Class: Social Engineering in Beijing. China Journal 51:1–26.

2005   Residential Space and Collective Interest Formation in Beijing's Housing Disputes. China Quarterly 184:934–51.

REFERENCES

Tsing, Anna Lowenhaupt
2005   Friction: An Ethnography of Global Connection. Princeton: Princeton University Press.

Tuladhar, Kamal
2004   Caravan to Lhasa: Newar Merchants of Kathmandu in Traditional Tibet. Kathmandu: Tuladhar Family.

Turner, Frederick Jackson
1993[1893]The Significance of the Frontier in American History. *In* History, Frontier, and Section: Three Essays by Frederick Jackson Turner. Pp. 59–91. Albuquerque: University of New Mexico Press.

Uberoi, Patricia
2008   Aspirational Weddings: The Bridal Magazine and the Canons of "Decent Marriage." New Delhi: Sage.

Urban, Greg
2001   Metaculture: How Culture Moves through the World. Minneapolis: University of Minnesota Press.

Urrea, Luis Alberto
1993   Across the Wire: Life and Hard Times on the Mexican Border. New York: Anchor.

Urry, John
1973   Towards a Structural Theory of the Middle Class. Acta Sociologica 16:175–87.

Valuch, Tibor
2004   Changes in the Structure and Lifestyle of the Hungarian Society in the Second Half of the XXth Century. *In* Social History of Hungary from the Reform Era to the End of the Twentieth Century. G. Gyányi, G. Kövér, and T. Valuch, eds. Pp. 511–672. Highland Lakes: Atlantic Research and Publications.

van der Kroef, Justus
1956   The Changing Class Structure of Indonesia. American Sociological Review 21(2):138–48.

Van Leeuwen, Lizzy
2008   Lost in Mall: An Ethnography of Middle-Class Jakarta in the 1990s. Leiden, Netherlands: KITLV Press.

Verdery, Katherine
2003   The Vanishing Hectare: Property and Value in Postsocialist Transylvania. Ithaca: Cornell University Press.

Viswanath, Gita
2007   The Multiplex: Crowd, Audience and the Genre Film. Economic and Political Weekly 42(32):3289–94.

Voyce, Malcolm

2007 Shopping Malls in India: New "Social Dividing" Practices. Economic and Political Weekly 42(22):2055–62.

Wacquant, Löic J. D.

1991 Making Class: The Middle Class(es) in Social Theory and Social Structure. *In* Bringing Class Back In: Contemporary and Historical Perspectives. Scott G. McNall, Rhonda F. Levine, and Rick Fantasia, eds. Pp. 39–64. Boulder: Westview.

Walcott, Victoria

2001 Remaking Respectability: African American Women in Interwar Detroit. Chapel Hill: University of North Carolina Press.

Waldrop, Anne

2004 Gating and Class Relations: The Case of a New Delhi "Colony." City and Society 16(2):93–116.

Walker, Pat, ed.

1979 Between Labor and Capital. Boston: South End.

Walkerdine, Valerie, and Helen Lucey

1989 Democracy in the Kitchen: Regulating Mothers and Socializing Daughters. London: Virago.

Wang, Ya Ping, and Alan Murie

1999a Commercial Housing Development in Urban China. Urban Studies 36(9):1475–94.

1999b Housing Policy and Practice in China. New York: St. Martin's.

Wardle, Huon

2000 An Ethnography of Cosmopolitanism in Kingston, Jamaica. Lewiston: Edwin Mellen Press.

Warner, Judith

2005 Perfect Madness: Motherhood in the Age of Anxiety. New York: Riverhead.

Warner, Michael

2002 Publics and Counterpublics. New York: Zone.

Watts, Michael J.

1992 Space for Everything (A Commentary). Cultural Anthropology 7(1):115–29.

Weber, Max

1947 The Theory of Social and Economic Organization. A. M. Henderson and Talcott Parsons, trans. New York: Free Press.

1958 The Protestant Ethic and the Spirit of Capitalism. New York: Scribner's.

1968 Economy and Society: An Outline of Interpretive Sociology. Guenther Roth and Claus Wittich, eds. New York: Bedminster.

1981 From Max Weber: Essays in Sociology. H. H. Gerth and C. Wright Mills, eds. and trans. New York: Oxford University Press.

REFERENCES

Weeks, Kathi

2007   Life within and against Work: Affective Labor, Feminist Critique and Post-Fordist Politics. Ephemera: Theory and Politics in Organization (7)1:233–49.

Wekker, Gloria

2006   "What's Identity Got to Do with It?": Rethinking Identity in Light of the Mati Work in Suriname. *In* Feminist Anthropology. Ellen Lewin, ed. Pp. 435–48. Malden: Blackwell.

Weyland, Petra

1993   Inside the Third World Village. London: Routledge.

Whyte, Martin King, and William L. Parish

1984   Urban Life in Contemporary China. Chicago: University of Chicago Press.

Williams, Brett

1988   Upscaling Downtown: Stalled Gentrification in Washington, D.C. Ithaca: Cornell University Press.

Williams, Raymond

1973   The Country and the City. New York: Oxford University Press.

1977   Marxism and Literature. New York: Oxford University Press.

Willis, Paul

1977   Learning to Labor: How Working Class Kids Get Working Class Jobs. New York: Columbia University Press.

Wilson, Elizabeth

1992   The Invisible Flâneur. New Left Review 191:90–110.

Wilson, Peter

1973   Crab Antics: The Social Anthropology of English-Speaking Negro Societies of the Caribbean. New Haven: Yale University Press.

Winegar, Jessica

2006   Creative Reckonings: The Politics of Art and Culture in Contemporary Egypt. Stanford: Stanford University Press.

Wirth, Louis

1938   Urbanism as a Way of Life. American Journal of Sociology 44:1–24.

Wolf, Diane

1992   Factory Daughters: Gender, Household Dynamics and Rural Industrialization in Java. Berkeley: University of California Press.

Wolf, Eric

1982   Europe and the People without History. Berkeley: University of California Press.

Wong, Edward

2010   China's Export Economy Begins Turning Inward. New York Times, June 25.

World Bank

2003   Combating Corruption in Indonesia: Enhancing Accountability for

Development. Washington, DC: East Asia Poverty Reduction and Economic Management Unit.

Wright, Erik Olin

1989   A General Framework for the Analysis of Class Structure. *In* The Debate on Classes. Erik Olin Wright, ed. Pp. 3–43. New York: Verso.

Yudhoyono, Susilo Bambang

2010   Keynote Address. Sixth Assembly of the World Movement for Democracy, Jakarta, Indonesia, April 12. http://www.wmd.org/assemblies/sixth-assembly/remarks/keynote-speech-dr-susilo-bambang-yudhoyono (accessed April 16, 2010).

Zaloom, Caitlin

2006   Out of the Pits: Traders and Technology from Chicago to London. Chicago: University of Chicago Press.

Zâyid, Ahmad

2005   Tanâqudât al-hadâtha fî Misr. Cairo: al-‘Ayn li-1-dirâsât wa-1-buhûth al-insânîya wa-1-ijtimâ‘îya.

Zelizer, Viviana A.

1994   Pricing the Priceless Child: The Changing Social Value of Children. Princeton: Princeton University Press.

2005   The Purchase of Intimacy. Princeton: Princeton University Press.

Zhang, Li

2001   Strangers in the City: Reconfigurations of Space, Power, and Social Networks within China's Floating Population. Stanford: Stanford University Press.

2002   Spatiality and Urban Citizenship in Late Socialist China. Public Culture 14(2):311–34.

2006   Contesting Spatial Modernity in Late Socialist China. Current Anthropology 47(3):461–84.

2008   Private Homes, Distinct Lifestyles: Performing a New Middle Class. *In* Privatizing China: Socialism from Afar. Li Zhang and Aihwa Ong, eds. Pp. 23–40. Ithaca: Cornell University Press.

2010   In Search of Paradise: Middle-Class Living in a Chinese Metropolis. Ithaca: Cornell University Press.

Zhang, Xing Quan

1998   Privatization: A Study of Housing Policy in Urban China. New York: Nova Science Publishers.

Index

Page numbers in *italics* refer to illustrations.

Abaza, Mona, 44

Abeles, Vicki, 182, 183

Abu-Lughod, Janet, 281

accumulation, and parenting in U.S., 181–86

advertising, of private housing in China, 218–21

aesthetics: of class display in U.S. suburbs, 246; and controversy on gate in American suburb, 255–58, 264

Alegría, Tito, 190

Alexandria (Egypt), 35, 55n2

Althusser, Louis, 20, 278

Anderson, Benedict, 238

anthropology: and centrality of consumption in formation and transformation of working-class identity and lifestyle, 236n18; contributions of to class analysis, 27; and scholarship on Indonesia, 147, 166n3; and scholarship on middle class in India, 57–59; and studies of middle class in Caribbean, 88–91; and studies on spatialization of political-economic shifts, 268n6; and theories on contemporary forms of globalization, 4; and tradition of research among middle-class subjects, 28n1; and transition in attitudes toward ethnographic analyses of middle classes, 5–8

Antigua, and social systems of islands, 110

anxieties: and childhood in U.S., 172–76; corruption and consumption in Indonesia, 152, 155, 157–58, 164, 166–67n7; and middle classness in Caribbean anthropology, 88–91; and middle class in postcolonial feminism, 91–93. *See also* insecurity

Appadurai, Arjun, 69

architecture, and organicist school, 144n10. *See also* housing; landscape

Armbrust, Walter, 31

aspiration: and middle classness as emic concept, 19; and middle class in provincial Egypt, 31–55, 296n2; use of term, 84n3

Austin, Diane, 113n3

Babcock, Richard F., 245

Bakhtin, M. M., 247, 254, 268n12

Baksh-Soodeen, Rawwida, 114n7

Barbados, entrepreneurial model of marriage and new middle class in, 85–113, 173

Barrow, Christine, 95, 96, 114n6

Benveniste, Emile, 211n4

Between Labor and Capital (Walker 1979), 9–10

Blaut, James M., 297n7

Bodnár, Judit, 130

border crossing, and class distinction in northern Mexico, 190

Bourdieu, Pierre, 26, 45, 84n3, 215, 235n7, 278, 280, 294

Braudel, Fernand, 15, 277, 282–83, 288, 297n9

Brazil: and gated communities, 60, 79; middle class and economic crisis in, 196

Bren, Paulina, 144n7

Brenner, Suzanne, 150–51

Bride and Home Magazine (India), 63

Buchowski, Michal, 126

Bullard, Robert D., 291

Cairo (Egypt), 35

Caldeira, Teresa P. R., 60, 79, 153, 233, 245

Canada, and middle-class status in compared to Mexico, 200

capitalism: distinction between rise and spread of, 280–84; history of, 12–13, 277; identification of with state, 15–16; and insecurity of middle classes, 20; and link between consumption and middle classes, 24–25; and new family house in Hungary, 142; relationship of with class and consumerism in world historical time, 277–80

Caribbean: and cultural framework of reputation/respectability, 90–91, 93, 111; middle classness in anthropology of, 88–91; Marxism as dominant paradigm in social science research on, 6, 89. *See also* Barbados

Caribbean Community Single Market and Economy, 87

castes, and middle class in Nepal, 285, 286, 287, 289, 290, 298n14

Chakrabarty, Dipesh, 281

Chandrasekhar, C. P., 71

Chicago School, of sociology, 290–91

childhood: and children as accumulation strategies in U.S., 181–86; and investment in U.S., 176–78; security issues and anxiety about in U.S., 172–76; shifts in cultural forms and practices of in U.S., 170–72. *See also* parenting

China: and commodification of social relations, 154; new articulations of intimacy and marriage in, 114n10; private housing and middle-class lifestyle in, 213–34

Christian, Barbara, 89

circulation, and approach to publics, 191

civil society, and zoning ordinances, 245–46

class: balance between heuristic idea and lived experience of, 12; basic understanding of as sociocultural phenomenon, 8–9; and Caribbean framework of reputation/respectability, 93; complexity of distinctions in Egypt, 34; contributions of anthropology to analysis of, 27; and coordination of class containment by states, 15–20; dominance of income-bracket logics of in U.S., 237; and entrepreneurship in Barbados, 112; key ideas for understanding of in context of Nepal, 273–77; moral and market logics of in Nepal, 289; as ongoing process of "happening," 214; and postcolonial feminism in Barbados, 91–93; as process defined by consumer practices, 85; and publics in Mexico, 191–93; race and history of in Barbados, 89; and racial politics in U.S., 245; and relationship between aspiration and distinction in Egypt, 45–49; relationship of with consumerism and capitalism in world historical time, 277–80; spatialization of and global interjacency in Nepal, 290–95; specific and historical ethnic conceptions of status in Java and, 150; and status groups, 235n5; transformation in U.S. and shifts in moral logics of private property, 264. *See also* middle class

clothing, and women's Islamic dress in Indonesia, *160*, 161–63

Colomina, Beatriz, 174–75

colonialism, respectability and coercive

power of, 86, 90–91, 113n2

community: commodity cultures and making of in India, 71–75; and formation of class in China, 214–15; and role of women in India, 78; and spatial differentiation by private wealth in China, 230. *See also* neighborhoods

competition, and parenting practices in U.S., 179–80

"concerted cultivation," and parenting in U.S., 177–78, 179, 182, 185

conditions of possibility, and middle-class formation in context of Nepal, 274–76

consumerism: and middle-class identity in India, 64; and middle-class practice and subjectivity, 24; relationship of with class and capitalism in world historical time, 277–80

consumption: anthropological studies on centrality of to formation and transformation of working-class identity and lifestyle, 236n18; and formation of middle-class subjects in China, 214, 236n19; and middle-class housing in China, 230–34; and relationship between femininity and morality in Indonesian discourse on middle class, 147–48, 151–65; and understanding of middle classes, 23–26

Corrigan, Philip, 167n13

corruption, and anxieties about consumption in Indonesia, 152, 155, 157–58, 166–67n7

cosmopolitanism: and aspiration for social advancement in Egypt, 42; and middle-class identity in India, 79–82

Daniel, E. Valentine, 266

danwei (public housing units in China), 216–18, 235n8

Davis, Mike, 79–80, 233

De, Shobha, 64–65, 66

Dean, Jodi, 197, 204

debt, middle-class lifestyle and reliance on in Egypt, 51–52

De la Calle, Luis, 194–95, 197, 210

Delhi, and gated communities, 59

Derrida, Jacques, 269n22

Dharma Wanita (Women's Duty), 156–57, 158

Dick, Howard, 151, 166n6

dining table, symbolism of in provincial Egypt, *41*, 42, 44

diurnal rhythms, and gated communities in India, 69–71

Dixit, Kanak, 291

Dobriner, William Mann, 248

Domesticity at War (Colomina 2007), 174–75

domestic sphere and domesticity: and emergence of new national identity in India, 62–63; gendered state organizations and new category of modern femininity in Indonesia, 156–57

Douglass, Lisa, 113n3

Dresser, Denise, 193–94, 195, 199, 200, 209, 212n14

Dwyer, John P., 245

Dwyer, Rachel, 65, 66

Economics: and anxiety about future in U.S., 174; and increasing income of upper middle class in U.S., 240; middle class and crisis in Mexico, 196; parenting and investment in children in U.S., 176–78. *See also* capitalism; exchange; free trade; labor; market; poverty

education: and middle-class aspirations in Egypt, 37–38; and parenting in contemporary U.S., 179–181, 182

Egypt: marriage and motherhood in, 115n15; middle class and aspirations in provincial, 19, 31–55, 296n2, 298n23

Ehrenreichs, Barbara, 11, 235n4, 290

Engels, Friedrich, 10

entrepreneurship: neoliberalism and partnership marriage in Barbados, 85–113; and private housing in China, 223

environment: and anxiety about future in U.S., 174; wetlands regulations and development in U.S., 269n19

epochs, and history of capitalism, 277

exchange, and social relations, 283–84. *See also* free trade; market

exclusion: and assertion of middle-class status in Egypt, 48–49; and private housing in China, 229; and zoning ordinances in U.S. suburbs, 244–47, 255–58. *See also* segregation

Family: gender relations of production and reproduction and reworking of forms,

171–72; intersection of nation and gender with in Indonesian conceptions of distinction, 157–63. *See also* childhood; kinship; marriage; parenting

fashion industry, and Islamic dress in Indonesia, *160*, 161–63

Fehérváry, Krisztina, 56n4, 28n3, 84n2

Feminine Mystique, The (Friedan 1963), 175

femininity, and relationship between consumption and morality in Indonesian public discourse on social difference, 147–148, 163–65. *See also* gender

feminism and feminist theory: gender and social difference in Indonesia, 146–47; impact on marriage and parenting in U.S., 172; and invisible forms of labor, 22, 146; and middle class in postcolonial Barbados, 91–93; and writings on public spaces in India, 74–75

Ferge, Zsuzsa, 130

Ferguson, James, 17

Fernandes, Leela, 36, 291

Fernández-Vega, María Patricia, 196

fi n-nuss (halfway or in-between in Arabic), 46

flexibility, and women's attraction to entrepreneurship in Barbados, 103

Fogelson, Robert M., 267n1

Folbre, Nancy, 242

football fan culture, in Egypt, 32–33, 54–55

Fordism, Gramsci's writings on, 20–21

Foucault, Michel, 148, 159, 274

Freeman, Carla, 173

free trade, and neoliberalism, 16–17, 292, 293

Friedan, Betty, 175

Friedman, Sara L., 114n10

friendship, and female alliances of kinship and marriage in Caribbean, 102

frontier society, and local ideology of Tijuana, Mexico, 209

Gal, Susan, 115n17

gardens (*yuan* or *huayuan*), and private housing in China, 221–23

gate, controversy over design of in American suburb, 237–66

gated communities: growth of in U.S., 239; increase of in Nepal, 298n16; and narratives of space in India, 58–82;

popularity of in Indonesia, 167n10; and private housing in China, 218, 224

Geertz, Clifford, 150, 165n2, 179

Geertz, Hildred, 149

gender: and Caribbean framework of reputation/respectability, 93; and consumption in Indonesia, 156, 157–63; and rational debate in Mexico, 212n16; and social difference in Indonesia, 146–47; and West Indian tradition of separate spheres of sociality and leisure, 106–107. *See also* femininity; masculinity; patriarchy; women

Ghosh, Jayati, 71

Gilfoyle, Timothy, 296n1

globalization: anthropological theories on contemporary forms of, 4; and concept of interjacency in context of Nepal, 276, 290–95. *See also* free trade; neoliberalism; "new middle class"

Goffman, Erving, 263

Goodman, David, 223, 235n9

Goswami, Shrivatsa, 72

Gramsci, Antonio, 11, 20–21, 247, 266, 268n12, 295

Greece, and illegal migration from Egypt, 43

Grigsby, J. Eugene, 291

Habermas, Jürgen, 26, 130, 192, 197, 204, 210, 211–12n6, 296n5

habitus, Bourdieu's theory of, 215, 232, 235n7

Hardt, Michael, 21

Hartmann, Heidi I., 92

Harvey, David, 14

Hawley, J. S., 71–72

Hays, Sharon, 179

Heiman, Rachel, 15, 84n5, 167n10, 187n2, 292

Heryanto, Ariel, 149

Hinduism, and festivals in India, 71–73

Hirsch, Jennifer S., 96

historical category, class as, 274–75

historic commissions, in American suburbs, 248

history: of capitalism, 12–13, 277; and conceptions of status in Java, 150; of race and class in Barbados, 89; Hochschild, Arlie Russell, 22, 115n16–17

Hodge, Merle, 94

Holi (Hindu festival), 71, *72*, 73–74

hooks, bell, 92

housing: consumption and middle-class lifestyle in Indonesia, 153–57; interior decoration and middle-class identity in India, 75–77; middle-class lifestyle and private forms of in China, 213–34; middle-class lifestyle and standard of living in Egypt, 41–42, 43, 49; postsocialist middle class in Hungary and new forms of, 117–42. *See also* gated communities

humor, as type of criticism, 261, 263

Hungary, postsocialist middle classes and housing in, 56n4, 28n3, 84n2, 117–42

Hurston, Zora Neale, 92

Identity, shift from postcolonial to postnational concepts of in India, 83. *See also* middle class; nationalism

imagination, ambiguity of in social practice, 55

immigration. *See* migration

incarceration, new kind of middle-class culture of, 292

India: gated communities and narratives of space in context of middle-class identity in, 57–83; middle class and liberalization in, 196; and new patterns of class interjacency, 292

Indonesia: femininity and morality in discourses on middle class in, 145–65, 173, 297n6; and political suppression of anthropological studies of class analysis, 6

industrial townships, in India, 61–62

Inhorn, Marcia Claire, 115n15

insecurity, in ethnographic analyses of global middle class, 20–27. *See also* anxiety

Institute of the Americas, 212n7

interjacency, and middle-class formation in context of Nepal, 276, 277, 282, 283, 290–95

International Monetary Fund (IMF), 151

International Society for Krishna Consciousness (ISKCON), 72–73

Islam: and anxieties about consumption and corruption in Indonesia, 157; and image of pious woman in Indonesia, 156, 159, 161; and politics in Indonesia, 167–68n16; and reformism in urban middle classes in Egypt, 39; and research on middle class in Indonesia, 168n17

Italy, and illegal migration from Egypt, 43

James, C. L. R., 89

Jameson, E. A., 131

Janmasthami festival (India), 71–73

jieceng (Chinese term), 215–16, 227–34

Jiménez, Michael, 194, 197

Johnson, John, 212n8

Johnston, Robert D., 26

Jones, Carla, 84n1, 173, 297n6

Joseph, Joel, 67

Joshi, Sanjay, 26

Kamath, Lalitha, 59

Kant, Immanuel, 200

Kaplan, Martha, 293, 294, 298n19

Karl, Rebecca, 235n10

Kathmandu (Nepal), 271–96

Katz, Cindi, 103, 170

Keeler, Ward, 150

kelas menengah (Indonesian equivalent of "middle class"), 148–53

Kelly, John, 293, 294, 298n19

Kenedi, János, 133

Kincaid, Jamaica, 110

kinship, matrifocality and history of Caribbean, 95–96. *See also* family

Kirp, David L., 245

Koning, Anouk de, 36

Konrád, György, 130

Kopátsy, Sándor, 137

Kósa, László, 143n3

Labor: affective form of and entrepreneurial marriage in Barbados, 104–107; feminist critiques of, 147; immaterial and affective forms of, 21–23; and Marxist theory of middle class, 10; middle-class modes of consumption and new ideologies of, 279; migration of from Nepal, 295; migration of and post-industrial service economy, 292, 298n17; military suppression of organized in Indonesia, 151; neoliberalism and manipulation of transnational class relations, 17; rates of women's employment outside home in Indonesia, 166n4; urbanization and women's employment in India, 71

Lan, Pei-Chia, 154

landscape, and Olmsted's theory of landscape architecture, 238

land use, and controversy about gate in American suburb, 243

language training, and parenting in U.S., 176

Lareau, Annette, 177, 179, 180, 185

learning disabilities, and parenting in U.S., 181

Lee, Charles, 291

Lefebvre, Henri, 266, 291, 297n5

leisure: andn images of middle class in globalized media, 19; middle-class cultural consumption and new practices of in India, 66–67

Lewis, Linden, 99

Liechty, Mark, 13, 24, 29n4, 127, 155, 167n15, 211n5

LiPuma, Edward, 268n6

Loaeza, Soledad, 211n5

Locke, John, 245

Lomnitz, Claudio, 194, 212n12

Low, Setha M., 79

Lucey, Helen, 178

Mallet, Serge, 10

market, logics of and moral economies in Nepal, 284–90. *See also* free trade

marriage: and definition of womanhood via motherhood in Egypt, 115n15; expense of weddings and middle class in Nepal, 286; and heterosexual normativity, 113n4; and housework done by middle-class husbands in U.S., 115n16; middle-class lifestyle and cost of in Egypt, 41–42; neoliberalism and entrepreneurial form of in Barbados, 85–113

Marx, Karl, 10, 21, 182, 192, 295

Marxism: as dominant paradigm in Caribbean social science, 6, 89; tradition of in anthropology, 7–8

masculinity, and partnership marriage in Barbados, 103. *See also* gender

materiality: and importance of middle class

analysis for theory and politics, 8–12; middle-class status and family house in Hungary, 131–32, 139–41, 143n4

matrifocality, and partnership marriage in Barbados, 94–99, 107–11

Mazzarella, William, 167n11, 196

McKenzie, Evan, 239

media: images of middle-class lifestyles and leisure in globalized, 19; and Islamic fashion magazines in Indonesia, 163; magazines and middle-class identity in India, 64; portrayals of middle-class life on Hungarian state television, 117–119, 131, 143n1; and recent discussions on condition of middle classes, 3; and representations of new family house in Hungary, 134

Mehta, Udau, 245

Meillassoux, Claude, 298n17

Meltoff, Sarah Keene, 268n6

mental health, and parenting in U.S., 181

Mexico, middle class at northern border of, 189–211

middle class: anthropological studies of and framework for theorizing, 27; and aspirations in provincial Egypt, 19, 31–55; category of as shifting and ideologically loaded, 122; and controversy over gate in American suburb, 237–66; discursive and performative production of in Nepal, 271–96; emergence of as critical site for studying implications of globalization, 4; femininity and morality in discourses on in Indonesia, 145–65; gated communities and narrative of space in India, 57–83; historicizing of and comparisons of "old" and "new," 12–15; housing and lifestyle in China, 213–34; and insecurity, 20–27; materiality of and importance of studies of for theory and politics, 8–12; neoliberalism and entrepreneurial marriage in Barbados, 85–113; and northern border of Mexico, 189–211; and parenting in contemporary U.S., 169–86; postsocialist in Hungary and new forms of housing, 117–42; recent media discussions on condition of, 3; transition in anthropological attitudes toward ethnographic analyses of, 5–8. *See also* class; "new" middle class

Middle-Class: Poor No More, Not Yet Developed (De la Calle & Rubio 2010), 195, 196, 197–98, 199

migration: and aspiration to middle-class status in provincial Egypt, 43–44, 49–53; of labor and post-industrial service economy, 292, 298n17; and middle class in Mexico, 208

Mills, Amy, 68

Mills, C. Wright, 11, 22

Mitchell, Timothy, 293, 294, 298n19

modernism and modernity: conscious display of in Egypt, 39–40; and middle-class status in Mexico, 190, 210; and new family house in Hungary, 138–39; and processes of transnational consumerism in India, 83

mohulla (neighborhood), and narratives of space in India, 68–71, 76, 77, 78–79, 83

morality: and middle class in Nepal, 272, 284–90; and relationship between femininity and consumption in Indonesian discourse on social difference, 147–48, 164, 297n6. *See also* respectability

Mosse, George, 86, 272

Nader, Laura, 5

naming, of gated enclaves in India, 65

National Action Party (PAN), 195, 196, 198

nationalism: commitment of middle classes to in Egypt, 40; and discourses on social difference in Indonesia, 152–53

Negri, Antonio, 21

neighborhoods: and private housing in China, 224–27, 236n13; and security concerns in gated communities in India, 79–82. *See also* community; *mohulla*

neoliberalism: and concept of "social space," 294; and emergence of "new middle class," 13–14; and entrepreneurial marriage in Barbados, 93–94, 99–104; and gated communities in U.S., 238–39; impact of in Nepal, 295; and link between consumption and promotion of middle classes, 25; and middle-class ideologies in U.S., 242, 259, 264, 266; and middle-class nationalism in Egypt, 40; and political economy of Barbados, 87; and social

reproduction in U.S., 171; state and politics of class containment, 16–20; and state power in China, 233; and urban class segregation, 292; use of term in context of China, 235–236n11

Nepal, discursive and performative production of middle-classness in, 155, 167n15, 271–96

New Jersey, and zoning boards in middle-class suburbs, 237–66

Newman, Katherine S., 235n4

"new middle class": and aspirations in Egypt, 36–40; comparisons of with "old" middle class, 12–15; and consumption in Indonesia, 153; incomplete transformations between "old" and "new" in India, 77–79; and "old middle class" in context of American suburbs, 237; and private housing in China, 213

Nordholt, Henk Schulte, 150

normality, and markers of middle-class status in Egypt, 34

North American Wetlands Conservation Act, 269n19

O'Dougherty, Maureen, 196

"old middle class." *See* "new middle class"

Olmsted, Frederick Law, 238, 244

Omaxe group (India), 59

Ong, Aihwa, 14, 28–29n3

orang kayak baru (OKB), and "new middle class" in Indonesia, 153

"Parental involution," and parenting practices in U.S., 179, 180, 182

parenting: and black middle class in Barbados, 103–104; and middle class in contemporary U.S., 169–86. *See also* childhood; family

Party of the Institutionalized Revolution (PRI), 196, 198–200

pastoral ideal, and zoning in American suburbs, 247–48

patriarchy: and entrepreneurial marriage in Barbados, 107–11; society and class in Egypt, 35

Peacock, James, 165n2

Peirce, Charles S., 268n11

Pembinaan Kesejahteraan Keluarga (Family Welfare Program), 156–57

Perin, Constance, 244, 268n6

pharmaceuticalization, of daily life in U.S., 181

polgár, and historic middle class in Hungary, 129–30, 131

police, and gated communities in India, 67

politics and political science: and anxiety about future in U.S., 174; consumption and femininity as linked components of classed subjectivities in Indonesian cultural, 163–65; and Islam in Indonesia, 167–68n16; and materiality of middle classness, 8–12; and progressivism of middle class, 296–97n5; and promotion of middle classes by state, 15–20; of race and class in U.S., 245; space and citizen action among middle classes, 26–27. *See also* nationalism; neoliberalism; socialism; state

Poulantzas, Nicos, 10

poverty, terms for in Indonesia, 167n9

power, and concept of interjacency, 276

privacy, and middle-class housing in China, 229, 230

private property, and controversy on gate in American suburb, 237–66

privatization: and gated communities in U.S., 239; of public housing in China, 217, 233, 234n1; of state-owned housing in Hungary, 125

pronatalism, and state financing of housing in Hungary, 133

prostitution, and class in Nepal, 272, 296n1

psycho-physical transformation, of early twentieth-century working-class subjectivities, 21

public(s), and studies of class in Mexico, 191–98

public good: relationship of with private property in liberal democracy, 245–46; and zoning ordinances in American suburb, 248–52

public vs. private spheres: consumption and middle-class lifestyle in Indonesia, 153, 154; entrepreneurial marriage and affective labor in Barbados, 104–107; and gated communities in India, 62; and postcolonial feminism in Caribbean, 92

pueblo ("the people" in Mexico), 195–96, 197, 198, 210

Race: and Caribbean framework of reputation/respectability, 93, 111; and history of class in Barbados, 89; and politics of class in U.S., 245

Race to Nowhere (film 2010), 170, 178, 182–85

rational debate, concept of and middle-class status in Mexico, 201–209, 210–11, 211n3, 212n16

Read, Benjamin L., 236n20

Reagan, Ronald, 171

real estate industry, in China, 217. *See also* housing

Redfield, Robert, 189, 191

religion, class dimension of in Egypt, 39, 52–53. *See also* Hinduism; Islam

reputation, and African culture in Caribbean region, 90–91, 93, 111

resident welfare associations (RWAs), 59–60

respectability: and colonialism, 86, 90–91, 113n2; and definition of middle classes of early modern Europe, 86; and entrepreneurship in Barbados, 93–94; and markers of middle-class status in Egypt, 34; and middle-class housing in China, 227–34; and partnership marriage in Barbados, 94–99, 111

Rofel, Lisa, 154

Rosenthal, Larry A., 245

Ross, Andrew, 20

Rouse, Roger, 11, 12, 269n23

Roy, Srirupa, 61–62

Rubio, Luis, 194–95, 197, 210

Ruble, Blair A., 125

Ruiz, Olivia Teresa, 211n2

Safety. *See* security

Sahara Corporation, 58

Sassen, Saskia, 14

Sayer, Derek, 167n13

scale, and middle-class formation in context of Nepal, 276–77

Scheper-Hughes, Nancy, 6

Schielke, Samuli, 19, 33, 45, 84n7 , 167n8, 211n2, 296n2, 299n23

School for Advanced Research, and advanced seminars, 3–4, 27

Scott, Joan Wallach, 272

security: and anxiety about childhood in U.S., 172–76; and controversy about gate in American suburb, 249, 250,

251, 252–54, 259–61; and gated communities in India, 79–82; and middle-class lifestyle in Indonesia, 154; and private housing in China, 222, 225–27

segregation, of classes in urban areas, 292. *See also* exclusion

self-definition, middle-classness as category of in India, 57

Siegel, James, 151–52

"sightseers," implications of term in debate on gate in American suburb, 252–54, 257, 264

Skeggs, Beverly, 86

Smith, Neil, 233, 242, 267n5

snob zoning, 245, 246

socialism, and middle stratum in Hungary, 126–29, 142

social relations, and exchange, 283–84

social reproduction: and childhood in analyses of political economy and class formation, 169; and neoliberalism in U.S., 171; and parenting in contemporary U.S., 175, 178

"social space," and neoliberalism, 294

sociology, Chicago School of, 290–91

Soja, Edward W., 292, 294

space: gated communities and narratives of in India, 60–82; middle-class subjectivity and power of, 26

Spock, Benjamin, 177

sports. *See* football fan culture

Srivastava, Sanjay, 75, 167n10

Stable Living Project (China), 225

standard of living, and middle-class aspirations in provincial Egypt, 41–45

state: and housing in Hungary, 132–33; and issues of consumption, family, and gender in Indonesia, 157–63; and narratives of space in India, 67–82; promotion of middle classes by and coordination of class containment, 15–20. *See also* politics and political science

"steel towns," in postcolonial India, 61–62

Stewart, Susan, 164

Stoler, Ann Laura, 166n3

"student management systems," 175–76

suburbanization: and controversy over gate in U.S., 237–66; and housing in Hungary, 143n3

Swarowsky, Daniela, 45

Taylor, Lawrence, 21

Thomas, Deborah, 113n3

Thompson, E. P., 12, 211n5, 214, 215, 274–276, 280, 283

Tijuana (Mexico), 189–211

Tilley, Christopher, 143n4

training seminars, on feminine role in consumption in Indonesia, 158–59

trespass, and private property in U.S., 252–54

Turner, Frederick Jackson, 209

Uberoi, Patricia, 62–63

undue hardship, and zoning variances in American suburb, 248–52, 260

United States: class and new role of in global economy, 292–293; class and sociospatial segregation in, 290–91; and controversy over gate in middle-class suburb, 237–66; and housework done by middle-class husbands, 115n16; middle-class parenting in contemporary, 169–86; references to in debate on middle class in Mexico, 199, 210

urbanism, and gated communities in India, 65

urban renewal, and American suburbs, 242

Urrea, Luis Alberto, 190

Van der Kroef, Justus M., 166n7

Van Leeuwen, Lizzy, 157

Vijayabaskar, M., 59

Voyce, Malcolm, 58

Waldrop, Anne, 59

Walkerdine, Valerie, 178

Wardlow, Holly, 96

Warner, Michael, 191, 261, 268–69n12

wa sat (middle or center in Arabic), 46

Weber, Max, 149, 157, 168n18, 235n4–5, 277, 278, 280, 289, 297n9

Weeks, Kathi, 115n17

Wekker, Gloria, 113–14n4

wetlands, and environmental regulations in U.S., 269n19

"white collar," in Chinese context, 220

Williams, Raymond, 15, 137, 239, 274, 280

Willis, Paul, 235n3

Wilson, Elizabeth, 167n14

Wilson, Peter, 86, 90–91, 112

Wolf, Eric, 297n7

women: and administration of gated communities in India, 78; femininity and morality in discourses on middle classness in Indonesia, 145–65; marriage and motherhood in definition of in Egypt, 115n15; and middle-class aspirations in Egypt, 35; rates of employment outside home in Indonesia, 166n4; and regendering of public spaces in India, 70; urbanization and employment of in India, 71. *See also* femininity; gender

Wright, Erik Olin, 10–11

Yeh, Rihan, 56n5, 84n1, 167n12, 296n3

Yudhoyono, Susilo Bambang, 165n1

Zang, Xiaowei, 235n9

Zelizer, Viviana, 155

Zhang, Li, 56n3, 84n2, 154

zhongchan jieceng, use of term in China, 216, 218, 220, 230, 232

zoning boards and ordinances, in American suburbs, 237–66

School for Advanced Research Advanced Seminar Series

PUBLISHED BY SAR PRESS

CHACO & HOHOKAM: PREHISTORIC REGIONAL SYSTEMS IN THE AMERICAN SOUTHWEST
Patricia L. Crown & W. James Judge, eds.

RECAPTURING ANTHROPOLOGY: WORKING IN THE PRESENT
Richard G. Fox, ed.

WAR IN THE TRIBAL ZONE: EXPANDING STATES AND INDIGENOUS WARFARE
R. Brian Ferguson & Neil L. Whitehead, eds.

IDEOLOGY AND PRE-COLUMBIAN CIVILIZATIONS
Arthur A. Demarest & Geoffrey W. Conrad, eds.

DREAMING: ANTHROPOLOGICAL AND PSYCHOLOGICAL INTERPRETATIONS
Barbara Tedlock, ed.

HISTORICAL ECOLOGY: CULTURAL KNOWLEDGE AND CHANGING LANDSCAPES
Carole L. Crumley, ed.

THEMES IN SOUTHWEST PREHISTORY
George J. Gumerman, ed.

MEMORY, HISTORY, AND OPPOSITION UNDER STATE SOCIALISM
Rubie S. Watson, ed.

OTHER INTENTIONS: CULTURAL CONTEXTS AND THE ATTRIBUTION OF INNER STATES
Lawrence Rosen, ed.

LAST HUNTERS–FIRST FARMERS: NEW PERSPECTIVES ON THE PREHISTORIC TRANSITION TO AGRICULTURE
T. Douglas Price & Anne Birgitte Gebauer, eds.

MAKING ALTERNATIVE HISTORIES: THE PRACTICE OF ARCHAEOLOGY AND HISTORY IN NON-WESTERN SETTINGS
Peter R. Schmidt & Thomas C. Patterson, eds.

CYBORGS & CITADELS: ANTHROPOLOGICAL INTERVENTIONS IN EMERGING SCIENCES AND TECHNOLOGIES
Gary Lee Downey & Joseph Dumit, eds.

SENSES OF PLACE
Steven Feld & Keith H. Basso, eds.

THE ORIGINS OF LANGUAGE: WHAT NONHUMAN PRIMATES CAN TELL US
Barbara J. King, ed.

CRITICAL ANTHROPOLOGY NOW: UNEXPECTED CONTEXTS, SHIFTING CONSTITUENCIES, CHANGING AGENDAS
George E. Marcus, ed.

ARCHAIC STATES
Gary M. Feinman & Joyce Marcus, eds.

REGIMES OF LANGUAGE: IDEOLOGIES, POLITIES, AND IDENTITIES
Paul V. Kroskrity, ed.

BIOLOGY, BRAINS, AND BEHAVIOR: THE EVOLUTION OF HUMAN DEVELOPMENT
Sue Taylor Parker, Jonas Langer, & Michael L. McKinney, eds.

WOMEN & MEN IN THE PREHISPANIC SOUTHWEST: LABOR, POWER, & PRESTIGE
Patricia L. Crown, ed.

HISTORY IN PERSON: ENDURING STRUGGLES, CONTENTIOUS PRACTICE, INTIMATE IDENTITIES
Dorothy Holland & Jean Lave, eds.

THE EMPIRE OF THINGS: REGIMES OF VALUE AND MATERIAL CULTURE
Fred R. Myers, ed.

CATASTROPHE & CULTURE: THE ANTHROPOLOGY OF DISASTER
Susanna M. Hoffman & Anthony Oliver-Smith, eds.

URUK MESOPOTAMIA & ITS NEIGHBORS: CROSS-CULTURAL INTERACTIONS IN THE ERA OF STATE FORMATION
Mitchell S. Rothman, ed.

REMAKING LIFE & DEATH: TOWARD AN ANTHROPOLOGY OF THE BIOSCIENCES
Sarah Franklin & Margaret Lock, eds.

TIKAL: DYNASTIES, FOREIGNERS, & AFFAIRS OF STATE: ADVANCING MAYA ARCHAEOLOGY
Jeremy A. Sabloff, ed.

GRAY AREAS: ETHNOGRAPHIC
ENCOUNTERS WITH NURSING HOME
CULTURE
Philip B. Stafford, ed.

PLURALIZING ETHNOGRAPHY: COMPARISON
AND REPRESENTATION IN MAYA CULTURES,
HISTORIES, AND IDENTITIES
John M. Watanabe & Edward F. Fischer, eds.

AMERICAN ARRIVALS: ANTHROPOLOGY
ENGAGES THE NEW IMMIGRATION
Nancy Foner, ed.

VIOLENCE
Neil L. Whitehead, ed.

LAW & EMPIRE IN THE PACIFIC:
FIJI AND HAWAI'I
Sally Engle Merry & Donald Brenneis, eds.

ANTHROPOLOGY IN THE MARGINS
OF THE STATE
Veena Das & Deborah Poole, eds.

THE ARCHAEOLOGY OF COLONIAL
ENCOUNTERS: COMPARATIVE
PERSPECTIVES
Gil J. Stein, ed.

GLOBALIZATION, WATER, & HEALTH:
RESOURCE MANAGEMENT IN TIMES OF
SCARCITY
Linda Whiteford & Scott Whiteford, eds.

A CATALYST FOR IDEAS: ANTHROPOLOGICAL
ARCHAEOLOGY AND THE LEGACY OF
DOUGLAS W. SCHWARTZ
Vernon L. Scarborough, ed.

THE ARCHAEOLOGY OF CHACO CANYON:
AN ELEVENTH-CENTURY PUEBLO
REGIONAL CENTER
Stephen H. Lekson, ed.

COMMUNITY BUILDING IN THE TWENTY-
FIRST CENTURY
Stanley E. Hyland, ed.

AFRO-ATLANTIC DIALOGUES:
ANTHROPOLOGY IN THE DIASPORA
Kevin A. Yelvington, ed.

COPÁN: THE HISTORY OF AN ANCIENT
MAYA KINGDOM
E. Wyllys Andrews & William L. Fash, eds.

THE EVOLUTION OF HUMAN LIFE HISTORY
Kristen Hawkes & Richard R. Paine, eds.

THE SEDUCTIONS OF COMMUNITY:
EMANCIPATIONS, OPPRESSIONS,
QUANDARIES
Gerald W. Creed, ed.

THE GENDER OF GLOBALIZATION: WOMEN
NAVIGATING CULTURAL AND ECONOMIC
MARGINALITIES
*Nandini Gunewardena &
Ann Kingsolver, eds.*

NEW LANDSCAPES OF INEQUALITY:
NEOLIBERALISM AND THE EROSION OF
DEMOCRACY IN AMERICA
*Jane L. Collins, Micaela di Leonardo,
& Brett Williams, eds.*

IMPERIAL FORMATIONS
*Ann Laura Stoler, Carole McGranahan,
& Peter C. Perdue, eds.*

OPENING ARCHAEOLOGY: REPATRIATION'S
IMPACT ON CONTEMPORARY RESEARCH
AND PRACTICE
Thomas W. Killion, ed.

SMALL WORLDS: METHOD, MEANING,
& NARRATIVE IN MICROHISTORY
*James F. Brooks, Christopher R. N. DeCorse,
& John Walton, eds.*

MEMORY WORK: ARCHAEOLOGIES OF
MATERIAL PRACTICES
Barbara J. Mills & William H. Walker, eds.

FIGURING THE FUTURE: GLOBALIZATION
AND THE TEMPORALITIES OF CHILDREN
AND YOUTH
Jennifer Cole & Deborah Durham, eds.

TIMELY ASSETS: THE POLITICS OF
RESOURCES AND THEIR TEMPORALITIES
*Elizabeth Emma Ferry &
Mandana E. Limbert, eds.*

DEMOCRACY: ANTHROPOLOGICAL
APPROACHES
Julia Paley, ed.

CONFRONTING CANCER: METAPHORS,
INEQUALITY, AND ADVOCACY
Juliet McMullin & Diane Weiner, eds.

DEVELOPMENT & DISPOSSESSION: THE
CRISIS OF FORCED DISPLACEMENT AND
RESETTLEMENT
Anthony Oliver-Smith, ed.

GLOBAL HEALTH IN TIMES OF VIOLENCE
*Barbara Rylko-Bauer, Linda Whiteford,
& Paul Farmer, eds.*

THE EVOLUTION OF LEADERSHIP:
TRANSITIONS IN DECISION MAKING FROM
SMALL-SCALE TO MIDDLE-RANGE SOCIETIES
*Kevin J. Vaughn, Jelmer W. Eerkins, &
John Kantner, eds.*

ARCHAEOLOGY & CULTURAL RESOURCE
MANAGEMENT: VISIONS FOR THE FUTURE
Lynne Sebastian & William D. Lipe, eds.

ARCHAIC STATE INTERACTION: THE
EASTERN MEDITERRANEAN IN THE BRONZE
AGE
*William A. Parkinson &
Michael L. Galaty, eds.*

INDIANS & ENERGY: EXPLOITATION
AND OPPORTUNITY IN THE AMERICAN
SOUTHWEST
Sherry L. Smith & Brian Frehner, eds.

ROOTS OF CONFLICT: SOILS, AGRICULTURE,
AND SOCIOPOLITICAL COMPLEXITY IN
ANCIENT HAWAI'I
Patrick V. Kirch, ed.

PHARMACEUTICAL SELF: THE GLOBAL
SHAPING OF EXPERIENCE IN AN AGE OF
PSYCHOPHARMACOLOGY
Janis Jenkins, ed.

FORCES OF COMPASSION: HUMANITARI-
ANISM BETWEEN ETHICS AND POLITICS
Erica Bornstein & Peter Redfield, eds.

ENDURING CONQUESTS: RETHINKING THE
ARCHAEOLOGY OF RESISTANCE TO SPANISH
COLONIALISM IN THE AMERICAS
*Matthew Liebmann &
Melissa S. Murphy, eds.*

DANGEROUS LIAISONS: ANTHROPOLOGISTS
AND THE NATIONAL SECURITY STATE
*Laura A. McNamara &
Robert A. Rubinstein, eds.*

BREATHING NEW LIFE INTO THE EVIDENCE
OF DEATH: CONTEMPORARY APPROACHES
TO BIOARCHAEOLOGY
*Aubrey Baadsgaard, Alexis T. Boutin, &
Jane E. Buikstra, eds.*

THE SHAPE OF SCRIPT: HOW AND WHY
WRITING SYSTEMS CHANGE
Stephen D. Houston, ed.

NATURE, SCIENCE, AND RELIGION:
INTERSECTIONS SHAPING SOCIETY AND
THE ENVIRONMENT
Catherine M. Tucker, ed.

THE GLOBAL MIDDLE CLASSES:
THEORIZING THROUGH ETHNOGRAPHY
*Rachel Heiman, Carla Freeman, &
Mark Liechty, eds.*

THE ARCHAEOLOGY OF LOWER CENTRAL
AMERICA
  Frederick W. Lange & Doris Z. Stone, eds.

CHAN CHAN: ANDEAN DESERT CITY
  Michael E. Moseley & Kent C. Day, eds.

DEMOGRAPHIC ANTHROPOLOGY:
QUANTITATIVE APPROACHES
  Ezra B. W. Zubrow, ed.

THE DYING COMMUNITY
  Art Gallaher, Jr. & Harlan Padfield, eds.

ELITES: ETHNOGRAPHIC ISSUES
  George E. Marcus, ed.

ENTREPRENEURS IN CULTURAL CONTEXT
  *Sidney M. Greenfield, Arnold Strickon,
  & Robert T. Aubey, eds.*

EXPLORATIONS IN ETHNOARCHAEOLOGY
  Richard A. Gould, ed.

LATE LOWLAND MAYA CIVILIZATION:
CLASSIC TO POSTCLASSIC
  Jeremy A. Sabloff & E. Wyllys Andrews V, eds.

LOWLAND MAYA SETTLEMENT PATTERNS
  Wendy Ashmore, ed.

METHODS AND THEORIES OF
ANTHROPOLOGICAL GENETICS
  M. H. Crawford & P. L. Workman, eds.

THE ORIGINS OF MAYA CIVILIZATION
  Richard E. W. Adams, ed.

PHOTOGRAPHY IN ARCHAEOLOGICAL
RESEARCH
  Elmer Harp, Jr., ed.

RECONSTRUCTING PREHISTORIC PUEBLO
SOCIETIES
  William A. Longacre, ed.

SIMULATIONS IN ARCHAEOLOGY
  Jeremy A. Sabloff, ed.

STRUCTURE AND PROCESS IN LATIN
AMERICA
  Arnold Strickon & Sidney M. Greenfield, eds.

THE VALLEY OF MEXICO: STUDIES IN
PRE-HISPANIC ECOLOGY AND SOCIETY
  Eric R. Wolf, ed.

Participants in the School for Advanced Research advanced seminar, "The Middle Classes: A Global Perspective," chaired by Rachel Heiman and Aihwa Ong, March 28–April 3, 2009. *Standing, from left*: Aihwa Ong, Rihan Yeh, Carla Freeman, Rachel Heiman, Krisztina Fehérváry; *seated, from left*: Hai Ren, Samuli Schielke, Cindi Katz, Mark Liechty. Photo by Jason S. Ordaz.